A Companion to Marx's *Capital*

VOLUME TWO

A Companion to Marx's *Capital*

VOLUME TWO

David Harvey

VERSO
London • New York

First published by Verso 2013

1 3 5 7 9 10 8 6 4 2

Verso
UK: 6 Meard Street, London W1F oEG
US: 20 Jay Street, Suite 1010, Brooklyn, NY 11201
www.versobooks.com

Verso is the imprint of New Left Books

ISBN-13: 978-1-78168-121-3 (pbk)
ISBN-13: 978-1-78168-122-0 (hbk)

British Library Cataloguing in Publication Data
A catalogue record for this book is available from the British Library

Library of Congress Cataloging-in-Publication Data

Harvey, David, 1935–
A companion to Marx's Capital. Volume 2 / David Harvey.
    pages cm
  Includes bibliographical references and index.
  ISBN 978-1-78168-122-0 (hardback) — ISBN 978-1-78168-121-3 (pbk) —
ISBN 978-1-78168-184-8 (ebk) (print)
  1. Marx, Karl, 1818-1883. Kapital. I. Marx, Karl, 1818-1883. Kapital. II. Title.
HB501.M37H336 2013
335.4'1—dc23
                                    2013018584

A catalog record for this book is available from the Library of Congress

Typeset in Minion Pro by Hewer UK Ltd, Edinburgh
Printed in the US by Maple Press

Contents

A Note on the Texts Used

The texts used are as follows:

K. Marx, *Capital, Volume II* (London: Penguin Books in association with *New Left Review*, translated by David Fernbach, 1978), page numbers cited directly.

K. Marx, *Capital, Volume I* (London: Penguin Books in association with *New Left Review*, translated by Ben Fowkes, 1976), citations referenced as C1 followed by the page number.

K. Marx, *Capital, Volume III* (London: Penguin Books in association with *New Left Review*, translated by David Fernbach, 1981), citations referenced as C3 followed by the page number.

K. Marx, *Grundrisse* (London: *New Left Review* and Penguin Books, translated by Martin Nicolaus, 1973), citations referenced as *Grundrisse*, followed by page number.

Whereas I worked from a transcript of the lectures in compiling the written version of the Volume I *Companion*, I did not follow the same procedure in this case. While I have often mined Volume II for particular insights, I did not have the appreciation that comes from teaching it on a regular basis. So I had to learn quite a bit more about the volume as a whole. Before giving the lectures, I therefore compiled lengthy notes on the materials from Volume II and the relevant chapters of Volume III and subsequently went back over these to correct them after the lectures were given. This formed the basis for the first version of the text. I then reread the original texts one more time and came up with further corrections and comments. As so often happens when reading Marx, consecutive readings revealed new insights and layers of meaning. Thus there are some differences and divergences not only in the manner of presentation but also, occasionally, in substantive interpretation between the lectures and this written version. Interpreting Marx is always an ongoing and incomplete project, and this is what often makes it so interesting to read and then reread him.

I want to thank the students who participated in the preliminary seminar on Volume II and those who patiently listened to the lectures at the Union Theological Seminary. Their pertinent questions were always helpful, while Crystal Hall, Priya Chandresakaran, Nkosi Anderson and Chris Caruso graciously and helpfully agreed to interview me about the text for the video version. I am also deeply indebted to Chris Caruso, who both led the film crew and manages my website, and Chris Nizza who edited the video so expertly. Finally, Maliha Safri, kindly read the first draft of the text and suggested some clarifications and reformulations. She is in no way responsible for my interpretations.

Introduction

My aim, as with the *Companion* to Volume I of *Capital*, is "to get you to read this book." I wish I could add "in Marx's own terms" but, as I shall shortly show, it is particularly difficult in this case to understand what those terms might be. But, first, I need to persuade you of the importance of undertaking a careful study of Volume II and treating it on a par with Volume I. The case for so doing is, in my view, unassailable.

In the *Grundrisse* (e.g. 407), Marx unequivocally asserts that capital can be understood only as a "*unity of production and realization*" of value and surplus-value. By this, he means that if you cannot sell in the market what has been produced in the labor process then the labor embodied through production has no value. Volume I of *Capital* concentrates its attention on the processes and dynamics of the *production* of value and surplus-value, laying to one side any difficulties that might arise out of the conditions of their *realization*. Marx assumes, in effect, that a market always exists and all commodities produced can be sold at their value. Volume II takes exactly the opposite tack: what turn out to be the fraught and often unstable processes of *realization* of surplus-value are put under the microscope while assuming there are no difficulties in the realm of surplus-value production. If, as is unfortunately generally the case, the much-studied Volume I is overemphasized while Volume II is neglected and treated as secondary, then, at best, we can get only half of the story of Marx's understanding of capital's political economy. In fact, the implications of the failure to take Volume II seriously are far worse: we fail to understand fully what is said in the first volume because its findings need to be placed *in a dialectical relation* to those of Volume II if they are to be properly understood.

The unity of production and realization, like that of the commodity, is a *contradictory unity*: it internalizes an opposition between two radically different tendencies. To ignore its contradictory character would be like trying to theorize capital without mentioning labor, or gender by talking about men and forgetting about women. It is out of the contradictory relations between production and realization that crises frequently arise. Ricardo and his school, Marx notes, "never understood the really modern crises, in which this contradiction of capital discharges itself in great thunderstorms which increasingly threaten [the accumulation of capital] as the foundation of society and of production itself" (*Grundrisse*, 411).

Marx clearly warned us of all this in the first chapter of Volume I. In the analysis of commodity production, he initially lays aside questions of use-value as if they do not matter, as if the discovery of "the manifold uses of things is the work of history" and therefore outside of the purview of political economy. But he then goes on to conclude that "nothing can be a value without being an object of utility. If the thing is useless, so is the labour contained in it; the labour does not count as labour, and therefore creates no value" (C1, 131). No realization, then no value—and certainly no surplus-value. Volume II studies those conditions that might lead to the value and surplus-value created potentially in production not being realized in monetary form through exchange in the market.

The idea of a deep contradiction between the conditions for the production and realization of surplus-value is so important that I think it wise to provide an initial indication of how it might work in practice. In Volume I, Marx focuses on the implications for the laborer of the ruthless pursuit of surplus-value by capital. The culmination of this enquiry in chapter 25 on "The General Law of Capitalist Accumulation" concludes that the lot of the laborer is bound to grow worse, that "the accumulation of wealth at one pole" is "at the same time accumulation of misery, the torment of labour, slavery, ignorance, brutalization and moral degradation at the other pole, i.e. on the side of the class that produces its own product as capital" (C1, 799). This idea of the increasing impoverishment and immiseration of the working classes has entered with a vengeance into the folklore of the Marxist interpretation of capital. But it is a contingent proposition. It presumes that there are *absolutely no problems* arising in the realization of value and surplus-value in the market, and that the manner in which surplus-value is distributed between rents, interest, profit on merchants' capital, taxes, and profits on direct production have *no relevance*.

In Volume II, however, we find the following statement, which is radically at odds with the Volume I formulation:

Contradiction in the capitalist mode of production. The workers are important for the market as buyers of commodities. But as sellers of their commodity—labour power—capitalist society has the tendency to restrict them to their minimum price. Further contradiction: the periods in which capitalist production exerts all its forces regularly show themselves in periods of over-production; because the limit to the application of the productive powers is not simply the production of value, but also its realization. However, the sale of commodities, the realization of commodity capital, and thus of surplus-value as well, is restricted not by the consumer needs of society in general, but by the consumer needs of a society in which the great majority are always poor and must always remain poor. (391)

Lack of aggregate effective demand in the market, in short, can act as a serious barrier to the continuity of capital accumulation, and working-class consumption is a significant component of that effective demand. By the end of Volume II, therefore, Marx is talking (albeit somewhat reluctantly) about how working-class demand, along with the manipulation of working-class wants, needs and desires, becomes critical for the achievement of that form of "rational consumption" that will support continuous capital accumulation.

Capitalism as a social formation is perpetually caught in this contradiction. It can *either* maximize the conditions for the production of surplus-value, and thereby threaten the capacity to realize surplus-value in the market; *or* keep effective demand strong in the market by empowering workers, and thereby threaten the ability to create surplus-value in production. In other words, if the economy does well according to the Volume I prescriptions, it is likely to be in trouble from the standpoint of Volume II, and vice versa. For example, capital in the advanced capitalist countries tended toward a demand management stance consistent with the Volume II propositions (emphasizing the conditions for realization of value) between 1945 and the mid-1970s but, in the process, increasingly ran into problems (particularly those of a well-organized and politically powerful working-class movement) in the production of surplus-value. After the mid-1970s, it therefore shifted (after a fierce battle with labor) toward a supply-side stance more consistent with Volume I. This emphasized cultivating the conditions for surplus-value production (through reducing real wages, crushing working-class organization and generally disempowering workers). The neoliberal counterrevolution, as we now call it, from the mid-1970s onwards resolved the preeminent problems of surplus-value production, but it did so at the expense of creating problems of realization, particularly from the early 1990s onwards. How these problems in aggregate effective demand were papered over by the extension of credit is a complicated history that culminated in the crash of 2008. This general story is, of course, a gross oversimplification, but it provides a neat illustration of how the contradictory unity of production and realization has been manifest historically. It has also been manifest in shifts in bourgeois economic theory. For example, Keynesian demand management dominated economic thinking in the 1960s, whereas monetarist supply-side theories came to dominate after 1980 or so. It is important to situate these histories in terms of the underlying contradictory unity of production and realization as represented by the first two volumes of *Capital*.

There is, however, one way that the contradiction between production and realization might be attenuated or even effectively managed, and that is by resort to credit. This is so because there is nothing in principle that prevents credit being supplied to sustain in equal measure both production and realization of values and surplus-values. The clearest example of this is when financiers lend to developers to build speculative tract housing while lending mortgage finance to consumers to purchase that housing. The problem, of course, is that this practice can all too easily produce speculative bubbles of the sort that led into the spectacular crash of 2007–08, primarily in the housing markets of the United States but also in Spain and Ireland. The long history of booms, bubbles and crashes in construction testifies to the importance of phenomena of this sort in capital's history. But the interventions of the credit system have plainly also been constructive in certain ways and played a positive role in sustaining capital accumulation through difficult times.

Partly for this reason, I decided to incorporate those parts of Volume III that deal with merchant and finance capital along with the credit system into this Volume II reading. Theoretically, this maneuver makes sense because Volume II opens with a study of three integrated circuits of capital—those of money, production and the commodity. But Marx treats of these circuits and their inner relations in purely technical terms, without considering the class agents that arise specifically charged with managing the disposal of capital in the different forms of money, production and commodity. The producers are very prominent in Volume I, of course, but the distinctive roles of the merchants and the financiers are only taken up in Volume III. What we find there is a history of how credit is the fount of all manner of insanity and speculative craziness, which then raises the obvious question as to why capital tolerates such excrescences, particularly since they underpin massive destructions of value of the sort we have recently witnessed. The answer to this conundrum actually lies in Volume II, though Marx does not specifically mention it. In fact, Marx systematically excludes credit from his analysis throughout the whole of Volume II (an exclusion that many readers, including me, find annoying and frustrating). But what we see from Volume II is that, without a credit system, capitalists would be forced into hoarding more and more capital to cover problems of fixed-capital circulation, differential turnover, working and circulation times, and the like. When capital is hoarded it becomes inactive and dead. If more and more capital ends up in that state, then this will act as a serious drag upon the dynamics of accumulation, to the point where the circulation of capital will likely gum up and ultimately grind to a halt. The credit system is, therefore, vital to release all this hoarded and inactive money capital. It helps return it into active use. But it does so at a cost. The Pandora's box of speculative credit activity has to be opened, and all sorts of unsavory things pop out. Marx does not explicitly point all of this out, but it is a clear implication that flows from the analysis of a creditless economy laid out in Volume II.

The final reason I have for incorporating some of Volume III into the context of Volume II is that it helps highlight the holistic nature of Marx's political-economic enquiry. By situating the Volume II reading in relation to the other two volumes of *Capital*, we better appreciate the contents and meaning of this volume in relation to Marx's overall project. But we also establish a clearer basis for understanding the nature of Marx's general project. It has long been my view, for example, that we should not cite passages from this or that volume as if they are pure and untrammeled truths, but always treat even firmly stated propositions (such as the increasing impoverishment of the workers in Volume I) as contingent statements that exist in relation to the total vision that Marx was seeking to represent. The truths that Volume II has to tell are vital to our overall understanding in themselves, of course.

But they are always situated truths in relation to the evolving framework of Marx's ongoing project.

With respect to the actual text of Volume II, I approach the challenge of devising an adequate reading of it with a mix of excitement and trepidation. Excitement because, for me (and I know I am not alone in this), some of Marx's most interesting and innovative ideas and insights are to be derived from a close reading of it. Constructed from the standpoint of circulation of capital in its different forms (the circulations of money, commodities and productive activities) rather than from the standpoint of production, it proposes a radically different model of how capital works to that set out in Volume I. It is, to use my favorite metaphor, capital seen through a different window on the world. From the two windows of the two volumes we see quite different patterns of relations and activities. Yet the view from each window is objectively described and truthfully portrayed. A general theory of what Marx calls "the laws of motion of capital," I have always thought, would have to come from triangulating between the two perspectives—a task that has never been satisfactorily accomplished, in part because Volume II is incomplete and its vision blurred. Volume II is also, for a variety of reasons, the least-read and least-considered of the three volumes of *Capital*.

I am personally indebted to Volume II in many ways. This is because it deals with how capital circulation constructs its own world of space and time. It helps explain why the history of capitalism has been characterized by speed-up and the reduction of cost and time barriers to spatial movement. It sets these trends against the background of the ongoing reproduction and expansion of the class relations that lie at the very heart of what capital is about. It has provided a more secure theoretical foundation for me to understand the political economy of urbanization and the dynamics of uneven geographical development. I have therefore drawn much inspiration from it in my own work. In *The Condition of Postmodernity*, for example, I coined and to some extent popularized the phrase "time-space compression" to capture the successive ways in which capital has knitted together a world of circulation of money, commodities, people, information and ideas in ever tighter, more complex and concentrated ways. This idea came from my reading of Volume II.

My trepidation arises because this volume is a rather boring book (and that may be an understatement). It lacks the literary style, the sparkle and the humor, the irony and devastating put-downs that help make Volume I such a readable tome. There are no bloodsucking vampires and table-turnings in Volume II, hardly any references at all to the immense cast of literary characters—Shakespeare, Cervantes, Goethe, Balzac, to say nothing of learned references to the Greeks and Enlightenment philosophers—that strut the stage in Volume I. The translator, David Fernbach, doubtless fearing he might be blamed for the uninspired qualities of the writing, points out the enormous stylistic differences between the first and the later volumes of *Capital*. Volume I "is palpably presented to the public as a work of science that is also a work of world literature," whereas the content of Volume II follows "much more in the wake of the less purple passages of Volume I." Those of you familiar with the first volume will know what he means. For most of Volume II, Marx seems content to assume the persona of the dry and dusty accountant of so many days or hours producing a commodity, and so many more days and hours getting it to market for sale. The subject matter, writes Fernbach, "is to a far greater extent technical, even dry." The book is above all "renowned for the arid deserts between its oases," and this "has caused many a non-specialist reader to turn back in defeat" (80). The amazingly important insights of the book are, to put it bluntly, buried in turgid prose and tedious arithmetic calculations.

The problem is not only one of written style. Volume II also lacks the compelling and clear narrative (some would call it dialectical) structure that is so persuasive in Volume I. This is, to some degree, explained by the incomplete and often inconclusive nature of the work. The threads that bind the volume into a whole are there, but it takes a lot of work to excavate them, and in some instances they are plainly frayed, if not broken. The only way the reader can make sense of the whole is to pick up the most prominent threads and try to weave them into some config- uration that makes sense. It takes imagination and patience to do that, and even then it is hard to be sure that what one comes up with is what Marx really had in mind. It is therefore sometimes said of commentaries on Volume II that they reveal more about the commentators than about Marx. This is surely to some degree true in my case. The problem is that there is no other way to read this volume productively.

Beneath this general difficulty lies also the question of how Engels created the texts of both Volumes II and III that have come down to us. Recent scholarship on Marx's original notebooks and drafts seems to indicate that Engels's interventions were substantial, and sometimes more than a little questionable. Some even go so far as to suggest that we should attribute the authorship of these volumes to Engels rather than to Marx. The raw and unedited notebooks and drafts have already been published in German and, as Marx scholars probe more deeply into them, there may be some very substantial reinterpretations in the offing. I cannot anticipate what these might be, but I think it only right to inform readers of such a possibility. Meanwhile, I can only proceed with the text as we currently have it.

Volume II is written at a high level of abstraction, and thus lacks the grounded qualities of Volume I. When Marx takes up the theory of absolute surplus-value in Volume I, for example, he illustrates it with a long history of struggle over the length of the working day. The relevance of the concept to daily life and politics is clear (remember Mary Ann Walkley, who died of overwork?). He does not usually bother with such examples in Volume II, and when he does—when he consults the railway manuals for ideas on how to handle maintenance, repair and replacement of fixed-capital items such as rail ties and rolling stock—it is only to find more appropriate abstractions on the basis of accountancy information. We are therefore left to imagine what a long illustrative chapter on, say, changing turnover times, equivalent to that on the working day in Volume I, might look like. It is not that Marx lacked for illustrative materials: circulation times (the time from production to market) were changing dramatically with the coming of the railroads and the telegraph. We can easily insert our own examples of such time-space reconfigurations today (such as the impact of the internet and cell phones). But, with chapter after chapter lacking any attempt to illustrate abstract and technical findings with materials drawn from daily life (let alone from the historical-geographical evolution of capitalism), it is very easy to become turned off.

Even worse is the lack of politics. Engels, as Ernest Mandel points out in his introduction to the Penguin edition, feared that "the second volume will provoke great disappointment, because it is purely scientific and does not contain much material for agitation" (11). This is, again, something of an understatement. The moral outrage that courses through Volume I and animates it at every turn is missing. Class struggle disappears, as do active class relations. The devastating ironic passages of Volume I are not to be found. There is no call for revolution. Marx seems interested only in the nuts and bolts of how capital circulates. He sheaths his acerbic critical sword (except when it comes to Ricardo's and Adam Smith's "errors") and for the most part gives us passive descriptions.

While the potentiality for disruptions and crises is perpetually being probed, the catalysts that turn such potentialities into realities are largely absent. It sometimes seems as if a self-perpetuating capitalist system can accumulate forever, with just a few hiccups and minor disruptions here and there. Rosa Luxemburg bitterly complained that the abstracted reproduction schemas developed at the end of Volume II showed on paper that "accumulation, production, realization and exchange run smoothly with clockwork precision," adding ironically (given the way that Marx calculated, not always correctly, tedious arithmetic examples of expanding accumulation from one year to the next) that "no doubt this particular kind of 'accumulation' can continue ad infinitum, just as long, that is to say, as ink and paper do not run out."

I do not mention all this to put readers off before they start, but to forewarn everyone of some of the difficulties and challenges that lie ahead. There are good reasons why this is by far the least read of the three volumes of *Capital*. The warning that Marx posted in one of his introductions to Volume I needs reiteration, but with redoubled force: "There is no royal road to science, and only those who do not dread the fatiguing climb of its steep paths have a chance of gaining its luminous summits" (C1, 104). Sticking with Volume II, I can assure you, is not only essential but well worth it in the long run. The view from some of the luminous summits is as unexpected as it is problematic and enlightening.

Because of the evident difficulties, I have taken certain liberties in presenting this text to first-time readers. I have added in tangible examples (contemporary if possible) to illustrate the principles that Marx is uncovering. I have added some comments on political implications and possibilities. I have also imported materials from elsewhere, particularly from the *Grundrisse*, to support and elaborate on some of the key ideas that are here incompletely presented. Even more dramatically, I elected, as already noted, to bring all of the materials from Volume III concerning merchants' capital and money, finance and banking capital into contact with the purely technical presentation on the circulation of money and commodity capitals laid out in Volume II. These far more lively (if incomplete and often frustrating) materials from Volume III deal with the roles of merchants and financiers as agents in the rise of a capitalist mode of production. They also help explain why it is so important to disaggregate the circulation of capital, as is done in Volume II, into its components of money, commodity and productive activity. By combining the activities and behaviors of the social agents—the merchants, the financiers and the bankers—with the technical aspects of capital accumulation, we gain a far richer understanding of how capital works.

It is also in Volume III that Marx comes the closest to analyzing actual crises—those of 1848 and 1857. Looking at how Marx did this is helpful in wrestling with what happened in the crisis that unfolded in global capitalism after 2007, and makes this reading far more relevant to contemporary circumstances. I do not claim that Marx provides answers to the conundrum of how to explain our recent difficulties. But there are some instructive parallels between Marx's time and ours. For example, his commentary on how the "mistaken" Bank Act of 1844 in Britain intensified and prolonged the commercial and financial crises of 1848 and 1857 bears an eerie resemblance to the unfortunate role of the European Central Bank in deepening and prolonging the crisis in Europe after 2008.

The necessity to go beyond the text of Volume II in order to understand it is mandated by its incomplete form. It is simply impossible to get much out of the book without speculating on its possibilities. I do not claim that my speculations and interpretations are right, or that I have privileged insights that others lack. But I do hope to demonstrate that the book becomes so much more interesting and exciting when approached in this way. If you remain constrained by the dry and technical manner of its presentation, you will emerge pretty desiccated by the experience. A more expansive and speculative reading allows you to import your own political fire into a text that on the surface seems to provide very little material for political activism.

Volume II is about the motion of capital, the "metamorphoses" that it undergoes as it moves through the different states of money, production, and commodities in a continuous stream. Whereas the labor process and the production of surplus-value dominate the argument in Volume I, these are viewed in Volume II as mere moments en route not only to the realization of surplus-value as capital in the marketplace but also to the perpetual renewal through capital circulation of the powers of domination of capital over social labor. The temporality (and to a lesser degree spatiality) of circulation is brought sharply into focus. The continuity of capital circulation, presupposed in Volume I, becomes a major preoccupation. We deal with questions of turnover time and of speed-up, with the complexities that arise because more and more capital circulates as fixed capital—not only the machines and the factories, but the whole complex of transport networks, built environments and physical infrastructures.

The circulation process of capital is here presented as the lifeblood that courses through the body politic of capitalism in the desperate quest to reproduce the capital-labor class relation. The potential barriers, blockages and imbalances within these processes of circulation form a field of contradictions which cry out for analysis. They also provide potential foci for political agitation. Anticapitalist politics have to grapple with the findings (tentative though they may be) of Volume II if they are to succeed. Though there is plenty of potential red meat for the political agitator buried in these pages, many of the findings do not sit easily with some of the political presuppositions that the Marxist left (heavily influenced by Volume I) has traditionally embraced. Problems are posed—such as the future of money and credit—that are not easy to resolve through classic forms of class struggle that focus on the workplace. Volume II defines what has to be reconstituted or replaced in the sphere of circulation if we are not all to starve when the revolution comes.

Marx opens Volume II by stating that the subject of his enquiry is rooted in the chapter on money in Volume I. This is discouraging, since the money chapter, being long, tedious and challenging, is where many people give up on that volume. I therefore advised first-time readers when reading Volume I to push on through this chapter as best they could to get to the more interesting materials on the other side. But here, in Volume II, we are invited to linger and expand upon this chapter at length. It is easier to do so once you recall the definition of capital, given in chapter 4 of Volume I, as a *process* and not a *thing*. The basic process is a continuous flow of value transiting through different states (entailing changes of form, or "metamorphoses" as Marx calls them):

$$\begin{matrix} & LP & \\ M\text{-}C & \ldots P \ldots & C'\text{-}M + \Delta M \\ & MP & \end{matrix}$$

If you are curious to know what kind of process this really is, then Volume II provides insights—such as the drive toward speed-up and the deepening tension between fixed and circulating capital—that are both revealing and surprising.

In pursuing his enquiries, Marx is never shy of making dramatic simplifying assumptions. These allow him, he frequently argues, to explore the dynamics of capital circulation and accumulation in their "pure state." Thus, on the very first page of Volume II, we read:

> In order to grasp these forms in their pure state, we must first of all abstract from all aspects that have nothing to do with the change and constitution of the forms as such. We shall therefore assume here, both that commodities are sold at their values, and that the circumstances in which this takes place do not change. We shall also ignore any changes of value that may occur in the course of the cyclical process.

The assumption that commodities exchange at their values (we abstract from the daily volatility of market prices) is familiar from Volume I, and we can, I think, presume that the "circumstances" to which Marx refers are those of perfectly functioning, legally defined and competitive market exchange set out in chapter 2 of Volume I. The "pure state" also assumes a closed system. There is no trade with some "outside"—unless otherwise specified—while capital is completely dominant within a closed system. The real kicker comes in the last sentence. "Changes of value" arise out of the changing productivity of labor. This is achieved through the technological and organizational changes outlined in the theory of relative surplus-value that dominates much of the text of Volume I. In Volume II, Marx excludes the theory of relative surplus-value from his purview and builds a model of an economy in a static technological and organizational state. At the outset of chapter 20, for example, he forcefully reiterates the assumption: "As far as revolutions in value are concerned, they change nothing . . ." (469). So the theory we are about to explore is one in which the technological and organizational dynamism that so dominates the argument in Volume I (and which constitutes such a revolutionary force in *The Communist Manifesto*) is held to one side in order to explore some other crucial aspects of the laws of motion of capital.

So what is it, then, that Marx is after in Volume II? Once surplus-value is produced (a process we understand very well from Volume I), then how does it get realized and then continue to circulate as accumulating capital? And, as it circulates, what particular forms of capital does it necessarily engender? Marx was obviously aware that the class configurations of merchants, bankers and financiers, and landlords existed in some relation to the industrial capitalist who, in Volume I, is depicted as the direct and sole appropriator of the surplus-value produced by wage labor. He also knew that these other forms of capital preexisted the rise of capitalist production and the factory system, and that they therefore played critical historical roles in the construction of a capitalist mode of production. Marx refuses, however, to conceptualize them as "mere residuals" of the transition from feudalism to capitalism. What he wants to know is how and why these other forms of capital are socially necessary to the survival of a capitalist mode of production in a "pure state," and in what ways they might become the locus of contradictions and crises.

The idea of "capital in a pure state" is important for Marx. It is always possible, when faced with a crisis, to say that the crisis is due to some impurity or malfunction of a "pure" and therefore perfect capitalist mode of production. We have heard that a lot from neoliberals in the last few years: the problem is not, they say, any deep contradiction within the neoliberal model of market capitalism itself but a failure to follow neoliberal dictates properly. Their solution is to drive capital back even further toward its pure state through a politics of austerity and an increasing emasculation of state powers. What Marx seeks to show is that crises are inherent in, necessary and endemic to the survival of a capitalist mode of production in all its purity. Not only can no amount of regulatory tinkering set that matter aright, but the closer the economy converges on its pure state, the deeper the crisis will likely become (which is where Europe with its austerity politics seemed so clearly to be headed in 2012).

What Volume II also shows, however, is that independent and autonomously forming crisis tendencies always exist within the circulatory system. For conventional Marxists this is not always welcome news. It poses the problem of how to wage class struggle against, say, the merchants, the bankers, currency traders and the like, and to understand the many activities in which they engage (insurance, hedging, betting on derivatives, collateralized debt obligations, credit default swaps, and so on). We need to establish what the contradictions are and figure out what the impacts of independent and autonomously forming commercial and financial crises might be. We also need a better understanding of the role of financial giants, like the infamous "vampire squid" known as Goldman Sachs, along with Citibank, RBS, HSBC, Deutsche Bank, and so on, and likewise to unpack the role of merchant capitalists such as Walmart, Ikea and Carrefour in the political economy of our own times.

Marx imposes draconian restrictions and exclusions on what is or is not admissible in the theoretical world he is constructing throughout all of *Capital*. This is particularly evident in Volume II.[1] Where do these restrictions come from, and how can they be justified? The credit system and the circulation of interest-bearing capital are frequently mentioned, for example, only to be shunted aside, usually with the comment that a consideration of such a form of circulation "does not belong here." But why not? An examination of fixed-capital circulation or of differential turnover times in the absence of a credit system does not seem on the surface to make much sense. So why does Marx systematically exclude credit from consideration throughout Volume II, all the while admitting that everything changes when the credit system intervenes?

It is hard to answer this question without probing into the deeply fraught relationship between Marx's "scientific" political-economic writings (*Capital*, the *Grundrisse* and *Theories of Surplus Value*) on the one hand and his historical writings (such as the *Eighteenth Brumaire of Louis Bonaparte* and *The Civil War in France*) on the other. Marx points to this tension on the very first page of *Capital*. Having defined the commodity as a unity of use- and exchange-values, he shunts the question of use-value aside (only, as we have seen, to resurrect it shortly thereafter) saying that "to study the uses of things is the work of history." From this and many other statements, we can reasonably conclude that Marx clearly understood political economy and history as two distinctive fields of enquiry. This raises the general question of how to understand the significance of the political economy. This is a particularly pertinent question to be asked of Volume II. Answering it, I believe, helps us to understand the exclusions that characterize Volume II.

---

1   The only set of studies on this volume is that of Christopher John Arthur and Geert A. Reuten, eds., *The Circulation of Capital: Essays on Volume Two of Marx's Capital* (London: Macmillan, 1998).

The political-economic writings are, of course, by no means devoid of historical content. The capitalist mode of production, which is their theoretical object of enquiry, is presented as an historical construct that arose out of feudalism, and which has the potential if not the necessity to evolve into some other social order, called "socialism" or "communism." The historical writings and the journalistic commentaries, on the other hand, make scant reference to political-economic theory and the laws of motion of capital—though they do, of course, document the turbulence of actual class struggles. The one exception is *The Communist Manifesto*, written in 1848, in which many of the themes later explored in *Capital* are easily discerned. We are, however, left to impute the political-economic content in the early historical works such as the *Eighteenth Brumaire*, which analyzes the aftermath of the economic crisis and revolutionary movements of 1847–48 in France. It takes considerable effort to exhume the economic content of *The Civil War in France*, which centers on the Paris Commune of 1871.[2] The focus is almost exclusively on fluid and often seemingly accidental political dynamics. Key concepts in Marx's political economy—the production of an industrial reserve army, the falling rate of profit, the theory of relative surplus-value, and the like—rate no mention even in historical texts written after the first volume of *Capital* was already published.

The difference between these two literatures would not be so troubling were it not for a seemingly unbridgeable divide between the fluid, accidental and voluntaristic tone of the historical and political writings, on the one hand, and the rigorously scientific and lawlike political economy on the other. There seem to be two Marxisms—the deterministic and the voluntaristic—that are never destined to meet, except through a rather arid debate, fuelled largely by Engels and turned into dogma by Stalin, on whether the transition to communism was a scientific question and whether dialectical materialism constitutes a theory of history.

In the introduction to the English version of the *Grundrisse*, Marx outlines the principles that guide his political-economic enquiries. These help explain the rules of engagement that Marx observed in constructing his theoretical edifice, while shedding light on where the

---

2   K. Marx, *The Eighteenth Brumaire of Louis Bonaparte* (New York: International Publishers, 1963); K. Marx and V. I. Lenin, *The Civil War in France* (New York: International Publishers, 1989).

gap between history and theory comes from. I have concluded that he rigorously (and if one wanted to be critical, as to some degree I am, one would say "rigidly") stuck by these principles in writing all of *Capital* (and there is no better place to examine this practice than in Volume II). This framework permitted him to transcend the particularities of his own times (such as the details of the crisis of 1857–58 that inspired his preparatory writings in the *Grundrisse*) and to produce a tentative though incomplete alternative theory of the laws of motion of capital. These laws animate, he held, the dynamics of all historical and geographical situations in which the capitalist mode of production predominates. But the achievement of this general theory came at a cost. The general framework Marx sets out constitutes a straitjacket that limits the applicability of these laws and leaves us a lot of work to do to understand particular historical movements and conjunctures.[3]

Marx sought a political economy that would be truly scientific. This science would, he hoped, have a power analogous to that of the knowledge structures of physics and chemistry. The law of value and surplus-value operates, Marx held, like a law of nature, albeit of capitalism's historical nature. Several times he compares value to the force of gravity. A better analogy would be the laws of fluid dynamics, which underpin all theorizing about the dynamics of atmospheres and oceans, and innumerable other phenomena where fluids of any sort are in motion. These laws cannot be mechanically applied to fields such as weather forecasting or climate change without all manner of modifications, and even then there are plenty of excesses that remain inexplicable. Marx's laws of motion of capital are very much of this sort. They do not and cannot explain all aspects of the prevailing economic climate let alone predict tomorrow's economic weather. This does not mean that Marx's political economy is irrelevant. No one in the physical sciences would dismiss the laws of fluid dynamics just because they do not provide exact predictions of tomorrow's weather.

Marx's general method goes something like this. He assumes that the legions of political economists and commentators who have written on the topic since the seventeenth century have made honest and good-faith

---

3   A more detailed version of the argument that follows can be found in David Harvey, "History versus Theory: A Commentary on Marx's Method in Capital," *Historical Materialism* 20: 2 (2012), 3–38.

attempts to understand the complicated economic world that was emerging around them. There were, of course, "vulgar" economists, who sought to justify the class privileges into which they were often born—but this was not true of William Petty, James Steuart, Adam Smith, David Ricardo, and so on. But even the vulgar economists, by the crassness of their arguments, revealed something very important about the inner nature of capital (as Marx shows in his amusing dissection of "Senior's Last Hour" in Volume I of *Capital*). By exploring critically (with the aid of dialectics) their formulations and the inner contradictions in their arguments, Marx aimed, as he declared in his Preface to *Capital*, to construct an alternative account of the laws of motion of capital.

Marx established his new political-economic science through a critique of classical political economy rather than through direct historical, anthropological and statistical enquiry and induction. This critique, most explicitly attempted in *Theories of Surplus Value* but also permanently present in *Capital* and the *Grundrisse*, accords a good deal of authority (some would argue far too much, and there are quite a few instances where I agree with that criticism) to the collective understandings of bourgeois political economy and bourgeois representations (as with, for example, the reports of the factory inspectors in England, the country where industrial capitalism was, according to Marx, most advanced). So how does he construe the general approach of the bourgeois political economists? And how did classical political economy frame its subject?[4]

"Production," he says in the *Grundrisse*,

> appears as the point of departure, consumption as the conclusion, distribution and exchange as the middle. . . . Thus production, distribution, exchange and consumption form a regular syllogism; production is the generality, distribution and exchange the particularity, and consumption the singularity in which the whole is joined together. . . . Production is

---

4   It is all too easy to confuse Marx's presentation of the arguments of the classical political economists with what he claims as his own. For example, the statement cited above from the *Grundrisse*, that the falling rate of profit is "the most important law of modern political economy," refers in the first instance to the political economy of Ricardo. The degree to which Marx accepted this law is therefore an open question that has to be settled by further study of his writings. Broadly speaking, he accepted the general thrust of the law, but radically reformulated the mechanism by which it worked.

determined by the general natural laws, distribution by social accident. ... exchange stands between the two as formal social movement; and the concluding act, consumption, which is conceived not only as a terminal point but also as an end in itself, actually belongs outside of economics except insofar as it reacts in turn upon the point of departure and initiates the whole process anew. (*Grundrisse*, 108–9)

This statement is foundational for understanding Marx's approach in *Capital*. Notice, then, the distinctions here invoked between *generalities* (production), which are deterministic and lawlike; *particularities* (exchange and distribution), which are accidental and conjunctural (for example, outcomes of social struggles that depend on the balance of forces deployed); and *singularities* (consumption), which I take to be unpredictable and potentially chaotic. Note also that the singularities of consumption belong largely "outside of economics" (and, presumably, within the realm of history as suggested on the first page of *Capital*). The general framework suggested here is laid out in Figure 1.

Figure 1: The "Weak Syllogistic'" Framework for Analysis that Marx Adopts in *Capital*

Universal Production	Universality	Natural Law	Determinate	Metabolic Relation to Nature	Evolution (Darwin)
Social Production	**Generality (Land, Labor, Capital, Money, Value)**	**Social Laws**	**Determinate**	**Laws of Motion of Capital**	**Political Economy**
Distribution	Particularity (Rent, Wages, Profit, Interest, Commercial Profit, Taxes)	Accidental and Contingent	Indeterminate	Outcomes of Class and Factional Struggles; Uneven Geographical Development	History, Geography, Geopolitics
Exchange	Particularity (Property Rights, Juridical Individuals, Competition, Centralization, Monopoly)	Accidental and Contingent	Indeterminate	Institutions, Competition versus Monopoly; Collective and Associated Forms of Capital and Labor	State Forms, History, Geography, Geopolitics
Consumption	Singularity	Chaotic	Unpredictable	Human Passions, Beliefs, Desires, Motivations, Socialities and Political Subjectivities (Affects)	Cultural and Psychological Analysis; Production of Human Wants, Needs, Desires

While this syllogism "is admittedly a coherence," it is, says Marx, "a shallow one." So he rejects it in favor of a dialectical conception of how production, distribution, exchange and consumption might be brought together within the totality of relations comprising a capitalist mode of production. After many pages discussing the inner and dialectical relations between, for example, production and consumption, and then production and distribution, and finally production and exchange, he reaches his conclusion. Production, distribution, exchange and consumption "form the members of a totality, distinctions within a unity. . . . Mutual interaction takes place between the different moments. This is the case with every organic whole" (*Grundrisse*, 99–100). The organic whole (totality) of a capitalist mode of production that Marx has in mind is not purely Hegelian (though it may well derive from revolutionizing Hegel's conceptions rather than simply turning them right-side-up). Its structure is ecosystemic, comprising relations within what Gramsci and Lefebvre call an "ensemble" or Deleuze an "assemblage" of moments. "Nothing simpler for a Hegelian than to posit production and consumption as identical," complains Marx. "And this has been done not only by socialist belletrists but by prosaic economists themselves, e.g. Say" (*Grundrisse*, 93–4).

One would expect that Marx would choose this dialectical and organic formulation to construct his alternative theory. But, from his practice in *Capital*, it becomes clear that he sticks to the shallow syllogistic framework given by classical political economy even as he uses organic thinking and dialectical-relational analysis to build his critique and explore alternatives. He sticks throughout as closely as he can to the bourgeois conception of a lawlike level of generality—of production—and excludes the "accidental" and social particularities of distribution and exchange (until he gets to discuss them in the latter part of Volume III), and even more so the chaotic singularities of consumption, from his political-economic enquiries. Thus both Volumes I and II presume that it does not matter how the surplus-value might be divided between interest, rent, profit on merchants' capital, profit of production and taxes. He also assumes that all commodities, with the exception of labor, are traded at their value (consumer desires are always manifest in ways that allow value to be realized in a trouble-free manner). There is, therefore, no theory of consumerism in Marx's *Capital* (an unfortunate gap given that consumption now accounts for some 70 percent of economic activity in the United States—compared to some 30 percent in China, which was probably closer to the general level in Marx's time).

Even more interestingly, Volume I is extremely weak in its discussion of the particularity of the distributive share that accrues to labor as wages. The question of what determines the value of labor-power is dealt with in two pages. It comprises a long list of all sorts of factors (everything from climate to the state of class struggle and the degree of civilization in a country) before declaring that labor-power is not a commodity like any other because it incorporates a moral element, but that in a given society at a given time its value is known. The analysis then proceeds on the presumption that the value of labor-power is fixed (which we know it never is). The later chapters on wages are pathetically thin. There is no attempt to come up with a theory of wage determination. All Marx does is to repeat the theory of surplus-value for the umpteenth time and add the insight that the practices of paying wages by the hour or by the piece mask even further what surplus-value might be about. He also records that there is a problem of trade between nations when the cost of reproduction, and therefore the value of labor-power, differs.

In Volume II, Marx likewise analyzes the commodity and money circuits of capital without any mention of distribution—interest on money capital and profit on commercial capital—and excludes any analysis of the credit system even though he freely concedes innumerable times that credit is a necessity and that everything looks different when it is taken into account. Again and again, we find exclusions of this sort from the analysis. The exclusions are almost always justified on the grounds that they do not lie within the field of generality with which Marx is exclusively concerned. This practice is found right throughout *Capital*. "It is outside the scope of our plan," Marx writes in his opening to what would seem a crucial chapter on "Credit and Fictitious Capital" in Volume III, "to give a detailed analysis of the credit system and the instruments it creates (credit money, etc.). Only a few points will be emphasized here, *which are necessary to characterize the capitalist mode of production in general*" (emphasis added).

I should add a caveat here. The exclusions are occasionally transcended (as in the case of the value of labor-power about which Marx has to say something). Marx typically handles such situations by a brief description of the problem (for example, the relation to nature or the consumer desires of workers), and adds a few assertions as to its significance before returning to the generality of production. He rarely devotes more than a few paragraphs (and sometimes only a sentence or two) to such issues.

So why does he stick with the bourgeois structure of knowledge so rigidly when he has already laid out an alternative dialectical, relational and organic way to understand how capital works? I really do not have a good answer to this question. All I know for sure is that this is clearly what he does (the textual evidence is overwhelming). My best hypothesis is that, if Marx's fundamental aim was to subject classical political economy to critique on its own terms, then he had to accept the general nature of those terms in order to identify their inner contradictions and deconstruct their absences. So, if bourgeois theorists presupposed a non-coercive free market, then he had to as well (as he does in the second chapter of Volume I). If the distinctions between generalities, particularities and singularities were foundational to the bourgeois mode of thought, then he had to work on that foundation too. This is the only answer I can give, but it is not fully satisfactory, because he abandons some bourgeois terms but not others. He will have no truck in Volume I with questions of supply and demand or of utility, for example (and we will shortly see why). He never bothers to explain the rationale for his choices. But it is overwhelmingly obvious that these are the choices he makes throughout.

The three levels of generality, particularity and singularity are not the whole story. There is a fourth level—that of universality—which concerns the metabolic relation to nature. Marx objected strongly to the habit of the classical political economists of presenting production "as encased in eternal natural laws independent of history." Marx rejects this "naturalization" of the political economy of capitalism. He takes every opportunity he can to attack this naturalistic view of things (including the Ricardian/Malthusian view that the profit rate was bound to fall because of natural scarcities and rising rents). The generalities of the capitalist mode of production cannot, he insists, be explained by appeal to the universalities of natural law.

While Marx accepts that "capitalist production" is the lawlike generality that he wants to understand, he refuses the idea that it is natural in the sense that the natural sciences would understand that term. Capitalism is lawlike but the laws (including those of private property relations) are a product of human action. These laws should be distinguished from those that derive from our embeddedness in a world governed by natural laws (such as those of physics, chemistry and Darwinian evolution). These latter laws are considered immutable: we cannot live outside of them. In Volume I of *Capital*, Marx writes: "Labour . . . as the creator of use values, as useful labour, is a condition of human existence which is independent of all forms of society." It is "an eternal and natural necessity which mediates the metabolism between man and nature and therefore human life itself" (C1, 133). The labor process "is the universal condition for the metabolic interaction between man and nature, the everlasting nature-imposed condition of human existence, and therefore it is independent of every form of that existence, or rather it is common to all forms of society in which human beings live" (C1, 290). We can only do as nature does.

The focus of Marx's scientific enquiry is to uncover how the general laws of capitalist political economy came to be, how they actually function, and why and how they might be changed. And he wants to do this without invoking the universality that describes our ever-evolving metabolic relation to nature.

Marx takes these distinctions between universality, generality, particularity and singularity from bourgeois political economy even as he injects into them relational and dialectical meanings and critical strategies drawn from Spinoza and Hegel. He threatens, in the *Grundrisse*, to make them his own by embedding them in the concept of an organic totality. The problem would then be to understand how these different "moments"—the universal metabolic relation to nature, the general production of surplus-value, the particularities of its distribution and exchange relations and the singularities of consumption—interrelate. He then has to show how to isolate the lawlike character of production from everything else, and why it is so important to do so.

Marx's political economy operates primarily at the level of the lawlike generality of production. But why prioritize production? Marx holds that "production predominates not only over itself, in the antithetical definition of production, but over the other moments as well. The process always returns to production to begin anew" (*Grundrisse*, 99). What does this strange wording mean? It would be wrong to interpret the production that "predominates" over itself as the material production of goods and services, as the concrete labor process, or even as the production of commodities. This is, unfortunately, a very common misreading. It leads to that erroneous interpretation of Marx as saying that social relations, ideas, human desires, and so on, are all determined by physical material practices. This is an erroneous productivist and physicalist reading of Marx, and it is not what Marx's historical materialism is about.

The production that "predominates" within a capitalist mode of production is *the production of surplus-value*, and surplus-value is a *social* and not a physical, material relation. It is, after all, the production of surplus-value that is the fundamental focus of Volume I of *Capital*. The mobilization by capital of material labor processes is geared to the production of surplus-value. What Marx means when he says that production predominates over itself in the "antithetical definition of production" is that concrete material labor processes that are surplus-value producing are all that matter. Material production processes that do not produce surplus-value are valueless. In Marx's grander scheme of things, of course, this means that the emancipatory possibilities available to human beings through the sensual physicality of the labor process are perverted and dominated by the social necessity to produce surplus-value for others. The result is universal alienation of human beings from their own potential capacities and creative powers. Some of the most powerful passages in the *Grundrisse* and *Capital* hammer home this point.

The production of surplus-value through the circulation of capital is, in short, the pivot upon which the lawlike character of a capitalist mode of production turns: no surplus-value, no capital. This was the fundamental break that Marx made with classical political economy. Marx continues: "That exchange and consumption cannot be predominant is self-evident. Likewise, distribution as distribution of products; while as distribution of the agents of production it is a moment of production. A definite production thus determines a definite consumption, distribution and exchange as well as *definite relations between these different moments*. Admittedly, however, *in its one-sided form*, production is itself determined by the other moments" (*Grundrisse*, 99). "One-sided" refers to the material labor process rather than to the social production of surplus-value. So what does "determine" mean here?

The "law" of a capitalist mode of production actually takes the following form: all manner of contingent and accidental structures of distribution and exchange and a grand diversity of consumption regimes are possible in principle, *provided that they do not unduly restrict or destroy the capacity to produce surplus-value on an ever-expanding scale.* A relatively egalitarian social-democratic structure of distribution in, say, Scandinavia can coexist with a brutal, unequal and authoritarian neoliberal regime of distribution in, say, Chile in the 1980s, provided that surplus-value is produced in both places. There is no unique pattern of distribution, system of exchange or specific cultural regime of consumption that can be derived from the general laws for the production of surplus-value. But—and this is a big "but"—*the possibilities are not infinite.* If any one of the moments, including the relation to nature, assumes a configuration that unduly restricts or undermines the capacity to produce surplus-value, then either capital ceases to exist or all-round adaptations within the totality of relations must occur. This is what "determines" means.

Such adaptations can occur incrementally, most often either through competition, state interventions or uneven geographical developments, in which configurations achieved in one space of the global economy out-compete others in producing surplus-value (much as the Chinese are now doing and the Japanese and Germans did in the 1980s). Changes can also occur through violent shakeouts: hence the significance of both localized and global crises and even wars (please note: I am not saying all wars and armed struggles occur solely for this reason).

Distribution, exchange and consumption reciprocally affect each other. But they also affect the production of surplus-value. This is so, Marx concedes, for a very simple reason: "Ground rent, wages, interest and profit figure under distribution while land, labour and capital figure under production as agents of production." Capital itself, Marx points out, "is posited doubly, (1) as agent of production, (2) as source of income, as a determinant of specific forms of distribution. . . . The category of wages, similarly, is the same as that which is examined under a different heading as wage labour, the characteristic which labour here possesses as an agent of production appears as a characteristic of distribution." So, while Marx sidelines the distributive aspects (the particularities of actual wage and profit rates, as well as interest rates, rents, taxes, profits on merchant capital) as contingent and accidental, and as therefore not lawlike (though this does not exclude empirical or historical generalizations), he foregrounds the crucial roles of land, wage labor, capital, money and exchange in the lawlike production of surplus-value. As a result, the factors of production loom large while the agents and rewards that attach to them are excluded from the picture (as is the case most obviously in Volume II). This leads many students to ask: Where is the agency in all of this political-economic theory? The answer is that Marx is merely following classical political economy. In his historical writings he does not have to do so.

So, let us look a little more closely at how he handles the particularities and the singularities that are so rigorously (rigidly?) excluded from his general theory.

THE PARTICULARITIES OF EXCHANGE

In the second chapter of the first volume of *Capital*, Marx assumes that "men are henceforth related to each other in their social process of production in a purely atomistic way. Their own relations of production therefore assume a material shape which is independent of their control and their conscious individual action." Marx here accepts the Smithian vision of a "hidden hand" of a perfectly functioning competitive market. The laws of motion of capital that Marx constructs also rest upon this fiction. The result, as we know, is Marx's compelling theoretical critique of free-market utopianism. The inevitable outcome, says Marx, is wealthier capitalists at one pole and ever more impoverished workers at the other. Such a system could not possibly produce, therefore, a result that would redound to the benefit of all, as Smith presumed.

This utopian vision of a perfectly functioning market never was and never could be realized. But what happens when exchange does not conform to this utopian vision? There are two areas in particular that call for attention.

Supply and Demand

When first reading Marx, many students ask: What happened to supply and demand? The answer Marx gives is: "If demand and supply balance, the oscillation of prices ceases, all other circumstances remaining the same. But then demand and supply also cease to explain anything." The price of labor, for example, "at the moment when demand and supply are in equilibrium, is its natural price, determined independently of the relation of demand and supply." Marx deals, for the most part, exclusively in the so-called "natural" or equilibrium prices presumed in classical political economy. The reason that shoes cost more on average than shirts has nothing to do with differentials in demand for shoes relative to shirts. It is determined by labor content (both past and present). Supply and demand and price fluctuations are vital for bringing the economy into equilibrium, but they have nothing to say about where that equilibrium might lie.

But we know, both theoretically and in practice, that supply and demand do not always come into equilibrium. There are many systemic reasons, such as asymmetries of information and of power, and politically managed currency exchange rates (such as that practiced by the Chinese), that distort prices and dictate a path of development that is very different from that which Marx, drawing on Smith, theoretically allowed. Marx, for the most part, rules these distortions out by assumption. But there are instances when he has to allow them into the picture because of their systemic relevance. In the case of the price of labor, for example,

> capital acts on both sides at once. If its accumulation on the one hand increases the demand for labour, it increases on the other the supply of workers by "setting them free" [through technologically induced unemployment] while at the same time the pressure of the unemployed compels those who are employed to furnish more labour, and therefore makes the supply of labour to a certain extent independent of the supply of workers. The movement of the law of supply and demand of labour on this basis completes the despotism of capital.

But as soon as workers figure this out, and form institutions and organize through trade unions to protect their interests, then "capital and its sycophant, political economy, cry out at the infringement of the 'eternal' and so to speak 'sacred' law of supply and demand" (C1, 793–4).

But, in both Volume II and Volume III, we encounter an even more damning reason why this equilibrium assumption cannot hold. It is both inevitable and necessary that the relation between supply and demand *not* be in equilibrium if capital is to survive. This is so because the total demand set in motion by capital is c + v (this is what capital lays out on wages and purchase of means of production) and the total supply is c + v + s (this is the total value produced). Capital's interest is to maximize the surplus-value, which increases the gap between demand and supply. So where does the extra (effective) demand come from to buy the surplus-value? Marx's very interesting answer is given in chapter 9, below.

The Coercive Laws of Competition

"The coercive laws of competition" play a vital role throughout *Capital*. "Competition," Marx argues in the *Grundrisse* (730; 752), "is the mode generally in which capital secures the victory of its mode of production." It "executes the inner laws of capital; makes them into compulsory laws towards the individual capital, *but it does not invent them. It realizes them*" (emphasis added). Like supply and demand, competition is treated as a mere executor and enforcer of inner laws of motion of capital that are established by other forces.

With respect to absolute surplus-value and the extension of the working day, for example, the spread of the appalling practices he describes does not depend in any way on the good or ill will of the individual capitalist. "Under free competition, the immanent laws of capitalist production confront the individual capitalist as a coercive force external to him" (C1, 381). With respect to relative surplus-value, innovations in productivity are similarly impelled forward by competition for market advantage. "While it is not our intention here," he says,

> to consider the way in which the immanent laws of capitalist production manifest themselves in the external movement of the individual capitals, assert themselves as the coercive laws of competition, and therefore enter into the consciousness of the individual capitalist as the motives which drive him forward, this much is clear: a scientific analysis of competition is possible only if we can grasp the inner nature of capital, just as the apparent motions of the heavenly bodies are intelligible only to someone who is acquainted with their real motions, which are not perceptible to the senses. Nevertheless, for the understanding of the production of relative surplus-value . . . there is a motive for each individual capitalist to cheapen his commodities by increasing the productivity of labour. (C1, 433)

In considering the impulsions that force individual capitalists to reinvest a part of their surplus-value in expansion, he invokes similar processes:

The development of capitalist production makes it necessary constantly to increase the amount of capital laid out in a given industrial undertaking, the competition subordinates every capitalist to the immanent laws of capitalist production, as external coercive laws. It compels him to keep extending his capital so as to preserve it, and he can only extend it by means of progressive accumulation. (C1,739)

Pressures to equalize the rate of profit, so essential to the argument that leads into the theory of a falling profit rate, similarly presume the operation of the coercive laws of competition.

But what happens when the enforcing power of competition is, for some systemic reason, ineffective? There is, Marx concedes, always a tendency for monopoly to be the final outcome of competition. But monopoly, oligopoly and the centralization of capital can also arise for other reasons. When barriers to entry into a particular line of production are high because of the massive amounts of capital initially required (as in building railroads), then "the laws of centralization of capital," with the help of the credit system, must take over. In fact, in any line of production where there are pronounced economies of scale, then something like an oligopolistic situation may result. To all this I add my own particular caveat: that, in a world of high transport costs, local industries, even those of small scale, are protected from competition. Falling transport costs from the mid-1960s onwards (with containerization being one of the unsung heroes of the process) changed the geography of competition remarkably.

Two important points then follow. When monopolistic and oligopolistic organization dominates, the laws of motion of capital (and even value itself) look very different. This was reflected in the theories of (state) monopoly capitalism that were articulated during the 1960s by Baran and Sweezy and the French Communist Party. The dynamics outlined by Lenin when he associated imperialism and monopoly capitalism into a specific configuration likewise depart significantly from the laws which Marx lays out in *Capital*.[5] This is an instance where the laws of motion are themselves clearly in motion.

---

5   Paul Boccara, *Études sur le capitalisme monopoliste d'État, sa crise et son issue* (Paris: Éditions Sociales, 1974); Paul Baran and Paul Sweezy, *Monopoly Capital* (New York: Monthly Review Press, 1966); V. I. Lenin, "Imperialism: The Highest Stage of Capitalism," in *Selected Works*, Vol. 1 (Moscow: Progress Publishers, 1963).

Phases of monopolization are, however, often followed by phases where the restoration of the power of the coercive laws of competition surges to the forefront of political concern. This happened towards the end of the 1970s throughout much of the capitalist world. It was, after all, central to the neoliberal agenda. Competition can be, as capitalists frequently complain, "ruinous," but monopoly can all too easily produce, as Baran and Sweezy argued, "stagflation." Capitalist state policies frequently attempt to regulate the balance between monopoly and competition either one way (through nationalization of the "command-ing heights" of the economy) or another (by anti-merger and monopoly legislation or by surrendering, willingly or unwillingly, to privatization and global competition).

In the cases of both supply and demand and competition, then, ques-tions arise as to the power of the enforcers to do their work. Laws mean nothing, after all, without effective enforcement. Whenever this issue comes up in *Capital*, as when the "laws of centralization of capital" are broached in Volume I, Marx characteristically turns away and says, "these laws cannot be developed here," even as he argues that centraliza-tion constitutes, with the aid of the credit system and joint stock companies, "new and powerful levers of social accumulation" (C1, 780). This does not diminish the relevance of Marx's focus on the laws as dictated by decentralized competition. But it does play an important role when it comes to figuring out how well those laws are being enforced in actual situations and why those laws may be changing. The ever-unresolved tension between decentralized competition and centralized monopoly power can even, under certain circumstances, become a trig-ger for crisis formation.

THE PARTICULARITIES OF DISTRIBUTION

Matters get even more interesting when it comes to the relations between the particularities of distribution and the general laws of motion of capi-tal. While Marx concedes that distributions must be integrated into those laws whenever they affect production directly, this occurs only under special circumstances (most particularly, of course, with respect to the relative shares of wages and profits in Volume I). He excludes any consideration of how the surplus-value might be distributed between rent, interest, profit on commercial capital and taxes in Volume I. In

Volume II, he avoids credit and interest even though he refers to their importance innumerable times (rent and profit on merchants' capital are likewise excluded). The circulation of commodity capital is also highlighted, but there is barely a mention of profit on commercial capital. This is why I find it so interesting, in teaching Volume II, to import all of the materials about merchants' capital (understood by Marx as both commercial and money-dealing capital) from Volume III into the purely technical presentations of Volume II on the circulation of money and commodity capitals (the circuit of production capital having been covered in Volume I). Not only does it attach a notion of class agency to the technical relations, but it opens up the revolutionary perspective that Engels feared was so lacking.

Volume II demonstrates, for example, the existence of a potential gap between where surplus-value is produced (in the labor process) and where it might be realized in circulation. If commercial (commodity) capital is powerful enough—as in the case of, say, Walmart—then much of the surplus-value produced may be realized by the merchants. The money capitalists can also take a huge cut, as can the landlords and the taxman, leaving the direct producers with the slenderest of profit margins (this is one of the reasons that any attempt to measure falling profit rates by looking only at money profits in the production sector alone is so hazardous). Organized labor can seem to procure a larger share of the value produced through struggles at the point of production, only to have that share recuperated by the capitalist class as a whole by the money-gouging retailers, the debt-peddling bankers and financiers, the landlords and, of course, the taxman, who often seems to specialize in taxing the poor to return surplus-value to the corporations and to the capitalists in the form of lucrative tax breaks and subsidies.

Throughout *Capital* Marx states that both merchants' capital and interest-bearing capital are "antediluvian" forms of capital that preceded the rise of a capitalist mode of production. He takes pretty much the same position with respect to landed property. The problem is then to understand how these prior means of extracting surpluses are rendered subservient to the rules of the capitalist mode of production. Usury, which played such an important role in undermining feudalism, had to be revolutionized so that it became interest-bearing capital operating within freely functioning money markets. Merchants, who once made their money buying cheap (or by robbery and stealing) and selling dear, can appropriate only that share of the surplus-value that accrues to them by virtue of the services they render to surplus-value production and realization. Rents on land and resources are fixed in relation to superior surplus-value production conditions; and rent levels can guide resource and land uses in ways that might optimize surplus-value production. This is broadly how Marx approaches these aspects of distribution. The rules of a capitalist mode of production supposedly discipline the distributional arrangements and the distributional shares (or, as Marx puts it in the *Grundrisse*, production of surplus-value "predominates" over distribution).

Financiers, merchants and landlords may or may not be more powerful than industrial capitalists in particular places and times. However, Marx treats their remunerations in a pure capitalist mode of production as being exclusively made up of deductions out of the surplus-value that comes from the exploitation of living labor in production. Their rate of return is sensitive to how much surplus-value is produced, which depends in part on their own indirect contribution (or lack of it) to surplus-value production. Distributional arrangements thus impinge upon the generalities of production in ways that Marx is reluctant to allow.

THE SINGULARITY OF CONSUMPTION

The production of surplus-value depends on its realization through consumption. Consumption cannot, therefore, be kept entirely outside of political economy as a general category because it reacts "upon the point of departure [of capital accumulation] and initiates the whole process anew." In the *Grundrisse*, Marx spends several pages going over the ways in which consumption and production of surplus-value relate. It is important to distinguish, Marx says, between (a) productive consumption on the part of the capitalist who needs raw materials, intermediate inputs, machinery, energy and the like in order to set a labor process in motion and (b) individual "final" consumption on the part of workers, capitalists and the various "unproductive classes" (military, state officials, and so on) that make up any social order. Consumption is necessary to complete the realization of the surplus-value produced in commodity form. But the demand has to be backed by an ability to pay. The capitalist, in short, recognizes only one kind of demand: *effective* demand.

So what is it, then, that lies outside of economics and political economy? To term consumption a "singularity" is to characterize it as something that is outside of the range of rational calculation, that is potentially uncontrollable, chaotic and unpredictable. The actual state of wants, needs and desires (and thus the qualities and politics of daily life) are therefore sidelined in the general theory. Capital is treated as agnostic as to what use-values to produce to satisfy final consumption, and seems indifferent as to whether people want horses and buggies or BMWs. The capitalist seems to say to the consumer: Whatever you fancy, want, need or desire, we will produce, provided you have enough money to pay for it. The issue of the historical and geographical development of actual consumption patterns and cultural lifestyles is thereby evaded. In Volume I of *Capital* Marx assumes that an effective demand always exists, that commodities (with the exception of labor-power) are traded at their value. This permits Marx to produce a general theory of capital accumulation that has the same relevance over entirely different final consumption regimes. This is the advantage that comes from abstracting from any distinctive regime of use-values. Had he locked himself into the consumption habits of mid-nineteenth-century Britain, we would no longer read him in the way we do.

But there are some general forces at work that call for elaboration. If a commodity is no longer wanted, needed, fancied or desired as a use-value, then it has no value. Both old and new uses and needs must therefore be stimulated to keep accumulation going. The problem is that, while "commodities are in love with money . . . 'the course of true love never did run smooth'. . . . Today the product satisfies a social need. Tomorrow it may perhaps be expelled partly or completely from its place by a similar product" (C1, 202–3). A vast industry has grown up since Marx's time to stimulate demand through fashion, advertising, emphasis upon lifestyle choices, and the like. But human curiosity and desire is not a blank slate upon which anything can be written. One need only look at the alacrity with which young children deploy their desires to play when given an iPad to recognize that Steve Jobs's brilliance lay as much in his understanding of human wants, needs, desires and powers as in his technical sophistication.

The manipulation and mobilization of human desires has been central to the history of capitalism, but Marx excludes it from the political economy precisely because it is the work of history to deal with it. But it is not entirely outside of theoretical elaboration.

Laborers, for example, exercise choices in how and on what they spend their money, so the state of their wants, needs and desires can become important. Maintenance of the necessary balances between the different sectors of the economy may require, Marx suggests, bourgeois manipulation of mass consumption to make the workers' consumption "rational" in relation to accumulation. Bourgeois philanthropy is therefore often about channeling laborers' consumption habits in ways favorable to accumulation. This was later most clearly exemplified in Henry Ford's use of social workers to monitor and direct workers' consumer habits when he introduced the $5 eight-hour day into his factories. The distinction between luxury goods and wage goods also becomes important because the dynamics of bourgeois consumption and of workers' consumption are qualitatively different.

Throughout *Capital*, the manifold ways that consumption can affect production are largely depicted in formal and technical terms, rather than as social relations and ways of daily life that have dynamics of their own. Marx avoids any specific characterization of the nature and form of final consumption habits, and he certainly avoids any mention of cultural preferences, fashion and aesthetic values or the compulsions of human desires (the role of sexuality in shaping consumerism, for example). But we can clearly see in Marx's presentation certain imperatives that explain why China is now the biggest market for BMWs when, a few years ago, the streets were full of bicycles.

Part of the work that Marx left us to do, therefore, is to pull together a far better understanding of contemporary consumerism than we typically possess. Traditional methodologies of political-economic enquiry do not work very well in this sphere (which is probably why Marx resisted bringing too many of the facts of consumption within the field of political economy). This applies as much to productive consumption—the application of labor in the labor process to consume materials in commodity production. The difficulty of controlling the singular character of laborers at work has come to be recognized, particularly through the work of Mario Tronti and Antonio Negri, as having great revolutionary potential precisely because of its singular character.[6]

---

6   Antonio Negri, *Marx Beyond Marx: Lessons on the Grundrisse* (London: Pluto Press, 1991); Harry Cleaver, *Reading* Capital *Politically* (Leeds–Edinburgh: Anti/Theses/AK Press, 2000).

In recent times, studies galore of consumption and consumerism have been produced, mainly in the field of cultural studies; but unfortunately all too many of them fail to situate their topic in relation to the totality of relations that Marx envisaged. Indeed, many such studies are conceived as antagonistic to the lawlike character of capital accumulation. There is, obviously, a sense in which this antagonism is correct, which is precisely why Marx held consumption to be about singularities, not generalities. But insofar as the ultimate aim of historical work (as opposed to lawlike political economy) is to understand a capitalist mode of production as an organic totality in evolution—so any attempt to understand our current conjuncture requires that we bring the world of consumption, of political subjectivities, and of the aesthetic, cultural and political preferences of individuals within the frame of enquiry, not as a substitute for the political economy but as a foundational and complementary field of analysis.

Of course, the world of human desire is not beyond the marked influence of the laws of motion of capital. The way that capital has changed our material world has implications for how our mental conceptions and our psychological make-up, our wants, needs and desires, our self-understanding have also changed. When the laws of motion of capital produced suburbanization as one answer to the persistent problem of overaccumulation, then tastes, preferences, wants, needs, desires and political subjectivities all shifted in tandem. And once all of these become embedded in a culture, then the rigidity of those cultural preferences came to form a serious barrier to revolutionary change. If, for example, it becomes necessary to revolutionize and reject suburban ways of life in order to open new paths either for capital accumulation, or even more compellingly for the transition to socialism through re-urbanization, then the fierce attachments of powerful political constituencies to suburban lifestyles and cultural habits will first have to be confronted, and eventually overcome.

It is undeniable that Marx operates throughout most of the three volumes of *Capital* within the "shallow syllogistic" framework derived from classical political economy, and that he largely confines his theoretical investigations to the level of generality within a purely functioning capitalist mode of production. In the texts that have come down to us, he marginalizes and frequently excludes questions of universality (the relation to nature), particularity (of exchange relations and distributions) and singularity (of consumption and of consumerisms), even as he recognizes in various study plans (such as that in the *Grundrisse*) that he would need further books on, for example, competition (actually there is a not very informative chapter on this topic in Volume III), the state, and the world market, to complete his project. When he does hit a point in *Capital* where the framework does not work, as we will see in the chapters on the circulation of interest-bearing capital, then he finally goes beyond it. But Marx does not attempt to re-specify what the laws of motion might look like under those new conditions where the framework is broken.

Volume II of *Capital* is written almost entirely in the shadow of the "shallow syllogistic" framework that Marx tended to impose upon all his political-economic enquiries. Rarely does he venture beyond that framework. While far-reaching and enlightening in some directions, the theoretical world he depicts is rigorously limited in others. Confining himself so tightly within the level of generality permitted Marx to construct an understanding of capital that transcended the historical particulars of his own time. This is why we can still read him today—even Volume II—and make sense of so much of what he has to say. On the other hand, this framework makes for difficulties of any immediate application to actually existing circumstances. This is the work we are left to do. We can better appreciate the nature of that work, however, when we understand the self-imposed limits of Marx's general theory and what, within its limitations, that theory can do for us. It is in the spirit of that question that I propose to take on the contents of Volume II. And it is to that exciting but daunting task that I now turn.

CHAPTER ONE

The Circuits of Capital (Chapters 1–3 of Volume II)

Capitalists typically start the day with a given amount of money. They go into the marketplace and buy means of production and labor-power, which they put to work using a particular technology and organizational form to produce a new commodity. This commodity is then taken to market and sold for the initial amount of money plus a profit (or, as Marx prefers to call it, a surplus-value). This is the basic form of the circulation of capital that Marx works with in Volume I of *Capital*. Put schematically, capital is defined as value in motion: *Money—Commodities......Production......Commodity'—Money'* (where M' can also be represented as M + DM, or in these chapters as *m*, the surplus-value). The central thesis Marx works with is that labor has the capacity to create more value (a *surplus*-value) than the value it can command as a commodity on the market. The freshly produced commodity, "impregnated" with surplus-value, is what is sold for a profit on the market. The reproduction of capital then depends on the recycling of all or part of M' back into the purchase, once more, of labor power and means of production to engage in a fresh round of commodity production.

"In Volume I," Marx writes, "the first and third stages [M-C and C'-M'] were discussed only insofar as this was necessary for the understanding of the second stage, the capitalist production process. Thus the different forms with which capital clothes itself in its different stages, alternately assuming them and casting them aside, remained uninvestigated. These will now be the immediate object of our enquiry" (109).

In the first three chapters of Volume II, Marx disaggregates the circulation process into three separate but intertwined circuits of *money* capital, *productive* capital and *commodity* capital. In the fourth chapter, he examines the circuit of what he calls "industrial capital," which is the unity of the three different circulation processes taken as a whole. In effect, Marx looks at the circulation process from the three different perspectives of money, production and the commodity. The general framework is laid out in Figure 2.

Figure 2

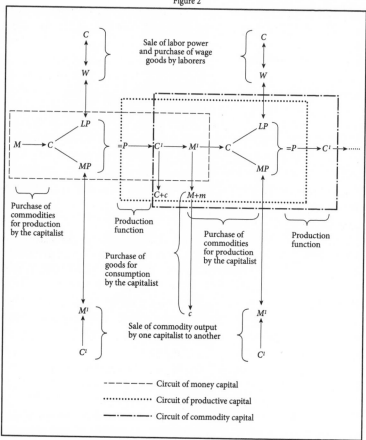

On the surface, this whole approach appears rather simplistic, even banal. He takes the continuous flow of circulation and boxes off three different circulation processes within it. It hardly seems worthwhile. But, through this tactic, he reveals and dissects the difficulties and contradictions inherent within the logic of the circulation process. From each window or perspective we get to see a rather different reality, and this allows us to identify points of potential disruption.

Throughout these chapters, Marx is preoccupied with three things, two of which are very explicit, while the third is implicit. The first is the idea of metamorphosis. This language derives from Volume I, chapter 3, where Marx makes much of the "metamorphoses" that occur within what he calls the "social metabolism" of capital. Metamorphoses are about changes in the form that capital assumes—from money to productive activity to commodity. Marx is interested both in the character that capital assumes as it enters and for a while dwells in each of these different states, and in how capital moves from one state to another. The central question that he poses is: What different possibilities and capacities attach to these different forms, and what difficulties arise in the move from one form to another? The analogy that might help here is that of the lifecycle of the butterfly. It lays its eggs; these become caterpillars that crawl around looking for food, before becoming a chrysalis within a protective cocoon. A beautiful butterfly suddenly emerges from the cocoon, and the butterfly flits around at will before laying its eggs to initiate the cycle anew. In each state the organism exhibits different capacities and powers: as an egg or as a chrysalis, it is immobile but growing; as a caterpillar it crawls around in search of food; and as a butterfly it can flit around at will. And so it is with capital. In its money state, capital can flit around butterfly-like pretty much at will. In its commodity form, capital, like the caterpillar, wanders the earth in search of someone who wants, needs or desires it, and has the money to pay for it and ultimately consume it. As a labor process, capital is for the most part rooted in the "hidden abode of production" (as Marx calls it in Volume I), in the place of the material activity of transforming natural elements through the production of commodities. It is usually locked in place at least during the time taken to make the commodity (transport, as we shall see, is an important exception).

For me, these distinctions are immediately meaningful. The differential spatial and geographical mobilities of capital in these different states have enormous implications for understanding the processes we now lump together under the heading of "globalization." Each "moment" in the circulation process—money, productive activity, commodity—is expressive of different possibilities. Money is the most geographically mobile form of capital, the commodity somewhat less so, while production processes are generally much harder (though by no means impossible) to move around. Within this general characterization there is a lot of variability. Some forms of commodity are easier to move around than others, and ease of movement is also relative to transportation capacities (containerization made shipping bottled water from France or Fiji to the US possible). The differential empowerment of the different factions of capital has huge consequences for how capital operates on the world stage. To empower finance capital relative to other forms of capital (such as production and merchant capital) is to invite the sort of hypermobility and "flitting around" of capital that has characterized capitalism over the last few decades. Marx does not take up such topics, but there is no reason why we cannot. Marx concentrates on other features of the metamorphoses that occur, and the differences and contradictions that can potentially arise.

This leads to the second major question in which Marx is interested. This concerns the potential for disruptions and crises within the circulatory process itself. In Volume I he made clear that the transitions from one moment to another are never free of tensions. It is generally easier to go, for example, from the universal form of value (money) into the particular form of value (the commodity) than it is to go in the other direction (commodities may be "in love with money," but "the course of true love never did run smooth," he observes). There is also no immediate necessity that impels anyone who has sold to use the money they receive to buy. Individuals can hold or hoard money. This underpins Marx's scathing attack upon Say's law in Volume I. Say held that purchases and sales are always in equilibrium, and therefore that there can never be any general crisis of overproduction (a proposition that Ricardo also accepted). But the holding of money (hoarding), as Keynes was later also to point out, is a permanent temptation, given that money is a universal form of social power appropriable by private persons. Hoarding is also, Marx shows, socially necessary (and throughout Volume II we will find frequent instances where this is so). But if everyone holds money and no one buys, then the circulation process gums up and eventually collapses. "These forms therefore imply," says Marx in Volume I, "the possibility of crises, though no more than the possibility. For the development of this possibility into a reality a whole series of conditions are required, which do not yet even exist from the standpoint of the simple circulation of commodities" (C1, 209). Volume II is in part concerned to show how these possibilities might be realized, though it does so in a frustratingly muted and technical way.

Marx also pointed out in Volume I that autonomously forming monetary crises are a very real possibility. With the quantity and prices of commodities constantly shifting, ways have to be found to adjust the supply of money to accommodate to the volatility in commodity production. Here a hoard of money becomes absolutely necessary. It provides a reserve of money to be drawn upon at times of hyperactivity. When money becomes money of account, then the need for commodity money (gold and silver) can be evaded. Balances can be settled up at, say, the end of the year, thereby reducing the demand for actual money (specie, coins, notes). But using money of account creates a new relationship, that between debtor and creditor. And this produces, Marx argued in Volume I, a contradiction, an antagonism, that

> bursts forth in that aspect of an industrial and commercial crisis which is known as a monetary crisis. Such a crisis occurs only where the ongoing chain of payments has been fully developed, along with an artificial system for settling them. Whenever there is a general disturbance of the mechanism, no matter what its cause, money suddenly and immediately changes over from its merely nominal shape, money of account, into hard cash. Profane commodities can no longer replace it. (C1, 236)

In other words, you cannot settle your bills with more IOUs; you have got to find hard cash, the universal equivalent and representation of value, to pay them off. If hard cash cannot be found, then

> the use-value of commodities becomes valueless, and their value vanishes in the face of their own form of value. The bourgeois, drunk with prosperity and arrogantly certain of himself, has just declared that money is a purely imaginary creation. "Commodities alone are money," he said. But now the opposite cry resounds over the markets of the world: only money is a commodity. As the hart pants after fresh water, so pants his soul after money, the only wealth. In a crisis, the antithesis between commodities and their value-form, money, is raised to the level of an absolute contradiction. (C1, 236–7)

Does the analysis in Volume II shed light on this issue? The answer is both yes and no. In Volume II, Marx lays the basis for understanding the conditions that might convert the possibilities of circulatory crises into realities. But there is no compelling argument proffered as to why such possibilities *must* rather than *might* become realities, and under what conditions. In part, this derives from Marx's reluctance to integrate the particularities of distribution into his arguments. Marx refrains from any analysis of the role of credit in Volume II, because it is a fact of distribution and a particularity. But it becomes plain as a pikestaff, throughout Volume II, that credit has major effects within the generality of production, and therefore on the actual laws of motion of capital. In the absence of any consideration of how the particularities of distribution and exchange work, a general theory of crisis formation seems a non-starter.

The third and more implicit question that arises in these chapters concerns the definition of the "essence" of capital itself. I am not sure that the term "essence" is right here, but I think these chapters do offer the possibility of reflecting on the different forms that capital can assume, and ask if there is any priority to be given to any one of the forms, as opposed to saying that capital is simply "value in motion" or the total circulation laid out in Figure 2, and that is that. Is one of the circuits of capital more important than the others even though none of them can exist without the others? We need to pay attention to these questions here, because they have deep political implications. But Marx himself makes no attempt to tease out these political meanings. That is something we have to do.

Having outlined the general formula for the circulation of capital on the first page of Volume II, Marx states the assumptions upon which his inquiry will be based. He assumes "that commodities are sold at their values and that the circumstances in which this takes place do not change. We shall also ignore any changes of value that may occur in the course of the cyclical process" (109). The absence of any systematic concern for technological and organizational change in Volume II is, as already noted, a huge departure from the focus of Volume I. Holding the productivity of labor constant (in effect abstracting from the creation of relative surplus-value) makes the whole of Volume II unrealistic. But Marx plainly felt that this was the only way he could identify key relationships in the world of capital circulation that could be synthesized into a far more realistic working model of capital circulation and accumulation later on.

The first link (metamorphosis) in the chain of exchanges that make up capital circulation is the use of money to purchase labor-power and means of production. Money capital here "appears as the form in which capital is advanced." The word "appears" suggests, as is often the case, that all is not exactly as it seems. "As money capital, [money] exists in a state in which it can perform monetary functions, in the present case of general means of purchase and payment. . . . Money capital does not possess this capacity because it is capital, but because it is money." Not all money is capital, and not all buying and selling, even of labor-power (such as in the case of personal services or home help), is caught up in the circulation and accumulation of capital. What converts money functions into money capital "is their specific role in the movement of capital," and this depends on their relationship to "the other stages of the capital circuit." Only when embedded in the total circulation process of capital does money function as capital. Then, and only then, does money become "a form of appearance of capital" (113). So there is money, and then money functioning as capital. The two are not the same.

When money is used to buy labor-power—$M\text{-}LP$—then the money actually drops out of the circulation of capital, even as laborers use their money wages to buy commodities that they, under the control of capitalists, have produced. The laborers give up their commodity (labor-power) in order to get the money to buy the commodities they need to live, thus returning money to the circulation of capital. They live in a $C\text{-}M\text{-}C$–type circuit (or, as Marx prefers to notate it, an $L\text{-}M\text{-}C$ circuit), as opposed to the $M\text{-}C\text{-}M'$ circuit of capital. In this $L\text{-}M\text{-}C$ movement, Marx argues, "the capital character vanishes though its money character remains" (112). He later expands on this theme:

> The wage labourer lives only from the sale of his labour-power. Its main-tenance—his own maintenance—requires daily consumption. His payment must therefore be constantly repeated at short inter-vals . . . Hence the money capitalist must constantly confront him as money capitalist, and his capital as money capital. On the other hand, however, in order that the mass of direct producers, the wage labourers, may perform the act $L\text{-}M\text{-}C$ [where L is the sale of their labor power], they must constantly encounter the necessary means of subsistence in purchasable form, i.e. in the form of commodities. Thus this situation in itself demands a high degree of circulation of products as commodities, i.e. commodity production on a large scale. (119)

The movement $M\text{-}LP$ is often, and in Marx's view erroneously, viewed as "the characteristic moment of the transformation of capital into produc-tive capital," and therefore "as characteristic of the capitalist mode of production." But "money appears very early on as a buyer of so-called services, without its being transformed into money capital, and without any general revolution in the general character of the economy" (114). For capital circulation truly to begin requires that labor-power first appear upon the market as a commodity. "What is characteristic is not that the commodity labour-power can be bought, but the fact that labour-power appears as a commodity." Money can be spent as capital "only because labour-power is found in a state of separation from its means of production," and because the owner of means of production is in a position to take

> control of the continuous flow of labour-power, a flow which by no means has to stop when the amount of labour necessary to reproduce the price of labour-power has been performed. The capital relation arises only in the production process because it exists implicitly in the act of circulation, in the basically different economic conditions in which buyer and seller confront one another, in their class relation. It is not the nature of money that gives rise to this relation; it is rather the existence of the relation that can transform the mere function of money into a function of capital. (115)

So here, then, is the first major precondition for the circulation of capital to occur: "*The class relation between capitalist and wage-labourer is . . . already present*" (115; emphasis added). This was a major theme in Volume I, particularly in the sections on primitive accumulation. Marx here reiterates that the existence of labor-power as a commodity "implies the occurrence of historic processes through which the original connection between means of production and labour-power was dissolved" (116).

"The transformation of money capital into productive capital" occurs when "the capitalist effects a connection between the objective and the personal factors of production insofar as these factors consist of commodities." If the laborer is to be put straight to work, the capitalist has to "buy the means of production, i.e. buildings, machines, etc. before he buys labour-power" (114). But this requires that such commodities—the means of production—are also readily available in the market. "For capital to be formed and to take hold of production, trade must have developed to a certain level, hence also commodity circulation and, with that, commodity production" (117). Only in this way can the objective factors (means of production) be brought together with the subjective power of labor in production.

The second major precondition for the circulation of capital to occur is this: *general commodity production for the market must already exist.* Only then will the capitalist find means of production available in the marketplace, and only then will wage laborers find the consumption goods required to reproduce themselves. If these prior conditions do not hold, then money cannot function as capital.

Marx is here disabusing us of the idea that capital is primarily to be understood in money terms, and he goes to considerable lengths to explain why (116). But, once the class of wage laborers exists and is able to reproduce itself, then a transformative dynamic gets set in motion:

> The same circumstance that produces the basic condition for capitalist production, the existence of a class of wage labourers, encourages the transition of all commodity production to capitalist commodity production. To the extent that the latter develops, it has a destroying and dissolving effect on all earlier forms or production, which, being pre-eminently aimed at satisfying the direct needs of the producers, only transform their excess products into commodities. It makes the sale of the product the main interest, at first apparently without attacking the mode of production itself; this was, for example, the first effect of capitalist world trade on such peoples as the Chinese, Indians, Arabs, etc. Once it has taken root, however, it destroys all forms of commodity production that are based either on the producers' own labour, or simply on the sale of the excess product as a commodity. It firstly makes commodity production universal, and then gradually transforms all commodity production into capitalist production. (120)

After these historical transformations have occurred, then capital can freely begin to circulate in a "pure" manner:

> It goes without saying, therefore, that the formula for the circuit of money capital: $M-C...P...C'-M'$, is the self-evident form of the circuit of capital only on the basis of already developed production, because it presupposes the availability of the class of wage-labourers in sufficient numbers throughout society. As we have seen, capitalist production produces not only commodities and surplus-value; it reproduces, and on

an ever-extended scale, the class of wage labourers and transforms the vast majority of the direct producers into wage labourers. (118)

I have elsewhere argued, not only in relation to Marx's statements in Volume I but also on my own account, that Marx is predisposed to what I call a "dialectical and co-evolutionary theory of social change."[1] This idea is compatible with the way the argument is set up in Volume II. It seems the only way to get out of an endless "chicken and egg" kind of debate on the origins of capitalism. Both the class relation and generalized commodity production (and by implication the money form) must precede the rise of capital, but the rise of capital generalizes these preconditions.

The second stage in the circulation of capital is that of production capital. Marx does not spend too much time elaborating on this because it is, after all, the foundational form for the analysis of Volume I. This stage entails the productive consumption of both the labor-power and the means of production in a labor process.

> The movement presents itself as $M-C...P$, the dots indicating that the circulation of capital is interrupted; but its circuit continues with its passage from the sphere of commodity circulation into that of production. The first stage, the transformation of money capital into productive capital, thus appears as no more than the prelude and the introduction to the second stage, the function of productive capital.

The particular way that labor-power and means of production are brought together "is what distinguishes the various economic epochs of the social structure." In the capitalist case,

> the separation of the free worker from his means of production is the given starting point . . . The actual process which the personal and material elements of commodity formation, brought together in this way, enter into with each other, the process of production, therefore itself becomes a function of capital—the capitalist production process, whose nature we have gone into in detail in the first volume of this work. All

---

1   David Harvey, *The Enigma of Capital: and the Crises of Capitalism* (London: Profile, 2010), chapter 5.

pursuit of commodity production becomes at the same time pursuit of the exploitation of labour; but only capitalist commodity production is an epoch-making mode of exploitation which in the course of historical development revolutionizes the entire economic structure of society by its organization of the labour process and by its giant extension of technique, and towers incomparably above all earlier epochs. (120)

Both means of production and labor-power are thereby transformed into "forms of the capital value advanced." As such, they "are distinguished as constant and variable capital." The "means of production are no more capital by nature than is human labour-power" (121). Marx then summarizes, for the umpteenth time, the theory of surplus-value: "In the course of its functioning, productive capital consumes its own components, to convert them into a mass of products of a higher value" such that the "product is therefore not only a commodity, but a commodity impregnated with surplus-value." Productive capital, he insists throughout, is "the only function in which capital value breeds value" (131).

In the third stage of the process, we need to confront capital in the form of commodity capital. In exactly the same way that capital in money form can only perform money functions and that, as productive capital, it can only do as production does, so capital in commodity form "must perform commodity functions" (122). The function of C' (the commodity impregnated with surplus-value)

is now that of every commodity product, to be transformed into money and sold, to pass through the phase of circulation C-M. As long as the now valorized capital persists in the form of commodity capital, is tied up on the market, the production process stands still. The capital operates neither to fashion products nor to form value. According to the varying speed with which the capital sheds its commodity form and assumes its money form, i.e. according to the briskness of the sale, the same capital will serve to a very uneven degree in the formation of products and value, and the scale of the reproduction will expand or contract.

We here introduce a very important new dimension into Marx's theoretical framework. The speed of transition from one state to another is a very important variable. It is affected by "new forces independent of the magnitude of value which affect the degree of effectiveness of capital, its expansion and its contraction" (124). Speed-up, turnover time, and the like, when driven onwards by the coercive laws of competition, alter the temporal frame not only of the circulation of capital but also of daily life. The nature of these "new and independent forces" that underpin speed-up calls for investigation. This forms one of the fascinating spheres of enquiry in Volume II.

That act of circulation C'-M' takes the "surplus-value that is simultaneously borne along by the commodity capital" and realizes it in money form, thus concluding the third phase of the metamorphoses of capital. But the surplus-value, it is important to remember,

> first came into the world within the production process. It is thus now entering the commodity market for the first time, and moreover in the commodity form; this is its first form of circulation and hence the act c-m is its first act of circulation or its first metamorphosis, which thus still has to be supplemented by the opposite circulation act, the converse metamorphosis m-c [the lower-case letters indicate that Marx is here talking only of the motion of the surplus-value, not the total capital, C' and M' respectively].

The production of surplus-value is in fact the production of capital, and the reinvestment of all or part of the surplus-value is foundational to the reproduction of capital.

In all of this, two things stand out. "Firstly, the ultimate transformation of capital value back into its original money form is a function of commodity capital. Secondly, this function includes the first formal transformation of the surplus-value from its original commodity form into the money form" (127). As a result, "capital value and surplus-value now exist as money, i.e. in the form of the universal equivalent." We here get a hint of something that will become increasingly significant as the text unfolds: the distinctive and vital role of commodity capital in the overall circulation process, as the converter of the surplus-value impregnated in the commodity into money form.

> At the end of the process, the capital value is thus once again in the same form in which it entered it, and can therefore open the process afresh and pass through it as money capital. And indeed because the initial and concluding form of the process is that of money capital (M),

we call this form of the circuit the circuit of money capital. It is not the form of the value advanced, but only its magnitude, that is changed at the end. (127)

The circuit of money capital thus reflects "the way in which the initial and concluding form of the process is that of money capital" (124). Once the surplus-value is realized as capital, as "value that has bred value," as the "purpose and result" of the circulation process, then M "no longer appears as mere money, but is expressly postulated as money capital, expressed as value that has valorized itself" ("the goose that lays the golden eggs," as Marx called it in Volume I). As soon as the capital- ized surplus-value re-enters the circulation process, however, it does so simply as money, in which the distinction between the initial money capital recuperated and the surplus-value is obliterated. It returns, once more, to performing purely money functions. So, while we may care conceptually to distinguish between "*money* capital" (money that gets used as capital) and "money *capital*" (capital that has gone back to the money form) both "money capital and commodity capital are modes of existence of capital. The specific functions that distinguish them can thus be nothing other than the distinctions between the money func- tion and the commodity function."

Yet, "the commodity capital, as the direct product of the capitalist production process, recalls its origin and is therefore more rational in its form, less lacking in conceptual differentiation, than the money capital, in which every trace of this process has been effaced, just as all the particular useful forms of commodities are generally effaced in money" (131).

While the difference is effaced, we need to hang on to the "conceptual differentiation," for it is this that reveals the secret of capital's laws of motion. The surplus-value that is converted into money, m, can then be spent. But on what? A part goes to bourgeois consumption (spent on both necessities and luxuries, as Marx will later explain). But a part will also be spent as money capital, and hence underpin the expansion of accumulation.

Throughout this presentation, Marx insists upon a whole series of seemingly picayune distinctions. Why does he do this? The answer to this question becomes more apparent in the final section, where he considers the circuit as a whole. "Capital appears," Marx writes, as a value that passes through a sequence of connected and mutually determined transformations, a series of metamorphoses that form so many phases or stages of a total process. Two of these phases belong to the circulation sphere, one to the sphere of production. In each of these phases the capital value is to be found in different form, corresponding to a different and special function. Within this movement the value advanced not only maintains itself, but it grows.

Within this "total process" that forms a "circuit," definite functions and categories can be defined:

> The two forms that the capital value assumes within its circulation stages are those of *money capital* and *commodity capital*; the form pertaining to the production stage is that of *productive capital*. The capital that assumes these forms in the course of its total circuit, discards them again and fulfils in each of them its appropriate function, is *industrial capital*—industrial in the sense that it encompasses every branch of production that is pursued on a capitalist basis. (132–3)

Industrial capital is an unfortunate term, given current connotations of the word, but what Marx plainly means by it is that circulation of capital which passes through a labor process that creates surplus-value, and which is then realized and reproduced by passing through the other moments in the overall process. "Money capital, commodity capital and productive capital thus do not denote independent varieties of capital, whose functions constitute the content of branches of business that are independent and separate from one another. They are simply functional forms of capital, which takes on all three forms in turn."

By restricting himself to this purely formal analysis, Marx obviates the need to discuss the distinctive agents who do indeed attach to these functions as distinctive businesses. Finance and money capitalists attach themselves to the money function, producer capitalists to the functions of production, and merchant (commercial) capitalists to commodity capital. Historically, the totality of the circuit of industrial capital in aggregate therefore has to engage not only the intertwining of the different circuits but also all the activities of the different active agents—distinctive factions of capital that extract distributive shares from the total surplus-value. Nowhere in Volume II, however, does

Marx examine these factional roles. He prefers everything to be kept on a purely logical, formal plane. I think the reason he takes this tack is that, were he to introduce the historical roles of the different agents and the struggles that have occurred between them, the whole account would become so blurred as to hide what Marx regards as foundational functions. Indeed, at various points in Volume II, he subjects Adam Smith to critique (see 269–71) for believing that these factions of capital were entirely independent and autonomous forms of capital. Marx sees them as differentiated but inexorably intertwined within the single form of industrial capital.

Marx then interjects a very important observation:

> The circuit of capital proceeds normally only as long as its various phases pass into each other without delay. If capital comes to a standstill in the first phase, M-C, money capital forms into a hoard; if this happens in the production phase, the means of production cease to function, and labour-power remains unoccupied; if in the last phase, C'-M', unsaleable stocks of commodities obstruct the flow of circulation.

The idea of obstructions and blockages to the circulation process is here broached, but only in a purely formal way:

> It lies in the nature of the case, however, that the circuit itself determines that capital is tied up for certain intervals in the particular sections of the cycle. In each of its phases industrial capital is tied to a specific form, as money capital, productive capital or commodity capital. Only after it has fulfilled the function corresponding to the particular form it is in does it receive the form in which it can enter a new phase of transformation. (133)

The implication is that capital cannot flow smoothly and continuously through the circuits, but that it necessarily experiences pauses in its motion. In what follows, these potential obstructions, pauses and blockages will frequently be examined, though without any reference to the interests and agency of the various factions of capital involved. This permits us to see clearly the obstacles that might hinder the continuous circulation of capital. It also points to measures that might prevent obstacles becoming insuperable blockages. The disadvantage is that it leaves the Volume II analysis in a dry and desiccated state of formal distinctions, leaving it to us, when we read Volume III, to remember the formal basis upon which much of the actual theory of historical crisis might be predicated.

In the course of this chapter Marx also inserts some remarks on the role of the transport and communication industries in the circulation process (135). Since this is taken up again at the end of chapter 5, I shall delay consideration of this issue until then.

So what, then, is the general picture that emerges? We have a circuit of industrial capital of the following sort:

$$\begin{array}{c} \text{LP} \\ \text{M-C...P...C} + c - M + \Delta\, m \\ \text{MP} \end{array}$$

We see immediately (Figure 2) that this can be disaggregated into three distinctive circuits all conditional upon each other—the money capital circuit, the circuit of productive capital, and the commodity capital circuit. The circuit of money capital must successfully negotiate the conditions that pertain to the production and commodity circuits if surplus-value is to be realized. The same conditionality applies to the circuits of production and commodity capital. A disruption in any one circuit will have catastrophic consequences for the others. The possibility therefore exists for distinctive crises in the circulation process as a whole. When we bring forward from Volume III the disaggregation of the capitalist class into various factions of producers, merchants and financiers, with distinctive interests and perspectives embedded in one rather than another of the circulatory processes, then even more persuasive reasons come into view to worry about the stability of the overall circulation process of what Marx calls industrial capital.

It remains to assess the significance of the money capital form to the overall circulation process of industrial capital. Money is not only the starting point but the end point of the process. Yet the money form, recall, is the representation of value, and this is the only way we get some tangible measure of the surplus-value produced: "It is precisely because the money form of value is its independent and palpable form of appearance that the circulation form $M...M'$, which starts and finishes with actual money, expresses money making, the driving motive of capitalist production, most palpably. The production process appears simply as an unavoidable middle term, a necessary evil for the purpose of money making" (137). Money may be the ultimate fetish, but it really is, for the capitalist, the holy grail because "enrichment as such appears as the inherent purpose of production." Without "the glittering money form" there would be no motivation for the capitalist, and without the realization of capital in its money form there would be no tangible measure of reward.

But realization depends on consumption—not only the productive consumption of other capitalists, but also the final consumption of others. For the first time in Volume II, we hit the idea that the consumption of the working classes may have a role to play (138). But Marx then adds an interesting comment on interstate trade and mercantilism. The mercantilists, he notes, preach

> long sermons to the effect that the individual capitalist should consume only in his capacity as worker, and that a capitalist nation should leave the consumption of its commodities and the consumption process in general to other more stupid nations, while making productive consumption into its own life work. These sermons are often reminiscent in both form and content of analogous ascetic exhortations by the Fathers of the Church. (139)

There are those, like Kevin Phillips, who believe we have been through a phase of mercantilism these last few decades, with the US playing the role of the most stupid nation (engaging in debt-fuelled consumerism) while the Chinese and the Germans save and accumulate huge trade surpluses at the expense of the US consumer. When the Obama administration approached the G20 meeting in Seoul, in the fall of 2010, with a proposal to reduce the trading imbalances within the global system, the Chinese and the Germans took the lead in rebutting the proposal. So it seems some form of mercantilism is indeed alive and well—and the US still seems happy to play the role of the most stupid nation.

The summary remarks with which Marx closes the chapter are important: "The circuit of money capital is thus the most one-sided, hence most striking and characteristic form of appearance of the circuit of industrial capital, in which its aim and driving motive—the valorization of value, money making and accumulation—appears in a form that leaps to the eye (buying in order to sell dearer)." As usual with Marx, we have to recognize that "appears" does not mean "is": "The circuit of money capital remains the permanent general expression of industrial capital, insofar as it always includes the valorization of the value advanced." From the standpoint of production, however, "the money expression of the capital emerges only as the price of the elements of production." While there are compelling reasons to look upon the circuit M-M' as preeminent, because not only does it appear as a beginning but it facilitates the flow of purchasing power to the laborers in the form of wages and the flow of profits to capitalists to facilitate their consumption, there is "in its form a certain deception," even an "illusory character" (141). This "illusory character" and "the corresponding illusory significance it is given, is there as soon as this form is regarded as the sole form, not as one that flows and is constantly repeated; i.e. as soon as it is taken not just as one of the forms of the circuit, but rather as its exclusive form." Marx's fundamental point is that the money circuit cannot exist "in itself," but necessarily "refers to other forms" (142). When we look at the perpetual repetition of capital circulation through its different forms (money, production, commodities) we see that money "forms an evanescent prelude to the constantly repeated circuit of productive capital." From this standpoint, "the capitalist production process is the basic pre-condition, it is prior to all else" (143).

ON CHAPTER 2: THE CIRCUIT OF PRODUCTIVE CAPITAL

The significance of the circuit of productive capital is so obvious that Marx does not bother to state it: it is, after all, in the "hidden abode" of production and only there that surplus-value is produced. From the standpoint of productive capital, the movement through circulation appears as an irritating necessity before getting back to the real game, that of producing surplus-value through the labor process: "the entire circulation process of industrial capital, its whole movement within the circulation phase, merely forms an interruption, and hence a mediation, between the productive capital that opens the circuit . . . and closes it" (144). But, as we should by now expect, there are plenty of pitfalls and perils encountered in the movement through the commodity and money forms. The formal requirements are that the value and the surplus-value congealed in the commodity must be realized in money form through a sale, and that the recuperated original money and some part of the profit then be used to purchase the means of production and the labor-power required to repeat the production process on an expanding scale. Formally the circulation steps to be navigated look like C'-M' followed by M-C, and an additional circulation of the surplus-value in money form, m-c.

Two cases are then considered. The first is that of simple reproduction, in which all of the surplus-value is consumed away and there is no reinvestment of the surplus (as in chapter 23 of Volume I and chapter 20 of Volume II), and the second is that of expanded reproduction (as in chapter 24 of Volume I and chapter 21 of Volume II). While Marx holds that simple reproduction is impossible under capitalism, he spends far more time on it, in part, I suspect, because he found it easier to establish the formal relations and conditions that must be realized if industrial capital is to continue on its merry way. He holds that these conditionalities carry over (though in more convoluted form, depending on the capitalists' choice of relative allocations for reinvestment or consumption) to the far more realistic model of expanded reproduction.

In the case of simple reproduction, the surplus-value m must all be spent on personal consumption. If the capitalist class simply holds money and fails to consume, then commodity capital cannot be realized in money form. For the first time, therefore, we see the importance of bourgeois consumption to the stabilization of capitalism: "m-c is a series of purchases made with the money that the capitalist spends, whether on commodities as such or on services, for his esteemed self and family. These purchases are fragmented, and take place at different times. The money therefore exists temporarily in the form of a money reserve or a hoard destined for current consumption" (146). This money "is not advanced but spent." So the bourgeois already must have the money in hand.

This is an interesting theme that we will encounter several times in Volume II. Where does the extra money come from to buy the surplus-value? The bourgeoisie buys the surplus-value congealed in commodities with its own money to augment personal consumption. This presupposes, of course, that productive capital is making the commodities that the bourgeoisie wants to consume (though Marx does not make the point here). The circulation m-c (the lower cases denote we are dealing not with the whole capital but the surplus part only), "presupposes the existence of the capitalist . . . and is conditional on his consumption of surplus-value" (149).

In passing, Marx notes that the manner in which the bourgeois pays for commodities depends to some degree on the nature of the commodity produced. Marx makes mention of the interesting case (to me, at least) of the London building trade, "which is conducted for the most part on credit, [and in which] the contractor receives advances in various stages as the building of the house progresses" (148). Furthermore, final commodity consumption can be "completely separated in time and space from the metamorphosis in which this mass of commodities functions as his commodity capital" (150). How commodities and payments move over time and space is here hinted at, but not developed as a field of analysis. This is the sort of thing that I have tried to follow up in some of my own work.

The recuperated original money capital has to circulate back into the field of productive consumption through the purchase of labor-power and means of production. But while the original M was advanced, the recirculated money has to be reconceptualized as money capital that has already been produced and valorized through the movement C'-M'. This change in signification is important. It echoes the view set out in Volume I that, after a while, labor reproduces the equivalent of the whole value of the capital originally advanced. The value circulating should by rights, in Marx's interpretation of Locke's argument that property accrues to those who mix their labor with the land to create value, belong to the laborer and not to the capitalist (who has, in effect, consumed away the original capital). The M that re-enters production is, Marx notes, "an expression of past labor" and not of money capital pure and simple.

But there are inevitably temporal gaps in the circulation process. The "difference in time between the execution of *C-M* and that of *M-C* may be more or less considerable." The temporality of circulation is important. Marx here immediately notes some curiosities. In some instances "*M* can represent for the act *M-C* the transformed form of commodities that are not yet present on the market at all." Pre-payments on commodities not yet made are possible. Even workers can pay in advance for a commodity not yet produced—in effect paying out of the wages of future labor. The possible timing arrangements are endlessly complicated and, as we will see later, the role of the credit system soon becomes crucial.

But there are also structural reasons why the movement from commodity to the purchase of both labor-power and means of production can become difficult. "If the second metamorphosis $M-C$ comes up against obstacles (e.g. if the means of production are unattainable on the market), then the circular flow of the reproduction process is interrupted, just as if the capital was tied up in the form of commodity capital. The difference, however, is that it can last out longer in the money form" (154). In Volume I it was generally taken that the passage $C-M$ was more difficult than that of $M-C$ because money is the universal equivalent and the commodity a particular equivalent. But we here encounter another story, because productive capital requires highly specific means of production in order to be reproduced. If the supply of iron ore dries up, then steel production cannot be reproduced. Heavy reliance on fixed capital in steel production (for example, blast furnaces) makes any disruption of supply of this sort very costly for the steel producer. Reproduction also presumes, though Marx does not make the point, that workers with the requisite skill continue to be readily available. But at least M cannot spoil, so for circulation to get stuck at this point is less problematic than it is for much of capital stuck in the commodity form (particularly if the commodities are perishable). The timely conversion of money into the elements for productive consumption is a necessity for the reproduction of productive capital. Marx then takes yet another swipe at the economists who adhered to Say's law: "A replacement of commodity by commodity conditioned by surplus-value production is something quite other than an exchange of products that is simply mediated by money. But this is how the matter is presented by the economists, as proof that no overproduction is possible."

We then need to consider the consumption of the workers. They live through participation in an $L-M-C$ circuit, giving up their labor-power in order to get the money to buy commodities to survive at a certain standard of living. This takes money value out of the circulation of capital only then immediately to put it back again, in a "company store" kind of relation made much of in Volume I. "The second act, i.e. $M-C$ [the purchases of wage goods by workers] does not fall into the circulation of the individual capital, although it proceeds from it. The constant existence of the working class, however, is necessary for the capitalist class, and so, therefore, is the consumption of the worker mediated by $M-C$"(155). We will later see, in chapters 20 and 21, how all of this looks from the standpoint not of individual capitalists but of the aggregate circulation of capital taken as a whole.

Notice how this is all being conceptualized here. The money, when in the hands of the capitalist and about to be transformed into variable capital through the purchase of labor-power, is functioning as capital. But that same money no longer functions as capital once it is in the hands of the workers. It too undergoes a metamorphosis of form, for it is now simply money in the hands of a buyer in the marketplace and, as such, can be used in any way the worker needs, wants or pleases. Once workers have spent their money on commodities and it is back in the hands of the capitalist, then it can revert to the form of capital provided the capitalist does not use it for consumption. This is Marx's relational way of working in full sight. And it is important to note it, because if the worker gambles away (or even saves) his or her earnings rather than spending them on commodities, then the continuity of the circulation process gets broken. Hence the concern, at the very end of Volume II, for establishing a "rational consumerism" on the part of the working classes as a condition for stable accumulation. The problem would not be identified if it was conceptualized as if the circulation of money capital were in total control at every point in this process. While Marx elsewhere typically depicts the working class as a whole as being locked into a "company store" relation to capital with respect to consumption, he is here opening up a way to problematize that assumption.

None of this, Marx holds, is affected in principle by the interventions of the merchant capitalists who may take over the job of mediating the conversion of C'-M' because, in the final analysis, "the whole process follows its course, and with it also the individual consumption of the capitalists and the worker that is conditional on it. This point is an important one in considering crises." If there is a crisis of some sort, we should not, therefore, attribute it fundamentally to the operations of the merchant capitalist (i.e. don't blame Walmart). We need to look deeper into the roles of bourgeois and working-class consumption as potential sticking points:

> As long as the product is sold, everything follows its regular course. . . . Then this reproduction of capital can be accompanied by a more expanded individual consumption (and hence demand) on the part of the workers. . . . The

production of surplus-value and with it also the individual consumption of the capitalist can thus grow, and the whole reproduction process finds itself in the most flourishing condition, while in fact a great part of the commodities have only apparently gone into consumption, and are actually lying unsold in the hands of retail traders, thus being still on the market. One stream of commodities now follows another, and it finally emerges that the earlier stream had only seemed to be followed up by consumption. . . . The earlier streams have not yet been converted into ready money, while payment for them is falling due. Their owners must declare themselves bankrupt, or sell at any price in order to pay. This sale, however, has nothing to do with the real state of demand. It only has to do with *demand for payment*, with the absolute necessity of transforming money into commodities. At this point the crisis breaks out. It first becomes evident not in the direct reduction of consumer demand, the demand for individual consumption, but rather in decline in the number of exchanges of capital for capital, in the reproduction process of capital. (156–7)

Marx distinguishes between final consumer demand on the part of workers and of capitalists, on the one hand, and the intercapitalist trading and demand for commodities involved in maintaining productive consumption. He here advances the very original view that crises can arise out of the capital-capital relation in organizing flows of commodities and monetary payments with respect to productive consumption. What may appear as a problem of lack of effective demand on the part of workers and of capitalists in the field of individual consumption may in fact be due to problems of circulation arising out of the purchase and sale of means of production. Is this a general theory of crisis, or a possibility that arises out of an examination of the circulation of productive capital? My general view is always in the first instance to take such statements as contingent, as possibilities that can be seen from a certain perspective under the given assumptions. This does not mean that such statements may not ultimately prove to have a broader generality, but that we have to *show* how the particular perspective illuminates crisis tendencies within capitalism.

In Volume II, for example, Marx makes seemingly quite contradictory statements with respect to the role of working-class effective demand and consumption:

Contradiction in the capitalist mode of production. The workers are important for the market as buyers of commodities. But as sellers of their commodity—labour-power—capitalist society has the tendency to restrict them to their minimum price. Further contradiction: the periods in which capitalist production asserts all its forces regularly show themselves to be periods of over-production; because the limit to the application of the productive powers is not simply the production of value, but also its realization. However, the sale of commodities, the realization of commodity capital, and thus of surplus-value as well, is restricted not by the consumer needs of society in general, but by the consumer needs of a society in which the great majority are always poor and must always remain poor. (391)

But elsewhere he says this:

It is a pure tautology to say that crises are provoked by a lack of effective demand or effective consumption. The capitalist system does not recognize any forms of consumer other than those who can pay. . . . The fact that commodities are unsaleable means no more than that no effective buyers have been found for them. . . . If the attempt is made to give this tautology the semblance of greater profundity, by the statement that the working class receives too small a portion of its own product, and that the evil would be remedied if it received a bigger share, i.e., if its wages rose, we need only note that crises are always prepared by a period in which wages generally rise, and the working class actually does receive a greater share in the part of the annual product destined for consumption. From the standpoint of these advocates of sound and "simple" (!) common sense, such periods should rather avert the crisis. It thus appears that capitalist production involves certain conditions independent of people's good or bad intentions, which permit the relative prosperity of the working class only temporarily, and moreover always as a harbinger of crisis. (486–7)

This second statement is more in accord with the spirit of argument in chapter 2, so it is clear that Marx felt the arguments constructed from the standpoint of productive capital had more general salience. This leaves us with the difficulty of deciding which of these formulations to follow. My own view (and you will also have to come to terms with this on your own account) is that circumstances arise, as in the late 1960s and early 1970s, when the rising share of labor in the national product was indeed a harbinger if not a fundamental locus of crisis in global capitalism as it was then constituted. It is impossible to make such an argument about the crash of 2007–09. The distributive share taken by the working class, no matter whether it is too high or too low, important though it may be, cannot explain the crisis tendencies of capital. Other formulations are required. We have to pay careful attention to what is said in Volume II (as well as elsewhere, of course) to figure out what these formulations might be. At this point, from the perspective of productive capital, we have at least part of the theory of crisis formation firmly in place.

When capital circulation encounters obstacles such as to "suspend the function of M-C," then the money transforms into "the involuntary formation of a hoard." This money "thus has the form of latent money capital, money capital that lies idle" (158). Later Marx will also call it "fallow capital" (164). These are important terms in the following argument.

The section on expanded reproduction contains nothing surprising. We know from Volume I that, for the capitalist, "the constant enlargement of his capital becomes a condition for its preservation." The only interesting question is what proportion of the surplus-value is capitalized as fresh capital, and for that there is no golden rule. The circuit $P....P'$ "does not express the fact that surplus-value is produced, but rather that the produced surplus-value is capitalized"(160). Again, this changes our conception of what the circulation process is all about. The first step in this capitalization is to put aside a certain amount of money realized from the sale of commodities preparatory to launching into expansion. This hoard of latent or fallow money capital is necessary because, in most lines of business, a certain minimum amount of capital is required in order to launch the expansion (to build a larger factory, invest in machinery, and so on). This may require that "the capital circuit must be repeated several times" before sufficient monetary power is acquired to satisfy the minimum requirements for expanded reproduction to proceed. This makes for the inevitability of hoarding in money form as "a functionally determined preparatory stage that proceeds outside the circuit of capital, and paves the way for the transformation of surplus-value into really functioning capital. . . . As long as it persists in the state of a hoard, it does not yet function as money capital, it is still money capital lying fallow; not interrupted in its function . . . but rather as yet incapable of performing this function" (164). Plainly, this is a situation, as Marx immediately concedes, where the credit system has a crucial role to play. Without it, more and more capital would be rendered "fallow" and the hoards would become a serious barrier to fluent accumulation. But that is not to be dealt with here.

ON CHAPTER 3: THE CIRCUIT OF COMMODITY CAPITAL

One of the more surprising aspects of Volume II is the attention Marx pays to the circuit of commodity capital. The reason for this has already been prefigured in the study of the circuit of productive capital. To the obvious difficulty of transforming particular forms of embodied value and surplus-value into the universality of the money equivalent, we must now add a further difficulty of finding the necessary commodities in the marketplace to meet the needs of productive consumption in specific labor processes. Capitalists have to depend on other capitalists to produce their means of production. It is therefore primarily in this circuit that we encounter the problem of specific interrelations and interdependencies between capitalists. And, as Volume II progresses, it becomes more and more evident that these intercapitalist relations are fraught with the possibility of crises of adequate supply, as well as the more obvious problem of possible crises arising out of lack of effective demand.

Marx's analysis at this point is, however, confined largely to formal functions and technicalities. There are a number of peculiarities to this circuit of commodity capital. To begin with, the commodity is impregnated with surplus-value that has yet to be realized. Whereas in the cases of both money and productive capitals, the surplus-value "vanishes" when the circulation process begins anew, such that money can only do as money does, and productive activity proceeds also on its own terms, in the case of commodities we are dealing—both at the beginning and the end of the circulation process—with a commodity impregnated with surplus-value. We are therefore looking at a form of circulation $C'....C'$, and in the case of expanded reproduction this would mean $C'....C''$. What this emphasizes is that it is in the commodity circuit that both the realization of the surplus-value in money form and the absorption of surplus product and value—not only in individual consumption but also in productive consumption—become imperative for the continuity of the circulation of industrial capital as a whole.

The second peculiarity is that of the role of productive consumption. "In the circuit of an individual industrial capital, C' as C appears not as the form of this capital but as the form of another industrial capital, insofar as the means of production are the product of this other capital. The act M-C (i.e. M-mp) of the first capital is for this second capital C'-M''" (168). The problem is that the surplus-value is hidden within the commodity form as a surplus product (a specific use-value) and that it is impossible to separate the value and the surplus-value in the way that becomes possible when the commodity value is realized in the money form. Whereas it is possible to take the realized M' and disaggregate it into $M + m$, and then decide how much of m to capitalize in expanding production, this cannot be done with a forklift truck. It might be possible with certain products, and Marx uses the example of yarn, in which it is in principle possible to separate the original value of C from C'. This provokes Marx to launch into one of his complicated and seemingly interminable calculations of how this might be done.

But behind all this there lies a distinction that prevails in this circuit that vanishes in the others: there is both a surplus product (the expanded use values embodied in the commodity) and a surplus-value, and a condition for the realization of the latter is the location of a home for the former. The specificity of use-values cannot be evaded. Conversely, if the decision is made to expand production by capitalizing part of the surplus-value in money form, then there must be surplus use-values on the market available for purchase as additional means of production for particular activities: "Reproduction on an expanded scale, with productivity otherwise remaining the same, can take place only if the material elements of the additional productive capital are already contained in part of the surplus product to be capitalized" (179). This is a very important condition and, plainly, any failure to meet it will seriously impair the smooth functioning of capital accumulation.

Productive consumption is not, of course, the only form of consumption involved in this circuit:

In the form C'....C', the consumption of the entire commodity product is presupposed as the condition for the normal course of the circuit of capital itself. The individual consumption of the worker and the individual consumption of the non-accumulated part of the surplus product comprise, taken together, the total individual consumption. Thus consumption in its entirety—both individual and productive consumption—enters into the circuit of C' as a precondition. (173)

But all of this is presupposed, he goes on to say, as a social rather than as an individual act. From this then follows the most important conclusion:

> Precisely because the circuit $C'...C'$ presupposes in its description the existence of another industrial capital in the form $C(=L+mp)$ (and mp comprises other capitals of various kinds, e.g. in our case machines, coal, oil, etc.), it itself demands to be considered not only as the *general* form of the circuit . . . hence not only as a form of motion common to all individual industrial capitals, but at the same time as the form of motion of the sum of individual capitals, i.e. of the total social capital of the capitalist class, a movement in which the movement of any individual industrial capital simply appears as a partial one, intertwined with the others and conditioned by them. If we consider, for example, the total annual commodity product of a country, and analyse the movement in which one part of this replaces the productive capital of all individual businesses, and another part goes into the individual consumption of the different classes, then we are considering $C'...C'$ as a form of motion of both the social capital and of the surplus-value or the surplus product produced by this. (176–7)

The circuit of commodity capital is special. It allows us to look at the aggregate flow of both surplus-value and surplus product (values and use-values) in the economy as a whole. It does so precisely because it has to focus on relations between individual capitals as they intertwine their activities and calculate their inputs and outputs in the economy as a whole. It introduces us to a very important idea of proportionality in those inputs and outputs from the standpoint not only of the individual capital but also of capital as a whole. The theme of proportionality—how much steel needs to be produced as means of production to support the activities of all manner of other sectors, and how much iron ore is needed to produce the steel—is in fact one of the major themes of Volume II. And this raises the issue of the mechanisms that assure that these proportionalities are roughly achieved. Can the market do it?

Does the equalization in the rate of profit guarantee it? If not, will this all result in crises of disproportionality? This mode of thinking was, as Marx points out at the end of this chapter, pioneered by Quesnay. It will form the basis for Marx's innovative expansion and development of Quesnay's formulations in chapters 20 and 21.

Notice that, in this chapter, use-values and values, surplus-value and surplus product, frequently appear hand in hand in ways that could not be observed in the study of the other circuits. When steel is sold as a means of production, it introduces the issue not only of physical flows of use-values but also of the balance of value transfers, and the two are not necessarily going to reflect each other neatly. In the case of the other circuits, surplus-value "vanishes" (because money is just money and can only do as money does, and because production contains no sign of the production of previous surplus-value production in its initiating moment, even as it produces it). With respect to the other circuits, we can focus exclusively on the individual industrial capital and pay no mind to aggregate conditions. These aggregate conditions come to the fore only in the case of commodity capital, where the surplus-value is embodied in the commodity at the outset and where the specific use-values required to continue production (of, say, steel) become crucial. It is from this perspective alone that we can study and unravel the aggregate laws of motion and the necessary physical use-value and value proportionalities that facilitate the reproduction of capital.

The way in which all of this integrates into the capital-circulation process as a totality is taken up in the next chapter.

CHAPTER TWO

The Three Figures of the Circuit and the Continuity of Capital Flow (Chapters 4–6 of Volume II)

ON CHAPTER 4 : THE DIFFERENT CIRCUITS OF CAPITAL AS A WHOLE

In my examination of the first three chapters of Volume II, I looked at the circulation process of capital through the three different windows of money, production and commodity. In the fourth chapter Marx puts the circuits back together in order to analyze the unity. The language is a bit convoluted, but I think the point is clear: the different circuits are intertwined, curling around each other and constantly in motion in relation to each other. The movement of each is a condition for the movement of all. "Valorization of value" (by which Marx means the production and realization of surplus-value) is "the determining purpose, the driving motive." When looked at as a whole, "all the premises of the process appear as its result, as premises produced by the process itself. Each moment appears as a point of departure, of transit, and of return. The total process presents itself as the unity of the process of production and the process of circulation; the production process is the mediator of the circulation process, and vice versa." Marx likens this whole to a

> constantly rotating orbit, every point simultaneously a starting point and a point of return . . . The reproduction of the capital in each of its forms and at each of its stages is just as continuous as is the metamorphosis of these forms and their successive passage through the three stages. Here, therefore the entire circuit is the real unity of its three forms. (180, 181)

The dominant language is one of continuity, succession, coexistence and the fluidity of capital's movement through the three circuits. This language is counterposed to another: that of interruptions and possible disruptions. "The circuit of capital is a constant process of interruption;

one stage is left behind, the next stage embarked upon; one form is cast aside, and the capital exists in another; each of these stages not only conditions the other, but at the same time excludes it" (182). The interruptions, like those in the lifecycle of the butterfly, are omnipresent and inevitable. They threaten the continuity of capital's motion, but they do not necessarily engender crises. By studying them we can hope to understand why crises might take particular forms—why, for example, a crisis might *appear* at one moment as a surplus of commodity capital that cannot be disposed of, or at another as an excessive hoard of money capital lacking investment opportunities, or at yet another as a scarcity of means of production or labor-power for the further expansion of accumulation. Capital flow can be blocked at any one of a number of different transitional points.

Marx counterposes these interruptions to the "continuity" that "is the characteristic feature of capitalist production, and is required by its technical basis, even if it is not always completely attainable" (182). The technical and social necessity for continuity of capital flow is far more important here than it was in Volume I. "Each different part of the capital runs in succession through the successive phases of the circuit, can pass over from one phase and one functional form into the other; hence industrial capital, as the whole of these parts, exists simultaneously in its various phases and functions, and thus describes all three circuits at once" (183).

So we have four terms to contend with: money capital, productive capital, commodity capital and "industrial capital"—the last understood as the unity of the three circuits. Any individual industrial capital will typically have different portions of its capital in each of the different circuits at any one moment. Part of it will be absorbed in production, part will be in money form, and part in commodity form. But this "coexistence," Marx insists, "is itself only the result of the succession." The necessity for continuous movement through the different circuits trumps all else. The immediate consequence is that, if

the commodity is unsaleable, then the circuit of this part is interrupted and its replacement by its means of production is not accomplished; the successive parts that emerge from the production process as C' find their change of function barred by their predecessors. If this continues for some time, production is restricted and the whole process brought to a standstill. . . . Every delay in the succession brings the coexistence into disarray, every delay in one stage causes a greater or lesser delay in the entire [industrial] circuit, not only that of the portion of the capital that is delayed, but also that of the entire individual capital. (183)

While Marx does not make the point, this situation potentially empowers workers. Work interruptions and strikes affect not only productive capital but all the other moments of circulation, and in the case of commodity capital can disrupt the flow of necessary means of production to other capitals:

As a whole, then, capital is simultaneously present, and spatially coexistent, in its various phases. But each part is constantly passing from one phase or functional form into another, and thus functions in all of them in turn. The forms are therefore fluid forms, and their simultaneity is mediated by their succession. Each form both follows and precedes the others. . . . The particular circuits simply constitute simultaneous and successive moments of the overall process. . . . It is only in the unity of the three circuits that the continuity of the overall process is realized, in place of the interruption we have just delineated. The total social capital always possesses this continuity, and the process always contains the unity of the three circuits. (184)

Then comes a critical commentary of the greatest importance. But it is stated in such a flat way (as is so typical of this volume) as to make it all too easy to miss its significance. The introductory line is in fact quite stunning in its implications: "Capital, as self-valorizing value, *does not just comprise class relations*, a definite social character that depends on the existence of labour as wage labour" (emphasis added). With this statement Marx opens the way to saying that contradictions and crises can arise in the circulation process outside the class struggle between capital and labor that centers Volume I. The capital-labor relation is not the only locus of contradiction within the laws of motion of capital. Contradictions can emerge from within the circulation and valorization process itself. There is something inherently fragile and vulnerable within the circulation of industrial capital. The task is to reveal what it is.

Marx then examines some of the ways in which the contradictions within this circulation process "grasped as a movement" play out in practice. "Those who consider the autonomization . . . of value as mere abstraction forget that the movement of industrial capital is this abstraction in action." The word "autonomization" signals a particular kind of problem. Value may be an abstraction, but it has real consequences (or, in the language of Volume I, value is "immaterial but objective"). Contradictions within the overall process of circulation play out autonomously, and by this Marx means in ways that are autonomous from the capital-labor contradiction. "Here value passes through different forms, different movements in which it is both preserved and increases and is valorized." The moment of valorization (realization of surplus-value) is just as important as that of production. To illustrate, Marx abandons his assumption of no technological and organizational change to consider "the revolutions that capital value may suffer in its circulatory process; it is clear that despite all revolutions in value, capitalist production can exist and continue to exist only so long as the capital value is valorized, i.e., describes its circuit as value that has become independent, and therefore so long as the revolutions in value are somehow or other mastered and balanced out" (185). From the perspective of individual industrial capital, the hope is that the impacts of the drive for relative surplus-value via technological and organizational change described in Volume I can "somehow" be absorbed, "mastered and balanced out." But notice the language of autonomy and independence.

Let us look at the circulation process from the standpoint of the commodity circuit, which plays such an important role throughout Volume II.

If the social capital value suffers a revolution in value, it can come about that (the) individual capital succumbs to this and is destroyed, because it cannot meet the conditions of this movement of value. The more acute and frequent these revolutions in value become, the more the movement of the independent value, acting with the force of an elemental natural process [that is, a general law of motion of capital] prevails over the foresight and the calculation of the individual capitalist, the more the course of normal production is subject to abnormal speculation, and the greater becomes the danger to the existence of the individual capitals. These periodic revolutions in value thus confirm what they ostensibly refute: the independence which value acquires as capital, and which is maintained and intensified through its movement. (185)

This is nothing short of a theoretical evocation of the perils of devaluations of capitals through what we now call deindustrialization. From the 1980s onwards, a massive wave of plant closures hit older industrial cities like Detroit, Pittsburgh, Baltimore, Sheffield, Manchester, Essen, Lille, Turin and the like. Lest it be thought that this phenomenon was confined to the advanced capitalist countries, the losses of the traditional textile industry of Mumbai and the distress of older industrial areas of Northern China were just as violent. Whole communities that had focused on industrial work were destroyed almost overnight. Some 60,000 jobs in steel were lost in Sheffield over a three-year period in the 1980s, for example. The desolation this wrought was everywhere apparent. When people looked for explanations, they were told it was all the result of a mysterious force called "globalization." When trade unions and social movements protested and sought to stem the hemorrhaging of jobs and livelihoods, they were told the mysterious force was both inevitable and unstoppable.

Looking backwards, we can see that this mysterious force had long been at work (though not given the name of "globalization" until the 1980s). From the 1930s there had been a steady drift of jobs in the textile industries in the United States from traditional working-class centers such as New York and Boston and the many other smaller mill towns of New England southwards down the so-called "Fall Line" towns (so-called because of the water power that originally encouraged mill location where the Appalachian rivers crossed onto the Atlantic flood plains) that stretched from Lowell to Baltimore. The jobs were drifting to the US South (the Carolinas in particular), and even spilling over the border into Mexico. In Britain during the 1960s, textile jobs were falling off as competition from the then British colony of Hong Kong became fiercer. Job relocations and community destructions have long been the way of the capitalist world.

Marx here offers us a way to cast all this in a particular theoretical light. When elaborated upon, the theory shows how and why crises of this sort, which are not total systemic crises but widespread localized destructions, are inevitable within a capitalist system. Industrial capitals in competition with each other promote revolutions in technologies and organizational forms that in turn produce value revolutions. This is the supposedly mysterious force (appearing like a force of nature, and therefore supposedly outside of human control) that deindustrializes whole industrial regions.

Stated more formally: individual capitalists organize their production of value in search of relative surplus-value, but in so doing produce new value relations that can return to destroy them. Not only does capital produce the means of its own domination; it also produces the means for its own destruction. Hence the Oedipal rage with which capitalists frequently respond to the crises of capitalism that destroy them. Have they not played the game correctly, calculated and planned the production of surplus-value as they should? Have they not performed according to the rule book of bourgeois virtue? How, then, have they not received their just rewards and, even worse, how have they now been cast into the darkness of bankruptcy? But instead of raging against capitalism— the system—they rage against the foreign producers, the immigrants, the speculators, and the others who are in fact merely the secret and hidden agents of capital's inner laws of motion.

Many people reading Marx have a problem with the concept of value as an abstraction, a social relation that is immaterial but objective in its consequences. But "value" is no more abstract and mysterious than the popularly accepted force called "globalization." What is odd is that so many people easily accept the latter (because we became habituated to it?), while often balking at the former as far too abstract. But the virtue of Marx's superior concept is that we see more clearly how this abstraction is created, and how the forces that it assembles work—how we become, as Marx puts it elsewhere, a victim of capital's abstractions. From the very beginning of *Capital*, we learned that value is constituted out of the socially necessary labor deployed through "the movement of industrial capital" through production and circulation. The abstraction of value (and its representation in money form) becomes a regulatory force by way of the hidden hand of market competition.

Recall, however, that if labor does not produce a use value that somebody wants, needs or desires, then it is not socially necessary labor: the unity of production and circulation is already presumed in the very first section of Volume I. Value is, therefore, an abstract social relation collectively produced by individual industrial capitals. But individual industrial capitals then have to submit to the laws they themselves have collectively created. And in so doing, many of them end up succumbing to or being destroyed by the very value revolutions they are perpetually creating. We see them in effect digging their own graves. Instead of some mysterious force called "globalization" that seems to descend from the ether with such destructive and irresistible power, we here have a theory which internalizes the self-destructive dynamic through which capitalists produce the very conditions of their own demise. To accept this theory, all we have to do is to recognize "the independence which value acquires as capital, and which is maintained and intensified through its movement." Why is that harder to accept than some vacuous term like "globalization"?

But the import of these passages is, of course, that not all industrial capitals are destroyed. So the question of which capitals survive, and of what sort and where they are, must obviously be raised even though Marx does not here care to do so (presumably it is too "particular" to be of immediate interest). You must, however, excuse my obvious pleasure, as someone who works on uneven geographical development, regional change and the changing paths of urbanization, to find my interests so neatly tied into the general corpus of Marx's political economy by way of these short passages.

In order to move in this direction, however, Marx has to abandon his general exclusion in Volume II of changes in productivity, of technological and organization change, from his theorizing. This prompts some reflections on his part as to why that exclusion was so necessary. If value changes are perpetually occurring within the circulation process—and it is the latter which is the focus of his attention in Volume II—then all sorts of consequences follow. When the value of means of production falls, then money capital is "set free" even as the simple reproduction of productive capital is maintained. If the value of means of production rises, then more money capital is needed just to keep the same productive capital functioning. "The process takes place quite normally only if value relations remain constant." The smoothness, continuity and fluidity that are so important to the circulation of industrial capital as a whole can be sustained only under conditions of zero technological change. As soon as new technologies are introduced, this introduces value revolutions and instability into the circulation process. For instance, a new technology comes in and the relative need for material inputs and labor-power changes. This will clearly disrupt preceding flow relations:

> In practice it runs its course as long as disturbances in the repetition of the circuit balance each other out; the greater the disturbances, the greater the money capital that the industrial capitalist must possess in

order to ride out the period of readjustment; and since the scale of each individual production process grows with the progress of capitalist production, and with it the minimum size of the capital to be advanced, this circumstance is added to the other circumstances which increasingly turn the function of industrial capitalist into a monopoly of large-scale money capitalists, either individual or associated. (187)

This is an important argument. A reserve of money power is needed to deal with uncertainties in the circulation process stemming from technological changes. Better, therefore, to be a money capitalist rather than a production capitalist at times of rapid technological change. This may have something to do with the increasing ascendancy of finance and money capital relative to industrial capital over the last thirty years or so. By introducing the figure of the money capitalist here, however, Marx departs even further from the assumptions (no specific agents) upon which he has hitherto based his purely formal argument. The production of a tendency towards monopolization, as a way to control the uncertainties, interruptions and disruptions that inevitably arise from value revolutions, is also an important idea. It relates back to Marx's arguments concerning the increasing centralization (as opposed to concentration) of capital as laid out in Volume I. The actual history of capitalism has often been marked by such tendencies towards centralization and monopolization, and again it is easy to see how this helps capitalists deal with the vicissitudes and uncertainties that derive from the fiercely competitive but destabilizing drive to procure relative surplus-value through technological changes. Monopoly power allows capital to control the pace of potentially disruptive technological changes.

Marx then briefly sets aside yet another of his tacit assumptions: that capital is working within a closed economy and that all means of production are produced by other industrial capitalists. What happens when means of production are procured from some other place where capital relations have yet to be established? Once they enter into the orbit of capital they become commodities just like all the others, thanks mainly to the agency of merchant capitalists who procure them from elsewhere. The circuit of industrial capital here

> cuts across the commodity circulation of the most varied modes of social production. . . . Whether the commodities are the product of production

based on slavery, the product of peasants (Chinese, Indian ryots), of a community (Dutch East Indies), of state production (such as existed in earlier epochs of Russian history, based on serfdom), or of half-savage hunting peoples, etc.—as commodities and money they confront the money and commodities in which industrial capital presents itself.

Capital can integrate with noncapitalist modes of production.

The character of the production process from which (commodities) derive is immaterial; they function on the market as commodities, and as commodities they enter both the circuit of industrial capital and the circulation of the surplus-value borne by it. Thus the circulation process of industrial capital is characterized by the many-sided character of its origins, and the existence of the market as a world market. (189–90)

From the *Communist Manifesto* on, Marx and Engels had been acutely aware that they were living in an era in which the creation of the world market was proceeding at a rapid pace (through the coming of the railroads, the steamships and the soon to be dominant telegraph, which permitted commodity prices to become almost instantaneously known in all the major port cities of the world). They were also very sensitive to the ways in which the circulation of industrial capital was intersecting with this world, both transforming it (as capitalist production became more and more hegemonic) and being transformed by it (as cheap raw materials and other commodities could be procured from noncapitalist social formations). There are two points that Marx here makes about this process. Firstly, the reproduction of productive capital requires the reproduction of the means of production, and this means that "the capitalist mode of production is conditioned by modes of production lying outside its own stage of development." But its "tendency" is "to transform all possible production into commodity production" and "the main means by which it does this is precisely by drawing this production into its circulation process. . . . The intervention of industrial capital everywhere promotes this transformation, and with it too the transformation of all immediate producers into wage-labourers." Whether this occurred peacefully or not, and to what degree it entailed imperialist and colonial practices, is left unsaid.

Secondly, "whatever the origin of the commodities that go into the circulation process of industrial capital . . . they confront industrial capital straight away in its form of commodity capital," and they therefore have "the form of commodity-dealing or merchant's capital; and this by its very nature embraces commodities from all modes of production" (190). This leads to some brief reflections (which we will elaborate upon later) on the role of merchant capital, of wholesale and retail merchants, in the capitalist mode of production. Similarly, the role of money-dealing capital also enters in with, as usual, some invocation of the credit system. We will return later to these questions of the roles of merchants and money capitalists.

There is a third point that Marx later hints at (195). The continuity of flow that is so essential to the circulation process of capital demands that supplies of commodities from noncapitalist social formations and producers be assured on a steady rather than an episodic and insecure basis. Once commodities from the noncapitalist world are drawn into the circulation process of industrial capital, steps have to be taken to ensure that the flow of these commodities continues unhindered. This is most assuredly one of the reasons for the establishment of some power relation, most conspicuously that of colonialism and imperialist domination, along with agreements with foreign potentates (such as the Saudis), through which the cooperation of the noncapitalist suppliers of key commodities involved in the reproduction of capital circulation is assured on a continuous basis.

Matters of this sort are barely hinted at here. But, as I began by arguing at the outset, once we let our imaginations roam on the basis of Marx's arguments, then Volume II appears a more and more fecund source for further theory-construction on all manner of topics, such as uneven geographical development, systems of commodity exchange with noncapitalist social formations, and culminating in the transformation, either through commerce or through colonialism or imperialist domination, of much of the world into one vast market where capital circulation ultimately reigns supreme. The actual materials of the text, however, are rather dry and cryptic. In themselves, these passages appear rather casual and tangential. But when we reflect as to where these ideas might lead, there opens up an amazing theoretical terrain which, when supplemented with the insights from Marx's other works, have all manner of implications for our understanding of how capital becomes grounded in particular situations, including those of a non-capitalist world.

Marx at this point merely adds some historical generalizations. "Natural economy, money economy and credit economy [are] the three characteristic economic forms of motion of social production" (195). The money economy and the credit economy "merely correspond to the different stages of development of capitalist production; they are in no way different independent forms of commerce as opposed to natural economy." Within capitalism, the distinction between money and credit economies basically refers to the "mode of commerce" between producers. In natural economy the mode of commerce is barter.

I have to say I do not find these categories and this periodization particularly illuminating. The distinctions are taken without any critical commentary from Adam Smith, and the periodization has no historical basis whatsoever. This is one of those moments where Marx merely regurgitates bourgeois mythology without question. It is, however, significant that Marx does underline that "the credit economy" requires a distinctive mode of analysis. But he says absolutely nothing here about what that distinctive mode of analysis might be. The historical relation between modes of commerce, along with the historical significance of usury and credit, are much better handled by Marx elsewhere (as we will see below).

The final section of the chapter poses a conundrum of great consequence for the whole of Volume II, and hence for the whole corpus of Marx's political economy. It therefore warrants a very close reading.

Marx is very reluctant, as I noted in the first chapter, to get into questions of supply and demand (since, when in equilibrium, "they cease to explain anything"). But, at this point in Volume II, he encounters a situation where he cannot avoid them. The problem arises out of a consideration of where the final demand comes from to realize the surplus-value:

> The capitalist casts less value into circulation in the form of money than he draws out of it, because he casts in more value in the form of commodities than he has extracted in the form of commodities. In so far as he functions merely as the personification of capital, as industrial capitalist, his supply of commodity value is always greater than his demand for it.

If his supply and demand matched one another in this respect, this would be equivalent to the non-valorization of his capital; it would not have functioned as productive capital. . . . The greater the difference between the capitalist's supply and his demand, i.e. the greater the additional commodity values that he supplies over the commodity value he demands, the greater the rate at which he valorizes his capital. His goal is not simply to cover his demand with his supply, but to have the greatest possible excess of supply over demand. What is true for the individual capitalist, is true for the capitalist class. (196–7)

The capitalist class demands means of production (c), so this is one source of demand. But this is much less than the value of the commodities that will be produced (c + v + s). The capitalist class provides the workers with purchasing power (v). The worker "converts his wages almost wholly into means of subsistence, and by far the greater part into necessities," so that "the capitalist's demand for labour-power is indirectly also a demand for the means of consumption that enter into the consumption of the working class." If we ignore workers' savings and "leave the matter of credit out of consideration[!]" then the "maximum limit of the capitalist's demand is c + v, but his supply is c + v + s." This means that the greater the surplus-value produced (or the higher the rate of profit), "the smaller his demand in relation to his supply" (197–8). Equilibrium between supply and demand therefore not only seems impossible, but is also undesirable from the standpoint of capital.

This points to what I call "the capital surplus disposal or absorption problem." The capitalist begins the day with a certain amount of money equivalent to c + v, and ends the day with a monetary equivalent of c + v + s. So where does the demand to buy the surplus-value at the end of the day come from? If it were just a matter of finding more money, then someone, somewhere (in Marx's day the gold producers, for example—and Marx will later on consider their potential role—and in our day the Federal Reserve) could simply supply it. But we have to solve the problem in value rather than money terms. If the surplus-value is to be realized in exchange, then we have to explain where the value equivalent of the surplus-value comes from in the final instance to accomplish that exchange. Theoretically, we have to answer this question without going outside of capitalism (the noncapitalist sources of both demand and supply that Marx considered earlier in the chapter) or assuming the existence of some class of conspicuous consumers (such as landlords and other feudal remnants, like the Crown and the Church) whose sole role is to produce nothing but to consume to the hilt in order to keep supply and demand in balance. This latter option (along with foreign trade), by the way, was how Malthus dealt with this same problem of insufficient effective demand to absorb the surpluses being produced. He went so far as to justify the existence of parasitic classes engaging in conspicuous consumption, such as the clergy, state functionaries (including the monarchy) and an idle aristocracy—because they played a crucial harmonizing role in an otherwise discordant capitalism. Marx, obviously, would want no truck with such a solution even if it could be sustained in the long run (which it could not).

Having introduced (as usual) some complications, such as those of turnover time and fixed capital investment (both of which will warrant separate chapters later), Marx seeks to solve the problem from the standpoint of reproduction. If the capitalist class itself consumes the whole of the surplus-value and recycles the value of constant and variable capital back into production, then demand and supply are brought back into equilibrium. But this means that the whole of the surplus-value must be purchased and consumed by the capitalist class. The capitalists must, in short, use their own stores of value (how obtained we do not know, though primitive accumulation presumably has something to do with it) to buy (realize) the surplus-value produced at the end of the day.

The logic behind this is impeccable in a way. Imagine a two-class society of capitalists and laborers. Plainly laborers cannot supply the extra demand to absorb the surplus (if anything, they are likely to exercise less demand over time with rising rates of exploitation). So the only class that can possibly supply the extra demand must be the capitalist class. They have to possess monetary (value) reserves at one point in time in order to realize the surplus-value they seek to appropriate at a later point in time. This sounds like a pretty weird system. It assumes, for example, an infinite desire on the part of the capitalists for an ever-expanding volume of consumption goods.

There is, however, one possible explanation for Marx's position. He began the chapter by saying that "all the premises of the process appear as its result, as premises produced by the process itself. Each moment appears as a point of departure, of transit, and of return." Could we say this is true of the capitalist class in general? On the first round of circulation, capital may indeed have to lay out the extra value (money) to purchase the surplus-value produced by the worker. But, once this is done, then the surplus-value produced by the workers belongs to the capitalists, while the capitalists have in effect consumed away their original capital. At the next round in the circulation process, the capitalists spend not their own money, but the money equivalent of the surplus-value they earlier appropriated from the workers. The capitalist class is thereby perpetually reproduced out of the production of surplus-value by the workers. The capitalists in effect supply the extra demand out of the surplus-value already produced by the workers and then appropriated by the capitalists. This was, of course, exactly the argument of chapter 23 of Volume I. The problem of where the extra demand comes from seems to disappear, because the workers have already produced it and all the capitalists have to do is to appropriate it. Or, as Marx began by saying, the premise (the effective demand of the capitalist) now appears as its result (the appropriation of surplus-value). This may work for simple reproduction, but given the general tenor of the argument in these chapters it is unlikely that this process can proceed continuously without interruptions and disruptions.

But, if the capitalist proceeds in this manner, then he is behaving as "a non-capitalist, not in his function as capitalist, but for his private requirements or pleasures." And this, says Marx, "is equivalent to assuming the non-existence of the industrial capitalist himself. For capitalism is already essentially abolished once we assume that it is enjoyment that is the driving motive and not enrichment itself." The distinction between enjoyment and enrichment seems here to be crucial to Marx's reasoning. To say that capitalism is founded on the personal desire for enjoyment would go against the argument Marx made in Volume I, chapter 24. Capitalism, he there argues, is based on "production for production's sake and accumulation for accumulation's sake" independent of the personal desires of the capitalists. While there is always a "Faustian moment" in which the desire for consumption and enjoyment conflicts with the necessity of reinvesting, the coercive laws of competition force capitalists willy-nilly towards the latter option. So it is insufficient to assume a capitalist persona besotted by the desire for consumer goods as the driving force of capital accumulation. It is even insufficient to assume that the driving force is the capitalist lust for more and more of the social power that the private appropriation of money allows (though this, as we shall see, is partially involved). The historical mission of the bourgeoisie is perpetual accumulation.

A system founded on the pursuit of pure pleasure and greed is, says Marx, "technically impossible. The capitalist must not only form a reserve of capital to guard against price fluctuations, and in order to be able to await the most favourable conjunctures for buying and selling; he must accumulate capital, in order to extend production and incorporate technical advances into his productive organism." Hoarding money to invest in large-scale and lumpy fixed capital, for example, withdraws money from circulation and thus diminishes the available demand: "the money is immobilized and does not withdraw from the commodity market an equivalent in commodities for the money equivalent that it has withdrawn for commodities supplied." This aggravates the gap between the value the capitalist is supplying to the market and the available demand.

When part of the surplus-value is reinvested in expanding production, the solution proposed above for the effective demand problem looks even fishier. Not only will the capitalist have to provide the wherewithal to purchase and realize the initial round of surplus-value production, but he or she will also have to find even more resources to realize the surplus-value produced from reinvestment. And that obligation will continue in perpetuity.

So the central problem is still left dangling: if, as seems to be the case, the demand cannot come from capitalist consumption, then from where on earth does it come? Marx provides hints but no definitive answer here. But it is, I think, significant that the chapter closes with this comment: "We have ignored credit here, and it pertains to credit if the capitalist deposits the money that he accumulates in a bank, for example, on current account bearing interest" (199). The hoarding necessary for fixed-capital formation could be organized through the credit system. This would certainly permit all of the hoarded value to be spent. This is, therefore, another of those points where the credit system seems set to play a crucial role of releasing more money power. But we have no idea here what that role might be, and how it might relate to the clear imbalance in demand and supply that arises from within the dynamics of the accumulation process.

The solution to the dilemma comes much later in Volume II, in several successive stages, culminating in the reproduction schemas at the end of the book. Rather than perpetuate the mystery (as Marx is prone to do), let me sketch in the broad outlines of how I interpret Marx's argument. Capitalist consumption is of two sorts: personal consumption (necessities and luxuries) and productive consumption. The latter entails recycling the original capital to produce yet another round of surplus-value production and reinvestment in expansion, which means an increased demand for more means of production and more wage goods for the extra laborers hired (presuming no labor-saving technological changes). The coercive laws of competition drive expansion (hence the emphasis on enrichment rather than enjoyment). The demand derived from expansion tomorrow (plus bourgeois consumption) provides the market for the surplus commodities produced yesterday.

The timing of all this is crucial. When disaggregated, we see that at any one moment some capitalists are spending on reinvestment while others are hoarding money in anticipation of future investments or reinvestments (in fixed capital, for example). Those reinvesting are furnishing extra demand, while those hoarding are withdrawing demand but still furnishing a supply. Is there a possibility of balancing aggregate supply and demand in this way? Only, it seems, if the credit system intervenes so that hoarded money becomes freely available for use by others (thanks to the operations of the banks) for even more reinvestment. The money derived from the sale of tomorrow's product is, in effect, needed to pay for the surplus-value produced today. This temporal gap between the capitalist's supply and the capitalist's demand can be bridged only with the aid of credit moneys (with which Marx studiously avoids engaging in Volume II). Capitalists do not actually have to borrow from anyone to do this. They can simply issue IOUs and engage in the long-standing practice of buying now and paying later. Hence arises an intimate association between the accumulation of capital and the accumulation of debt. Each is impossible without the other. Fighting to curb further debt creation (as the Republican Party seemed to be doing in 2011) is, in effect, a fight to end capitalism. This is why a politics of austerity, if endlessly pursued, will not only stymie growth, but in the end lead to a capitalist collapse.

There is no more than a brief hint of this solution and its attached problems in this chapter. I am here getting way ahead of myself. Indeed, Marx's reluctance to deal with the categories of credit and interest along with the personas of bankers and financiers leads him to evade a full statement in Volume II of how capitalists can balance supply and demand under a pure capitalist mode of production.

Reflections on the Definition of Capital

Marx does not make political arguments in Volume II. So what kinds of political insights can we infer from the text so far? One issue that jumps out in these chapters is the definition being given to capital. At a time when there is renewed talk of anticapitalist struggle, it is useful to define exactly what the struggle might be against.

In Volume I, capital is defined as value in motion. "Capital is money, capital is commodities," Marx says.

> In truth, however, value is here the subject of a process in which while constantly assuming the form in turn of money and commodities, it changes its own magnitude, throws off surplus-value from itself . . . Money therefore forms the starting point and the conclusion of every valorization process. . . . Value therefore now becomes value in process, money in process, and, as such, capital.

But, *nota bene*, Marx is here invoking how capital *appears* and not what it really is. In these passages, for example, he notes how capital "has acquired the occult ability to add value to itself. It brings forth living offspring, or at least lays golden eggs." In Volume I Marx shows how those golden eggs are laid by labor working under the direction and control of capital in the hidden abode of production.

But, in Volume II, "value in motion" is disaggregated into the circuits of money, commodity and productive capital. Is one of these circuits more defining of capital than the others? And, if so, are there critical transformative points within or between the different circuits that provide clear foci for political struggle? What are we to make of the contradictions within the circulation process that are not directly attributable to the tension within the capital-labor relation? What are we to make of the bald fact that if value is not realized in circulation then that value (along with any surplus-value) is lost?

Marx is very emphatic in these chapters that money is not capital. Money, he argues, can only perform money functions: the buying and selling of commodities. Besides, money forms arose well before capital arose as a dominant force over human affairs. But while capital cannot be reduced to money, there are some good reasons why capital can not only *appear* to be, but can also actually *become* money capital. Money is a form of social power appropriable by private persons. Desire for more money power animates many a capitalist, and this can certainly become one of the driving forces behind the desire for private accumulation. Furthermore, it is only in the money form that surplus-value becomes calculable. The capitalist knows how much money he laid out at the beginning of the circuit, and can easily figure the extra money he gets back. So it is hardly surprising that, when we think of capital, we think of it primarily in its money form. From this we can see how the fetish belief that money is capital can take root. It is important to recognize the power of this fetish belief. It really is the case that money power is both vitally important and an object of desire. But the fetishism of money, like that of the commodity so brilliantly laid out in Volume I, conceals an underlying social reality. Money cannot in itself create anything: it can only perform money functions. It is therefore delusional to think, Marx shows, that the money circuit is the pre-eminent circuit of capital. Yet, at a certain point in its circulation, industrial capital takes on the money form and, as it does so, it produces money capital.

Commodities can likewise perform only commodity functions. Commodities can exist without being products of capital. In fact, Marx argues, a whole world of commodity production and exchange, along with monetary and market forms, had to exist before capital itself could come into being. If there were no commodities already on the market, where would capitalists buy their means of production and workers the wage goods they need to survive? So commodification in general, and even direct commodity production, does not define capital. What *is* specific is that commodities under capitalism are impregnated with surplus-value, and commodities cannot impregnate themselves. But commodities cannot define capital, either. Important though it is throughout Volume II, the commodity circuit is not defining for capital.

Even more surprising is Marx's assertion that the buying and selling of labor-power, often taken as basic to the definition of capital, can exist without capital. Labor services could be paid for outside of the purview of any circulation of capital. There was plenty of that going on under feudalism. Read a Dickens novel and you will see it going on all over the place in London even when capitalism was well-established. This distinction is still important: if I pay a kid in my building to walk my dog in the afternoon, or if I give a case of beer to a neighbor who spends hours helping me fix up my porch, then none of this presupposes the existence or circulation of capital. Exchanges of labor services for money or other commodities, Marx notes, had to exist before capital could buy labor-power as a commodity. So while extensive proletarianization was a necessary precondition for the rise of capital, it does not define what the essence of capital is all about.

Marx also points out (161) that capitalist commodity production can only be carried out in the same way as "production in general," and so cannot in itself be differentiated from "the non-capitalist production process" by any particular physical attributes. Growing corn is, in the end, growing corn regardless of the mode of production. So physical practices of use-value production do not define capital. The same physical production process can in principle take place under feudal, capitalistic or socialist social relations.

The essence of capital, we are forced to conclude, is the class relation between capital and labor in production that facilitates the systematic production and appropriation of value and surplus-value. This definition of capital is consistent with Marx's argument in the introduction to the *Grundrisse* that it is production, understood as production of surplus-value (not physical production), that predominates over all the other moments of distribution, exchange, consumption and, most of all, over the physical process of production itself. The reproduction of capital is always to be understood as the reproduction of the class relation between capital and labor (as chapter 23 of Volume I makes very clear).

The narrative that emerges from Marx's account is this: all of these elements of money, commodities, the buying and selling of labor services, and a given physical and technical capacity for production had to preexist the rise of capital. Together they constituted the necessary preconditions for the emergence of that class relation between capital and labor that facilitates the systematic production and appropriation of surplus-value. It is this last central feature, however, that is the defining specificity of capital. If, therefore, we want to talk about "the communist hypothesis" or an anticapitalist politics, then the core goal must be the abolition of this class relation in production.

It is tempting then to conclude that it should in principle be possible to construct socialism, and even communism, in a world of monetization, commodification, and even the trading of labor services, provided that the class relation between capital and labor is erased from the world of production (replaced, for example, by the "associated laborer" to whom Marx usually appeals whenever he gives consideration to alternatives). After all, if all of these features preexisted the rise of capital, why could they not continue to play a crucial role under socialism or even communism?

But there is a more complicated narrative that emerges out of these chapters. Once the class relation between capital and labor becomes dominant in production, then it entails a transformation of the preconditions that gave rise to it. The circulation of money and commodities and the functioning of labor markets are transformed so as to support and even mandate and discipline the reproduction of class relations in production. In these chapters, we see that the three circuits of money, commodity, and productive capital are so intertwined with each other that one cannot be changed without changing all the others. This does not mean that change is impossible. Indeed, it is precisely because a disruption at one point of a circuit has immediate impacts on all the others that change *becomes* possible. And what Marx shows us is that disruptions are inevitably occurring anyway, thereby offering abundant opportunities for political interventions. The whole system, once we understand it well, appears as both fragile and vulnerable.

While it is true that money, commodities, and the exchange of labor services logically and historically preceded the rise of capital as a class relation, these exchanges at that time functioned under radically different social conditions. When most individuals either exercised some control over their own means of production or were (as under slavery and serfdom) assured of a permanent (albeit tightly circumscribed) position in the social order, the direct producers were always in a position to reproduce themselves wholly or partly outside of market exchange. Some may have been forced by extreme hunger or crop failures into involuntary exchange of either commodities or labor services, but much of the exchange was of surpluses over and above those needed for social reproduction. The exchanges occurred outside of the discipline exercised by exchange-value. It is still the case, under those conditions called "partial proletarianization," that some large segments of the global labor force that have access to land and other family or kinship resources can return to such conditions when unemployed, sick, or disabled. This is the case in contemporary China, for example, where many of the costs of social reproduction are borne in the rural areas. Even more callously, this is how US agribusiness unloads the costs of social reproduction on Mexico by employing illegal immigrants to work with carcinogenic pesticides, until they become too sick and have to return to the Mexican villages from whence they came to be cared for or to die.

In these opening chapters of Volume II, Marx directs our attention to a general point: that, as the class relation between capital and labor came to dominate in production (spreading far afield even in Marx's day), so this had a transforming impact upon the form and functioning of money, commodities, and labor markets. Once money becomes money *capital*, Marx notes, it becomes not only the aim and object of the capitalist's fetish desire. It also assumes very different functions and, particularly in the form of the credit system, is organized solely to support the reproduction of the class relation. The different circuits of capital are enmeshed and intertwined in such a way that each supports and on occasion contradicts the others, even as the class relation and the production of surplus-value remain at the center of the capitalist mode of production. Capital "is a movement, a circulatory process through different stages, which itself in turn includes three different forms of the circulatory process. Hence it can only be grasped as a movement, and not as a static thing." This is consistent with Marx's dialectical conception of "totality," as also laid out in the introduction to the *Grundrisse*. While the specificity of capital lies in the class relation in production that facilitates the creation of surplus-value, its generality lies in the circulation process of industrial capital that is constituted as a unity of the circuits of money, production, and commodity capitals.

It would be delusional to believe, therefore, that changes in production could be far-reaching without the mandating of radical changes in the functioning of the other circuits. The transition to socialism or communism entails not only a fierce combat to eradicate the class relation between capital and labor in production. It also requires the rolling back, or perhaps the reconstruction, of these other circuits in order to show how monetization, commodification and the trading of labor services might be transformed to support associated laborers in production. If, for example, something akin to money is needed to facilitate exchange, then how can we prevent money from becoming money capital, and the social power that inheres in money from being appropriated by that class that will then use it to produce and appropriate surplus-value for itself? Exchange of commodities is one thing, but exchange-value as the regulator of all human transactions is quite another. Without such ancillary transformations, the abolition of class relations in production appears impossible.

This conclusion finds support in the long and often vainglorious history of attempts to reorganize capitalist production on noncapitalist lines, particularly under the rubric of associated labor. Attempts at workers' control, self-management, *autogestión*, and factory cooperatives (of the sort that sprung up in Europe in the 1970s or in Argentina after the crisis of 2001) have invariably suffered, and in some instances been destroyed, from having to deal with the controlling powers of hostile merchants' and finance capital. The dream of *autogestión* and workers' control has often crashed on the rocks of the powers of money and commodity capital and the laws of exchange-value to discipline them. The driving force to valorize value and thereby extract surplus-value is hard to ward off. And it is perhaps significant that the longest-lasting workers' cooperative that has survived—Mondragon, which was founded in Spain's fascist period, in the Basque country, in 1956—did so in part because it set up its own credit institutions and marketing functions, thus casting its political strategy across all three circuits. It continues to survive and flourish, and in most of the 200 enterprises it now controls the differentials in rewards to participants are still held for the most part at 3-to-1 (compared to 400-to-1 or more in US corporations).

The difficulties confronted by forms of associated labor largely derive from the perpetuation of the capitalist laws of value which, as we earlier saw, dominate and often destroy individual capitals. Once any enterprise enters into a world where these laws of value hold sway, it is subject to the disciplinary power of those laws. Staying out of range of that disciplinary power is difficult, if not impossible. In order to survive, Mondragon and the recuperated factories in Argentina had to find a way to compromise with the law of value. This leads us to a general and, on the surface at least, dispiriting conclusion, for which Marx has already prepared us in his analysis of the devaluation and deindustrialization of capital: the class relation between capital and labor in production cannot be abolished without the abolition of the laws of motion of capital and the abolition of that immaterial and objective force of the law of value that anchors those laws of motion. But Marx is often drawn to a co-evolutionary theory of historical transformation. If we apply the lineaments of such a theory to this case, then a strategy for anticapitalist struggle begins to emerge. While the class relation between capital and labor lies at the center of the definition of capital, it is so deeply embedded in other facets of the circulation process as to make it hard to dislodge without demolishing or replacing the supports that surround it. While we can remain faithful to the principle of associated workers, of worker autonomy and self-management, and honor the long history of attempts to implement such ways of producing and living, we also have to confront all the other facets of social change required to emancipate the social world from the domination of capital.

While communism has at the end of the day to abolish the class relation between capital and labor, it does not necessarily have to abolish money (or its equivalent), or the exchange of goods and of labor services. It would, as did capital before it, have to find ways to restructure all of these other circulatory processes in ways supportive of associated labor, instead of supportive of the class relations of capital. This poses some very general and seemingly quite difficult questions on the future role and very nature of money, commodification, and markets. How, for example, might labor services be traded, and how could labor move fluidly from one line or place of production to another? And how would divisions of labor be coordinated to a social purpose? Would there be labor and commodity exchanges? The transition to communism would entail the transformation of all these other circulatory processes so that they no longer operate in support of capital. But the experience of trying to create communism through the total abolition of all these supplementary forms, as occurred in North Korea, would suggest that this is not possible either.

Marx, while not a utopian, seems to favor the idea of associated laborers autonomously controlling and deciding what use-values they produce, and by what means, as the basis of a revolutionary alternative to a ruthless capitalism based on exchange-values and surplus-value appropriation. But this, as we will see when we examine the aggregate conditions of reproduction in the last two chapters of Volume II, cannot happen without some kind of directing and coordinating mechanism or authority of governance, and without conscious planning of how use-values are to be produced in a coordinated way. All of this is, of course, a very long way away from Marx's actual text. But I think Volume II does invite reflection on such processes and problems. This is what turns a rather dull book into a much more interesting exercise in creative political thinking.

But there is one other crucial political point to be made here. In many parts of the world—the United States in particular—the idea of socialism or communism is associated primarily with dictatorial forms of centralized state power. A perfectly valid distrust of the state and of the exercise of state power is everywhere observable. But here is Marx suggesting that the core imaginary of an alternative communist society is that of freely associating laborers controlling their own production process and exercising autonomy in the workplace within a decentralized economy. There is, it turns out, immense public sympathy with that idea. I recall seeing a public opinion poll some years back that indicated that most Americans thought worker control a good idea. And when the workers at Republic Windows and Doors in Chicago sat in and occupied their factory in the crisis of 2008, they were treated by the mainstream press even in the United States more as local heroes than as commie-pinko villains. If you ask the most vociferous opponents of socialism, including those in the Tea Party, whether they agree or not with worker rather than state or government control, they will almost certainly reply affirmatively. Many people are, it turns out, in favor of at least this version of the communist hypothesis. What emerges from these chapters, therefore, is not only a clearer definition of capital, but a conception of a communist alternative that even many Americans might willingly endorse.

CHAPTERS 5–6 OF VOLUME II IN GENERAL

The next two chapters deal with the time and costs that attach to the circulation processes described in the preceding chapters. Marx here embarks upon an investigation into the temporality of continuous capital accumulation. Even though he focuses exclusively on the laws of motion of capital, it is not hard to recognize how these processes necessarily impinge upon and shape the temporalities of daily life for everyone living under a capitalist mode of production. Buried in the details of these chapters is, in fact, a profound enquiry into the ruling but ever-changing temporality and perpetually emergent spatiality of a capitalist mode of production. What, then, does the time-space evolution of capital look like? What forces lie behind it, and why does it take the particular trajectory it does? These questions should be borne constantly in mind while working through the details.

There is one basic idea that is fundamental for understanding Marx's argument in these chapters. It derives from his long-standing insistence that value and surplus-value cannot be produced through acts of exchange. Value is created in production, and that is that. From this it follows that the time and labor expended on circulation in the market is unproductive of value. A lot of time and labor effort is taken up by circulation in the market. Marx considers this lost time and lost expenditure of labor time in relation to the production of value. There are many incentives, therefore, to find ways to reduce it. One consequence is capital's historical and continuing fascination with speed-up. The expenditure of labor on transforming a commodity into money or vice versa is unproductive labor (unproductive not in the sense that the labor is useless or unnecessary, or performed by idle, lazy and unproductive workers, but unproductive because it does not produce value). A lot of labor is, of course, employed in circulating commodities, and capitalists such as merchants, wholesalers, and retailers organize that labor and take profit from it in part by exploiting the workers they employ in the same way that production capitalists do. But as far as Marx is concerned this is still to be categorized as unproductive labor. This is a controversial issue, and it has been the subject of substantial and interminable debate, some of which is well described in Ernest Mandel's "Introduction" to this Volume II (though there are plenty of scholars who dispute Mandel's interpretation[1]).

I am not inclined to go into this controversy in detail. But there are some general points that need to be made even if they cannot be resolved here. For example, there is a potential difficulty that arises in relation to Marx's formulation in Volume I. In chapter 16, he shifts his focus from

---

1   For a critique of Mandel's arguments in the Introduction to Volume II, see Patrick Murray, "Beyond the 'Commerce and Industry' Picture of Capital," in Christopher John Arthur and Geert A. Reuten, eds., *The Circulation of Capital: Essays on Volume Two of Marx's* Capital (London: Macmillan, 1998), 57–61.

the individual to the "collective laborer." He plainly has in mind a factory in which the direct producers on the line are mixed together with cleaners, maintenance workers, and other support staff, and Marx is happy to include all of them as part of the collective production process, even though some of them individually do not apply their labor-power to the commodity being produced. As I noted in the *Companion* to Volume I, there is a problem of defining exactly where the collective labor begins and ends. Does it include designers, managers, engineers, maintenance workers, cleaners and traders operating from within the factory? If it is the productivity of the collective rather than the individual laborer that really matters, as Marx insists here, then we need to know over what group of workers the productivity is to be calculated, and who the "associated laborers" are who produce the value. What happens when various functions that were once a part of collective laboring within the factory (such as cleaning and graphic advertising design) are subcontracted out? Do they suddenly shift from being a part of the collective productive labor to the category of unproductive labor? There has been a marked systematic trend, particularly over the last forty years or so, for capitalist firms to rely increasingly on subcontracting, presumably to come to a far more "lean and mean" definition of the collective laborer they employ, and so bolster their individual profit rate (though the aggregate effects upon surplus-value production are murky at best). Cleaning, maintenance, design, marketing, and so on are increasingly organized as "business services," and it is very hard to tell (as Marx himself concedes, as we shall see) when these activities need to be classified as productive of value or unproductive, though necessary. These problems exist within putative socialist forms (one of the criticisms of Mondragon is that it increasingly relies on subcontracting, and therefore survives at the expense of exploitation elsewhere).

I cannot address this question here, except to signal that we are here in the midst of an accounting nightmare (which, in my view, is insoluble) and a resultant mass of controversies (at which Marxists have long excelled). I leave you to study these problems at your leisure. In so doing, you will find that the distinction between productive and unproductive labor is very important in Adam Smith's writings, and that Marx devotes much of the first volume of *Theories of Surplus Value* to examining Adam Smith's views and subjecting them to critique, in order to better define his own. But I am personally not persuaded that Marx found a reasonable answer to the problem. I do not think anyone else has either, which is why there is such a legacy of controversy.

In the absence of a clear accounting solution to the division between productive and unproductive labor, we are left with the problem of how to proceed in a way that preserves Marx's intuitive insights while recognizing the difficulty (impossibility?) of operationalizing the distinctions. The intuitive insight derives from the analysis of the three circuits of capital. There is the moment of production (the labor process) which founds the productive circuit. But that circuit cannot be completed without negotiating the conditions of circulation defined by money and by commodities. Labor is plainly involved in all three circuits, and the continuity of the circuit of industrial capital (the whole process) depends upon the conditions of continuity defined in all three circuits. The notion that trumps all others is the necessity of continuity and speed (acceleration) of flow, and what has to be done to ensure this continuous movement.

If this were the only consideration then we might argue for including all labor involved in production, circulation, and realization as part of the collective labor of maintaining and reproducing capital (this could also be extended to include household labor devoted to the reproduction of labor-power). In other words, we could say that all laborers involved in the circuit of industrial capital ought to be considered productive workers. But this would, in Marx's view, gloss over and mask something very important. If value and surplus-value are produced only at the point of production in the productive circuit, then the expenses involved and labor expended within the circulation of industrial capital have to be paid for by deductions from the value and surplus-value produced in production. Plainly, the extent of these deductions is a matter of deep concern, both individually and socially, to the reproduction of capital. If all the value and surplus-value produced were absorbed in costs of circulation, then who would bother to produce? Strategies to reduce these deductions, as well as to minimize the lost time in circulation, have therefore played an important role in capital's history, and we experience the results of these strategies in our daily lives.

This is where the impulse perpetually to revolutionize the time-space configurations of capitalism through speed-up (even of our consumption, for example) and the "annihilation of space though time" (as Marx puts it in the *Grundrisse*) comes from. Conversely, it also follows that excessive power to impose these deductions (or fail to facilitate the speedy motion of capital through the circuits) can be the generator of crises. If all power lies with the money capitalists (the financiers) and the commodity capitalists (the merchants), then what impacts does this have on the production of value upon which these factions of capital ultimately depend? It could be, for example, that the global economic distress that set in after 2007 was due either to the excessive (and, as we shall see, largely fictitious) profits extracted from the unproductive money and commodity circuits (for example, by Goldman Sachs and Walmart) that sucked energy out of the pursuit of productive activities or, conversely, to such degraded conditions in the productive circuit as to provoke capital flight into the unproductive money and commodity circuits, where accumulation could proceed through dispossession rather than through production. How we might establish the truth of either of these propositions is an intriguing question. But the question readily presents itself: If value can be produced in circulation, then why bother to produce? Marx does not pose this question in that form here, but it is implicit in the analysis. I would far rather take up this question than get lost in some accounting quagmire. And this is the question that seems to correspond most closely to Marx's intuitive understanding. It also happens to be of great contemporary relevance. Bearing all this in mind, let us see how Marx handles the details.

CHAPTER 5 OF VOLUME II

Chapter 5 begins with the seemingly simple distinction between circulation time (how long capital spends in the sphere of circulation in the transition from commodity to money) and production time (how long capital spends in the sphere of active production). The sum of circulation and production times is later defined as the turnover time of capital (204). But there are complications. Fixed capitals (machines, and so on) can spend a long time in the sphere of production whether they are being used or not. There is a key difference, to be taken up in a later chapter, between the total capital *applied* in production (this includes all of the fixed capital, such as machinery and buildings) and the capital actually consumed or *used up* (which only includes that part of the fixed capital used up in the active production process). This distinction only makes sense, however, over a given period of time. Marx often assumes that period to be one year, unless otherwise stated. Furthermore, "the periodic interruption of the labour process, at night for example, may interrupt the function of these means of labour, but it does not affect their stay in the place of production" (200). Production also requires a certain reserve (an inventory) of means of production on hand in the event of sudden shortages in the market for inputs or other unforeseen fluctuations.

This leads Marx to distinguish between functioning time, or what he later calls "working time" (the time when surplus-value is actively being produced through productive consumption), and production time (which includes the time capital is held in reserve, or is not being actively used in the production process). Just to add another wrinkle to the problem, situations often arise in which the production process continues even though no labor is being expended—as, for example, "when wheat grows in the earth or wine ferments in the cellar" (201). For all of these reasons, the production time is nearly always much greater than the working time.

When capital is not actively being used, it reverts to being what Marx calls *latent capital* that functions "in the production process without being involved in the labour process. . . . Its idleness forms a condition for the uninterrupted flow of the production process. The buildings, apparatus, etc. that are necessary for storing the productive reserve (the latent capital) are conditions of the production process and hence form components of the productive capital advanced." But idle capital does not produce value and surplus-value, even though it is a necessary "part of the life" of productive capital:

> It is clear that the nearer the production time and working time approach to equality, the greater the productivity and valorization of a given productive capital in a given space of time. The tendency of capitalist production is therefore to shorten as much as possible the excess of production time over working time. But although the production time of capital may diverge from its working time, it always includes the latter, and the excess itself is a condition of the production process. (202)

Circulation time is the time taken to sell the commodity and then reconvert the money capital into means of production and labor-power. "Circulation time and production time are," Marx writes, "mutually exclusive. During its circulation time, capital does not function as productive capital, and therefore produces neither commodities nor surplus-value" (203). This means that

> the expansion and contraction of the circulation time hence acts as a negative limit on the contraction or expansion of the production time ... The more that the circulation metamorphoses of capital are only ideal, i.e. the closer the circulation time comes to zero, the more the capital functions, and the greater is its productivity and self-valorization. If a capitalist works to order, receives payment on the delivery of his product, and is paid in his own means of production, then his time of circulation approaches zero. (203)

Classical political economy, Marx observes, missed the importance of analyzing production and circulation times. There consequently arose the fetish illusion among many of them, as well as among the capitalists themselves, that surplus-value could derive "from the sphere of circulation," because "longer circulation time is the basis for a higher price." This produces the illusion that "capital possesses a mystical source of self-valorization that is independent of its production process and hence of the exploitation of labour." Beguiled by the fetish belief (which still persists) that value can originate in circulation, it is impossible to understand why capital internalizes a drive towards speed-up and increasing efficiency in circulation. After all, if value can be produced through circulation, then why struggle to reduce circulation times? Slower times would yield more value.

It is unfortunate that Marx merely lays all this out in a purely formal way, without any attempt to indicate its historical relevance. But it is not hard to connect the dots and expand upon the history. Marx, for example, refers back to the Volume I description (C1, 367–9) of how capital internalizes "the drive towards night work" as a way "to shorten the excess of production time over working time" (201). He could, however, have gone much further. Had he here introduced "the coercive laws of competition," as he did when developing the theory of relative surplus-value in Volume I, then he would have derived a powerful logical argument for capitalists' perpetually seeking out competitive advantage by finding means to shorten the gap (and the cost) between production and working times. He would likewise have pointed to the imperative for capital to shorten circulation times and seek out greater efficiencies in distribution (the Walmart syndrome, if you will). I often think how much richer and more appealing Volume II would have appeared if Marx had inserted even a brief chapter, like that on the working day in Volume I, which described the history of technological and organizational shifts designed to reduce the gap between production time and working time as well as circulation times. We would then have understood why it is that capital has so fiercely pursued the speeding up of the temporality of everything. The less the time spent in any of these phases, the faster capital recuperates surplus-value.

The initial "natural" reproductive cycle of hogs, for example, has been accelerated from one to three litters a year; the efficient slaughter and dismembering of the hogs is performed on an assembly line and the packing and shipping is orchestrated as a just-in-time delivery system to supermarkets that exercise tight computerized inventory controls. The only wayward moment in the whole process lies with the singularity of consumer choices. How many pork chops will consumers in New York City buy today? This is the world that capital has produced. What we encounter in this chapter is an explanation of the imperatives within capital that necessarily make it so.

The basic form of commodity circulation is defined in Volume I as C-M-C. The circulation time is broken down "into two opposing phases"—the time needed for its transformation from money into commodity inputs into production, "and the time it needs for its transformation from commodity into money." In Volume I, Marx had argued that there is an asymmetry, because it is easiest to move from the universal representation of value—money—to the particularity of value as embodied in the commodity. But here Marx presents these relations in a rather different light. For the capitalist seeking to buy means of production, the conversion from money into commodities involves a transformation "into those commodities which form the specific elements of productive capital in a given sphere of investment." This is very different from the situation of final consumers with money to spend, who can just as easily purchase shirts if they cannot find shoes. The capitalist producer, by contrast, faces specific purchasing requirements:

The means of production may not be present on the market, needing first to be produced, or they may have to be drawn from distant markets,

> or there may be dislocations in their normal supply, changes of price, etc. in short, a mass of circumstances that are not recognizable in the simple change of form M-C, but require for this part of the circulation phase either less time or more. Just as C-M and M-C are separated in time, so they may also be separated in space, the selling and the buying markets being in different places. (205)

The geographical and spatial conditions of supply of means of production therefore impose constraints on capitalist production because of the time taken to bring these means of production to the point of production where laboring takes place.

But it is not only time taken that is important: "In factories, for example, buyers and sellers are frequently even different persons" and since these agents of circulation (such as the merchants) are "just as necessary for commodity production . . . as agents of production," so both require payment (205). In short, capitalists face all sorts of potential supply constraints and costs when it comes to procuring the use-values required as a precondition of production. They also have to face constraints created by other factions of capital, or by different state powers with geopolitical ambitions. I need rare earth metals to produce wind turbines. But 95 percent of the production and world trade of rare earth metals is controlled by China. When Japan was involved in a conflict with China over jurisdiction in territorial waters, Chinese customs officials held up the shipment of rare earth metals to Japan, leaving Japanese producers high and dry. Innumerable barriers of this sort can affect the transformation of money into commodities as means of production.

Marx's general point is well-taken: the metamorphosis from money into means of production is potentially problematic. The longer it takes to secure those means of production, the more capital is locked up in an unproductive state. Conversely, improvements of access to supplies increase the overall productivity of capital deployed, and hence expands the basis for surplus-value production. But this does not gainsay the greater significance of the sale that realizes the surplus-value: "M-C is in normal conditions a necessary act for the valorization of the value expressed in M, but it is not a realization of surplus-value; it is a prelude to its production, not an appendix to it" (205). The realization of the surplus-value has enormous significance.

The specifics of commodity use-values come to play a much more significant role in Volume II than they did in Volume I. And this is true both for the transition M-C and for the movement to final consumption, C'-M'. "The very form of the existence of commodities, their existence as use values, sets certain limits to the circulation of the commodity capital C'-M'." If "they are not sold within a definite time, then they get spoiled and lose, together with their use-value, their property as bearers of exchange-value. Both the capital value contained in them and the surplus-value added to it are lost." The problem is that

the use-values of different commodities may decay at different speeds. . . . The limitation of the circulation time of commodity capital imposed by the spoiling of the commodity body itself is the absolute limit of this part of the circulation time. . . . The more perishable a commodity, the more directly after its production it must be consumed, and therefore sold, the smaller the distance it can move from its place of production, the narrower therefore is its sphere of spatial circulation, and the more local the character of its market. Hence the more perishable a commodity . . . the less appropriate it is as an object of capitalist production. Capitalism can only deal in commodities of this kind in populous places, or to the extent that distances are reduced by the development of means of transport. The concentration of the production of an article in a few hands, however, and in a populous place, can create a relatively large market even for an article of this kind, as is the case with the big breweries, dairies, etc. (206)

Here, too, technological innovations in the sphere of circulation, the most important of which have undoubtedly been canning and refrigeration (along with keg beers!), have played a critical role in capitalist history for obvious reasons. These brief passages also provide, of course, much grist for the economic geographer's mill of knowledge of how capital accumulation might work through and across space to produce distinctive locational structures and geographical linkages. Supply chains of means of production, along with commodity chains destined for final consumption in spatially distinct and often distant markets, are constantly being reshaped and re-formed into more efficient configurations by the coercive pressures of competition. We will take up Marx's views on transport and communications in general, along with an understanding of locational requirements, at the end of this chapter.

One final point needs to be made. Marx came to these questions on working, production, circulation, and turnover times rather late in the day. He did not, for example, include any analysis of turnover time in Volume III (most of which was written earlier). Engels recognized that changing turnover times had an impact upon the rate of profit. He therefore inserted a tentative chapter on this topic in Volume III. He was, I think, right to do so. I therefore think it very important to bear all of these issues, including those of costs taken up in the next chapter, very much in mind in any reading of Volume III.

CHAPTER 6 OF VOLUME II

Labor-power is required to circulate commodities, and the activity of circulation imposes costs. The sphere of circulation thus arises as a distinctive field of capitalist endeavor that is the special province of a distinctive class faction—merchants. The transition M-C-M takes up time and energy, absorbs labor, and offers the opportunity for financial gain to merchant capitalists. Those who work in this circulation sphere may use it as "an opportunity to appropriate an excess quantity of value," but this labor, Marx insists, "increased by evil intent on either side, no more creates value than the labour that takes place in legal proceedings increases the value of the object in dispute." This labor "does not create value, but only mediates a change in the form of value" (208). This is true of all those who work on the buying and selling of commodities, no matter whether it is the capitalist himself or laborers employed by the capitalist. Here "we have a function which, although in and for itself unproductive, is nevertheless a necessary moment of reproduction. . . . One merchant . . . may, by way of his operations, shorten the buying and selling time for many producers. He should then be considered as a machine that reduces the expenditure of useless energy, or helps set free production time" (209). This merchant is useful "because a smaller part of society's labour-power and labour time is now tied up in these unproductive functions"(210). The remaining necessary costs (*faux frais*) have to be deducted from the value and surplus-value created in production.

We immediately encounter an oddity that is analogous, as Marx points out, to the application of machinery. While machines cannot produce value, as he argues in Volume I, they can be a source of relative surplus-value both individually (capitalists with superior machinery earn excess profits) and socially (the reduction in the cost of wage goods because of rising productivity reduces the value of labor-power). So something that is not a source of value can be a source of surplus-value. This proposition seems to carry over to the activities occurring within the sphere of circulation. While value is not created in this sphere, surplus-value can be realized within it. It is realized individually when a capitalist (for example, a merchant) employs labor-power at its value but overworks it to gain surplus-value for himself. The social form is realized when merchant capitalists reduce the average necessary costs of circulation by excessively exploiting the labor-power they employ (which accounts for the often dismal and highly exploitative conditions of labor encountered in this sector). Less then has to be deducted from value production to cover the *faux frais* of circulation. In the same way that the gains to be had from rising productivity are open to being divided between workers and capitalists, so the gains from rising productivity and increasing rates of exploitation in circulation can be divided between merchant and production capitalists. But, in this instance, we are looking at relations between capitalists, rather than between capitalists and workers. In fact, there is far more in Volume II about relations between capitalists than there is about the class relation between capitalists and workers. "It is businessmen who face businessmen here, and 'when Greek meets Greek then comes the tug of war'" (207). Watch out for this "tug of war" as we go forward.

Marx then takes up the costs of bookkeeping. While clearly a cost of circulation, it is quite different from normal buying and selling costs. "As the supervision and ideal recapitulation of the process, [bookkeeping] becomes ever more necessary the more the process takes place on a social scale, and loses its purely individual character; it is thus more necessary in capitalist production than in the fragmented production of handicraftsmen and peasants, more necessary in communal production than in capitalist" (212). (Does this last remark imply a key role for bookkeepers under socialism?) Necessary costs likewise attach to the provision and renewal of the money supply:

> The commodities that function as money go neither into individual nor into productive consumption. They represent social labour fixed in a

form [money] in which it serves merely as a machine for circulation. Apart from the fact that a part of the social wealth is confined to this unproductive form, the wear and tear of money requires its steady replacement, or the transformation of more social labour—in the product form—into more gold and silver. These replacement costs are significant in nations where there is a developed capitalism. (213)

The necessary costs associated with money supply tend to grow over time (Marx does not contemplate electronic moneys): "This is a part of the social wealth that has to be sacrificed to the circulation process" (214).

"The costs of storage" are, however, treated as a major issue. For the individual capitalist, these costs have a "value forming effect" and "form an addition to the selling price" of commodities. "While costs that make commodities dearer without increasing the use-value are *faux frais* of production from the social point of view, for the individual capitalist they can constitute sources of enrichment" (214). This is so because these costs are actually continuations of the costs of production even though they are incurred within the circulation process itself. The sort of issue that Marx has in mind here would be something like the cost of refrigeration, which does not add anything useful to the product but does prevent the decay of use-value and hence preserve value that would otherwise be lost. Again, I think the details are historically important, and we need to treat these as crucial in the struggle for competitive advantage, such as Walmart's use of optimal scheduling, just-in-time delivery systems, and the like. What is being managed here is the inventory, and there are two crucial questions: How much will be held, and who will hold it? The inventory in my refrigerator is close to zero because I can walk out onto the streets of New York City any time of the day or night and pick up something to eat. The retailers carry the bulk of the inventory (though when a hurricane threatened, there was a massive wave of panic buying, so the supermarkets had empty shelves). People who live in remoter areas keep much more inventory at home. This is all idle capital in Marx's view, and reducing it releases this idle capital for productive use. There is, therefore, a whole history of inventory management that attaches to the history of capitalism (and a terrific book or PhD thesis to be written on the topic).

Marx then examines the costs that arise in relation to stock formation, but I am not inclined to follow this in any detail. The important point has already been made: stocks and inventories are necessary to capital accumulation for a variety of reasons, but they take capital away from active production and maintain it in a latent or idle state. "The flow of the production and reproduction process . . . requires that a mass of commodities (means of production) is constantly present on the market, i.e. forms a stock" (215). In that state, the capital is clearly unproductive. Improvements in stock or inventory management will release capital from this nonproductive activity. For this reason, stock and inventory management has had a hugely important role in the history of capital. Firms like Walmart and Ikea are super-efficient at this, and therefore gain relative to their competitors. The Japanese auto companies out-competed Detroit in the 1980s through the introduction of a just-in-time scheduling system that dramatically reduced the need for inventories at different points within the flow of production.

All of this confirms Marx's insistence on the necessity to maintain the continuous flow of capitalist production. But this requires that a mass of commodities constantly be available on the market. This "commodity stock . . . appears for M-C as the condition for the flow of the reproduction process and for the investment of new or additional capital" (215). But the

> persistence of commodity capital as commodity stock requires buildings, stores, containers, warehouses, i.e. an outlay of constant capital; it equally requires that payment be made for the labour-power employed in placing the commodities in their containers. Furthermore, commodities decay and are subject to the damaging influence of the elements. Additional capital must thus be expended to protect them from this, partly in objective form as means of labour, and partly in labour-power.

These circulation costs "are distinguished from those mentioned [earlier] in as much as they do enter into the value of commodities to a certain extent and thus make commodities dearer" (216). They are, in short, expenses attributable to production, because the commodity is not truly finished until it is on the market in saleable form. Some value can therefore be created in what appears to be circulation. This porosity makes the accounting nightmare even worse: placing a commodity in a container adds to its value while time taken sitting in the warehouse entails deductions from value (for example, the rent of the warehouse).

It is impossible to imagine a purely functioning capital-circulation process without adequate stocks and inventories in place. These stocks can take three forms—stocks of inputs into productive capital, stocks in the houses and larders of final consumers, and stocks of commodity capital on the market (in wholesale and retail stores) awaiting purchasers. To some degree, these forms are mutually interchangeable. A large and easily accessible stock of commodity capital on the market would render a small stock of productive capital inputs more feasible for producers. Stores stocked with goods reduce the need for stocks in the household.

There is a general tendency for the mass of this stock of capital to grow, however, the more that capital develops. This growth "is both premise and effect of the development of the productive power of labour" (218). But the quantity of stock that a capitalist must have on hand "depends on various conditions which essentially all derive from the greater speed, regularity and certainty with which the necessary mass of raw material can be constantly supplied in such a way that no interruption arises. The less these conditions are fulfilled . . . the greater must be the latent part of the productive capital" (219). So "it makes a great difference, for example, whether the mill-owner has to have sufficient cotton or coal on hand for three months, or only for one." The development of the means of transport here has a crucial role to play. "The speed with which the product of one process can be transferred to another process as a means of production depends on the development of the means of transport and communication. The cheapness of transport here plays a great role in this connection. The constantly repeated transportation of coal, for example, from the mine to the spinning mill will be cheaper [the text says "dearer" which must be wrong!] than the storage of a larger amount of coal for a longer period, if transport is relatively cheap" (219–20). But there are other means to smooth the flows: "The less dependent the mill-owner is for the renewal of his stocks of cotton, coal, etc., on the direct sale of his yarn – and the more developed the credit system . . . the smaller the relative sizes of these stocks need to be, in order to secure a continuous production of yarn independent of the accidents of sale." I here note a tacit association in Marx's thinking between transport and credit conditions in assuring the continuity and flow of continuous capital accumulation. These two elements have in fact jointly played a crucial role in reshaping the time-space relations of capitalism.

But, again, we confront the problem that "many raw materials, semi-finished goods, etc. require lengthy periods of time for their production." If, therefore,

> there is to be no interruption of the production process, then a definite stock of these must be present for the whole period of time in which new products cannot replace old. If this stock in the hands of the industrial capitalist declines, this only means that it increases in the form of a commodity stock in the hands of the merchant. The development of the means of transport, for example, permits cotton lying in the import dock to be quickly delivered from Liverpool to Manchester, so that the manufacturer can renew his stock of cotton in relatively small portions according to his needs. But then the same cotton exists in even greater amounts as a commodity stock in the hands of the Liverpool merchants" (220).

This leads to a general conclusion. First, the quantity of stocks producers need to keep on hand depends on the ease and cost of transportation. Secondly, "the development of the world market and the consequent multiplication of sources of supply for the same article has the same effect. The article is supplied bit by bit from different countries and at different points in time" (220).

It is, for example, very helpful if the cotton harvest in Egypt or India occurs at a different time of year from that of the United States.

Marx closes with further consideration of "the extent to which these expenses enter into the value of commodities." Costs of storage are a positive loss for the individual capitalist. The purchaser will not pay for them since they are not part of the socially necessary labor time. Even when the capitalist speculates and holds back in anticipation of rising prices, then the speculative gamble is the capitalist's alone. But there is a distinction here between voluntary and involuntary stock formation. The latter arises simply from the fact that a certain stock is socially necessary, and so, Marx argues, it can be considered as constituting part of the value of commodities, as part of the socially necessary expenses involved in all forms of capitalist production. "However rapidly the particular elements of this stock may flow, a part of them must always stand still in order for the stock to remain in motion" (221). Here Marx explicitly enunciates another vital general topic: the relation between fixity and motion in the whole dynamics of capitalism.

The distinction between productive and unproductive activity, and hence between productive and unproductive labor, is thus even harder to distinguish in practice. As I have noted several times, this makes for an accounting nightmare in which a night watchman in a warehouse is unproductive while a worker packing a container is judged productive. Anyone looking for a simple accounting solution should at this point freak out. My own conclusion is to give up on the accountancy and concentrate on the material consequences of the effects of speed-up, inventory cost management, and the like, that Marx has identified as crucially necessary to capitalism's development. These questions become even more prominent as we turn to integrate the question of transport and communications, and by implication the production of space, into Marx's theoretical presentation.

The Question of Transportation and Communications

Circulation costs, the locking up of capital in stocks and inventories, are crucially affected by transport relations. This is a topic taken up several times in these first chapters. Transportation, Marx argues, is an unusual branch of industry. It does not produce an objective thing like corn or iron bars, and it is consumed as it is produced (it has zero circulation time). But it is productive of value. Change in spatial location is its product: for example, "the yarn finds itself in India instead of England." So "what the transport industry sells is the actual change of place itself." The "exchange value of this useful effect is still determined, like that of any other commodity, by the value of the elements of production used up in it (labour-power and means of production), plus the surplus-value created by the surplus labour of the workers occupied in the transport industry" (135).

These remarks occur early on in the first chapter, but at the end of chapter 6 Marx elaborates further:

The 'circulating' of commodities, i.e. their actual course in space, can be resolved into the transport of commodities. The transport industry forms on the one hand an independent branch of production, and hence a particular sphere for the investment of productive capital. On the other hand, it is distinguished by its appearance as the continuation of a production process *within* the circulation process and *for* the circulation process. (229)

This is so because "the use-value of things is realized only in their consumption, and their consumption may make a change of location necessary, and thus also the additional production process of the transport industry. The productive capital invested in this industry thus adds value to the products transported, partly through the value carried over from the means of transport, partly through the value added by the work of transport. The latter addition of value can be divided, as with all capitalist production, into replacement of wages and surplus-value" (226–7). Changes in location can be small-scale, like the movement "from the carding shop into the spinning shed" or over longer distances to faraway final markets. In all these cases, "the absolute magnitude of value added by the transport of commodities stands in inverse proportion to the productive power of the transport industry and in direct proportion to the distance covered." This rule is modified by the character and nature of the commodities transported—size and weight, but also "fragility, perishability and explosiveness of the article." Rate schedules can be very complicated: "The railway magnates have shown greater genius in inventing fantastic species than have botanists and zoologists" when it comes to deciding how much to charge per mile on this or that commodity.

The importance of the dynamics involved here are only weakly hinted at, so let me elaborate. Systematic improvements in transport and communications since Marx's time have reduced both the cost and the time of movement of commodities over space, and radically transformed locational possibilities and requirements. This has been so because time and space relations are jointly implicated in determining the turnover time of capital in general, as well as in particular industries. Marx does not make the point here, but in the *Grundrisse* he makes a great deal out of the need to diminish the friction of distance in order to shorten aggregate turnover time. It is, I think, testimony to the incompleteness of Volume II that he does not take up here concepts such as the perpetual tendency toward "the annihilation of space through time" that can be found in the *Grundrisse*. The general case for the role of innovations in transport and communications in the formation of the world market is also made much more strongly in the *Communist Manifesto*.

How many innovations over the last 200 years have been about speeding up and accelerating turnover time? How many have been about reducing the friction of distance as a drag upon the spatial movement of commodities and information? How many have been about jointly producing both effects? Instead of seeing all this history as an accident, or as being due to some human longing to transcend both time and space, we have in Volume II the lineaments of an explanation of how capital internalizes a necessity for perpetual time-space transformations within its own laws of motion. Unfortunately, Marx did not attempt to connect his brilliant intuitions in the *Communist Manifesto* and the *Grundrisse* with the technicalities of production, circulation, and turnover times highlighted in Volume II.

But there is one point made here that is of great significance:

> The circulation of commodities can also take place without their real physical movement. . . . A house that is sold by A to B circulates as a commodity, but it does not get up and walk. Movable commodity values, such as cotton or pig-iron, can remain in the same warehouse while they undergo dozens of circulation processes, and are bought and resold by speculators. What actually moves here is the property title to the thing and not the thing itself. (226)

Had Marx cared to elaborate further, he might have observed that the conditions and possibilities of spatial mobility look very different within the money, commodity and productive circuits of capital, and that the circulation of both present and future property titles (and claims to future labor) on the world market was destined to become an ever more prominent feature affecting the laws of motion of capitalist development.

As in any other industry, competition within the transport and communications industry can be intense and lead to a rapid proliferation of innovations that affect the productivity, efficiency, and spatial range of the industry. This is a story complicated somewhat by the fact that competition in the industry is often restricted to what is called "monopolistic competition"—because once a rail line is set up between, say, Washington and New York, it is difficult to envisage several other rail lines being built to compete. But there are all sorts of innovations that permit spatial competition to modify the geographical conditions under which capital operates (including of course so-called "modal switches" in which, say, trucking proves more flexible, efficient, and cheap than, say, rail transport).

CHAPTER THREE

The Question of Fixed Capital (Chapters 7–11 of Volume II)

GENERAL INTRODUCTORY REMARKS

For Marx, fixed capital is a vital if problematic category. Some commentators have gone so far as to suggest it punches a fatal hole in Marx's labor theory of value. I will explain why I do not agree later. Since fixed capital has cropped up several times in preceding chapters, it is not surprising that it receives special attention here. But the Volume II presentation is rather less stimulating than it is elsewhere. When I sought to reconstruct Marx's views on fixed-capital formation and circulation in *The Limits to Capital* (see pages 685–743), for example, I found myself referring far more to the *Grundrisse* than to Volume II. There the presentation is far more flamboyant:

> Nature builds no machines, no locomotives, railways, electric telegraphs, self-acting mules etc. These are products of human industry; natural material transformed into organs of the human will over nature or of human participation in nature. They are *organs of the human brain, created by the human hand*; the power of knowledge objectified. The development of fixed capital indicates to what degree general social knowledge has become a *direct force of production*, and to what degree, hence, the conditions of the process of social life have come under the control of the general intellect and been transformed in accordance with it. To what degree the powers of social production have been produced, not only in the form of knowledge, but also as immediate organs of social practice, of the real life process. (*Grundrisse*, 706)

I think of this quote whenever I look at the skyline of New York City or fly into London, São Paulo, Buenos Aires, or wherever, and I find myself thinking of these places, for both good and ill, as "organs of the human brain, created by the human hand; the power of knowledge objectified." I see the offices, factories, workshops, houses and hovels, schools and hospitals, pleasure palaces of all kinds, streets and back alleys, highways, railroads, airports and ports, parks and iconic memorials not only as mere physical objects but as a humanly constructed material world, a constitutive site of daily life for millions of human beings, produced through human labor, endowed with social meaning, and a world through which vast amounts of capital circulate on a daily basis, amortizing loans and creating vast flows of rent and interest payments, all the while indulging the speculative fantasies, dreams, and coldly calculated expectations of property owners both great and small. The capitalist city is, surely, the most stunning example of the power of a certain kind of desire, knowledge, and practice objectified.

But, in the *Grundrisse*, Marx also identifies, at the heart of this undoubtedly magnificent achievement, a profound contradiction that finds an echo in Volume II.

"The development of the means of labour into machinery is not an accidental moment of capital, but is rather the historical reshaping of the traditional, inherited means of labour into a form adequate to capital." (This idea is powerfully echoed in chapter 15 of Volume I on machinery and large-scale industry, which Marx applauds as the unique and only appropriate technological basis for a capitalist mode of production.)

> The accumulation of knowledge and of skill, of the general productive forces of the social brain, is thus absorbed into capital, as opposed to labour, and hence appears as an attribute of capital, and more specifically as *fixed capital*, in so far as it enters into the production process as a means of production proper. *Machinery* appears, then, as the most adequate form of *fixed capital*, and fixed capital, in so far as capital's relations with itself are concerned, appears as the most adequate form of capital as such. In another respect, however, in so far as fixed capital is condemned to an existence within the confines of a specific use-value, it does not correspond to the concept of capital, which, as value, is indifferent to every specific form, and can shed or adopt any one of them as equivalent incarnations. In this respect, as regards capital's external relations, it is *circulating capital* which appears as the adequate form of capital, and not fixed capital. (*Grundrisse*, 694)

We have seen repeatedly how continuity, fluidity and speed-up are essential qualities of capital flow, but now we encounter a category designed to facilitate that fluidity but which itself is not fluid, but fixed. A part of the capital has to be fixed in order for the rest of capital to keep in motion. When we go beyond the image of fixed capital as mere machine, we find ourselves conjuring up a picture of capital building whole landscapes of cleared fields and factories; of highways and railways; of ports, harbors and airports; of dams, power stations and electric grids; of gleaming cities and massive industrial capacity. This landscape that capital builds to facilitate its operations imprisons capital accumulation in a world of fixity that becomes increasingly sclerotic in relation to the fluidity of circulating capital. This world, and the capital embodied in it, is always vulnerable to the "butterfly qualities" of money capital, and even to the more pedestrian but also unpredictable shifts and flows of capital in commodity and productive form. This presages crisis formation of a distinctive sort. Money capital flits away, leaving fixed capital high and dry and subject to savage devaluation. I put the contradiction this way: capital builds a whole landscape adequate to its needs at one point in time, only to have to revolutionize that landscape, to destroy it and build another one at a later point in time in order to accommodate the perpetually expansive forces of further capital accumulation. What gets left behind are desolate, devalued landscapes of deindustrialization and abandonment, while capital builds another landscape of fixed capital either elsewhere or on the ruins of the old. This is what Schumpeter called "creative destruction." This process has periodically devalued and revolutionized the geographical landscapes of capital circulation and accumulation in literally earth-moving, if not earth-shaking ways.

The deep, crisis-prone contradiction between fixity and motion is palpable: and fixed capital is at the center of it all. The trouble with fixed capital is precisely, in short, that it is fixed, when capital is all about value in motion. This opposition constitutes a fascinating problem. And it has been and still is a frequent source of crises that are independent in principle (though not always in practice) from the crises that arise out of the perpetually contested capital-labor relation. Such crises occur when the fixity can no longer accommodate the expansionary motion. The latter has to break with the constraints imposed by that part of capital that is fixed. The result is the devaluation of large swathes of fixed capital, as circulating and highly mobile money capital moves elsewhere (deindustrialization from the mid-1970s onwards left behind abandoned factories and warehouses, decaying physical infrastructures—even shrinking cities, like Detroit).

While these contradictions do find their way into Volume II, they are far more forcibly portrayed in the *Grundrisse*. It is therefore helpful to read the Volume II presentation with these passages from the *Grundrisse* in mind. For one thing, it makes for a more thrilling ride. But it also highlights vital understandings that might otherwise remain submerged. Why Marx did not incorporate brilliant if somewhat purple passages of this kind into Volume II, written nearly twenty years later, is a mystery. It may be due to his desire to be seen as rigorously scientific and factual. He certainly seems far more concerned here to plunge into the minutiae of, for example, the distinctions between repair and replacement of fixed capital as revealed in the railway engineering manuals of the time. But I suspect that Marx sets aside broader questions because he has a very specific and limited objective in Volume II. As indicated in the brief introductory materials of chapter 7, the real object of his inquiry is the turnover time of capital. He knows that he cannot investigate that fully without dealing with the complications that attach to the turnover time of long-term fixed capital investments. This concern narrows his focus and leads him, I suspect, to lay to one side the more general significance of fixed capital in the historical geography of a capitalist mode of production. Nevertheless, the presentation does help illuminate how the world we live in became the way it is, and how the processes of accumulation through fixed-capital formation actually work. But Volume II also disappoints on the technical terrain: several vital systemic issues raised in the *Grundrisse* and elsewhere in *Capital* are missing. This is almost certainly due to the incompleteness of Volume II. So, in what follows, I shall indicate where some of the more gaping holes lie in the analysis, and how they might be plugged with materials from the ancillary works.

The overall framework for Marx's thinking on fixed capital emerges only in bits and pieces in these five chapters. Whether this has to do with the manner of Engels's reconstruction of the materials, I cannot say, but the result is that I find it necessary to jump around in the text—and I apologize in advance for so doing—rather than try to follow the presentation as if it were a clearly unfolding argument.

Marx's foundational position on fixed capital is best articulated, for example, in the later chapters that subject Adam Smith's and Ricardo's views to critique in excruciating detail (chapters which for the most part warrant only cursory study, unless you are interested in the history of political economy and Marx's opinions on the Physiocratic school of thought). "Bourgeois political economy," writes Marx,

> held instinctively to Adam Smith's confusion of the categories "fixed and circulating capital" with the categories "constant and variable capital" and uncritically echoed it from one generation down to the next for a whole century. It no longer distinguished at all between the portion of capital laid out on wages and the portion of capital laid out on raw material, and only formally distinguished the former from constant capital in terms of whether it was circulated bit by bit or all at once through the product. The basis for understanding the real movement of capitalist production, and thus capitalist exploitation, was thus submerged at one blow. All that was involved, on this view, was the reappearance of value advanced. (297)

Even Ricardo, who did have some primitive conception of the theory of surplus-value, "commits very great errors as a result of confusing fixed and circulating capital with constant and variable capital." He never managed to overcome the fact that "he starts his investigation on a completely false basis"(301).

While Marx does invoke this "basic error" in his opening argument on fixed capital (241), he does not elaborate on its significance. So what is at stake here? In Volume I, Marx clearly distinguishes between variable capital—the purchase of the labor-power that has the capacity to create value and surplus-value—and the constant capital (means of production) whose value does not quantitively change even as it undergoes a change of material form. From this it becomes very clear that surplus-value arises from the exploitation of living labor in production.

But the study of fixed capital requires that we categorize the elements entering into production in a different way. These are all those elements that transfer their value fully into the finished commodity in a given turnover time. These elements include labor inputs (the subject of labor), raw materials (the objects of labor), and ancillary materials like energy (the means of labor). All of these elements are lumped together as "circulating capital." Their values enter into and exit the production process completely in a given turnover period. Then there are the machines, buildings, and other elements that remain behind after the turnover is complete, and which can be used again and again over several turnover periods. In a given turnover time, only a portion of the value of these means of labor is transferred to the final product. These elements are called "fixed capital." Figure 3 below depicts how these categories relate to those of variable and constant capital.

Figure 3

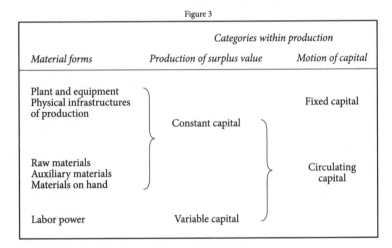

No theory of surplus-value can be derived from the categories of fixed and circulating capital. The fixation of the bourgeois economists upon these categories therefore had the effect (either conscious or not) of disguising the role of labor in producing surplus-value (profit). But this does not mean that the distinction between fixed and circulating capital is unimportant for Marx. It affects the aggregate turnover time of capital in general, and thereby the overall dynamics of accumulation. But, in Marx's book, it can never do so at the expense of "submerging" the theory of surplus-value production.

There is another potential source of linguistic confusion which Marx attributes to Adam Smith, but which he himself to some degree repeats. "Circulating capital" in these chapters means all the capital that is used up in a given turnover time relative to the fixed capital left over to be used again later. "Circulating capital," in the earlier chapters on the circuits of capital, refers to that capital that is out there circulating in the marketplace before returning to production. These are two completely different definitions of the term. Marx highlights this potential confusion relatively late in the game, and again only in the context of the critique of Adam Smith (271). He therefore proposes at one point to distinguish between "capital of circulation" on the market and "circulating and fixed capital in production." In practice, Marx often substitutes the term "fluid capital" for "circulating capital" in chapter 8, and uses the contrast between "fixed" and "fluid" capital to develop his analysis. These terms do indeed appear far more appropriate, but he does not stick with them throughout. I will continue to use the term "circulating capital" in the sense that Marx means it in this chapter (with an occasional concession to fluidity). But please remember that circulating capital means something different here than it did in the earlier chapters on the production, circulation, and realization of capital. The categories of circulating and fixed capital arise solely in relation to production, and do not carry over into the money and commodity circuits of capital (as Adam Smith erroneously supposed).

To restate the definitions: circulating capital is here all that capital—both constant and variable capital—used up in a single turnover period; fixed capital is that part of constant capital that carries over from one turnover period to another. Bearing all these issues and definitions in mind, let us turn to a closer reading of the textual materials.

THE "PECULIARITY" OF FIXED CAPITAL

"One part of the constant capital," Marx observes at the opening of chapter 8, "maintains the specific use form in which it enters the production process, over and against the products it helps to fashion. It continues to perform the same functions over a shorter or longer period in a series of repeated labour processes. Examples of this are factory buildings, machines, etc." (237). The word Marx repeatedly uses to describe the circulation of fixed capital is *peculiar*. "The peculiarity of this part of constant capital, the means of labour in the strict sense, is this . . ." he states at the outset of the second paragraph. Again, in the middle of the next page, we read "the circulation of the part of capital considered here is a peculiar one" (238). So what, exactly, is peculiar about it, and why does this peculiarity matter?

"In the first place it does not circulate in its use form. It is rather its value that circulates, and this does so gradually, bit by bit, in the degree to which it is transferred to [the commodity]." A part of the value always remains fixed in the machine or the factory as long as it continues to function, and the fixed capital always remains distinct and apart from the commodities that it helps to produce. "This peculiarity is what gives this part of the constant capital the form of *fixed capital*. All other material components of the capital advanced in the production process, on the other hand, form, by contrast to it, circulating or *fluid capital*" (238).

The materiality of fixed capital does not get incorporated into the commodity, but its value does. So fixed capital does not circulate in its material but in its ideal (socially determined) value form. Fixed capital (machinery, for example) materially functions as a *means of labor* as opposed to the *objects of labor* (the raw materials and other means of production) that are transformed into commodities to be sold on the market. Fixed capital shares this character of being a *means of labor* with certain other constant capital ancillary inputs into production. Energy—coal for the steam engine or gas for lighting—does not enter into the material use-value of the commodity produced either. Its value is added to the commodity as its physical being is used up in production. In the case of fixed capital, this using up lasts, however, over many turnover cycles while, in the case of energy inputs, they are "completely consumed in every labour process they enter into" (238). It is for this reason that the preceding chapter on the turnover time of capital is so crucial. Fixed capital is "fixed" in relation to turnover time, and turnover time varies a great deal from one industrial sector to another.

THE PHYSICAL LIFETIME OF FIXED CAPITAL

"This part of the constant capital gives up value to the product in proportion to the exchange-value that it loses together with its use-value." This implies some relation—which turns out to be rather problematic—between the value transferred to the product and the changing usefulness of, say, a machine. How and why might the usefulness of the machine change? It turns out that there are both physical and social reasons why such changes might occur.

The extent to which the value of such a means of production is given up or transformed to the product that it helps to fashion is determined by an average calculation; it is measured by the average duration of its function, from the time it enters the production process as means of production to the time it is completely used up, is dead, and has to be replaced by a new item of the same kind. (237)

What Marx appears to have in mind here is a machine with an average useful lifetime of, say, ten years. Some capitalists may be lucky and be able to use their machine for eleven years, while others will need to replace it earlier. What matters in the value transfer into the commodity is the social average life of the machine rather than the individual lifetime. No customer will be willing to pay me more for the commodity I produce simply because the lifetime of my machine turns out to be shorter than the social average.

Over the course of its useful lifetime, the value of the fixed capital

steadily declines, until the means of labour are worn out and therefore distributed in value, in a longer or shorter period, over the volume of products that has emerged from a series of continually repeated labour processes. As long as a means of labour *still remains effective*, and does not yet have to be replaced by a new item of the same kind, some constant capital value remains fixed in it, while another part of the value originally fixed in it passes over to the product and thus circulates as a component of the commodity stock. The longer the means of labour lasts and the more slowly it wears out, the longer the constant capital value remains fixed in this use-form. But whatever its degree of durability, the proportion in which it gives up value is always in inverse ratio to the overall duration of its function. If two machines are of equal value, but one of them wears out in five years and the other in ten, then the first gives up twice as much value in the same space of time as the second does. (238; emphasis added)

But Marx does not immediately explain what is meant by "still remains effective," or what happens when machines cease, for some reason or other, to be effective even before their value is fully used up. At the outset of this chapter it seems that "effective" is understood in purely physical terms—that it is the rate of physical decay and wearing-out that matters—but later on it is understood in more social terms. Curiously,

Marx does not immediately mention the problem of so-called "moral depreciation" that he identified in Volume I. This occurs when employers of an older machine have to compete with others possessed of newer and more "effective" and cheaper machines. Only on page 250, and then in the subsequent chapter, on page 264, does the term "moral depreciation" enter into the discussion, and then without too much comment. This is a crucial question, and we will return to it later.

Behind it, however, lies the thorny question: When and why does a machine have to be replaced? When the machine is physically worn out? Or do situations arise in which the machine has to be replaced earlier because more effective and cheaper machines are available on the market? This is something we encounter all the time. How often do we have to change our computers? Every two years? Do we change them because they are physically used up or because they have become outmoded? Most of the examples Marx gives in this chapter are of physical depreciation even as other social questions arise. I suspect that Marx's anxiety to go no further than the formal relations he can establish is playing an important role here. Certainly, much of the social and historical content is missing.

As he delves deeper into the formal aspects of the use and circulation of fixed capital, so he encounters both exceptional circumstances and a blurring of distinctions between fixed and fluid capital. The means of labor that are the material bearers of fixed capital, for example,

> are consumed only productively and cannot enter individual consumption . . . but rather maintain their independent shape vis-à-vis it until they are completely worn out. An exception to this is provided by the means of transport. The useful effect that these produce in their productive function, i.e. during their stay in the sphere of production—the change of location—simultaneously enters individual consumption, e.g. that of the traveler. The latter then pays for their use just as he pays for the use of other means of consumption. (239)

This exception is of particular interest to me, since it implies that the useful effect of "change of location" (and, hence, the production of spatial relations) applies not only to production (the movement of raw materials) but also to consumption (the movement of people). In other words, the production of "change of location" is itself a commodity, no matter who uses it and for what purpose (further production or final consumption). And of course, transportation is a sector that absorbs a vast amount of fixed capital, much of which (like railway and subway tunnels) lasts for a very long time (provided, of course, that it is maintained and repaired). Since, as we have seen, transport and communication are consumed as they are produced, much of their value exists ideally in the form of fixed-capital circulation. Both the locomotive and the rails on which it runs are forms of fixed capital (though with different qualities, as we shall see).

The distinction between fixed capital and the use of ancillary materials (like energy) also becomes "blurred" when the ancillary materials are used up bit by bit rather than all at once. This occurs "in the manufacture of chemicals, for example. The same is true with the distinction between means of labour on the one hand, and ancillaries and raw materials on the other. In agriculture, for instance, the materials added to improve the soil partly enter the plant product as formative elements. Their effect, however, is spread over a fairly long period." While, for example, irrigation ditches are clearly a form of fixed capital in agriculture, a dose of guano fertilizer can have an effect on yields over several production cycles, even though it looks like the application of fluid capital.

DUAL USAGES AND RELATIONS BETWEEN FIXED CAPITAL AND THE CONSUMPTION FUND

Then there is the difficult but intriguing problem of dual usage (represented as "joint products" in the language of contemporary economics). "An ox, as a draught animal, is fixed capital. If it is eaten, however, it no longer functions either as a means of labour, or as fixed capital" (239). In raising oxen, both commodity forms are being produced at the same time. It is the social decision on how to use the oxen that defines whether or not they are fixed capital:

> Here the distinction between means of labour and object of labour which is based in the nature of the labour process itself is reflected in the new form of the distinction between fixed capital and circulating capital. It is only in this way that a thing that functions as means of labour becomes fixed capital. If its material properties also allow it to serve for other functions than that of means of labour, then whether it is fixed

capital or not depends on these various functions. Cattle as draught animals are fixed capital; when being fattened for slaughter they are raw material that eventually passes into circulation as a product, and so not fixed but circulating capital. (241)

Marx returns to this theme much later and sets it in an even broader context:

The same thing, moreover, can function at one time as a component of productive capital, and at another time form part of the direct consumption fund. A house, for example, when it functions as a place of work, is a fixed component of productive capital; when it functions as a dwelling, it is in no way a form of capital in this capacity. The same means of labour can in many cases function at one time as means of production, at another time as means of consumption. (282)

This becomes particularly tricky when we think of a street, which can be used for production or just for walking.

Marx here raises the idea of a consumption fund. He does so, however, without any further elaboration. Plainly, consumption requires long-term aids just as does production—houses, crockery, knives and forks, and all the items that typically fill a house and permit people to consume, along with cars and trains and airplanes, which likewise facilitate our consumption. The use-value of the items in the consumption fund is, like fixed capital in production, consumed bit by bit, sometimes over many years. The residual value of these assets in the consumption fund is huge in contemporary societies, and many of these items (like cars, houses, and knives and forks) can be bought and sold on second-hand markets long after they have originally been produced.

Such items have, as Marx here indicates, a complicated relation to fixed capital, in that any one of them at any time can in principle be diverted or converted from consumption to production. Thus Marx complains that "Ricardo forgets . . . the house in which the worker lives, his furniture, his tools of consumption such as knives, forks, dishes, etc., all of which possess the same character of durability as do the means of labour. The same things and the same classes of things thus appear now as means of consumption, now as means of labour" (300).

Marx sees fixed capital as a highly flexible category that depends upon how things are used rather than upon their inherent physical characteristics. He complains vigorously of "the fetishism peculiar to bourgeois economics, which transforms the social, economic character that things are stamped with in the process of social production into a natural character arising from the material nature of these things" (303).

FIXED CAPITAL IN THE LAND

This unjustified "physicalism" or "naturalism" has yet another important dimension that needs to be considered, and which also contributes to the "peculiarity" of fixed capital as a category. An important distinction exists within the category of fixed capital itself. "Certain properties that characterize the means of labour materially are made into direct properties of fixed capital, e.g., physical immobility, such as that of a house. But it is always easy to show that other means of labour, which are also as such fixed capital, ships, for example, have the opposite property, i.e., physical mobility" (241). This distinction between mobile and immobile forms of fixed capital is not absolute. While sewing machines can be shifted with ease, blast furnaces are rarely moved, and then only because of vast expenditure of money (the dismantling and subsequent shipping of a whole iron-and-steel works from Germany to China is a recent example of such an effort).

> Some of the means of labour . . . are held fast in their place once they enter the production process as means of labour[:] machines for example. Other means of labour, however, are produced at the start in static form, tied to the spot, such as improvement to the soil, factory buildings, blast furnaces, canals, railways, etc. . . . On the other hand, a means of labour may constantly change its physical space, i.e. move, and yet be engaged throughout in the production process, as with a locomotive, a ship, draught cattle, etc. Immobility does not give it the character of fixed capital in the one case, nor does mobility remove this character in the other. But the circumstance that some means of labour are fixed in location, with their roots in the soil, gives this part of the fixed capital a particular role in a nation's economy. They cannot be sent abroad or circulate as commodities on the world market. It is quite possible for the property titles to this fixed capital to change: they can be bought and sold, and in this respect circulate ideally. These property titles can even

circulate in foreign markets, in the form of shares, for example. But a change in the persons who are the owners of this kind of fixed capital does not change the relationship between the static and materially fixed part of the wealth of a country and the movable part of it. (242)

Later on, in chapter 10, this theme is elaborated even further. An element of future fixed capital, such as a spinning machine, "can be exported from the country where it is produced and be sold, directly or indirectly, to a foreign country, whether in exchange for raw materials, etc. or for champagne. In the country where it was produced it then functions only as commodity capital, but never, not after its sale, as fixed capital." The same can be said of machine tools, steel girders and prefabricated building materials. They are commodity capital until they actually become fixed in some production process. "However, products that have been localized by being incorporated into the earth, and hence can only be used locally, e.g. factory buildings, railways, bridges, tunnels, docks, etc., soil improvements, and so on, cannot be exported body and soul. They are immobile. If they are not to be useless, they must function after their sale as fixed capital in the country in which they were produced. For the capitalist producer who builds factories speculatively or improves estates in order to sell them, these things are the form of his commodity capital. . . . But from the society's standpoint, they must ultimately function as fixed capital, if they are not to be useless, in the country in question, in a production process fixed by their own location" (288)

This locational fixity has implications for the geographical patterning of capitalist activity. If these commodities cannot be useful in the place where they are located, then they are useless and therefore have no value. Notice how the criteria of utility (usefulness) is here creeping into the discussion. It is one of those important categories of conventional economics which, like demand and supply, Marx tends to hold very much at arm's length. The application of the utility principle is not confined to the world of production. "It in no way follows . . . that immobile objects as such are automatically fixed capital; they may be dwelling houses, etc. that belong to the consumption fund and thus do not form part of the social capital at all, even though they form an element of the social wealth, of which capital is only one part" (288). Houses are for the most part fixed in space and place but, as we have seen in recent years, securitization of mortgages and their packaging in collateralized debt obligations allows some version of title to them (and we are now finding that the actual meaning and legal status of this title is more than a little obscure) to circulate internationally, with all sorts of devastating consequences. In the case of transportation, also, the locomotive may be mobile, but the track upon which it moves is not. "Property titles to a railway," however, "can change hands daily, and their owners can even make a profit by selling them abroad. The property titles are thus exportable, but the railway itself is not."

Throughout these passages we encounter again and again the tension between fixity and motion in the geographical landscape of capitalist activity. Planes, ships and locomotives which move across space depend crucially upon airports, harbors and train stations that do not. The value of fixed immobile capital depends crucially upon its use: an airport to which no planes fly has no value. But then planes that have no airports to which to fly have no value either. Notice that, in this instance, it is very clear that the geographical pattern of movement of the mobile forms of fixed capital (as well as the commodities they carry as commodity capital out there circulating on the market) is constrained by the need to valorize the often huge amounts of fixed immobile capital value embedded in place. The recuperation of the value of immobile fixed capital depends upon corralling the capital in motion to use the immobile capital in its particular location. This generates phenomena such as inter-urban competition, for example, over attracting or keeping highly mobile capital in town (often ending up with massive public subsidies to private corporations).

Place-specific rises in the valuation of immobile forms of fixed capital are not infrequent, and can become particularly violent when radical shifts occur in the geographical movement of commodities and people more generally. While Marx only hints here at the nature of this problem, the general question of regional and localized crises of deindustrialization and devaluation particularly of immobile forms of fixed capital can be derived from these passages. There is also a relation, which Marx fails to mention here, with land rent and property prices, which vary greatly from one place to another depending very much upon the qualities of the fixed capital assets embedded in place. This brings the whole history of capitalist urbanization into the orbit of some level of conformity to the laws of motion of capital. Conversely, it opens up the very real way in which urbanization in turn comes to play a crucial role in how those laws of motion might work. This has been one of my own major interests over the years, and it is through passages of this sort on the role of immobile fixed capital that I have found it possible to extend Marx's general theory into the arena of city building and the urban process. But Marx barely hints at the existence of such relations.

THE PRODUCTION OF SPACE

There is a particular wrinkle in Marx's account to which I attach great (though perhaps unwarranted) significance because of my personal research interests in urbanization. When Marx is considering how replacement of fixed capital embedded in the land might morph into expansion, he makes the following remark. It all depends, he writes,

> on the space available. In some buildings extra floors can be added, while others require horizontal extension and thus more land. While capitalist production is marked by the waste of much material, there is also much inappropriate horizontal extension of this kind (partly involving a loss of labour-power) in the course of the gradual extension of a business, since nothing is done according to a social plan, but rather depends on the infinitely varied circumstances, means, etc. with which the individual capitalist acts. This gives rise to a major wastage of productive forces. . . . The progressive reinvestment of the money reserve fund (i.e. of the part of the fixed capital that is transformed back into money) is most easily effected in agriculture. Here a spatially given field of production is capable of the greatest gradual absorption of capital. The same is true when natural reproduction takes place, as in the case of cattle breeding. (252)

In my work, I often appeal to the necessity for capital absorption through the production of space (with considerable emphasis upon the way in which it can be both speculative and wasteful as, for example, in the case of capitalist suburbanization). And here is Marx also talking about the spatial aspects of capital absorption—which are often wasteful because of capitalist competition and the failure of social planning. I do not point to this passage in order to suggest that Marx was a brilliant precursor of everything that has been written ever since on spatial questions, nor to suggest that the Marxist tradition of theorizing the production of space in the works of Henri Lefebvre and by the radical geographers in more recent times is legitimized by such a passage.[1] Rather, the implication is that if, as I think we should be, we are interested in integrating theories of the production of space into Marx's general theory of capital accumulation, then it must primarily be through systematic extension of the materials assembled both here and in the *Grundrisse* on the formation and the circulation of fixed capital, particularly of that part of fixed capital embedded in the land. The processes Marx here describes, for example, are not confined to agriculture. They are just as relevant to theorizing the growing of condominiums to absorb surplus capital as they are to the growing of cabbages. Crises in the production of space, the consequences of which we see all around us, derive ultimately from the contradictions between fixity and motion that Marx so clearly identifies.

CAPITAL CONSUMED V. CAPITAL EMPLOYED

The ideas broached in these chapters have other potentially fecund implications. There is, for example, the distinction between the "capital employed" in production and the "capital consumed" (240). Marx does not do much with this distinction beyond noting its existence, and that the former often outgrows the latter as capital develops. In particular, he does not explore the implications of this distinction for measuring the value composition of capital, which plays such a crucial role in his theory of the tendency for the rate of profit to fall. Obviously, the value composition of capital is much higher (and, all other things remaining equal, the rate of profit much lower) if the capital employed is considered the relevant magnitude. Most analysts would prefer capital used up, but the vast and increasing amount of capital employed gives intuitive heft to the falling-rate-of-profit theory ("just look at the enormous amount of physical fixed capital around in our society compared to simpler times," the argument goes, and "it is obvious that the value

1   Henri Lefebvre, *The Production of Space* (Oxford: Basil Blackwell, 1991); Neil Smith, *Uneven Development* (Oxford: Basil Blackwell, 1984); David Harvey, *Spaces of Capital: Towards a Critical Geography* (Edinburgh: Edinburgh University Press, 2001).

composition of capital is rapidly increasing"). A heavy wave of fixed-capital investment may increase the capital employed but have no impact on the capital consumed in a given turnover time. Indeed, if that investment helps to economize on the use of fluid constant capital, then it could be associated with a falling value composition of the capital consumed and a rising rate of profit. But the distinction between capital employed and capital consumed is also sensitive to changes in turnover times. Engels recognized the significance of all this to measures of the profit rate, and hence inserted a tentative chapter on the effect of changing turnover times on the rate of profit into the Volume III analysis.

The category of fixed capital depends, as we have seen, upon use by the user: "A machine that is the product and thus the commodity of the machine-builder is part of his commodity capital. It only becomes fixed capital in the hands of his buyer, the capitalist who employs it productively" (240). Once a new commodity is produced, furthermore, the distinction between the value of the fixed and circulating components that go into its production disappears. If uses change, then the fixed capital is either dissolved or instantaneously created. For example, as already noted, a house that is lived in is not fixed capital, but a factory is. But if I start making things in my house—set up sewing machines and hire some immigrants to make shirts—then the house suddenly becomes fixed capital. When a loft that once housed the production of garments gets converted into a living space, then it moves from the category of fixed capital into that of the consumption fund. Furthermore, capital is fixed only in relation to the turnover time of that part of capital that is defined as fluid. A machine making ice cream on a daily basis is fixed capital, but a similar kind of machine used in the production of an oceangoing tanker that takes two years to build will not be fixed capital if it is used up entirely in the production period.

THE HISTORICAL RELEVANCE OF MARX'S RELATIONAL DEFINITIONS

All these possibilities derive from Marx's relational way of defining fundamental categories like fixed capital. Put simply, the category of fixed capital is not itself fixed. Marx does not here attempt to assess the historical significance of shifting relational meanings. I have found them in my own thinking to be of major significance. In Walt Rostow's theory of "the stages of economic growth," for example, written in the

1950s as a "non-communist manifesto"—and an extremely influential text at the time, which students all had to read—a phase of strong fixed-capital formation (mainly basic infrastructures such as roads, dams and harbors) was portrayed as playing a pivotal role in creating the "preconditions" for subsequent economic growth in a country. The creation of these physical infrastructures provided the basis for a subsequent "take-off" into economic growth, which was then followed by "a drive to mass consumption." Creating mass affluence would build popular support for capitalist forms of development all around the world, and so reduce the threat of communism. This was the sequential path, Rostow argued, to compete with communist promises of affluence for all in the so-called undeveloped world. The preconditions phase of strong investment in fixed-capital infrastructures would, however, require sacrifices. Current consumption had to be curbed and belts tightened in order to allow for fixed-capital formation. Help from outside would also be important (and the primary mission of the World Bank was, and to a large extent still is, precisely to support and aid such infrastructural investments).

Rostow provided historical data to back up his developmental theory. Each country was treated as a developmental space, and the historical data he assembled showed how important a phase of strong fixed-capital formation had been in each as a precursor to strong economic growth. Leaving aside the odd idea that countries form "natural" and independent units of capitalist development, the problem Rostow ignored was that of the international capital flows that underpinned imperialist forms of expansion, as Lenin had long before described. Furthermore, Britain, which was the country where the capitalist "take-off" first occurred, did not conform to Rostow's model. There was no identifiable phase of heightened fixed-capital formation. Colonial and imperial dispossession and merchant capital plundering were here the important precursors. In fact the problem in Britain, as several economic historians like Postan pointed out, was that the country had a huge capital surplus (much as China does today) from the seventeenth century onwards.[2] The problem was to find profitable uses for the surpluses available. Fixed-capital formation in infrastructures (abroad as well as at

2   W. W. Rostow, *The Stages of Economic Growth: A Non-Communist Manifesto* (London: Cambridge University Press, 1960); M. M. Postan, *Medieval Trade and Finance* (Cambridge: Cambridge University Press, 1973).

home) provided one convenient channel for the absorption of such surpluses. Furthermore, it was pretty easy to convert much of the physical infrastructure built up for consumption in Britain into fixed capital for production. The putting-out system, whereby merchants left materials to be worked up in peasant cottages, in effect turned those cottages into the equivalent of factories (in much the same way that microfinance today turns peasant huts into the fixed capital of production). So there was something profoundly wrong with Rostow's "anti-communist" development theory, particularly with its emphasis upon sacrifice and austerity in the here and now for the sake of future capitalist development. What Rostow's program was really about was opening up the world to the flows of surplus capital being generated by imperialist powers, and legitimizing the "austerity" conditions that permitted a high rate of exploitation of labor-power as necessary to future prosperity. Capital exports and international capital flows did not, therefore, appear in Rostow's data.

Marx's alternative account in the *Grundrisse* (unfortunately missing from Volume II) is much more compelling:

> *The development of fixed capital indicates in still another respect the degree of development of wealth generally, or of capital.* . . . The part of production which is oriented towards the production of fixed capital does not produce direct objects of individual gratification, nor direct exchange values; at least not directly realizable exchange values. *Hence, only when a certain degree of productivity has already been reached—so that a part of production time is sufficient for immediate production—can an increasingly large part be applied to the production of the means of production.* This requires that society be able to wait; that a large part of the wealth already created can be withdrawn from immediate consumption, in order to employ this part for labour which is *not immediately productive* (within the material production process itself). This requires a certain level of productivity and of *overabundance* [emphasis added], and, more specifically, a level directly related to the transformation of circulating capital into fixed capital. *As the magnitude of relative surplus labour depends on the productivity of necessary labour, so does the magnitude of labour time*—living as well as objectified—*employed on the production of fixed capital depend on the productivity of the labour time spent in the direct production of products. Surplus population* (from this standpoint)

as well as *surplus production* is a condition for this. . . . The *smaller* the direct fruits borne by *fixed capital*, the less it intervenes in the *direct production process*, the greater must be this relative *surplus population and surplus production*; thus more to build railways, canals, aqueducts, telegraphs, etc. than to build the machinery directly active in the direct production process. Hence—a subject to which we will return later—in the constant under- and over-production of modern industry, constant fluctuations and convulsions arise from the disproportion, when sometimes too little, then again too much circulating capital is transformed into fixed capital. (*Grundrisse*, 707–8)

This is not only a brilliant theorization of how capitalist development got underway in Britain, but it is nothing short of an equally brilliant evocation of the developmental process that has been occurring in China over the last thirty years. It also points to the potential dangers of cyclical phases of overinvestment in physical infrastructures, and hence yet another mode of crisis formation in capitalist economies. The crises that attach to fixed-capital formation do, however, receive brief mention in Volume II, mainly in the context of Marx's analysis of "moral depreciation," which we will take up shortly. But, again, there is much more to be done on this topic.

There are, however, some more mundane applications of these ideas. Milton Friedman, in his panegyric to capitalist forms of development, famously begins his argument by celebrating sweatshops as the beginnings of capitalist development. The home and the dwelling are converted by a mere change of use into a form of fixed capital. This generates a very interesting contrast to conditions in our own times: the costly fixed capital of textile factories in Boston and Manchester has been converted over the last forty years to consumer uses, while backrooms and basements are converted into the fixed capital for sweatshop production from Los Angeles to Manila. When microfinance is extended to peasant women in Mexico and India to buy a sewing machine, the peasant hut is simultaneously converted into the fixed capital for production for free. This is a neat way to counter any tendency for the profit rate to fall, because it dramatically reduces the value of constant fixed capital inputs relative to labor.

I find Marx's relational way of treating fixed-capital formation extremely helpful in interpreting the history of capital. His account opens up all manner of theoretical possibilities. A lot can be hung upon

Marx's seemingly casual observation that an ox can either be used for consumption or function as fixed capital in production, because there are all sorts of things all around us that have that character—from pencils to houses, streets, and even whole cities. The fluidity of definition is as important as it is functionally creative. This is the sort of thing that is hard, if not impossible, to incorporate into conventional bourgeois economic theory, which cannot handle flexible definitions of categories. Fixed capital, obviously, must, in the view of conventional economists, have a fixed definition. Unfortunately, not all Marxist economists, as we shall see, understand how the relationality of Marx's definition works either. As a result, they repeat the mistakes of bourgeois theory.

MAINTENANCE, REPLACEMENTS AND REPAIRS

Marx pays considerable attention to the seemingly mundane problems posed by the different lifetimes of different components of the fixed capital (such as a railroad), and to questions of replacements, repairs and costs of maintenance. Without going into the details, there are some very important general points that should be noted.

The lifetime of fixed capital depends upon wear and tear, which is dependent on use (much-used highways, railroads, automobiles, etc. wear out faster) as well as upon environmental conditions and exposure to the elements. Even more importantly, "the various elements of fixed capital in a particular investment have differing lifespans, and hence also different turnover times. In a railway, for example the rails, sleepers, earthworks, station buildings, bridges, tunnels, locomotives and carriages all function for different periods and have different reproduction times, and so the capital advanced in them has different turnover times" (248). We all have experience with houses, cars, and all sorts of other elements in the consumption fund in which the parts have to be renewed on quite different temporal schedules. The distinction between replacement, on one hand, and reinvestment and expansion, on the other, as Marx points out, is thus often opaque. Is putting a new and much better roof on a house a replacement or a reinvestment in what will in effect be a new house? But fixed capital also requires maintenance. This is in part provided gratis by the laborers who keep the machines they mind in good working order simply by using them properly. But "additional labour" is "constantly necessary" to keep the machine in use, and Marx allocates this labor to fluid capital (253). Repairs, on the other hand, are considered "an additional component of value" to be added to the original fixed capital "according to need. . . . All fixed capital requires these later doses of additional capital outlay on means of labour and labour-power" (254). The implications of this for the understanding of turnover time (which is, as already noted, Marx's primary preoccupation here) are then spelled out:

> It is however assumed in assessing the average life of the fixed capital that it is constantly maintained in working condition, partly by cleaning (which includes keeping clean its site), partly by repairs . . . The transfer of value through the wear and tear of the fixed capital is calculated over its average period of life, but this average period is calculated on the assumption that the additional capital required to keep it in working order is continuously advanced. (255)

This begs the question, of course, as to what happens when capital, desperately seeking to economize on its costs of constant capital, defers repairs and maintenance on its fixed capital. This often happens, particularly with respect to the built environment. This has all manner of implications for the qualities of daily life, as well as for the general *effectiveness* of the fixed capital deployed. Twenty years of deferred maintenance on the New York City subway system, on bridges and tunnels, and on public school buildings makes for a very ineffective infrastructure for further capital accumulation. The issue of who bears the costs of maintenance and repair is also crucial. Marx uses the example of housing:

> In connection with contracts of rental for houses and other things that are fixed capital for their proprietors and are rented out as such, legislation has always recognized the distinction between normal deterioration, produced by time, the influence of the elements and normal wear and tear, and the occasional repairs that are necessary from time to time for maintenance in the course of the normal life of a house and its normal use. As a rule, the first fall on the landlord, the second on the tenant. Repairs are further divided into the ordinary and the substantial. The latter represent in part the renewal of the fixed capital in its natural form,

and also fall on the landlord, unless the contract expressly states the opposite.

Marx then cites the details of English law on the subject.

While Marx is inclined to get lost in technical details, I think it important to highlight the general point: as society evolves, so the whole question of maintenance, repairs and replacement of existing fixed capital (along with the consumption fund) not only absorbs increasing quantities of capital, but also requires increasing quantities of labor. In large metropolitan areas, like New York City, it could be that just as much capital and labor are deployed in maintenance, replacement and repair as are involved in the creation of new products (even allowing for the ambiguity of when replacement of parts becomes renewal of the whole). How all of this is to be accounted for in the production and circulation of values is an open question (if not, as more often than not with Marx, an accounting nightmare). But, plainly, having to invest substantial amounts of new fixed capital through replacements and repairs, along with escalating running costs of maintenance (think the New York subway system, or all those people erecting scaffolding and taking it down again), can put an enormous burden on society. For individual capitalists this changes the calculus on turnover time. At a certain point it may become more economical to abandon a fixed-capital investment (either mobile or immobile) because of escalating costs of repair and maintenance and start anew with different equipment, perhaps elsewhere.

MONETARY ASPECTS OF FIXED-CAPITAL CIRCULATION

Marx approaches the monetary aspects of fixed-capital circulation in the following way.

> The peculiar circulation of fixed capital gives rise to a peculiar turnover. The portion of value that it loses in its natural form through wear and tear circulates as a value portion of the product. Through its circulation the product is transformed from a commodity into money, and so is the portion of the value of the means of labour that is circulated by the product; its value trickles from the circulation process as money in the same proportion that this means of labour ceases to be a bearer of value in the

production process. Its value thus acquires a dual existence. A part of it remains tied to its use form . . . while another part separates off from this form as money. (242–3)

In what follows I shall attach considerable significance to this idea of the "dual existence" of the value of the fixed capital—part increasingly in the money form as recuperated from production over successive turnover periods, and part as a diminishing residual value of the fixed capital (such as a machine) that has not yet been fully used up.

The money acquired is gradually accumulated as a reserve fund over the lifetime of the fixed capital. In the absence of a banking and credit system, the capitalist has to hoard the money capital until it comes time to replace the machine. The money returns into circulation only with the purchase of the replacement (243). If all capitalists worked on the same schedule, then the effect would be to create periods of feast and famine in the monetary circulation. Fortunately, they do not do so, but there is nothing that says they all work so as to even out the monetary circulation either, and periods of intense technological innovation may indeed induce monetary feasts and famines in the absence of a credit system.

The monetary turnover time of the fixed capital therefore has very specific qualities that are very different from those of the fluid (circulating) capital. Ancillary materials, like energy, are consumed entirely during the turnover time it takes to produce and market the commodity, so the money equivalent to those materials circulates back regularly. The same is true for the constant capital elements that constitute the object of labor, and which reappear in the commodity. In the case of labor, variable capital is advanced on a regular schedule (for example, weekly) to the laborer, who then spends the money on commodities according to his or her needs. This latter transaction, as Marx will frequently emphasize in what follows, "is no longer between worker and capitalist as such, but between the worker as buyer of commodities and the capitalist as their seller." For "it is the worker himself who converts the money he receives for his labour-power into means of subsistence" (245). This point will return in what follows, for in this function as buyer, the worker has the relative autonomy of consumer choice even as the choices are to some degree forced by the fact that the worker must buy in order to live.

Recall that the distinction between fixed and fluid capital is of relevance only to productive capital: "It exists only for productive capital and only within it" (247). During the turnover time of the fixed capital, however, several turnovers of fluid capital are completed. The value of the fixed capital "is advanced all at once in its entirety. . . . The capitalist thus casts this [monetary] value into the circulation sphere all at once; but it is withdrawn from circulation again only gradually and bit by bit" (247). But during the lifetime of the fixed capital, the capitalist does not usually need to use this money for replacement: "This transformation of money back into the natural form of the instrument of production takes place only at the end of the latter's period of functioning, when the instrument of production has been completely used up" (248).

But the replacement schedule of fixed capital is affected by natural laws. "In the case of living means of labour, such as horses, for example, the . . . average life as means of labour is determined by natural laws. Once this period has elapsed, the worn-out items must be replaced by new ones. A horse cannot be replaced bit by bit, but only by another horse" (250). The "lumpiness" of fixed-capital investment, with respect to both original purchase and replacement, is therefore a noteworthy feature. It has monetary implications for how much money capital has to be withdrawn or thrown back into circulation at particular moments in time:

> Apart from the case where reproduction takes place bit by bit in such a way that new stock is added to the depreciated old stock at short intervals, a prior accumulation of money is necessary, of a greater or lesser amount according to the specific character of the branch of production in question, before this replacement can occur. This cannot be just any sum of money whatever; an amount of a certain size is required. (260–1)

All sorts of combinations are possible here. A railway cannot function until the whole line is completed, so much money must be laid out in advance—but track renewal can be carried out, unlike with a horse, on a piecemeal basis.

The monetary consequences of all this are again briefly invoked at the end of chapter 8 and, as usual, Marx ends up noting how everything looks different when the credit system is brought into play. In the absence of the credit system, a "part of the money present in society always lies fallow in the form of a hoard, while another part functions as means of circulation or as an immediate reserve fund of directly circulating money." As a result,

> the proportion in which the total quantity of money is divided between hoard and means of circulation constantly alters. In our present case, money that has to be accumulated on a large scale as a hoard in the hands of a big capitalist is thrown into circulation all at once on the purchase of fixed capital. . . . By way of the amortization fund in which the value of fixed capital flows back to its starting point in proportion to the wear and tear, a part of the money in circulation again forms a hoard. . . . There is a constantly changing distribution of the hoard existing in a society which alternatively functions as means of circulation, and is then again divided off from the mass of circulating capital as a hoard. With the development of the credit system, *which necessarily runs parallel* with the development of large-scale industry and capitalist production, this money no longer functions as a hoard but as capital, though not in the hands of its proprietor, but rather of other capitalists at whose disposal it is put. (261; emphasis added)

The "dual character" of the money and material aspects of fixed-capital circulation is thereby fundamentally modified. The monetary aspects are released from their bonding with the material depreciation process, and are freed up as potential money capital.

"MORAL DEPRECIATION"

The important problem of "moral deterioration," or "moral depreciation" as Marx called it in Volume I, is subject to rather cursory treatment in Volume II. Revolutions in production either cheapen fixed capital over time or lead to the production of better machines to replace existing ones before the lifetime of the latter is out. The result is to accelerate the depreciation, or what amounts to the same thing, reduce the effectiveness—the utility—of the old machines. This is, therefore, where we might expect a full explication of that tantalizing caveat of fixed capital "still being effective" that we noted at the outset of this chapter. Unfortunately, Marx does not enlighten us too much, except to note that "the volume of fixed capital that is invested . . . and has to last out for a definite average lifetime" acts as "an obstacle to the rapid general introduction of improved means of labour." From this derives an understandable reluctance to embrace technological changes and new forms of fixed capital until the old fixed capital has been fully amortized. Under conditions of monopoly control, this reluctance can lead to stagnation (though this is not a point that Marx cares to make). Against this, "competition forces the replacement of old means of labour by new ones before their natural demise, particularly when decisive revolutions have taken place. Catastrophes, crises, etc. are the principle causes that compel such premature renewals of equipment on a broad social scale" (250). This theme is taken up again in chapter 9. The lifetime of fixed capital is cut short

> by the constant revolutionizing of the means of production, which also increases steadily with the development of the capitalist mode of production. This also leads to changes in the means of production; they constantly have to be replaced, because of their moral depreciation, long before they are physically exhausted. . . . The result is that the cycle of related turnovers, extending over a number of years, within which the capital is confined by its fixed component, is one of the material foundations for the periodic cycle in which business passes through successive periods of stagnation, moderate activity, overexcitement and crisis. The periods for which capital is invested certainly differ greatly, and do not coincide in time. But a crisis is always the starting-point of a large volume of new investment. It is also, therefore, if we consider the society as a whole, more or less a new material base for the next turnover cycle. (264)

Accelerated depreciation entails devaluation of the existing fixed capital whose value has not yet been fully recovered through the production and sale of commodities. If this occurs on a widespread enough scale, then it can obviously result in crises. As Marx noted in Volume I, the implication for labor is in the form of shift- and night-work as a way to recuperate fixed-capital value as quickly as possible before the risk of moral depreciation hits home. But the general significance of the devaluation of large quantities of fixed capital due to "moral depreciation" or to other social forces (such locational shifts that leave fixed capital in place high and dry) is not emphasized at all in Volume II. It is picked up in the *Grundrisse*, both theoretically and historically. So we are left on our own to figure out some of the implications.

Generalized crises (which obviously entail value losses to capital), Marx suggests, may be good moments to renew or replace existing fixed capital. This is an idea that needs to be followed up. In a crisis, much of the existing fixed capital remains idle and devalued anyway (capital utilization is very low), so capitalists who have the monetary reserves might just as well junk it and move on (particularly since the costs of new fixed capital are likely to be low). A recent example of exactly this in the realm of public policy was the so-called "cash for clunkers" program launched by the federal government in 2008. Consumers were offered cash to ditch their old cars before their lifetime was up and to buy new ones. The aim was to keep the automobile market buoyant and the industry in business. Tax breaks for accelerated depreciation are another form of public policy incentive affecting renewal of and reinvestment in fixed capital. This occurred under Ronald Reagan in the early 1980s. It was a public subsidy to permit the accelerated write-off of the value of much existing and new fixed capital. It actually subsidized the movement of capital to the South and West and the deindustrialization of the Northeast and Midwest of the United States. Whether or not this is more generally "effective" depends, of course, on the existence in the wings of new technological or locational possibilities. The great depression of the 1930s was a remarkable period of technological and institutional renewal in the midst of crisis conditions in the United States. The result was a completely different model of fixed-capital engagement (based on the automobile, electrification, and the opening up of California) that bore fruits after World War II. It laid "the new material base for the next turnover cycle." Is there a similar process of reorganization of the fixed-capital milieu occurring in the midst of the present recessionary conditions? And if so, where? China? Marx's theoretical question is certainly worthy of investigation.

The general significance of these aspects of Marx's theory of crisis formation and resolution is not often remarked upon in the Marxist literature, even though there is considerable historical evidence for business cycles associated with waves of new technologies coming on line, and associated waves of extensive "moral depreciation" in the way that Marx briefly outlines. Measures of the utilization of capacity (i.e. largely fixed capital) are considered, after all, to be vital indicators of economic health. One only has to look at the vast wave of investment in fixed capital in China in response to the crisis conditions of 2008–09 to recognize how important these relations might be. On the one hand we can see how necessary it is that "there be constant over-production, i.e. production on a greater scale than is needed for the simple replacement and reproduction of the existing wealth—quite apart from any increase in population—for the society to have at its disposal the means of production to make good unusual destruction caused by accidents and natural forces" (257). While Marx obviously has in mind here the impacts of earthquakes and tsunamis, there is no reason not to extend this insight to the collapse of export markets of the sort China experienced in 2009. China has vast capital surpluses (as did Britain from the seventeenth to the end of the nineteenth century). It does not have to appeal for austerity (as Rostow and the current Republican Party in the United States do) to fund this vast wave of fixed-capital investment. However, as Marx so presciently signals, there is also a "material basis" here for the periodic crises "in which business passes through successive stages of stagnation, moderate activity, overexcitement, and crisis" (264). There are, in fact, innumerable ways in which the "moral depreciations" that occur in relation to fixed capitals of all sorts (including those immobilized in the land as vast physical infrastructures) can and regularly do morph into major disruptions and crises (particularly with respect to asset values) within the heart of a capitalist mode of production. While Marx signals the general possibility of this, he fails to elaborate in any depth. This is, in my view, a great pity. It leaves us with plenty of work to do even as it furnishes some very suggestive ideas to that end.

FIXED CAPITAL AND VALUE THEORY

There is a lot of debate, both in Marxist economics and in bourgeois theory, over how to value fixed capital. It is a very thorny and difficult problem. Marx provides us with three ways to do it. He introduces the problem by appealing to straight-line depreciation. A machine that lasts ten years recovers one tenth of its value every year, until its value is fully realized and its use-value fully used up, at which point the capitalist buys a new machine with the money that has been hoarded. The second means of valuing fixed capital is by way of replacement cost. The residual value in the machine is determined at any point in its lifetime by what it would cost to replace it with an equivalent machine. Thirdly, the value of the machine is dependent upon the social average lifetime and the general level of effectiveness of fixed capital deployed by competing capitalists in a given line of production. This is where the "moral depreciation" argument and the question of the "effectiveness" or "utility" (though Marx does not use this term) of the fixed capital dominate. Technological revolutions make new machines cheaper and/or more efficient and effective. This affects the value of the goods being produced. Rising productivity means lower commodity values, so the imputed social average value of existing fixed capital diminishes because the "level of effectiveness" or the usefulness of that existing fixed capital (such as a machine) diminishes. When commodity values plunge because of rising productivity (due to the availability of cheaper and more effective fixed-capital equipment), then individual capitalists cannot claim back the whole value of their fixed capital when they go to market. No purchaser is likely to listen when I say, "Please pay me more for this commodity because I have not yet amortized my older and clunkier forms of fixed capital."

But Marx leaves this determinant largely uninvestigated. The question of sunk capital values and the valuation of physical fixed capital over time is left in abeyance. The valuation of fixed capital is a horror story in bourgeois economics, and it is also viewed by many as deeply problematic in Marx. In particular, it is sometimes presented as the Achilles' heel in Marx's conception of the labor theory of value. There is no question that its "peculiarities" do challenge certain conceptions of that theory. If value is interpreted as that socially necessary embodied labor input that fixes the "true" value of a commodity for all time and which underpins the "natural" or equilibrium prices observed in the market, then Marx's relational approach to deciding when something is or is not fixed capital (vis-à-vis items in the consumption fund or in joint product situations) plainly subverts this whole framework. It has certainly been shown conclusively that the circulation of fixed capital cannot be reconciled with a theory of value that rests solely on past and present embodied labor time as fixed magnitudes. But this, I argued in *The Limits to Capital*, is Ricardo's labor theory of value and not Marx's:

> While Marx frequently equates socially necessary labour with embodied labour for the sake of convenience, the latter does not embrace all aspects of value as a social relation. Value, recall, "exists only in articles of utility,"

so that if an article loses utility, it also loses its value." This is so because "commodities must show that they are use-values before they can be realized as values" so that "if a thing is useless, so is the labour contained in it; the labour does not count as labour, and therefore creates no value."[3]

Now, for reasons laid out at the very beginning, Marx is reluctant to deal with specificities like demand and supply, and certainly does not want to get into any version of utility theory. So it is in general assumed that either the article is or is not a use-value. But it is not hard to see how the use-value of fixed capital changes over its lifetime depending upon its "effectiveness" (which is why I so underlined that word at the outset). More generally, I argue, "value is not a fixed metric to be used to describe a changing world, but a social relation which embodies contradiction and uncertainty at its very center. There is, then, no contradiction whatsoever between Marx's conception of value and the 'peculiarities' of fixed capital circulation. The contradiction is internalized within the very conception of value itself."[4]

There is one interesting way to make this whole argument more tangible, and indeed Marx hints at but does not pursue a more thorough application of the theory of joint products. At the end of a turnover period of, say, one year, two commodities have been produced jointly— the commodity and the residual fixed capital (in the form, say, of sewing machines). At the end of the turnover time, I have the option to treat both the shirts and the sewing machines as commodity capital and to realize the value of both. The partially used sewing machines have a value on the market, but with the built environment there is a problem. The secondhand market value of a whole industrial landscape is not easy to assess. Although there are now astounding stories of whole plants being dismantled in Germany and reassembled in China, the cost of the move is likely to diminish seriously the cost of acquisition of the devalued fixed capital. But then the anticipated future value may come into play (a form of fictitious capital that we will encounter later). Yet

3 David Harvey, *The Limits to Capital* (Oxford: Basil Blackwell, 1982), chapter 8; John E. Roemer, "Continuing Controversy on the Falling Rate of Profit: Fixed Capital and Other Issues," *Cambridge Journal of Economics* 3 (1979), 379–98; Ian Steedman, *Marx After Sraffa* (London: Verso, 1977).
4 David Harvey, *Limits to Capital*, 215.

this involves a considerable risk for the capitalist buying up the old partially devalued fixed capital in the land, and then hoping either to use it directly or convert it to other uses (for example, converting an abandoned cotton mill into condominiums).

All sorts of problems obviously exist in the field of valuing fixed-capital investments, old and new. Strategies emerge to deal with some of these difficulties, such as planned obsolescence or the leasing of fixed capital on an annual basis, such that the risk shifts from the producer who uses it to the owners who lease it (often in return for interest only). And, in practice, state and local governments often step in to provide certain elements of fixed capital in the land for little cost, to socialize both the burden and the risk of certain kinds of fixed-capital investments.

I mention all these problems and possibilities to illustrate the kind of complexity that attaches to what initially seems the very simple category of fixed capital. Marx takes up many but not all of these complexities, but does so in a relational way that emphasizes the fluidity and the instability of how the category works in and through the circulation and accumulation of capital in general. The unfinished character of Volume II means that there is still work to do on this topic, while Marx's reluctance to use all of his prior findings from the *Grundrisse* and elsewhere is somewhat puzzling. But, in spite of all these particular shortcomings, the question of the circulation of fixed capital in all its forms (mobile and immobile, in particular), and with all its relationalities (with the consumption fund, in particular), constitutes a major feature of Marx's critical search for an understanding of the laws of motion of capital in its "pure state." That this search brings Marx ever closer to the question of how the credit system operates in relation to fixed-capital formation, circulation and use, provides one compelling reason to interrogate more closely how the credit system itself functions within the rules of a pure capitalist mode of production.

CHAPTER FOUR

Merchants' Capital
(Chapters 16–20 of Volume III)

We now move into the "grand experiment" of seeing how Marx's theory looks when we seek to integrate the technical analysis of circulation processes laid out in Volume II with their corresponding distributional forms as presented in Volume III. In venturing into Volume III, we have to confront some immediate difficulties that derive from the nature of that text.

Engels had great difficulty reconstructing much of it from Marx's draft manuscripts. Part 4, on merchants' capital, was in a reasonable state, but Part 5, which deals with money capital, finance and credit "presented the major difficulty and this was also the most important subject in the whole book." That Engels viewed it so is, I think, of more than mere passing significance. I, too, think it of the greatest significance and regret that it has not been the center of a far more wide-ranging analysis and debate within the Marxist tradition of political economy.

The problem for Engels was that there was no "finished draft, or even an outline plan to be filled in, but simply the beginning of an elaboration which petered out more than once in a disordered jumble of notes, comments and extract material." After three attempts to rewrite it, Engels gave up and just arranged the materials as best he could, while making "only the most necessary alterations." The real difficulties began, Engels reports, after chapter 30, on "Money Capital and Real Capital." "From here on it was not only the illustrative material that needed correct arrangement, but also a train of thought that was interrupted continuously by digressions, asides, etc., and later pursued further in other places, often simply in passing. There then followed, in the manuscript, a long section headed 'The Confusion'" (C3, 94–5). These materials are, in short, in pretty bad shape.

It is hard, if not impossible, to reconstruct the general flow in much of Marx's argument. There are places where this can be done, but elsewhere I find it best to extract what seem to be key insights and ideas from a lengthy text, to see if some more general framework for analysis emerges—there is no option, for example, except to read the materials on speculation speculatively.

Marx begins Part 4 of Volume III with the following observation: "Merchant's or trading capital is divided into two forms or sub-species, commercial capital and money-dealing capital" (C3, 379). While there is an obvious overlap between commodity trading and money dealing (for example, trading frequently entails offering credit), Marx separates them out from each other in exactly the same way as he distinguishes between the money and the commodity circuits of capital in Volume II. But please note that when Marx uses the term "merchants' capital" he is combining both commercial capital (which we would normally call the activities of the merchant) and that of the bankers and money dealers.

Marx also makes clear his determination not to stray from his mission, as described in the introduction to the *Grundrisse*, to focus on the general laws of motion of capital even when he deals with the partic- ularities of distribution. We will, he frequently declares, only go into "such detail as is needed in order to analyse capital in its basic inner structure." He aims to locate the activities of merchants and money dealers in relation to these general laws. The trouble is that Marx is not always sure what is or is not relevant to the general laws. This is some- thing that we need to keep a critical eye on as we proceed.

This last problem relates to another of which we also need to be keenly aware:

> As the reader will have recognized in dismay, the analysis of the real, inner connections of the capitalist production process is a very intricate thing and a work of great detail; it is one of the tasks of science to reduce the visible and merely apparent movement to the actual inner move- ment. Accordingly, it will be completely self-evident that in the heads of the agents of capitalist production and circulation, ideas must necessar- ily form about the laws of production that diverge completely from these laws and are merely the expression in consciousness of the apparent movement. The ideas of a merchant, a stock jobber or a banker are necessarily quite upside-down. The ideas of the manufacturers are viti- ated by the acts of circulation to which their capital is subjected and by

the equalization of the general rate of profit. Competition, too, necessarily plays in their minds, a completely upside-down role. (C3, 428)

Notice what this implies. The self-presentations, self-perceptions and ideas of the agents of finance (as well as of capitalists in general) are delusional, not in the sense that they are crazy (though, as we will see, they often are) but *necessarily* deluded in the sense that Marx described in his theory of fetishism. In that theory, the surface appearance of market exchange signals (such as prices and profits), to which we must all perforce react, conceals the real content of our social relations. We necessarily act upon the basis of these market signals no matter whether we recognize that they mask something else or not. It is therefore not surprising to find bourgeois ideas and theory replicating the misleading signals in the world of consciousness and thought. Marx's general intent throughout *Capital* is to get behind and beyond the fetishisms of commodity exchange and see the world "right-side-up." This was, Engels surmises in his Preface, Marx's intent in analyzing "the confusion." This also explains why the materials Marx assembled in Part 5 after chapter 30 consisted "simply of extracts from the parliamentary reports on the crises of 1848 and 1857, in which the statements of some twenty-three businessmen and economic writers, particularly on the subjects of money and capital, the drain of gold, over-speculation, etc., were collected, with the occasional addition of brief humorous comments" (C3, 95). These statements were the basic raw materials that needed to be turned "right-side-up." Hardly surprisingly, the theory of commodity fetishism therefore makes an explicit reappearance in Part 5, en route to deriving the all-important category of "fictitious capital."

Marx's view on all this has immense contemporary significance. Not only do we now have to hand innumerable accounts of what happens on Wall Street (including Congressional Enquiries) that we are supposed to consider trustworthy, but we are overwhelmed with a rhetoric that says that banking is so complicated that only the expert bankers understand what it is they do. We therefore have to rely upon their expertise, we are told, to deal with the problems they created. But if Marx is correct, then we should not believe these bankers' accounts (even when "truthful" in the fetishistic sense), and certainly not trust them to devise institutional arrangements to control the inherent contradictions (most of which remain unrecognized) within the laws of motion of capital. The bankers and financiers are, in some ways, the very last people to trust, not because they are all fraudsters and liars (even though some of them patently are), but because they are likely to be prisoners of their own mystifications and fetishistic understandings. What Marx would have said of Lloyd Blankfein when he claimed, when pressed before a Congressional Committee, that his bank, Goldman Sachs, had merely been doing God's work, is not hard to imagine.

Banking and finance constitute, Marx concedes, a very complicated world. His insistence that we should only pay mind to those aspects of it that connect to the general laws of motion of capital turns out to be both helpful and frustrating. Marx's science searches for the actual inner movement in the midst of all the apparent chaos and the innumerable complications. We should strive to do no less. This saves us from getting bogged down in every detail of how this or that new financial instrument operates. But it is frustrating because Marx never completed his analysis of what was or was not relevant and, as we shall see, ran into some rather deep problems in seeking to do so. And he never completed his ambition to turn the views of the bankers right-side-up.

So let us first recall where the argument stands. We know from the analysis laid out at the beginning of Volume II that the circuit of industrial capital comprises three intertwining yet distinctive circulation processes: those of money, commodity and production capital. The money and commodity circuits (the monetization and commodification of exchange relations) had to preexist the rise of a distinctively capitalist mode of production driven by the logic of surplus-value production and appropriation, as laid out in Volume I.

The vital importance and special qualities of commodity capital within the overall circulation of industrial capital were singled out for examination in chapter 3 of Volume II. But Marx scrupulously refrained in that chapter from going any further than was necessary in order to understand the formal position of commodity capital in the overall dynamics of the circulation process. Here, in Volume III, he is prepared to go deeper and further—although, as we shall see, he is still reluctant to engage with the power relations between merchants and producers within any actually existing capitalist society.

Throughout *Capital*, Marx refers to these preexisting forms of capital as "antediluvian" (see Volume I, page 266, and chapters 20 and 36 of Volume III). How, then, are these antediluvian forms—commercial capital and usury in particular—which function independently and autonomously and with (or without) their own rules of conduct and exchange, disciplined to serve the needs of a rule-bound capitalist mode of production? Theoretically, the answer to this question entails specifying the distinctive and necessary roles of commercial and money-dealing capitals within a purely capitalist mode of production, and showing how their forms of operation (marked, as always, by certain pervasive contradictions) might affect the laws of motion of capital. This then leads into the further obvious question, first broached in the chapter on money in Volume I, of the role of commercial and financial crises, such as those which Marx experienced in 1848 and 1857 (and which we have been experiencing since 2007), in relation to the value theory and the overall dynamics of capital accumulation. These are the issues I will now take up.

ON CHAPTER 20 OF VOLUME III: HISTORICAL MATERIALS ON MERCHANTS' CAPITAL

I find it helpful to begin with a reading of chapter 20, which provides an overview of the historical role of the "antediluvian" forms of merchants' capital in the rise of a capitalist mode of production. Marx's historical reconstructions are, as we have seen, often suspect, but in this instance his account is suggestive, if not informative.

Marx opens the chapter with a critique of all those economists who see merchants' capital simply as one branch among many in the social division of labor:

> In commercial and money-dealing capital, rather, the distinctions between industrial capital as productive capital and the same capital in the sphere of circulation attain autonomy in the following way: the specific forms and functions that capital temporarily assumes in the latter case come to appear as independent forms and functions of a part of the capital that has separated off and become completely confined to this sphere.

Note the language: merchants' capital "attains autonomy" by "appearing" as a "separate and independent" form of capital. Even if Marx means here independent and autonomous from feudal social relations, this still leaves open the question of potential autonomy and independence relative to the laws of motion of capital, as earlier defined.

It is certainly erroneous, however, to see the activities of banking, wholesaling and retailing as in principle no different from value-producing activities like mining, metallurgy and agriculture within the overall division of labor. Yet this is how these sectors were typically viewed in classical political economy, and how they continue to be represented to this day in national accounts. Marx insists they are fundamentally different activities deriving from their relation to the flow of capital in the circulation sphere, rather than in production. The "confusions" of classical political economy were expressed, firstly, by an "inability to explain commercial profit and its characteristic features" and, secondly, through the "apologetic endeavour to derive the forms of commodity capital and money capital . . . from the production process as such." The idea that "production predominates" is correctly ascribed to Marx, but here he is saying that this cannot be the case in the narrowly deterministic sense that classical political economists typically proposed. "Smith. Ricardo, etc. . . . focused on . . . industrial capital . . . and were perplexed by commercial capital" because "value formation, profit, etc. derived from the examination of industrial capital cannot be applied directly to commercial capital. They therefore entirely ignored the latter" (C3, 440–1). The questions of how to deal with the role of merchants' capital is just as confused today as it was in Marx's time. So this is a great opportunity to sort the confusion out and ask some fundamental questions. Where does the profit on merchants' (commercial and money-dealing) capital come from—and how can it be justified in relation to the laws of motion of capital—when it is not in itself a branch of production that produces value? This is the problem that the substantive chapters will attempt to address purely from "the standpoint of the capitalist mode of production and within its limits."

But "trading capital is older than the capitalist mode of production, and is, in fact, the oldest historical mode in which capital has an independent existence." All that is required for its existence is "the simple circulation of commodities and money. . . . Whatever mode of production is the basis on which the products circulating are produced—whether the primitive community, slave production, small peasant and petty-bourgeois production, or capitalist production—this in no way alters their character as commodities [and] commercial capital simply mediates the movement of these commodities" (C3, 442). The extent of the trade depends, of course, on the mode of production. In a largely self-sufficient peasant society, only surpluses over and above basic needs will be traded, and so merchants will be restricted to trading in these surpluses. Their role expands and reaches "a maximum with the full development of capitalist production, where the product is produced simply as a commodity and not at all as a direct means of subsistence." Commercial capital "simply mediates the exchange of commodities," but "buys and sells for many people. Sales and purchases are concentrated in his hands and in this way buying and selling cease to be linked with the direct needs of the buyer (as merchant)." While Marx does not say this here, the merchant obviously stands to make gains from the economies of scale of his or her operation.

The wealth of the merchant "always exists as money wealth and his money always functions as capital," although its form is always M-C-M', which means that the aim and object of the merchant's operations must be the procurement of ΔM (C3, 443). The question is: Where does this ΔM come from, and what are the implications of its appropriation by the merchant?

There is, Marx asserts,

> no problem at all in understanding why commercial capital appears as the historic form of capital long before capital has subjected production itself to its sway. Its existence and its development to a certain level, is itself a historical precondition for the development of the capitalist mode of production (1) as precondition for the concentration of monetary wealth, and (2) because the capitalist mode of production presupposes production for trade. . . . On the other hand, every development in commercial capital gives production a character oriented ever more to exchange-value, transforming products more and more into commodities.

The existence of commercial capital may be a necessary condition for the transition into a capitalist mode of production, but "taken by itself, is insufficient to explain the transition" (C3, 444).

In the context of capitalist production, "commercial capital is demoted from its earlier separate existence, to become a particular moment of capital investment in general, and the equalization of profits reduces its profit rate to the general average. It now functions simply as the agent of productive capital."

We must, as I will shortly show, be very careful how we understand this statement. Marx's subsequent commentary can be misleading. He says, for example, that "where commercial capital predominates, obsolete conditions obtain," and that "trading cities," even within the same country, "exhibit a far greater analogy with past conditions than do manufacturing towns." This was, actually, a rather astute historical observation. In Britain, for example, capitalist production did not arise in the main commercial and trading cities such as Bristol and Norwich (which were dominated by conservative corporatist and guild forms of organization) but on the "greenfield" sites of villages with names like Manchester and Birmingham, where such forms of organization were absent. This led Marx to conclude that "the independent and preponderant development of capital in the form of commercial capital is synonymous with the non-subjection of production to capital," and so "stands in inverse proportion to the general economic development of society." In other words, a hegemonic merchant class would attempt to suppress the rise of the industrial form of capital, since its capacity to extract ultra-profits by exploiting weak and vulnerable producers would be curbed.

The transitional story that Marx tells runs like this: capital "appears first of all in the circulation process. In this circulation process, money develops into capital. It is in circulation that the product first develops as exchange-value, as commodity and money. Capital can be formed in the circulation process, and must be formed there, before it learns to master its extremes, the various spheres of production between which circulation mediates." Once capital has mastered the extremes, then "the production process is completely based on circulation, and circulation is a mere moment and a transition phase of production" (as described in the first chapters of Volume II). This leads to "the law that the independent development of commodity capital stands in inverse proportion to the level of development of capitalist production." There is "a decline in the supremacy of the exclusively trading peoples and in their commercial wealth" reflecting "the subordination of commercial capital to industrial capital" with "the progressive development of capitalist production" (C3, 446).

Marx illustrates the power of this law with some remarks on the nature of the carrying trade as organized through the Venetians, the Genoans and the Dutch, all of whom relied heavily upon "commercial capital in its pure form," and effectively built their wealth through positioning themselves as mediators in exchange and accumulators of money capital, by buying cheap and selling dear. While the commodities exchanged are an expression of human labor and have a value, "they are not equal values." But the more merchants transform the world of commodity exchange into one where, as he earlier argued, exchange becomes "a normal social act," so the value metric becomes increasingly hegemonic. This is an important point. The importance of the value concept and of the whole theory that Marx builds upon it depends historically upon the activities of merchant capitalists in creating exchange networks on the world market.

While this may be historically accurate, the supposed existence of such a "law" poses a serious problem for us. The rise of powerful forms of commercial capital (such as Walmart, Ikea, Nike, Benetton, the Gap, and so on) over the last thirty years suggests either that the "law" no longer holds, or that it requires a nuanced interpretation. Or are we simply being misled by surface appearances? We will return to this issue shortly.

"In the stages that preceded capitalist society," Marx continues,

> it was trade that prevailed over industry; in modern society it is the reverse. Trade naturally reacts back to a greater or lesser extent on the communities between which it is pursued; it subjects production more and more to exchange-value. . . . In this way it dissolves the old relationships. It increases monetary circulation. It no longer just takes hold of surplus production, but actually gobbles up production itself and makes entire branches of production dependent upon it. (C3, 448)

In its initial stages, commercial capital derives much of its wealth from "defrauding and cheating." When it held "a dominant position," it constituted "in all cases a system of plunder" which, we should note, goes entirely against the rules of free and fair market exchange generally presupposed in *Capital*, and plunges us back into the Volume I world of primitive accumulation. But as it becomes more regularized, so it becomes more rule-bound. And the rules are set, in theory at least, by what the capitalist mode of production demands, even as the development of trade promotes those demands.

> The development of trade and commercial capital always gives production a growing orientation towards exchange-value, expands its scope, diversifies it and renders it cosmopolitan, developing money into world

money. Trade always has, to a greater or lesser degree, a solvent effect on the pre-existing organizations of production, which in all their various forms are principally oriented to use-value. But how far it leads to the dissolution of the old mode of production depends first and foremost on the solidity and inner articulation of this mode of production itself. And what comes out of this process of dissolution, i.e. what new mode of production arises in place of the old, does not depend on trade, but rather on the character of the old mode of production itself. (C3, 449)

There is, therefore, no necessary movement towards a capitalist mode of production. How money "dissolves" the ancient community to become the community is a theme elaborated upon at some length and with great passion in the *Grundrisse* (see for example pages 224–8). Nevertheless,

there can be no doubt . . . that the great revolutions that took place in trade in the sixteenth and seventeenth centuries, along with the geographical discoveries of the epoch, and which rapidly advanced the development of commercial capital, were a major moment in promoting the transitions from the feudal to the capitalist mode of production. The sudden expansion of the world market, the multiplication of commodities in circulation, the competition among the European nations for the seizure of Asiatic products and American treasures, the colonial system, all made a fundamental contribution towards shattering the feudal barriers to production.

But while "the sudden expansion of trade and the creation of a new world market had an overwhelming influence on the defeat of the old mode of production and the rise of the capitalist mode," there occurred at some point a historic reversal in which it was no longer the expansion of trade and the world market that provided the impetus for capitalist production, but a shift in which the latter became the driving force, such that an industrializing nation (Britain) assumed a hegemonic role in capitalist development displacing commercial power (that of Holland). Those familiar with Giovanni Arrighi's history of shifting hegemonies within global capitalism—*The Long Twentieth Century*—will immediately see the historical validity of this point.[5] It was this that also drove

---

5   Giovanni Arrighi, *The Long Twentieth Century: Money, Power and the Origins of Our Times* (London: Verso, 1994).

the traders to become the cutting edge of colonial and imperialist practices, destroying Indian industry to create a market for goods produced in Britain.

"The transition from the feudal mode of production takes place in two different ways. The producer may become a merchant and capitalist," which is "the really revolutionary way. Alternatively, however, the merchant may take direct control of production himself." Marx later adds a third way in which "the merchant makes the small masters into his middlemen, or even buys directly from the independent producer; he leaves him nominally independent and leaves his mode of production unchanged" (C3, 454).

There are two perceptive points here. First, the overwhelming power of merchants' capital and its forms of organization just as often inhibited the development of full-fledged industrial capitalism as they promoted it. There is considerable historical evidence to support this view. But there is a more contemporary point. When the merchants retain control, they often preserve and retain old and backward forms of production organized on traditional lines. This

> stands in the way of the genuine capitalist mode of production and disappears with its development. Without revolutionizing the mode of production, it simply worsens the conditions of the direct producers, transforms them into mere wage-labourers and proletarians under worse conditions than those directly subsumed by capital, appropriating their surplus labour on the basis of the old mode of production. Somewhat modified, the same relationships are to be found in the manufacture of furniture in London, which is partly carried out on a handicraft basis. This is particularly the case in Tower Hamlets. (C3, 453)

The case of Tower Hamlets provides some very important insights:

> The whole of furniture production is divided into very many separate branches. One firm just makes chairs, another tables, a third chests and so on. But these firms are themselves conducted more or less on a handicraft basis, by one master with a few journeymen. Despite this, production is on too large a scale to work directly for private clients. The buyers are the proprietors of furniture stores. On Saturday the master goes to these stores and sells his products. . . . These masters need their

weekly sale simply to buy more raw materials for the coming week and to pay wages. Under these conditions they are really only middlemen between the merchant and their own workers. *The merchant is the real capitalist and pockets the greater part of the surplus-value,* (C3, 453; emphasis added).

Systems of production of this sort have long existed in the history of capitalism, and this form has proliferated (though in modern guise) over the past forty years, as merchant capitalist organizations like Benetton, Walmart, Ikea, Nike, and so on, almost certainly "pocket the greater part of the surplus-value" from the producers whom they subcontract. In what sense, then, can we still say that "production predominates?"

In Volume I, Marx concedes that capital was in his time constituted by all manner of different or "hybrid" labor systems (ranging from the factory to domestic workers). But there was a definite teleological thrust in which Marx seemed to assume that mixed and hybrid labor systems of the Tower Hamlets sort were transitional toward a factory system that would dominate over all else. In a purely capitalist mode of production the factory would be all there was. I challenged that teleological presumption in the *Companion* to Volume I. In my own studies of industrial organization in Second Empire Paris, I had found that the Tower Hamlets kind of organization was proliferating and not shrinking. But where Marx was right was in remarking the vicious exploitation entailed in such forms of labor organization. Zola, in his novel *l'Assomoire*, has a devastating description of the oppressive conditions lived by a husband-and-wife team making gold chain in their apartment on command from merchants who supplied the gold and collected the product on a monthly basis. And there is a good deal of evidence in the contemporary world that super-exploitation characterizes many of the subcontracting networks mobilized and organized by merchant capital (hence the scandals that burst into the mainstream press regarding Liz Claiborne clothing, Nike shoes, children making carpets and soccer balls—to be kicked around by soccer players earning millions—and harvesting cacao).

But the super-exploitation to be found here is significant in another way. As the factory system did indeed proliferate and grow, putting sometimes incredible competitive pressures on these other systems of production, then workers began to organize on the basis of factory labor, as Marx predicted. They formed unions and exerted political pressures of the sort that became generalized toward the end of the 1960s in many parts of the advanced capitalist world. It was under such political conditions that the turn toward older commercial forms of super-exploitation became far more attractive. Hence the rebirth of the merchant capitalists (and even the renewal of mercantilist practices and theories) and the proliferation of their super-exploitative networks and chains of dispersed and subcontracted production. But, in certain arenas and areas of production, such practices had never disappeared; they had always retained their competitive edge over factory production. Hong Kong, for example, is celebrated for such forms of workshop and family labor production—in contrast with, say, Singapore, which is more corporately organized, and South Korea, which took the classic path into large-scale factory production, and ended up with a strong labor movement of the sort that would be unthinkable in Hong Kong. The teleological presumption cannot, in my view, be sustained. Competition between different labor systems remains, I would argue, a vital aspect of contemporary global capitalism, which in turn implies different relative roles for producers vis-à-vis merchants. There are certain sectors, as well as certain spaces in the global economy, in which it would seem that the producers do indeed dominate the merchants, whereas there are other places and sectors where the opposite is true. In the automobile industry, for example, producers tend to dominate distributors, but in textiles it is almost always the other way round these days. In the case of General Motors, however, a hybrid form emerged in the form of General Motors Acceptance Corporation, which became an independent and autonomous branch of General Motors organizing credit (it eventually qualified as a bank in the crisis of 2008–09).

There is still a clear sense in which Marx's proposition that "production predominates," and that the activities of the merchants are rendered "subservient" to the requirements of a capitalist mode of production, remains true. Whereas merchant capitalists at one time lived off fraudulent and predatory practices of buying (or procuring) cheap and selling dear, they now have to organize the direct producers under their influence to maximize the production of surplus-value even as they, the merchants, appropriate the lion's share of that value. Marx's proposition concerning the subservience of merchants' capital to the requirement of surplus-value production therefore still holds good. This does not mean the merchant capitalists have to be or currently are subservient to the power of the producers. Nor does it mean that the merchants stop engaging in fraudulent practices of accumulation by dispossession (in which they have a lot of historical experience). In the recent foreclosure crisis in the United States, for example, a mortgage institution like Countrywide was shown to have defrauded millions of people of billions of dollars in asset values during the housing boom from 2000 to 2007.

Marx readily concedes the perpetuation and periodic return of such practices, but his intent is to locate the origins of the profits of merchant capital within the rules of a purely capitalist mode of production. This requires that he define the logic of merchant capitals' position, and the contributions they and the labor they employ make to the production and realization of surplus value within a purely functioning capitalist mode of production. This is the focus of the substantive analytic chapters on merchants' capital, to which we now turn.

ON CHAPTER 16 OF VOLUME III: COMMERCIAL CAPITAL

Marx opens his chapter on commercial capital (defined as that part of merchants' capital that deals primarily in commodities) by reminding us of its connectivity to the circulation of commodity capital as presented in Volume II. One part of the total social capital

> is always on the market as a commodity, waiting to pass over into money. . . . Capital is always involved in this movement of transition, this metamorphosis of form. In as much as this function acquires independent life as a special function of a special capital and is fixed by the division of labour as a function that falls to a particular species of capitalists, commodity capital becomes commodity-dealing capital or commercial capital. (C3, 379)

Our task, then, is to understand the role this "particular species" of capitalist plays in the accumulation of capital.

In order to get at commercial capital in its pure form, Marx reminds us that there are certain activities—most notably transportation—that are part of value production even though they are often carried out by commercial capital. Marx proposes to ignore these functions here (C3,

380). This leaves him with the bare distinction between circulating (or fluid) capital and capital engaging in production within the overall circulation of industrial capital. "Commercial capital" is

> nothing but the transformed form of a portion of the circulation capital which is always to be found on the market. . . . We refer here to a portion only, because another part of the buying and selling of commodities always takes place directly between the industrial capitalists themselves. We shall ignore this other portion of circulation capital completely in the present investigation, since it contributes nothing to the theoretical definition, to our understanding of the specific nature of commercial capital, and has moreover been exhaustively dealt with, for our purposes, in Volume II. (C3, 380)

The commercial capitalist "appears on the market as the representative of a certain sum of money that he advances as a capitalist," with the intent of gaining profit (Δm). In order to deal in commodities, "he must first buy them, and be therefore the possessor of money capital. . . . What then is the relationship between this commodity-dealing capital and commodity capital as a mere form of existence of industrial capital?" (C3, 381). This is the question.

The linen manufacturer realizes "the value of his linen with the merchant's money." As far as the manufacturer is concerned this completes the circuit of capital and frees him or her to use the money so gained to continue and if necessary expand production activities. But the linen itself is still on the market as a commodity. All that has happened is that its ownership has changed, and it is now in the hands of the merchant whose special business it is to realize the linen's value in the market. This special business is "separate from the other functions of industrial capital and hence autonomous. It is a particular form of the social division of labour, such that one part of the function which has to be performed in a particular phase of capital's reproduction process, here the phase of circulation, appears as *the exclusive function of a specific agent of circulation distinct from the producer*" (C3, 384; emphasis added). This implies that the "autonomy" of commercial or trading capital that had been so important historically is preserved within the framework of a capitalist mode of production. So what, exactly, does this "autonomy" allow?

First notice that what appears as a simple exchange of C-M for the producer now takes the form of an operation by the merchant of M-C-M' (C3, 385). "Thus the way that commodity capital assumes in commercial capital the form of an independent variety of capital is by the merchant advancing money capital that is valorized as capital and functions as capital, only because it is exclusively engaged in facilitating the metamorphosis of commodity capital in making it fulfill its function as commodity capital." The money capital advanced by the merchant is exclusively wrapped up in buying and selling, and "remains for ever penned into capital's circulation sphere" (C3, 386).

The benefit to the industrial capitalist is that the turnover time of his capital is shortened. His production process "goes forward without a break" because "as far as he is concerned, the transformation of his commodity into money has already taken place." This does not mean that the problem of circulation time is abolished. But, without the intervention of the merchant, "the part of the circulation capital that exists in the form of a money reserve would always have to be greater in proportion to the part employed in the form of productive capital, and the scale of reproduction would be accordingly restricted." The producer "can now regularly apply a greater part of his capital in the actual production process, leaving a smaller money reserve" (C3, 387). Furthermore, "if the merchant remains a merchant . . . the producer saves time in selling which he can apply to supervising the production process, while the merchant has to spend his entire time selling." This is what makes the activities of merchant capital logically consistent with the rules of a purely capitalist mode of production. Or, more accurately, this is what makes the emergence of an autonomous class of merchant capitalists within a capitalist mode of production both advantageous and logically necessary.

Marx then lists some of the important functions of the rise of a form of capital exclusively devoted to buying and selling. By selling the products of several different producers or of several different lines of production within the division of labor, they can compensate for and smooth out different turnover times while achieving certain economies of scale. The more efficient they are and the faster their own turnover time, the less capital they will require. They also have a role to play in increasing the velocity of circulation of their own money capital and of influencing the speed of consumption. This last point is, I think, now of great importance in our consumerist world, and could do with further elaboration. But

> commercial capital is nothing more than capital functioning within the circulation sphere. The circulation process is one phase of circulation, no value is produced, and thus also no surplus-value. The same value simply undergoes changes of form. Nothing at all happens except the metamorphosis of commodities, which by its very nature has nothing to do with the creation or alteration of value. If a surplus-value is realized on the sale of the commodity produced, this is because it already existed in the commodity . . . *Commercial capital thus creates neither value nor surplus-value*. (C3, 392; emphasis added)

But the indirect effects described in this chapter are of considerable significance:

> In so far as (commercial capital) contributes towards shortening the circulation time, it can indirectly help the industrial capitalist to increase the surplus-value he produces. In so far as it helps to extend the market and facilitates the division of labour between capitals, thus enabling capital to operate on a larger scales, its functioning promotes the productivity of industrial capital and its accumulation. In so far as it cuts down turnover time, it increases the ratio of surplus-value to the capital advanced, i.e. [raises] the rate of profit. And in so far as a smaller part of capital is confined to the circulation sphere as money capital, it increases the portion of capital directly applied in production. (392–3)

Capital, we have seen all along, is very much about maintaining the continuity, smoothness and fluidity of movement, and commercial capital plays a crucial role in doing this.

ON CHAPTER 17 OF VOLUME III: COMMERCIAL PROFIT

As was shown in Volume II, and firmly reasserted in chapter 16, "the pure functions of capital in the circulation sphere create neither value nor surplus-value." But the industrial capitalist always has some money capital tied up in circulation. "The time these operations require sets limits to the formation of value and surplus-value, objectively as far as the commodities are concerned and subjectively as concerns the capitalist" (C3, 394). The implication, of course, is that any relaxation of these limits can contribute to the capacity to produce even more surplus value, as was shown in the preceding chapter. We now have a situation where a special capital performs these functions:

> Commercial capital . . . stripped of all the heterogeneous functions that may be linked to it, such as storage, dispatch, transport, distribution and retailing, and confined to its true function of buying in order to sell, creates neither value nor surplus-value, but simply facilitates their realization, and with this, the actual exchange of commodities, their transfer from one hand to another, society's metabolic process. (C3, 395)

But this commercial capital is still capital and must, like any capital, "yield the average profit." If it yielded a higher rate than industrial capital, then a portion of the latter would switch into it (and vice versa if its rate was lower). "No species of capital finds it easier than commercial capital to change its function and designation."

Marx is here invoking the principle of the equalization of the rate of profit examined at length in Part 2 of Volume III. Since we have not considered this principle, let me inject a brief comment on its significance. Capital tends to flow, Marx argues, to wherever the rate of profit is highest (particularly under competitive conditions). Intuitively, this makes sense. The result is a tendency for the profit rate to equalize across all sectors of the economy, from textiles to agriculture to oil production. The problem is that this tendency does not lead capital to flow to the areas that are most prolific in the production of surplus-value. Capital-intensive sectors (sectors with high value or organic composition of capital) capture surplus-value from labour-intensive (low-value or organic composition) sectors. This misallocation of investment in relation to value and surplus-value production has all manner of complicated consequences (including a tendency for the rate of profit to fall, because the profit rate, not surplus-value production, is necessarily the incentive to which the capitalist responds, given market forces). The effects of this tendency are occasionally invoked in the chapters that follow. Here, however, Marx simply asserts that the rate of profit on commercial capital will tend to equalize with the rate of profit on industrial capital. Later on, there will be instances where he will argue that, if the rate of profit in general tends to fall, then so must the rate of return on commercial capital. The question of whether the rate of interest on money capital equalizes with the rate of profit on industrial capital will be taken up in subsequent chapters.

Returning to the text, it is clear, says Marx, that, if the rate of profit on commercial capital is equalized with that of industrial capital, and if investment in commercial operations yields no value or surplus-value in itself, then "the surplus-value that accrues to it in the form of the average profit forms a portion of the surplus-value produced by the productive capital as a whole." The question then becomes: "How does commercial capital attract the part of the surplus-value or profit produced by productive capital that falls to its share?" (C3, 395).

After the usual tedious detailed calculations, Marx exposes as an "illusion" the idea, promoted from the standpoint of commercial capital, that it adds value because it buys cheap from the industrial capitalists and sells dearer to the consumer. The difference in value between what it pays out and what it sells for is construed and appears as a measure of the distinctive value that it produces.

"Assuming the predominance of the capitalist mode of production, this is not the way commercial profit is realized." Although it appears as if "the merchant sells all commodities above their values" (C3, 397), commercial capital in fact "contributes to the formation of the general rate of profit according to the proportion it forms in the total capital" (C3, 398). If "we consider all commodities together, the price at which the industrial capitalist class sells them is less than their value" (C3, 399). Therefore, "the merchant's sale price is higher than his purchase price not because it is above the total value, but rather because his purchase price is below this total value." In other words, "the average rate of profit already takes into account the part of the total profit that accrues to commercial capital."

"Commercial capital is involved in the equalization of the rate of profit even though it is not involved in the production of surplus-value. The general rate of profit thus already takes account of the deduction from the surplus-value which falls to commercial capital, i.e. a deduction from the profit of industrial capital" (C3, 400). It then follows that "the bigger the commercial capital is in comparison with industrial capital, the smaller the rate of industrial profit, and vice versa. While Marx does not make the point, this is vital for understanding the increasing importance and power of commercial capital in recent times. Once it is conceded that the relationship between the profits of industrial and commercial capital is in some sense contingent, then all sorts of possibilities exist for lopsided power relations to distort and disturb the supposed equilibrium that Marx assumes will be achieved through the equalization of the rate of profit. It also means that the investment of industrial plus commercial capital earns a lower aggregate rate of profit than that on industrial capital alone (the latter measure had been used in all earlier calculations in Volume III).

Marx then goes on to point out that, when "all other circumstances are the same, the relative size of commercial capital (though retailers, a hybrid species, form an exception) will be in inverse proportion to the speed of its turnover, i.e. in inverse proportion to the overall vigour of the reproduction process" (C3, 400). Historically this had not been the case, because it was commercial capital (as we saw in the historical chapter) that first fixed the prices of commodities "more or less according to their values, and it is the sphere of circulation that mediates the reproduction process in which a general rate of profit is first formed." Historically, "commercial profit originally determined industrial profit." As the capitalist mode of production matured, however, this relationship was reversed in ways already described in the history chapter. What we see here is the externalization of a whole series of internal costs and burdens that already existed for the industrial capitalist by virtue of his having a portion of his total capital wrapped up in circulation times and costs. The industrial capitalist in effect passes on all those costs and temporal problems to a different capital that manages them as best it can, in return for receiving a portion of the surplus-value produced in the form of the average rate of profit.

Later in the chapter, Marx restates this idea more explicitly:

> Since commercial capital is nothing at all but the form in which a part of industrial capital functioning in the circulation process has become autonomous . . . the problem must at the outset be put in the form in which the phenomena peculiar to commercial capital do not yet appear independently but are still in direct connection with industrial capital, of which commercial capital is a branch. (C3, 412)

Commercial capital incurs costs, of course. Many of these costs are of a form similar to the *faux frais* of circulation considered in Volume II, and fixed capital (the office space) is also involved. "Price calculation, book-keeping, fund management and correspondence are all part of this." Although in the beginning "the office is always infinitesimally small in relation to the industrial workshop. . . . The more the scale of production grows . . . the greater also the labour and other circulation costs involved in the realization of value and surplus-value" (C3, 413).

The most significant question, however, is "the position of the commercial wage-labourers employed by the merchant capitalist, in this case the dealer in commodities" (C3, 406). The commercial capitalist could of course operate entirely on his or her own. But with the development of accumulation this is no longer feasible, so wage labor has to be employed. "From one point of view, a commercial employee of this kind is a wage-labourer like any other. It is purchased as variable capital (not as a service out of revenues). Its value is determined in the normal way by the value of labor-power. But then there is a difference: "The commercial workers . . . cannot possibly create surplus-value for [the commercial capitalist] directly" (C3, 406). While the commercial capitalist might gain extra by paying workers less than their value (and in practice, of course, this often happens), in a purely functioning capitalist mode of production such cheating is ruled out by assumption. Obviously, commercial capital does not pay for the unpaid labor employed by the industrial capitalist, and so is complicit with labor exploitation in that sense. So it "appropriates a portion of this surplus value by getting it transferred from industrial capital to itself." But

for the individual merchant, the amount of profit depends on the amount of capital that he can employ in this process, and he can employ all the more capital in buying and selling, the greater the unpaid labour of his clerks. . . . Their unpaid labour, even though it does not create surplus-value, does create his ability to appropriate surplus-value, which, as far as this capital is concerned, gives exactly the same result; i.e. it is its source of profit. Otherwise the business of commerce could never be conducted in the capitalist manner, or on a large scale. Just as the unpaid labour of the worker creates surplus-value for productive capital directly, so also does the unpaid labour of the commercial employee create a share in that surplus-value for commercial capital. (C3, 407–8)

The greater the rate of exploitation by commercial capital, the greater the share of surplus-value it can appropriate from industrial capital.

But there is a residual difficulty: How to account for the variable capital laid out for the purchase of labor-power by the commercial capitalist? Should it be included in the total variable capital employed by the total capital even though it is not surplus-value producing? Is it productive or unproductive labor? Marx concedes that there is still a lot to do to investigate this topic, and attempts to do so with his usual meticulous investigations, which I do not intend to repeat here. His tentative conclusion is that

> what the merchant buys with [his variable capital] is merely commercial labour, i.e. labour needed for the functions of capital circulation, C-M and M-C. But commercial labour is the labour that is always necessary for a capital to function as commercial capital, for it to mediate the transformation of commodities into money and money into commodities. It is labour that realizes value but does not create any. And only in so far as a capital performs these functions [does this capital] take part in settling the general rate of profit, by drawing its dividends from the total profit. (C3, 411–12)

The upshot is that the wages of the commercial laborer do not

> stand in any necessary relationship to the amount of profit that he helps the capitalist realize. What he costs the capitalist and what he brings in for him are different quantities. What he brings in is a function not of any direct creation of surplus-value but of his assistance in reducing the cost of realizing surplus-value, in so far as he performs labour (part of it unpaid). (C3, 414)

This emphasis upon the imperative to reduce costs puts fierce pressure on the efficiency, forms of organization, wage rates, and rates of exploitation associated with commercial capital.

Generally speaking, Marx opines, "the commercial worker proper belongs to the better paid class of wage-labourer; he is one of those whose labour is skilled labour above average labour. His wage, however, has a tendency to fall . . . Firstly, because the division of labour within the commercial office means that only a one-sided development of ability need be produced" and, "Secondly, because basic skills, knowledge of commerce and languages, etc., are produced ever more quickly, easily, generally and cheaply, the more the capitalist mode of production adapts teaching methods, etc., to practical purposes. The general extension of popular education permits this variety of labour to be recruited from classes which were formerly excluded from it and were accustomed to a lower standard of living. . . . With few exceptions, therefore, the labour-power of these people is devalued with the advance of capitalist production." (C3, 415)

What has subsequently happened to this class of laborers, and what its current status is, clearly require detailed investigation. Its condition has plainly changed since Marx's day.

Nevertheless, it is always crucial to realize—and this is the important point—that "the increase in this labour is always an effect of the increase of surplus-value, and never a cause of it" (C3, 415).

ON CHAPTER 18 OF VOLUME III: THE TURNOVER OF COMMERCIAL CAPITAL

"The merchant buys, transforming his money into commodities, then sells, transforming the same commodities again into money, and so on in constant repetition." The merchant, in short, engages in two sets of metamorphoses—M-C and C-M—but conducts those operations in the sphere of circulation alone. It then follows that the speed of turnover is, for the commercial capitalist, of the essence: "Just as the same shilling circulating ten times buys ten times its value in commodities, so the same money capital belonging to the merchant . . . realizes a total commodity capital of ten times its value." The only difference is that "the same money capital, irrespective of the pieces of money of which it is composed, repeatedly buys and sells commodity capital to the amount of its value and hence repeatedly returns to the same owner as M + ΔM" (C3, 418).

There are, however, limits and barriers to this turnover process:

Now commercial capital certainly facilitates the turnover of productive capital; but it only does this in so far as it cuts down the latter's circulation time. It has no direct effect on the production time, which also forms a barrier to the turnover time of industrial capital. This is the first limit to the turnover of commercial capital. Secondly, however ... this turnover is decisively restricted by the speed and volume of the total individual consumption. (C3, 418)

The implications of this last point are largely ignored in what follows, presumably because consumption, for Marx, is a "singularity" and, as he argues in the *Grundrisse*, outside of the purview of political economy (I can think of no other reason). But, historically, it has been very much the role of the commercial capitalist to stimulate consumer desires, titillate the public with the wares the industrial capitalist might have to offer, and ensure, as far as possible, that potential customers have the money (usually credit) at their disposal to absorb the product speedily and keep the consumption dynamic expanding at a pace consistent with the endless accumulation sought by industrial capital. But Marx characterizes this barrier of consumer turnover time as "decisive." I am surprised that more has not been made of this point.

Some of this is mentioned in the passages that follow. But the issues are largely technical, and arise out of the autonomy of commercial capital within the circulation sphere. "Given the tremendous elasticity of the reproduction process, which can always be driven beyond any given barriers, [the commercial capitalist] finds no barrier in production itself, or only a very elastic one." Furthermore, "given the modern credit system, [commercial capital] has a large part of the society's total money capital at its disposal, so that it can repeat its purchases before it has definitively sold what it has already bought." It is therefore, by virtue of its autonomy, perpetually extending beyond what the market will bear so as to drive "this process beyond its own barriers" (i.e. beyond the "decisive restriction" set by the capacity of consumers to use up the product):

Despite the autonomy it has acquired, the movement of commercial capital is never anything more than the movement of industrial capital within the circulation sphere. But by virtue of this autonomy, its movement is within certain limits independent of the reproduction process and its barriers. . . . This inner dependence in combination with external autonomy drives commercial capital to a point where its inner connection is forcibly re-established by way of a crisis. (C3, 419)

The language here is very important. Commercial capital is autonomous, and can drive the whole system well beyond its limits (in particular with the help of credit). But there is an inner connection with the laws of value and surplus-value production and realization, and it is this inner connection that is reasserted in commercial (and financial) crises. This is the general proposition with which Marx is working. We will see it very much in action in subsequent chapters dealing with the circulation of interest-bearing capital. We here begin to see why it might be that crises within capitalism so often appear in the first instance as commercial and financial crises.

In the paragraphs that follow, Marx adduces some evidence in support of this idea. He asserts, for example, that commercial crises typically originate in the wholesale trade and banking, rather than in the retail trade (I am not sure this is empirically true). The full employment of both capital and labor leads to overextension that can

> continue quite happily for a good while, stimulated by prospective demand, and in those branches of industry business proceeds very briskly, as far as both merchants and industrialists are concerned. The crisis occurs as soon as the returns of these merchants who sell far afield (or who have accumulated stocks at home) become so slow and sparse that the banks press for payment for commodities bought, or bills fall due before any resale takes place. And then we have the crash, putting a sudden end to the apparent prosperity. (C3, 420)

This actually shifts the problem to ask why the bankers suddenly demand payments (which we will examine later).

But I think it is clear what is happening in the text here: we are moving onto that terrain where the formation and role of commercial and financial crises are being tentatively broached in a context where there is a complicated relation between the autonomy of merchants' capital (commercial and money capital) and some inner connection with value and surplus-value production and realization.

One of the ways in which the inner connection is asserted is through the equalization of the rate of profit, which is, however, sensitive to the different turnover times of industrial and commercial capital. The turnover of commercial capital "can mediate the turnovers of various different industrial capitals" simultaneously or in succession (C3, 420).

The turnover of industrial capital, on the other hand, is set by the periodicity of production and reproduction, in which circulation time also "forms a limit . . . which may have a more or less constricting effect on the formation of value and surplus-value through its effect on the scale of the production process . . . and hence on the formation of the general rate of profit" (C3, 424). Reducing the turnover time of industrial capital by reducing circulation time can raise the rate of profit. Commercial capital receives (in theory) the general rate of profit no matter what its turnover time. So, while commercial capital cannot increase its own rate of profit by accelerating its turnover time, it can affect the general rate of profit because less commercial capital is required for realization to be completed. "The absolute size of the commercial capital required stands in inverse proportion to the speed of its turnover." Furthermore, "circumstances that shorten the average turnover of commercial capital, such as the development of means of transport, for example, reduce in the same proportion the absolute magnitude of this commercial capital and hence raise the general rate of profit" (C3, 425).

There is, Marx argues, a "double effect" at work. Faster turnover is reducing the quantities of commercial capital required, while the general expansion of the scale and diversity of commodification is increasing the demand for commercial capital to deal with the rapidly increasing mass of commodities being produced. The result is "that not only does the mass of commercial capital grow, but so too does that of all the capital invested in circulation, e.g. in shipping, railways, telegraphs, etc." (C3, 426). Marx also concedes that a great deal of "semi-functioning commercial capital also grows . . . with the increased ease of entry into the retail trade, with speculation and a surplus of unoccupied capital" (C3, 426). The role of surplus capital in *Capital* always intrigues me. It keeps on cropping up as an issue, but is rarely highlighted as a foundational problem (I am on record as saying it is).

Marx closes out this chapter with some acerbic observations on how fetish conceptions and beliefs can all too easily be constructed out of the complex intertwining of merchant and productive activities: "All superficial and distorted views of the overall reproduction process are derived from consideration of commercial capital and from the notions that its specific movements give rise to in the heads of the agents of circulation." He even goes so far as to suggest that, "in the heads of the agents of capitalist production and circulation, ideas must necessarily form about the laws of production that diverge completely from [reality such that] the ideas of a merchant, a stock-jobber or a banker are necessarily quite upside-down." Even competition, he asserts, "necessarily plays in their minds a completely upside-down role."

"From the standpoint of commercial capital, therefore, turnover itself seems to determine price. On the other hand, while the speed of industrial capital's turnover, in so far as it enables a given capital to exploit more or less labour, has a determining and delimiting effect on the mass of profit and hence on the general rate of profit as well, commercial capital is faced with the rate of profit as something external to it, and this rate's inner connection with the formation of surplus-value is entirely obliterated." This turns out to be a generic problem when we enter into the realm of distribution, and we will encounter this phenomenon again when dealing with the circulation of interest-bearing capital. All trace of connection to surplus-value production is obliterated on the surface of society, and this is the source of all manner of fetish beliefs.

The power of this world of appearance is redoubled by the fact that individual commercial capitalists can indeed gain extra profit in competition by accelerating their turnover in relation to the social average. "In such a case he may make a surplus profit, just as industrial capitalists make surplus profits if they produce under more favourable conditions than the average" (this is what the theory of relative surplus-value in Volume I presents). Furthermore, "If the conditions that enable him to have a quicker turnover can themselves be purchased, e.g. the location of his sales outlet, he may pay extra rent for this; i.e. a part of his surplus profit is transformed into ground-rent" (C3, 430). This takes us into the realm of relations of commercial capital to land rent, and the ways this relation gets structured in urban settings (just look at the stores on Madison Avenue or Oxford Street and you will get Marx's meaning here).

Chapter 19 is a transitional chapter that leads into Part 5, dealing with money and finance capital and the credit system. It largely focuses on "the purely technical movements that money undergoes in the circulation process of industrial capital," but goes on to make clear that "these movements, having acquired autonomy as the function of a special capital which practises them, and them alone, as its specific operations, transform this capital into money-dealing capital." As a result, a definite part of the total capital now separates off and becomes autonomous in the form of money capital, its capitalist function consisting exclusively in that it performs these operations for the entire class of industrial and commercial capitalists. . . . The movements of this money capital are thus again simply movements of a now independent part of the industrial capital in the course of its reproduction process. (C3, 431)

The language of "autonomy" and "independence" of this form of capital is crucially important, and has all manner of implications for the analysis that later follows. Since the most important theses in this chapter are, however, elaborated upon later in the context of Marx's studies of money capital and finance, I shall not consider them further here.

CHAPTER FIVE

Interest, Credit and Finance (Chapters 21–26 of Volume III)

GENERAL REMARKS

I begin with an overview of Marx's argument in these first few chapters on money capital because, as is often the case with Marx, it is difficult to see the wood for the trees. The overall flow of argument is in fact very interesting, and the links that bind these chapters together are quite strong.

I must first remind you, however, that the text we have was painstakingly reconstructed by Engels from Marx's manuscripts. While most would agree that his was a stirring effort to be faithful to Marx's intent, subsequent studies of the original manuscripts have suggested that not all of Engels's choices might have been right. It was Engels, for example, who created the chapter headings out of a continuous manuscript. So it is hardly surprising that the links between the chapters are so strong. You will also notice that several long passages have been inserted by Engels himself in an effort to complete, correct or update Marx's own work. I will not dwell upon these problems here. I shall proceed as if the text before us is an accurate if incomplete sketch of Marx's views.

Marx begins by observing that there is something more to money in its role as capital than we have hitherto appreciated. Possession of money opens the way to (and is a necessary precondition for) the production of surplus-value and, consequently, the production of capital. Money capital (defined as money used to produce surplus-value) can consequently take on commodity form. It has both an exchange-value (a price) and a use-value. Its use-value is that it facilitates the production of surplus-value. Its exchange-value (price) is interest. This is a very different reading from that set out in Volume II, where Marx held that money as capital can only do as money does, i.e. be used for buying and selling. This conceptual shift is significant. I don't think it is about Marx just changing his mind or being inconsistent. Nor is it one of those examples of how relational meanings change as the context of the study unfolds. So what is going on here?

It is always wise, I think, when confronted with questions of this kind to examine the overall movement of Marx's argument. The significant clue in these chapters is Marx's explicit resurrection of the concept of fetishism, which has a vital place in the very first chapter of Volume I. The real foundations of capital (i.e. surplus-value production), he argued there, lie buried under surface appearances that are real but misleading. We really do go into a marketplace and use money to buy commodities (including labor-power). The problem is that these market relations mask the sociality and sensuality of the labor congealed in the production of commodities and the whole process that brought the commodities to market. Marx's project is to get behind these surface appearances.

So why does Marx return to the fetish nature of surface appearances at this point in the third volume of *Capital*?[1] Nowhere else in *Capital* does he do this so explicitly. Here he proclaims that "the fetish character of capital and the representation of this capital fetish is now complete" (C3, 516). He almost sounds gleeful and triumphalist about it. Interest-bearing money capital is, he proclaims, "the capital mystification in the most flagrant form."

I attach great significance to these remarks. It seems to me as if Marx, having defined the fetish at the outset as an external, objective and real barrier to true understanding, can now return to its very heart with a deep internal and subjective understanding of its destructive and potentially violent powers. We can, in short, now hope to get inside the head of the Wall Street speculator.   But who among us can truly claim that we are immune to the fetish siren of the pure lust for money and to its seemingly limitless powers of endless accumulation at a compounding rate? Can we now hope to understand what has entered our own heads too?

To put it more technically, money is portrayed in Volume I as the consummate fetish (it simultaneously represents and hides the sociality of labor). How money circulates as capital is the subject of investigation in Volume II. Here, in Volume III, the circulation of interest-bearing

---

1   This question takes center stage in Enrique Dussel, *Towards an Unknown Marx: A Commentary on the Manuscripts of 1861–3* (New York: Routledge, 2001). This text deserves close study.

capital reappears as the consummate fetish form of capital's circulation. But we should now understand how it is that money capital appears to have the magical and occult power to create ever more money in and by itself. This power has real effects. It "distorts" and "mystifies" (these are the words that Marx favors) the laws of motion of capital with dizzying and dire effects. Capital is therefore perpetually in danger of falling victim to its own fetish forms, and the false and fictitious understandings that flow therefrom.

So how does Marx put flesh upon the bones of this argument?

The price (exchange-value) of the money capital commodity is called interest, and the circuit of money capital now appears as the circulation of interest-bearing money capital. There is, however, no "natural rate of interest" of the sort that bourgeois theory proposed. Recall that Marx viewed "natural" price (the price of commodities when supply and demand are in equilibrium in the market) as an approximation to value. But in this case a "natural price" cannot exist.

So what determines the rate of interest, given that there is no inherent value to money capital as a commodity, or any "natural" rate of interest? It is set in the first instance, Marx argues, by the supply and demand for money capital. But, so far throughout *Capital*, Marx has held that supply and demand, being "particularities," explain nothing when they are in equilibrium. There is no "natural" point of equilibrium here. To believe so would be to accept the truth of a tautological proposition: that a value can be put on value. The interest rate is also set, he says, through competition. But the coercive laws of competition are also viewed as particularities, as the enforcers of inner laws of motion of capital that are not dictated by competition. Both supply and demand and competition have hitherto been dismissed as "particularities" (as the formulation given in the *Grundrisse* has it). Yet, at this point, they move center stage and explain everything. This is a huge conceptual shift.

We have here, I would like to suggest, a deep stress point in Marx's analysis. His reluctance (to the point of obsessive refusal) to deal in particularities in Volume II contrasts with the necessity of dealing with them here in order to understand the circulation of interest-bearing capital.

This then poses the question of the relation between these particularities and the general laws of motion of capital. It is in this context that the movement from the underlying reality examined in Volume II to the fetish of surface appearances in Volume III makes sense. We see why capital cannot survive without its fetish forms, and how those fetish forms distort and mystify the general laws of motion. But then, as some bourgeois critics have noted, if capitalism actually works on the basis of its forms of appearance, then why not simply describe these forms and forget all this complicated stuff about underlying realities, value theory, and the like? Marx's answer to that would presumably be that the violent contradictions exhibited in the surface movement can only be both anticipated and understood through a study of the underlying dynamics that both produce the fetish forms and underpin the fetish interventions in capital's laws of motion. Our objective in reading these chapters is therefore to uncover how these relations between underlying laws and forms of appearance actually work.

Marx treats of interest as both "autonomous and independent" (his words), but subsumed under the world of value and surplus-value production. What he means by "subsumed under" is what has to be established. Put another way, the interest rate and the circulation of interest-bearing capital can move in autonomous and independent ways because they are particularities determined by the vagaries of supply and demand and competition. Are there, to invoke the language of the introduction to the *Grundrisse*, ways in which these particularities return to affect the generality of production in determinate rather than merely contingent ways? If so, how do the general laws of motion of capital work when these particularities operate freely? Or are the particularities in some way beholden to the general laws of motion of capital?

This question becomes paramount because Marx clearly recognizes that the mass of money capital that comes together on the money market can and does act as "the common capital of the class" (C3, 490). It was in this form that it produced the huge financial and commercial disruptions of 1847–48 and 1857, in much the same way as the crisis of 2007–09 has shaken capital to its roots in our own times. If the circulation of interest-bearing capital functions as the "common capital of the class," then how can we possibly exclude it from any specification of the general laws of motion of capital? I pose that question as starkly as I can because whatever answer is given has huge consequences for how we theorize crisis formation under capitalism in general, and how we might use Marx's insights to approach the analysis of recent events in particular.

The first step is to examine how the circulation of interest-bearing capital acquires its autonomy and independence vis-à-vis the surplus-value (profit) generated through the circulation of industrial capital. Marx begins by distinguishing between money capitalists (those who hold money power) and industrial capitalists (those who organize the production of surplus-value). The rate of interest is fixed by competition between these two class factions. This puts the power relation between money capitalists and industrial capitalists into a central position, historically if not theoretically.

The history of this relation is sometimes interpreted teleologically— finance capital has inevitably moved into an increasingly dominant position vis-à-vis industrial capital since 1980 or so, and this produces a different kind of capitalism—finance capital—one that has different laws of motion to those defined when industrial capital was dominant (as was supposedly the case in Marx's time). Marx does not generally make this argument (though there are passages that make it seem so). I would not make this argument either. But there is no question that the balance of forces between these two class factions (as well as between them and the other major class factions, such as landlords and merchants) has never been stable, and that shifting hegemonies have certainly occurred. In the work of Giovanni Arrighi, for example, the very plausible argument is constructed that hegemonic shifts in the global economy (for example, from Britain to the US in the first half of the twentieth century) were preceded by phases of financialization (of the sort that Hilferding, Hobson and Lenin described in the early 1900s).[2] The undoubted wave of financialization that has occurred since the 1970s would then seem to presage another hegemonic shift (from the US to East Asia?). Understanding capitalism's history, therefore, requires that we come to terms with the balance of forces actually existing between these different class factions in different times and places, and the consequences that flow from competition between them.

But Marx goes further. What initially appears as a relation between

---

2 Rudolf Hilferding, *Finance Capital: A Study of the Most Recent Phase of Capitalist Development* (New York: Routledge, 2006); John Atkinson Hobson, *Imperialism* (Ann Arbor, MI: University of Michigan Press), 1965.

class factions is actually internalized within the persona of the individual capitalist. All capitalists embrace two very distinctive roles.
Industrial capitalists must always hold some of their capital in money
form. They always have the option, therefore, to use their money to
produce more surplus-value (and profit) through the expansion of
production, or simply to lend it to someone else in return for interest.
The logic of this decision holds out enticing possibilities to the individual capitalist. What would you rather do? Go through all the trouble of
actually producing surplus-value (dealing with pesky workers, unrelia-
ble machinery or fickle markets), or just lend the money away to earn
interest and go and live in the Bahamas on the proceeds? The ambition
of many industrial capitalists in Britain, Marx records, was often to
engage with production up to the point where it allowed them to become
rentiers or financiers, and to retire to a country estate and live comfort-
ably off the rents. But if everyone becomes a rentier trying to live off
interest or rent and no one produces surplus-value, Marx observes, then
the interest rate would fall to zero, while the potential profit on reinvesting in production would soar to untold heights (C3, 501). We here
encounter at least one point where the circulation of interest-bearing
capital has to be subservient and submissive to surplus-value production.

This immediately leads to another question: Is there an equilibrium
of some sort between the profit rate on industrial capital and the interest
rate on money capital? Does interest join profit on commercial capital in
the equalization of the profit rate? In the case of commercial capital,
there is a metamorphosis (an actual transaction) in which capital in
commodity form is realized as money. But interest is very different,
because it is a relation of money to money. There is no metamorphosis
involved at all. The problem is also that money, as Marx insisted in
Volume I (C1, 253), can be accumulated without limit. Interest-bearing
capital, in short, seems to have the magical (fetish) power to grow at a
compound rate (it is the goose that seems to have the power to lay its
own golden eggs, as Marx put it in Volume I). I put money in a savings
account and it grows as if by magic. If money can be accumulated without limit, then so can money capital. This is the ultimate capitalist fetish
fantasy.

The fantasy of compound growth forever takes hold—a fantasy that
Marx highlights here by reference to this wonderful image from a tract

published in 1772—"a shilling put out to 6 per cent compound interest at our Saviour's birth would have increased to a greater sum in gold than the whole solar system could hold" (C3, 520). This might explain, by the way, why we had to go off the gold standard and in the end relinquish any commodity base to paper money. The global money supply is then limitless, because it is just numbers. The Federal Reserve adds a trillion or so to the money supply at the drop of a hat (adding gold bullion would be a completely different proposition). While the idea of accumulation without limit "beggars all belief," it actually underpinned, Marx shows, the monetary and commercial explosions of 1847–48 and 1857–58. Lending and borrowing relations can spiral out of control to produce more and more money in credit form (the proliferation of paper IOUs). This necessarily lends a fictitious character to all credit markets.

It is here, therefore, that Marx invokes the very important but underdeveloped concept of fictitious capital. This gives a more tangible shape and form to the fetish of money capital. Its role is taken up through an incomplete and somewhat confusing examination of the commercial and financial crisis of 1847–48, all of which is mixed up with a critique of the ideas of someone called Overstone. I re-emphasize, once more, that fetishism, as defined in Volume I, is real and objective even as it disguises underlying value relations. The commodity really does exchange for money in the supermarket, but it does so in a way that conceals information about the labor (value) that went into its creation. Fictitious capital has to be understood in the same way. It is not the product of the delirious brain of some Wall Street banker high on cocaine. It is a real form of capital—money which has become a commodity with a price. While the price may be fictitious, we are all nevertheless forced to respond to it (be it in paying a mortgage, seeking interest on our savings, or borrowing to get a business off the ground).

We will take up the details later. But one neat illustration of its significance arises out of Marx's discussion of the distinction between loan capital (money lent for the expansion of production) and money extended to discount bills of exchange (which facilitates the realization of value in the market). Money capital intervenes in the circulation of industrial capital at two different points—at both the beginning and the conclusion of its circuit. The same financier can lend to developers to build tract housing and then ensure the market for that housing by lending to purchasers to buy that housing. Money capital thereby facilitates the supply of commodities as well as the demand. It is easy to see how this can become a closed circuit (an asset bubble in, say, the production and realization of housing). This is where the interest rate and the profit rate intersect and interact in powerfully important and all too often speculative ways.

The flow of argument in these chapters moves, therefore, from the technical aspects of circulation into far deeper territory in which all the vulnerabilities, fragilities and potential points of disruption identified in Volume II are made more and more tangible. Money capital and, even more importantly, money capitalists become autonomous and independent, but in some way subordinate to surplus-value production. The fetish character of the money form permits the creation of fantasies and fictions that periodically explode as uncontrollable and violent financial and commercial crises.

But the two roles of money and productive capitalist are internalized within the same person. How individual persons perceive their situation and behave therefore has great importance for understanding the dynamics of capital accumulation. Marx was not at all comfortable with exploring such "singularities" as the inner workings of the spirit of entrepreneurship, the psychology of expectations, and the role of trust in financial affairs, but there are enough occasional asides in these chapters to suggest that he could see how important such questions might be in any full analysis (the psychological aspects of this were later to be taken up much more explicitly, of course, by Keynes, and "expectations" have now become a whole field of investigation in bourgeois economics).

The analysis laid out here helps understand the financial and economic crisis of 2007–09 and the whole sequence of financial crises that preceded it. But we have to be careful not to misinterpret Marx's meaning or overextend what we might possibly learn from his incomplete and frequently foggy theorizing in relation to the crises of 1847–48 and 1857–58.

The philosophical pivot on which Marx's more technical argument rotates is, I think, laid out in the following commentary.

> If interest is spoken of as the price of money capital, this is an irrational form of price, in complete contradiction with the concept of the price of a commodity. Here, price is reduced to its purely abstract form,

completely lacking in content, as simply a particular sum of money that is paid for something which somehow or other figures as a use-value; whereas, in its concept, price is the value of this use-value expressed in money. Interest, as the price of capital, is a completely irrational expression right from the start. Here, a commodity has a double value, firstly a value, and then a price that is different from this value, although price is the money expression of value. (C3, 475)

What we are looking at here is nothing less than the tautology of the value of value. We have actually encountered something close to this argument before. In Volume I Marx notes that

things which in and for themselves are not commodities, things such as conscience, honor, etc., can be offered for sale by their holders, and thus acquire the form of commodities through their price. Hence a thing can, formally speaking, have a price without having a value. The expression of price is in this case imaginary, like certain quantities in mathematics. On the other hand, the imaginary price form may also conceal a real value relation or one derived from it, as for instance the price of uncultivated land, which is without value because no human labour is objectified in it. (C1, 197)

The key example Marx cites here is of the rent and price of uncultivated land. He could also have pointed out that the same is true of money. But, in the Volume I chapter on money, it would have undoubtedly confused matters beyond belief in a chapter that confuses quite enough as it is. Now we see that the imaginary price form applies to money itself. This poses some very deep and particular problems: what does this fetish "imaginary price form" conceal in relation to "real value relations"? And how should we think about its role?

And what, exactly, does Marx mean by "irrational and contradictory" here? He does not mean that interest is irrational and contradictory in the manner of a Sarah Palin speech or a Groucho Marx monologue. If it were so, then we would have to dismiss the category of interest as whimsical and arbitrary, throw up our hands in frustration, and just laugh or weep, depending on the implications. Marx is, I believe, making an analogy with number theory (hence the allusion to "certain quantities in mathematics" in the Volume I, quote above), in which the distinction between rational and irrational numbers is crucial. The irrational numbers are those that cannot be reduced to a fraction, and include such well-known examples as Ö2 and π (which, far from being whimsical or arbitrary, is one of the most important constants in mathematical theory, fixing the ratio of a circle's circumference to its diameter).

Marx is saying in effect that there is something incommensurable, and therefore irrational and contradictory, going on in the determination of the interest rate. When I consulted Wikipedia on irrational numbers (not being an expert at all on such matters), I found something interesting. Hippasus was a Greek Pythagorean who proved the existence of irrational numbers, and he showed that they are (just like the interest rate) "incommensurable, irrational and contradictory." Since the Pythagorean position was broadly that all relations can be reduced to whole numbers and their ratios, this finding came as quite a shock to his fellow Pythagoreans. According to one legend, Hippasus made his discovery while out at sea, and was promptly thrown overboard. This is, of course, a typical reaction of academicians when someone disproves their favorite theory. Marx was long ago thrown overboard by the economists, who probably to this day would be horrified to hear that one of their most fundamental categories—the interest rate—is incommensurable, irrational and contradictory. But Marx is a strong swimmer in the tides of history. He keeps clambering back on board to remind everyone that this is indeed the case, as should be apparent to everyone who watched the events of 2007–09 in even the most cursory manner. Whether he will be thrown overboard yet again depends upon whether things settle down to a level satisfactory to the compound accumulation of capital and wealth without limit.

The irrationality and the contradictory character of interest on capital has to be appreciated in this number-theory sense. We can then more easily see how fictitious forms get produced and with what effects, in much the same way that constants like π can be used in engineering. Thinking this way puts us in a better position to understand both the practical and theoretical consequences that flow therefrom.

There are, however, two big and interrelated problems that then need to be addressed. First, to what degree does Marx's insistence on the fetish character of the interest that underpins the category of fictitious capital, alter our understanding of how the general laws of motion of capital work? While the distributive category of commercial capital appears absorbable into the general theoretical framework that Marx has hitherto constructed, this does not appear to be the case with the effects of the circulation of interest-bearing capital in relation to the circulation of industrial capital. Nor, in my view, and in spite of Marx's protestations to the contrary, is this the case with the other crucial "irrational number" in Marx's theory—land rent. Like interest, this is a form of fictitious capital that is real and has real consequences. When you come to Manhattan to live, you can't say that land rent and house prices are fictitious and that you are not going to pay anything for such a fiction. And most people who buy do so by paying interest on a mortgage—which is a form of fictitious capital.

So where does this leave us with respect to the forces that render the interest rate subservient and subordinate to the production of value and surplus-value? While it is clear that we cannot all live on interest or rents if no one produces value, and while there is also an overwhelming sense that in commercial and monetary crises such as those of 1847–48 and 1857–58, and in our case 2007–09, there is some kind of disciplinary power being exerted in which all the fantasies and fictions of speculative financial activity are brought back to the earthliness of real production, there are also disturbing indications in Marx's analysis that the power relation between finance and production might also be the other way around.

One indication of this is found in a seemingly interesting sidebar to Marx's analysis. When an industrial capitalist accumulates capital in money form and puts it in a bank to earn interest (which happens, as we saw, in relation to fixed-capital circulation because the capitalist has to hoard money capital for replacement), then that interest appears as a pure rate of return on the property right of ownership. This passive return on the pure property right contrasts with the active creation of surplus-value through the organization and superintendence of production. Why, therefore, would the capitalist not pay someone wages of superintendence to take care of production while they live on the return to the pure property right? Out of this arises an interesting and crucial distinction within the history of capitalism between ownership on the one hand and superintendence and management on the other. With these general points in mind, let us take up the details of the text.

ON CHAPTER 21 OF VOLUME III: INTEREST-BEARING CAPITAL

Marx begins by reminding us that the general rate of profit is created out of the activities of both industrial and merchant (i.e. commercial) capital, and that the profit rate is equalized between them. "Whether capital is invested industrially in the sphere of production, or commercially in that of circulation, it yields the same annual average profit in proportion to its size" (C3, 459). Money, however, is different. It acquires

> an additional use-value, namely the ability to function as capital. Its use-value here consists precisely in the profit that it produces when transformed into capital. In this capacity of potential capital, as the means to the production of profit, it becomes a commodity, but a commodity of a special kind. Or what comes to the same thing, capital becomes a commodity. (C3, 459–60)

The holder of money possesses the means to make surplus-value, and can lend that money to another in return for interest. The money capitalist and the producer share the surplus-value that the money capital can be used to produce. Interest is "a particular name, a special title, for a part of the profit which the actually functioning capitalist has to pay the capital's proprietor, instead of pocketing it himself." Thus does Marx acknowledge the power of pure ownership of capital as a right to claim a rate of return.

Commodity and money movements and exchanges occur all the time within the industrial circuit of capital and, at each moment, there is the potential for either to be deployed to make more surplus-value. But, in these transactions, money can only do as money does (i.e. facilitate buying and selling), and the commodity can only do as the commodity does (be sold for either final or productive consumption). But "with interest-bearing capital," says Marx,

> the situation is different, and this is precisely what constitutes its specific character. The owner of money who wants to valorize this as interest-bearing capital parts with it to someone else, puts it into circulation, makes it into a commodity *as capital*; as capital not only for himself but also for others. It is not only capital for the person who alienates it, but it is made over to the other person as capital

—to be used as such right from the start, as value that possesses the use-value of being able to create surplus-value or profit. "It is neither paid out nor sold, but simply lent; alienated only on condition that it is, first, returned to its starting point after a definite period of time, and, second, is returned as realized capital, so that it has realized its use-value of producing surplus-value" (C3, 464–5).

A possible source of confusion may arise because capital can be lent out in either money or commodity form. Factories and machines can just as easily be lent in return for interest as money. Indeed, certain commodities, "by the nature of their use-value, can be lent only as fixed capital, such as houses, boats, machines, etc. But all loan capital, whatever form it might have and no matter how its repayment might be modified by its use-value, is always a special form of money capital" (C3, 465). Hereafter, Marx subsumes loans in commodity form under the general form of the circulation of interest-bearing capital. One very important implication does follow, however. If property (houses, for example) and land can also be lent out, then an inner relation is surely established between rent and the circulation of interest-bearing capital. Marx does not note this inner relation here, but I have pursued it elsewhere, and the more I pursue it the more this seems to me a vital but missing link in Marx's political economy.

Marx concludes this part of the argument a few pages later (after a diversion to subject Proudhon's views to critique):

> The lending capitalist parts with his capital, transfers it to the industrial capitalist, without receiving an equivalent. But this is in no way an act of the actual cyclical process of capital; it simply introduces this circuit, which is to be effected by the industrial capitalist. This first change of place on the part of the money does not express any act of metamorphosis, neither purchase nor sale. Ownership is not surrendered, since no exchange takes place and no equivalent is received. (C3, 468–9)

After the industrial capitalist has used it to produce surplus-value, the money has to be returned to the lender. All of this is a matter of legal transactions.

> The initial act which transfers the capital from the lender to the borrower is a legal transaction that has nothing to do with the actual

reproduction process of capital [i.e. the labor process], but simply introduces it. The repayment which transfers the capital that has flowed back from the borrower to the lender again is a second legal transaction, the complement of the first; the one introduces the real process, the other is a subsequent act after that is completed. The point of departure and the point of return, the lending-out of the capital and its recovery, thus appear as arbitrary movements mediated by legal transactions. (C3, 469)

So what, then, is the relation between these legal transactions and the underlying realities of surplus-value production?

Capital as a special kind of commodity also has a kind of alienation peculiar to it. Here therefore the return does not appear as a consequence and result of a definite series of economic processes, but rather as a consequence of a special legal contract between buyer and seller. The period of the reflux depends on the course of the reproduction process; in the case of interest-bearing capital, its return as capital *seems* to depend simply on the contract between lender and borrower. And so the reflux of capital, in connection with this transaction, no longer appears as a result determined by the production process, but rather as if the capital lent out had never lost the form of money. Of course, these transactions are actually determined by the real refluxes. But this is not apparent in the transaction itself. (C3, 470)

In other words, the legal relations and contracts conceal a relation between the circulation of interest-bearing capital on the one hand and the production of surplus-value on the other. But the word "appear" recurs frequently in these sentences and, as I have often noted, that usually signals that something else is also going on that is not easily visible:

In the real movement of capital, the return is a moment in the circulation process. Money is first transformed into means of production; the production process transforms it into a commodity; by the sale of the commodity it is transformed back into money, and in this form it returns to the hands of the capitalist who first advanced the capital in its money form. (C3, 470)

But all these intermediate steps are eliminated from view in the legal contract that specifies M-M′ and nothing more. "The real cyclical movement of money as capital is the assumption behind the legal transaction by which the borrower of the money has to return it to the lender." Thus, Marx concludes, "lending is thus the appropriate form for its alienation *as capital*, instead of as money or commodity" (C3, 471).

The next step is to take up specifically the question of interest. The circulation process here considered has the form of M-M + ΔM, where ΔM is the interest, "or that part of the profit which does not remain in the hands of the functioning capitalist but falls rather to the money capitalist" (C3, 472). "With other commodities, the use-value is ultimately consumed, and in this way the substance of the commodity disappears, and with it its value. The commodity of capital, on the other hand, has the peculiar property that the consumption of its use-value not only maintains its value and use-value but in fact increases it." So the "use-value of the loaned money capital . . . appears as a capacity to represent and increase value." Again, "as distinct from an ordinary commodity, however, this use-value is itself a value, i.e. the excess of the value that results from the use of money as capital over its original magnitude. The profit is this use-value" (C3, 473).

This is a very important statement. In the same way that Marx argued in Volume I that, unlike other commodities, money never leaves circulation once it enters it ("circulation sweats money from every pore" was how he charmingly put it), so interest-bearing capital can continue circulating indefinitely. But we also see here how it can endlessly grow.

More specifically, "the use-value of money lent out is its capacity to function as capital and as such to produce the average rate of profit under average conditions. . . . The sum of value, the money, is given out without an equivalent"—again, a condition that marks this transaction off from other forms of commodity exchange—"and returned after a certain period of time. The lender remains the owner of this value throughout, even after it has been transferred from him to the borrower." This means that interest is, in effect, a rate of return to be attributed to pure ownership, as opposed to actual use. It is, however, "only by its use that it is valorized and realized as capital. But it is as *realized* capital that the borrower has to pay it back, i.e. as value plus surplus-value (interest); and the latter can only be a part of the profit he has realized. Only a part, and not the whole" (C3, 474). If it were the whole, then the industrial capitalist would have no incentive to produce.

This relation entails a relation "between two kinds of capitalist, the money capitalist and the industrial or commercial capitalist." So here, then, we have the introduction of the idea of different factions of capital in relation to each other, but each with distinctive concerns, interests and needs. What then follows is a disquisition on the irrationality and contradictory qualities of the price of money as already outlined above, concluding that, in spite of everything, "a price that is qualitatively distinct from value is an absurd contradiction" (C3, 476).

What, then, are the inner connections at work here that tie the interest rate to value production? Marx goes back to the beginning of his analysis:

> Money or a commodity is already potential capital in itself, just as labour-power is potential capital. For (1) money can be turned into elements of production, and is already, just as it is, simply an abstract expression of these elements, their existence as value; (2) the material elements of wealth possess the property of being already potential capital, because their complementary antithesis, the thing that makes them capital—namely wage-labour—is present as soon as capitalist production is assumed.

For these reasons, "money, and likewise commodities, are in themselves latent, potential capital, i.e. can be sold as capital; in this form they give control of the labour of others, give a claim to the appropriation of others' labour, and are themselves self-valorizing value" (C3, 477). Then follows the real kicker:

> Capital further appears as a commodity in so far as the division of profit into interest and profit proper is governed by supply and demand, i.e. by competition, just like the market prices of commodities. But here the distinction is just as striking as the analogy. If supply and demand coincide, the market price of the commodity *corresponds to its price of production* [emphasis added; see below], i.e. its price is then governed by the inner laws of capitalist production, independent of competition, since fluctuations in supply and demand explain nothing but divergences between market prices and prices of production.

This is a familiar argument from Volume I—that supply and demand cease to explain anything when in equilibrium. This is even true with wages:

> If supply and demand coincide, their effect ceases, and wages are equal to the value of labour-power. It is different, though, with interest on money capital. Here competition does not determine the divergences from the law, for there *is* no law of distribution other than that dictated by competition; as we shall go on to see, there is no "natural" rate of interest. What is called the natural rate of interest simply means the rate established by free competition. There are no "natural" limits to the interest rate. Where competition does not just determine divergences and fluctuations, so that in a situation where its reciprocally acting forces balance, all determination ceases, what is to be determined is something lawless and arbitrary. (C3, 478)

This is a big statement: the dynamics of capital accumulation become lawless and arbitrary. The whole edifice for rules of engagement that Marx set up in the *Grundrisse*, and that he has hitherto deployed throughout *Capital* to explore the generality of the laws of motion of capital, here appears to be stretched to breaking point. Whether or not the whole edifice crumbles depends on what happens in the subsequent chapters. As Marx says: "more about this in the next chapter"!

What is clear is that the avoidance of particularities that restricts the analysis in Volume II is here abandoned. If the result is "lawless and arbitrary," then what happens to the general laws of motion that have hitherto been Marx's main focus of concern? We have a very paradoxical situation. Competition is throughout envisaged as the enforcer of the inner laws of motion of capital; the enforcement mechanism is here understood to be determinant in the circulation of interest-bearing capital in its role as the common capital of the class—but the enforcer is lawless and arbitrary.

This constitutes a clear break with the framework given in the *Grundrisse*. Marx recognizes that he cannot accommodate the circulation of interest-bearing capital within the framework of assumptions that have hitherto guided his studies. While there may be ways to understand how and why this divergence occurs in the case of interest-bearing capital (as opposed to other aspects of distribution, such as rent and profit on merchants' capital, that Marx believed he had successfully incorporated within the framework), I cannot help but think it must have been difficult and stressful for him to confront where this break might take him. On the one hand, the nervous energy on display in these chapters suggests a certain exhilaration at leaving the constraints of the framework behind, while the loss of control (the indeterminacy and the autonomization) threatens the theoretical edifice he has constructed. It is no wonder that, as Engels reports in his introduction, Marx's health deteriorated markedly when writing these chapters. I sympathize, since it took me more than two years to write the two chapters on Marx's views on money capital and finance in *The Limits to Capital*, and I became pretty demented in the process.

There is another point of stress hidden in these paragraphs. Marx uses the term "prices of production" rather than "values." This change of language is significant, but we are not in a position to understand it here because it arose earlier in Volume III (chapters 9 and 10), out of an analysis of what happens when the profit rate is equalized through competition across industries operating with different value compositions. Briefly summarized, the effect of the equalization of the rate of profit is that commodities trade at prices of production formed by the value of constant and variable capital plus the value of the average rate of profit ($c + v + p$), rather than according to the formula earlier assumed which, was that commodity values were constituted as $c + v + s$. The result is that sectors with low value composition (high labor content) end up subsidizing sectors with high value composition (high constant capital content). We cannot go further into this here. While I do not think this has a huge impact upon what happens with the circulation of interest-bearing capital, it points to yet another foundational shift in Marx's analysis.

So what happens when competition moves from being the mere enforcer of the inner laws of motion of capital to become an active determinant of the lawlessness of capital accumulation? In several of the outlines that Marx sketched out of what *Capital* would look like as a series of books, he recognized that a book on competition would be logically required to complete the analysis. The book was never written (though there is a draft chapter included at the end of Volume III on "the illusions created by competition"). Here we are seeing exactly why such a book might be, and still is, needed.

There are a couple of minor asides in this chapter that are worthy of some comment. Firstly, Marx early on subjects to critique Gilbart's view on the "justice of transactions between agents of production" (C3, 460). This issue arises because the interest rate is a legal contract and not an exchange of commodities. In Marx's view, justice is a "natural consequence" of "the relations of production." While the "legal forms" appear as "voluntary actions of the participants, as the expressions of their common will and as contracts that can be enforced on the parties concerned by the power of the state," the content of this justice "corresponds to the mode of production and is adequate to it." So both slavery and cheating on the quality of commodities can be considered unjust from the standpoint of the capitalist mode of production, whereas wage-labor cannot.

Several times in *Capital*, Marx attacks the idea that there is some ideal, abstracted notion of justice outside of existing social relations. He does not entirely embrace the idea that Plato, in *The Dialogues*, attributes to Thrasymachus—that justice is that which the most powerful players in society dictate (a view that Plato endeavors to disprove in favor of some perfected ideal of justice); Marx resolutely refuses, however, to accept the Platonic universal ideal. Justice is embedded in the social relations of a given mode of production (the liberal theory of justice therefore derives from the rise of capital to dominance in social relations). The "just" rate of interest is that which is consistent with the continuous reproduction of capital. It is clearly distinguishable from usury. This should not be taken to mean that there is nothing contradictory in bourgeois conceptions of justice that might be played upon in the course of class struggles. But Marx rejects the idea that there is some Archimedean point from which some perfected version of justice and of ethics can be applied to judge the world. This is the major defect, he argues, in Proudhon's reasoning.

The second aside is the direct critique of Proudhon's views on interest and credit. As I have noted elsewhere, Marx is not always fair to Proudhon, but here I think he is quite right to point out that Proudhon's failure to understand the theory of surplus-value and its relation to the circulation of interest-bearing capital led Proudhon to suppose that some sort of free credit bank would mark the end of exploitation (C3, 467). For Marx, it is the exploitation of living labor in production that matters, and not the extraction of interest. Tinkering with the interest rate while ignoring the exploitation of living labor in production was, in Marx's view, ridiculous politics.

ON CHAPTER 22 OF VOLUME III:
DIVISION OF PROFIT AND THE RATE OF INTEREST

Marx recognizes that the rate of interest can fluctuate over the short term for all sorts of reasons. He abstracts from all these movements and the tendency to equalize the rate of interest on the world market in order to concentrate on "the way that interest acquires autonomy vis-à-vis profit" (C3, 480). He begins by assuming that there is "a fixed ratio between the total profit and the part of it paid to the money capitalist as interest" (C3, 481). This means that the average rate of profit ultimately determines the maximum limit of interest (C3, 482). If there is a tendency for the rate of profit to fall, as Marx often argues, then obviously the rate of interest must also tend to fall. But if the interest rate depends on conditions of supply and demand for money capital, then how does this vary over the industrial cycle? "If we consider the turnover cycles in which modern industry moves—inactivity, growing animation, prosperity, overproduction, crash, stagnation, inactivity, etc., cycles which it falls outside of our scope to analyze further—we find that a low level of interest generally corresponds to periods of prosperity or especially high profit, a rise of interest rate comes between prosperity and its collapse, while maximum interest up to extreme usury corresponds to a period of crisis." This is an empirical generalization, however, and not a theoretical statement. It also presumes no state intervention in the money supply of the sort that could drive the interest rate down to close to zero at the height of the crisis (as has been the case in the US since 2007). I say this because Marx is obviously struggling to get a handle on the supply and demand conditions for money capital as they fluctuate, and has no way to do it apart from empirical generalization of the moving relation between the rate of profit and the interest rate.

There are, he notes, some independent reasons (other than that given by the tendency of the profit rate to fall) for the rate of interest to fall. To begin with, there is a perpetual temptation for those who make money out of the production of surplus-value to retire, particularly as they age, simply to live off the interest of money capital and not be troubled by the uncertainties of production. Marx quotes George Ramsay's remark on "how much more numerous in proportion to the population is the class of *rentiers* . . . in England! As the class of *rentiers* increases, so also does that of lenders of capital because they are one and the same." This tendency is exacerbated by "the development of the credit system, the ever growing control this gives industrialists and merchants over the monetary savings of all classes of society through the mediation of the bankers, as well as the progressive concentration of these savings on a mass scale, so that they can function as money capital." This "must also press down the rate of interest" (C3, 484). For the first time, Marx here addresses a crucial question: the role of the financial system in assembling the initial capital for circulation (promising, as always, "more on this later"). The role of the financial system in mobilizing the savings of all classes and deploying those savings as money capital has been of increasing importance throughout the history of capitalism.

The problem, however, is that "the prevailing average rate of interest in a country, as distinct from the constantly fluctuating market rate, cannot be determined by any law. There is no natural rate of interest, therefore, in the sense that economists speak of a natural rate of profit and a natural rate of wages" (C3, 484). It is, therefore, "competition as such that decides, [and consequently] the determination is inherently accidental, purely empirical, and only pedantry or fantasy can seek to present this accident as something necessary" (C3, 485). But the effects of competition are mitigated by the fact that "custom, legal tradition, etc. are just as much involved," while "how the two parties who have claims on this profit [the industrial capitalists and the lenders] actually share it between them is as it stands a purely empirical fact, pertaining to the realm of chance, just as respective shares in the common profit of a business partnership are distributed among its various members" (C3, 486). This is very different with the relation between wages and profit (and, Marx claims, with the relation between rent and profit): "With interest . . . the *qualitative distinction* proceeds from the *purely quantitative division* of the same piece of surplus-value," whereas, in the case of wages and rents, it is the other way round. The landlord delivers a tangible commodity—land—and the laborer delivers labor-power, but the money capitalist delivers only money capital, which is the representation of value and which contributes nothing tangible to production.

The general rate of profit is determined, of course, by the factors that determine the surplus-value (the mass of surplus-value, the mass of capital advanced, and the state of competition). This contrasts with interest which, as we have seen, is determined through supply and demand. But there are two factors

> which favor the consolidations of the interest rate: (1) the historical pre-existence of interest-bearing capital and the existence of a general rate of interest handed down by tradition; (2) the far stronger direct influence that the world market exerts on the establishment of the interest rate, independently of the conditions of production in a country, as compared with the influence of the profit rate. (C3, 490)

Money, particularly in its credit form, is, as I remarked earlier, the "butterfly" form of capital that can flit around pretty much at will. Reports on interest rate movements on the stock markets are like "meteorological reports," yet there are convergences toward a generality of price on loan capital:

> On the money market it is only lenders and borrowers who face one another. The commodity has the same form, money. All particular forms of capital, arising from its investments in particular spheres of production or circulation, are obliterated here. It exists in the undifferentiated, self-identical form of independent value, of money. Competition between particular spheres now ceases; they are all thrown together as borrowers of money, and capital confronts them all in a form still indifferent to the specific manner and mode of its application. Here capital really does emerge, in the pressure of its demand and supply, as *the common capital of the class.* (C3, 490)

This is a pretty startling idea. How on earth can we uncover the general laws of motion of capital without understanding how money capital works as the common capital of the class?

> Money capital on the money market, moreover, really does possess the form in which it is distributed as a common element among these various spheres, among the capitalist class, quite irrespective of its particular application, according to the production requirements of each particular sphere. On top of this, with the development of large-scale industry money capital emerges more and more, in so far as it appears on the market, as not represented by the individual capitalist, the proprietor of

this or that fraction of the mass of capital on the market, but rather as a concentrated and organized mass, placed under the control of the bankers as representative of the social capital in a quite different manner to real production. The result is that, as far as the form of demand goes, capital for loan is faced with the entire weight of a class, while as far as supply goes, it itself appears *en masse* as loan capital. (C3, 491)

For all of Marx's attempts to reduce the "arbitrary and lawless" movements of interest rates deriving from competition and supply and demand conditions to empirical regularities and customary habits, there is at the core of all of this a deep asymmetry within the functioning of the financial and monetary system: individual capitalists have to procure money capital for particular projects from bankers who control a mass of the universal equivalent (which mirrors the asymmetry of the movements M-C and C-M noted in Volume I).

ON CHAPTER 23 OF VOLUME III: INTEREST AND PROFIT OF ENTERPRISE

The capitalist class is divided between money capitalists and industrial capitalists, and competition between them creates the rate of interest (C3, 493). So "how does it happen," Marx asks, "that even the capitalist who simply uses his own capital, and no borrowed capital, classes part of his gross profit under the special category of interest and takes particular account of it as such? And how does it subsequently happen that all capital, whether borrowed or not, is distinguished as interest-bearing capital from itself in its function as capital bringing a net profit?" (C3, 495). The answer to these questions requires that we

proceed from the assumption that the money capitalist and productive capitalist actually do come face to face, not just as legally separate persons but as persons who play quite different roles in the reproduction process, or in whose hands the same capital really does go through a double and completely different movement. The one simply lends the capital, the other applies it productively. (C3, 495)

What then emerges is the significance of the legal status of ownership of property. "The interest that he pays to the lender appears therefore as a part of the gross profit that accrues to *property in capital as such*" (C3, 497; emphasis added). Interest therefore

> appears as the mere fruit of property in capital, of capital in itself, abstracted from the reproduction process of capital in so far as it does not "work", i.e. function; whereas profit of enterprise appears to him as the exclusive fruit of the functions he performs with the capital, as the fruit of capital's movement and process, as process that appears to him now as his own activity, in contrast to the non-activity and non-participation of the money capitalist in the production process.

Interest "accrues to the money capitalist, the lender, who is simply the owner of the capital and thus does represent mere property in capital before the production process and outside it." This "mutual ossification and autonomization" (note the theme of autonomy here) "of the two parts of the gross profit, as if they derived from two separate sources, must now be fixed for the entire capitalist class and the total capital" and this is so "irrespective of whether the capital applied by the active capitalist is borrowed or not, or whether or not the money capitalist who owns the capital uses it himself." In fact,

> the person who applies the capital, even if he works with his own capital, breaks down into two persons, the mere owner of capital and its user; his capital itself, with respect to the categories of profit that it yields, breaks down into *owned* capital, capital *outside* the production process, which yields an interest, and capital *in* the production process, which yields profit of enterprise as capital in process. (C3, 498)

This then becomes a "qualitative division for the total capital and the capitalist class as a whole" (C3, 499).

The passivity of money capital as property commanding interest confronts the activism of the capitalist producer who uses the money capital to produce the surplus-value and receive profit of enterprise. This distinction not only applies to the whole capitalist class, but is internalized within the capitalist as person.

"Whether the industrial capitalist operates with his own capital or with borrowed capital in no way alters the fact that the class of money capitalists confronts him as a special kind of capitalist, money capital as an autonomous kind of capital, and interest as the separate form of surplus-value that corresponds to this specific capital" (C3, 500). But the individual capitalist "has the choice between lending his capital out as interest-bearing capital or valorizing it himself as productive capital, no matter whether it exists as money capital right at the start or has first to be transformed into money capital" (C3, 501). An entrepreneur can start up a business on borrowed capital, but once surplus-value is produced that entrepreneur can choose to lend out a part of that surplus-value to someone else rather than reinvest it.

But it would be "utter nonsense" to suppose that "all capital could be transformed into money capital." The idea that "capital could yield interest on the basis of the capitalist mode of production without functioning as productive capital, i.e. without creating surplus-value, of which interest is simply one part," is "still greater nonsense":

> If an inappropriately large number of capitalists sought to transform their capital into money capital, the result would be a tremendous devaluation of money capital and a tremendous fall in the rate of interest; many people would immediately find themselves in the position of being unable to live on their interest and thus compelled to turn themselves back into industrial capitalists. (C3, 501)

Here we see one clear point where the circulation of interest-bearing capital is subordinated to and dominated by surplus-value production.

So while there is no "natural rate of interest," there is some suggestion here that a balance of forces (or in the case of individuals, some balance of sentiments) would be necessary between the money capitalists on the one hand and the activities of surplus-value production on the other. Where that balance might lie we have at this point no means of knowing. (Is it purely conjunctural and accidental?) But that the consequence of chronic imbalance towards, say, money capital would be its devaluation is clearly signaled. Is this the kind of imbalance that is signaled by the very low rates of interest that have prevailed in Japan since 1990 and in the US since 2007?

Marx then examines the impact this has upon class relations. The antithesis and opposition between labor and capital occur at the point of production of surplus-value. But we are now looking at the relation between money capitalists and production capitalists. As a result, the antithesis to wage-labour is obliterated in the form of interest; for interest-bearing capital as such does not have wage-labour as its opposite but rather functioning capital; it is the capitalist actually functioning in the reproduction whom the lending capitalist directly confronts, and not the wage-labourer. . . . Interest-bearing capital is capital *as property* as against capital *as function*. But if capital does not function, it does not exploit workers and does not come into opposition with labour. (C3, 503)

The importance of this idea for thinking through the dynamics of class struggles cannot be overemphasized. Whereas the lines of opposition and struggle between workers and functioning capitalists are clear both in the labor process and in the labor market, the relation between workers and money capital as property is far more abstract and opaque. Worker mobilization against the power of money capital and its mode of circulation is much more problematic. Small businesses are much more likely to oppose the power of banks and financial institutions than are workers. Such struggles are hard to incorporate into the usual interpretations of class struggle. Historically, struggles against the powers of money capitalists (and against rentiers more generally) have tended to take (and continue to take) a populist form. The intuitive populism manifest in the "Occupy Wall Street" movement provides an excellent recent example.

But interest-bearing capital puts pressure on productive capital to produce surplus-value, and the higher the interest rate the more pressure it exerts. Producers can then say to workers that the high rate of exploitation they have to impose upon them reflects high rates of interest, and so divert attention from themselves to the greed and power of the bankers. The dynamics of class struggle can thus be displaced, and even distorted.

There is yet another, deeper complication. The internalization of the two different roles of money capitalist and production capitalist within the same person naturally leads the functioning capitalist to interpret his profit of enterprise

as independent of his property in capital and rather as the result of his functions as a non-owner, as a *worker*. He inevitably gets the idea into his head that his profit of enterprise—very far from forming any antithesis with wage-labour and being only the unpaid labour of others—is rather itself a wage, "wages of superintendence of labour", a higher wage than that of the ordinary wage labourer (1) because it is complex labour, and (2) because he himself pays the wages. (C3, 503–4)

Once things are conceptualized in this way, however, the capitalist can choose between doing the work himself (and paying himself the wages of superintendence), or paying someone else to do that work. It then becomes all too easy to forget that interest and profit of enterprise are "simply parts of surplus-value, and that such a division [between wages in general and wages of superintendence] can in no way change its nature, its origin and its conditions of existence" (C3, 504). The remainder of the chapter takes up the ramifications of such a choice.

The capitalist's logic runs as follows. If "interest represents mere ownership of capital," then in relation to surplus-value production it "is a relationship between two capitalists, not between capitalist and worker." It thus

gives the other part of profit the qualitative form of profit of enterprise, and subsequently of wages of superintendence. [The capitalist] obtains surplus-value not because he works as a *capitalist* but rather because, leaving aside his capacity as a capitalist, he *also* works. This part of surplus-value is therefore no longer surplus-value at all, but rather its opposite, the equivalent of labour performed. Since the estranged character of capital, its antithesis to labour, is shifted outside the actual process of exploitation, i.e. into interest-bearing capital, this process of exploitation itself appears as simply a labour process[!], in which the functioning capitalist simply performs different work from that of the workers. The labour of exploiting and the labour exploited are identical, both being labour.

All of this is mirrored, of course, "in the consciousness of the capitalist" (C3, 506).

In this way, "one part of the profit can be separated off as wages." In large-scale enterprises marked by a complicated, detailed division of labour, this wage can actually be paid to a manager. This "work of supervision and management necessarily arises" (note the necessity invoked here) "where the direct production process takes the form of a socially combined process," but the form of this association varies (C3, 507). Complicated cooperation relations in enterprises require a "conductor of the orchestra" (an image evoked in the chapter on cooperation in Volume I), and this form of productive labor can command a higher rate of remuneration. But the management of exploitation through domination and despotism also requires a governing authority. Marx here cites Aristotle to the effect that "domination in the economic domain as well as in the political, imposes on those in power the functions of dominating, so that, in the economic domain, they must know how to consume labour power." As soon as they become wealthy enough, "the master leaves the 'honor' of this drudgery to an overseer." The figure of the overseer had already been noted in the chapter on cooperation in Volume I. The question of the supervision of labor is, however, common to many modes of production. It is clear from Marx's examples that the management of slave labor was a vital precursor to capitalist management practices. Doctrines of racial inferiority played an important role in justifying the organization of the labor of distinctive "others." According to the "lawyer O'Connor" speaking in New York ("to thunderous applause"), the master ought indeed to command "just compensation for the labour and talent employed in governing [the slave] and rendering him useful to himself and to the society" (C3, 510). There is a considerable literature now that shows how the techniques of factory management that became common in Britain were pioneered on the West Indian sugar plantations through the management of large numbers of slave laborers.

"Mr Ure has already noted," Marx continues, "how it is not the industrial capitalists but rather the industrial managers who are 'the soul of our industrial system.'" However this may be, it is sure that "capitalist production has itself brought it about that the work of supervision is readily available, quite independent of the ownership of capital. It has therefore become superfluous for this work of supervision to be performed by the capitalist" (C3, 511). The wages for this management "appear as completely separate from profit of enterprise both in the workers' cooperative factories and in capitalist joint-stock companies." But the practices in both of these cases, which Marx briefly describes, are obviously very different:

> In the case of the cooperative factory, the antithetical character of the supervisory work disappears, since the manager is paid by the workers instead of representing capital in opposition to them. Joint-stock

companies in general (developed with the credit system) have the tendency to separate this function of managerial work more and more from the possession of capital, whether one's own or borrowed . . . (C3, 512)

This leads to an interesting conclusion:

> The confusion between profit of enterprise and the wages of supervision or management originally arose from the antithetical form that the surplus of profit over interest assumes in opposition to this interest. It was subsequently developed with the apologetic intention of presenting profit not as surplus-value, i.e. as unpaid labour, but rather as the wage that the capitalist himself receives for the work he performs. The socialists then raised the demand that profit should be reduced in practice to what it claimed to be in theory, i.e. simply to the wages of supervision.

But the false theory came more under pressure as the wages of supervision tended to fall due to deskilling. With the formation of workers' cooperatives and with the rise of joint-stock companies, "the last pretext for confusing profit of enterprise with the wages of management was removed, and profit came to appear in practice what it undeniably was in theory, mere surplus-value" (C3, 514).

But there is a final and very prescient twist in this chapter: "On the basis of capitalist production, a new swindle with the wages of management develops in connection with joint-stock companies, in that, over and above the actual managing director, a number of governing and supervisory boards arise, for which management and supervision are in fact a mere pretext for the robbery of shareholders and their own enrichment."

The contemporary significance of all of this calls for some commentary. In Marx's time, the wages of superintendence would likely be far less than the profit of enterprise actually generated. But once this distinction is introduced, then the balance of power between owners and superintendents can shift around in all manner of ways. In the case of joint-stock companies the superintendents—the CEOs and the management—have increasingly succeeded in feathering their own nests at the expense of owners. In a very influential book published in the 1930s, Berle and Means pointed to the rise of a distinctive managerial stratum that was radically reshaping the dominant class relations of

capitalism.[3] Marx (drawing upon Ure) anticipates the potential significance of the separation between ownership and management, and the
likelihood of the emergence of a managerial class. He does not anticipate its full flowering, partly because the joint-stock company form was
only just getting going. But he certainly sees the possibility of all manner
of "swindling" in the new forms being generated under what subsequently came to be called "money-management capitalism."

In the case of cooperatives, which were a popular socialist form at the
time (as in the case of Robert Owen), the question of managerial rewards
was also being posed. Plainly, if all institutions and corporations operated today on the Mondragon model (described earlier), we would be
living in a very different world. University presidents in the United
States would be receiving no more than $150,000 per year, as opposed
to well over $1 million, while adjunct teachers would be earning $50,000
instead of $20,000 (if they are lucky).

The conflict in our own times between owners and managers of
corporations is plainly of great significance economically, socially and
politically. The idea that capitalism is really about "other people's money"
was jokingly understood even in the latter half of the nineteenth century,
and this is what Marx is picking up on. But it is now a real issue, and is
not at all helped by the recent habit of paying managers in stock options,
which muddles the distinction between ownership and management.
Marx's commentaries on all of this therefore have contemporary significance, as does, even more importantly, his fundamental position that
the evolution of wages of superintendence as a form or remuneration
for capital is a mask for the extraction of surplus-value from the laborer
engaged in production.

ON CHAPTER 24 OF VOLUME III: FROM FETISHISM TO FICTITIOUS
CAPITAL

"In interest-bearing capital, the capital relationship reaches its most
superficial and fetishized form." So begins chapter 24, which is followed
by a chapter on "Credit and Fictitious Capital," thus initiating a transition in Marx's thinking in which the ultimate fetish—credit

---

3   Adolf A. Berle and Gardiner C. Means, *The Modern Corporation and Private
Property* (New York: Macmillan, 1932).

money—takes command of the laws of motion of capital to produce fictitious forms that mystify, distort, and ultimately undermine the laws of motion of capital accumulation that Marx has hitherto been concerned to theorize. The language here is quite stunning.

> Capital appears as a mysterious and self-creating source of interest, of its own increase. The thing (money, commodity, value) is now already capital simply as a thing; the result of the overall reproduction process appears as a property devolving on a thing in itself. . . . In interest-bearing capital, therefore, this automatic fetish is elaborated into its pure form, self-valorizing value, money breeding money, and in its form it no longer bears any marks of its origin. The social relationship is consummated in the relationship of a thing, money, to itself.
>
> . . .
>
> There is still a further distortion. While interest is simply one part of the profit . . . it now appears conversely as if interest is the specific fruit of capital, the original thing, while profit, now transformed into the form of profit of enterprise, appears as a mere accessory and trimming added in the reproduction process. *The fetish character of capital and the representation of this capital fetish is now complete.* In M-M' we have the irrational form of capital, the misrepresentation and objectification of the relations of production, in its highest power; the interest-bearing form, the simple form of capital, in which it is taken as logically anterior to its own reproduction process; the ability of money or a commodity to valorize its own value independent of reproduction—the capital mystification in the most flagrant form. (C3, 516; emphasis added)

This mystification is a "godsend" for vulgar economists, because they can then "present capital as an independent source of wealth, of value creation," having an "autonomous existence." But the far grander question is: To what degree do capitalists become so locked into the distortions of the fetish forms that they act irrationally in relation to their own reproduction? If the coercive laws of competition and all the market signals they receive point them in the wrong direction, then how can capital, left to itself, do anything other than dig for itself an ever deeper hole—if not a grave?

This issue has been on the cards right throughout *Capital.* It first and most conspicuously cropped up in the chapter on "The Working Day," in Volume I, where competition drives capital to so increase the length of the working day as to endanger the lives of those that produce the surplus-value. In this instance, it was state intervention to regulate the length of the working day that saved the capitalists from this "Après moi, le déluge" politics. So it is interesting that Marx here speaks explicitly of how "the fetish character of capital and the representation of this capital fetish is now complete." It is almost as if Marx's project throughout *Capital* has been to reveal the fetishisms that rule the capitalist system, and that he has here brought this project to completion.

The consequences are legion. One of the most crucial is how this fetish form (which Marx goes over in several compelling passages—citing Goethe's "the money's body is now by love possessed") produces the fancy and fantasy of compound interest. A certain Dr. Price, we learn, "was simply dazzled by the incredible figures that arise from geometric progression," as was the commentator who fantasized in 1772 that investing "a shilling at 6 per cent compound interest at our Saviour's birth would . . . have increased to a greater sum in gold than the whole solar system could hold" (C3, 520). Given this magical capacity, all existing debts (both public and private) could easily be retired with only a token of initial saving! This led the *Economist* to observe, in 1851: "Capital, with compound interest on every portion of capital saved, is so all-engrossing that all the wealth in the world from which income is derived, has long ago become the interest of capital," adding, significantly, that "all rent is now the payment of interest on capital previously invested in the land." To this, Marx acidly remarks that this implies that "by its own inherent laws, all surplus labour that the human race can supply" now apparently belongs to "capital in its capacity as interest-bearing capital" (C3, 521).

Marx brings this "absurdity" of automatically compounding growth forever back to earth by pointing out that "the accumulation process of capital may be conceived as an accumulation of compound interest, in so far as the part of profit (surplus-value) that is transformed back into capital, i.e. which serves to absorb new labour, may be called interest." But there is another reality: "a large part of the existing capital is always being more or less devalued in the course of the reproduction process," partly because of the rising productivity of social labor (which devalues the products of past labor, and which may also produce a falling rate of profit as laid out in the earlier chapters in Volume III). Wherein lies the balance between creation and destruction? The truth of the matter is this:

> The identity of surplus-value and surplus labour sets a qualitative limit to the accumulation of capital: *the total working day*, the present development of the productive forces and population which limits the number of working days that can simultaneously be exploited. But if surplus-value is conceived in the irrational form of interest, the limit is only quantitative, and beggars all fantasy.

The power of the fetish is that a reality is built around this fantasy. Interest-bearing capital "displays the conception of the capital fetish in its consummate form, the idea that ascribes to the accumulated product of labour, in the fixed form of money . . . the power of producing surplus-value in geometric progression by way of an inherent secret quality, as a pure automaton" (C3, 523). Consequences then follow as capital seeks to chain the use of both past and present labor to this fetish conception and its concomitant commitment to never-ending compound growth. It is not hard to spot the potential contradiction in all of this. While interest-bearing capital circulating within a monetary system that has no limits can spiral onwards and upwards into the stratosphere of compounding asset and fictitious capital values, the quantitative limits of real surplus-value production are quickly left behind, only to assert their limiting power in the course of a crisis.

ON CHAPTER 25 OF VOLUME III: CREDIT AND FICTITIOUS CAPITAL

After the quite stunning revelations of chapter 24, the two following chapters come as a bit of a disappointment, particularly given the promise of the title of chapter 25 to unpack the mysteries of the category of fictitious capital. This results partly from Marx's decision to refrain from any "detailed analysis of the credit system and the instruments it creates," including the development of state credit. He confines himself to examining "commercial and bank credit," because these are "necessary to characterize the capitalist mode of production in general." In other words, he returns to the level of generality, to the exclusion of all else. The wild assertions of the previous chapter are constrained by an attempt at sober analysis.

The credit system "is expanded, generalized and elaborated" as trade in commodities increases with capitalist development. Money is increasingly used as "money of account," as the practices of buying now and paying later become more common. Promises to pay can also circulate, and Marx lumps all such practices together under the heading of "bills of exchange." Since many of these bills cancel each other out through the balancing of debts and claims, so they function as money even though no metallic or government paper money is involved (C3, 525).

Marx cites a banker, W. Leatham (I think approvingly—though it is hard to tell), who attempted to calculate the volume of such bills of exchange circulating in Britain. It was clear that the nominal value of these bills far exceeded the amount of gold on hand. Leatham wrote that the bills of exchange were not

> placed under any control, except by preventing the abundance of money, excessive and low rates of interest or discount, which create a part of them, and encourage their great and dangerous expansion. It is impossible to decide what part arises out of real bona fide transactions, such as actual bargain and sale, or what part is fictitious and mere accommodation paper, that is, where one bill of exchange is drawn to take up another running, in order to raise a fictitious capital, by creating so much currency. In times of abundance, and cheap money, this I know reaches an enormous amount. (C3, 526)

Strikingly, this is the only explicit mention of the category of fictitious capital in this chapter. It is only in chapter 29 that Marx takes up the category on his own account. But here he does examine some of the practices involved in this trade in paper IOUs through which property rights change hands without the aid of conventional moneys.

This trade defines a new and very specific economic role, that of the money dealer—or banker—middlemen who specialize not only in the discounting of bills of exchange, but also "in the management of interest-bearing capital" and the borrowing and lending of money. "The business of banking consists . . . in concentrating money capital for loan in large masses in the bank's hands, so that, instead of the individual lenders of money, it is the bankers as representative of all lenders of money who confront the industrial and commercial capitalists. They become the general managers of money capital"—which is, recall, the common capital of the capitalist class. "A bank represents on the one hand the centralization of money capital, of the lenders, and on the other hand the centralization of the borrowers. It makes its profit in general by borrowing at lower rates than those at which it lends." Marx briefly describes the multiple functions of the various types of banks, and concludes by noting that the bank in effect interposes its own creditworthiness in between all lenders and borrowers, and can also in some instances issue banknotes that are "nothing more than a bill on the banker, payable at any time to its possessor and given by the banker in place of private drafts." The banks that issue notes are usually "a peculiar mishmash between national banks and private banks and actually have the government's credit behind them, their notes being more or less legal tender" (C3, 529). While Marx does not dwell on the point, what we are in effect seeing here is a banking system and banking functions that arise out of the activities of commercial exchange, but that "mishmash" together private and state functions in peculiar combinations. It was left to Engels, however, to insert a number of instances where this had gone badly awry, helping to produce the financial and commercial crises of 1847–48 and 1857–58.

ON CHAPTER 26 OF VOLUME III: THE ACCUMULATION OF MONEY CAPITAL

This chapter is largely made up of lengthy quotes from other commentators, along with extensive quotation from the evidence given in the Report of the Parliamentary Committee on the Bank Acts (with the evidence from Overstone being the main focus). While Marx does insert some critical commentary here and there, it is hard to identify any systemic critique. It is not clear whether Marx fully accepts some of the views he presents or is merely copying passages out for later critical examination.

He starts, for example, with a long quote from Corbet which I find particularly interesting. The steady accumulation of wealth in England in money form poses a problem for Corbet:

> Next in urgency, perhaps, to the desire to acquire money, is the wish to part with it again for some species of investment that shall yield either interest or profit; for money itself, as money, yields neither. Unless,

therefore, concurrently with this ceaseless influx of surplus capital, there is a gradual and sufficient extension of the field for its employment, we must be subject to periodical accumulations of money seeking invest-ment, of more or less volume, according to the movement of events. For a long series of years, the grand absorbent of the surplus wealth of England was our public debt . . . Enterprises which entail a large capital and create an opening from time to time for the excess of unemployed capital . . . are absolutely necessary, at least in our country, so as to the take care of the periodical accumulations of the superfluous wealth of society, which is unable to find room in the usual fields of application. (C3, 543)

Marx does not offer any commentary on this passage, either pro or con. But, at several points throughout *Capital*, what I call "the capital surplus disposal problem" does come into focus. I find it interesting that, in Corbet's account, the national debt, far from being the awful burden that it is so often presumed to be, is a welcome outlet, and that large-scale enterprises (for example, large public works, physical infrastructures, and urbanization projects) are also "absolutely neces-sary" if capital surpluses are to be absorbed. All of this fits with the general idea, of which I am personally rather fond, that the accumula-tion of wealth has to be paralleled by the accumulation of debt. Whether Marx would have come to that view explicitly I cannot tell. But he certainly does not reject it.

What we do know from this chapter is that Marx most certainly did disapprove of the so-called "currency principle," as advanced by Mr. Norman, then director of the Bank of England, and that he had nothing but contempt for the views of "the usurer logician" banker, Lord Over-stone. But since the substantive issues raised are taken up later in Marx's text, I will delay consideration of them until my next chapter.

CHAPTER SIX

Marx's Views on the Credit System (Chapters 27–37 of Volume III)

There is a rapid deterioration in the quality of Marx's text on the role of credit in relation to capital after chapter 28. As I have noted, it was after chapter 30 that Engels found that "the real difficulty" began:

> From here on it was not only the illustrative material that needed correct arrangement, but also a train of thought that was interrupted continuously by digressions, asides, etc., and later pursued further in other places, often simply in passing. There then followed, in the manuscript, a long section headed "The Confusion", consisting simply of extracts from the parliamentary reports on the crises of 1848 and 1857, in which the statements of some twenty-three businessmen and economic writers, particularly on the subjects of money and capital, the drain of gold, over-speculation, etc., were collected, with the occasional addition of brief humorous comments. (C3, 94–5)

After several attempts, Engels gave up on trying to reconstruct Marx's views on "the confusion," and confined his efforts simply to replicating the notes while emphasizing the occasional points of critical engagement.

I do not recommend any attempt at a close reading of chapters 30–35 on the first time through. But the challenge of trying to understand what "the confusion" is all about has to be addressed. Is Marx suggesting that bourgeois thought is confused and that his is not? If so, then he does a poor job at clarifying matters. Or does he mean that the contradictions run so deep with respect to the world of credit moneys as to produce damaging confusions and crises all around? Knowing Marx, he probably means both. Some commentary on this is surely called for. So I shall first offer my overview of what I think is going on before delving into individual chapters and commenting on the more relevant passages. I do so, I should make clear, without making any claim whatsoever to a definitive, let alone correct, reading.

THE GENERAL ARGUMENT

After sketching in the general role of credit in capitalist production in chapter 27, Marx devotes two chapters to considering the role of banks and bankers in providing liquidity (cash or banknotes) for either the production or realization of capital. The following three chapters, on money capital and real capital, focus mainly on what happens as fictitious capital takes on a life of its own, permitting all manner of speculations and inversions of power relations in ways that may have little to do with the actual production of surplus-value, even as the latter seems to exercise some sort of shadowy disciplinary power over the excesses within the financial system. The three technical chapters that follow are largely compiled from official reports, and it is hard to decipher Marx's own views, so I will not attempt to synthesize or interpret these materials here. The final chapter, on pre-capitalist relations, offers an interesting account of the history of credit as usury, and some provocative thoughts regarding political possibilities.

Some key threads run through these chapters. Marx clearly saw that profound consequences flowed from the consolidation of the credit system into the "common capital of the class," as already stated in chapter 22 and in his general introduction to merchant's capital. I cannot overemphasize the importance of this idea. It repositions the circulation of money capital as a kind of central nervous system guiding the capital flows that reproduce capital in general. It implies, furthermore, a socialization of capital that signals some radical change in its character. Joint-stock companies, for example, facilitate the emergence of collective and associated capitals, which, on the one hand, permit a vast extension in the scale, range and form of capitalist endeavors while, on the other hand, they open a path toward a world market in which associated labor and collective property rights might find an increasing place. Marx even thought joint-stock companies, because of their associative character, could become the basis for a transition to a noncapitalist mode of production. This seems today to be a quaint, if not astonishingly mistaken idea, but at the time there were some interesting reasons one might have thought of such possibilities.

The positive and negative possibilities inherent in the rise of the capitalist credit system were embodied, says Marx, in the person of the

French banker Isaac Péreire, who had "the nicely mixed character of swindler and prophet" (C3, 573). So let me digress a little (as Marx does in chapter 36) on what this "character" is about.

The Péreire brothers—Isaac and Émile—were schooled in Saint-Simonian utopianism in France in the 1830s, and put some of those utopian ideas, particularly regarding the power of associated capitals, into practice during the Second Empire (1852–70). Saint-Simon (1760–1825), whose "genius and encyclopedic mind" Marx, according to Engels, much admired (C3, 740), sought to give advice to the King. He sent many epistles suggesting this or that way of improving collective life so as to avoid the violence of change typified by the French Revolution, the excesses of which Saint-Simon deemed abhorrent. He was probably one of the first thinkers to propose something like the European Union. Had anyone listened, two world wars might have been avoided. He proposed rationalized and representative forms of government that would legislate for the benefit of all classes under benevolent monarchical rule. He also emphasized the importance of bringing both capital and labor (which included artisans and working capitalist entrepreneurs) together to produce very large-scale (and to some degree planned) projects and public works that would contribute to everyone's well-being. For this to happen required that the small amounts of money capital wastefully dispersed in society be assembled in associated form.

Louis Napoleon, who proclaimed himself Emperor in 1852 after a coup d'état in 1851, was a fan of Saint-Simon's ideas. He was sometimes referred to as "Saint-Simon on horseback." Louis looked to large-scale projects to mop up unemployed capital and labor after the crash and revolutionary movements of 1848. The Péreire brothers played an important role in this. They developed new credit institutions and assembled small amounts of capital into the associated forms that Saint-Simon had advocated, and thus came to dominate the world of Second Empire finance. Through their control over credit paper moneys, they became key participants in Haussmann's large-scale mission to absorb surplus capital and labor by rebuilding and transforming Paris. They were active in the construction of apartment buildings and new department stores, while they monopolized public utilities (such as gas lighting) and new transport and communications structures within the city. But the boom of the 1850s and early 1860s, along with the legendary rivalry between the Péreires and the conservative banking house of

Rothschild (the centerpiece of Zola's novel, *Money*), came to an end in the financial crash of 1867, which destroyed the Péreires' speculative credit empire. It could well be that Marx had this rivalry in mind when he wrote:

> The monetary system is essentially Catholic, the credit system essentially Protestant. "The Scots hate gold." As paper, the monetary existence of commodities has a purely social existence. It is *faith* that brings salvation. Faith in money value as the immanent spirit of commodities, faith in the mode of production and its predestined disposition, faith in the individual agents of production as mere personifications of self-valorizing capital. But the credit system is no more emancipated from the monetary system as its basis than Protestantism is from the foundations of Catholicism. (C3, 727)

Rothschild (while Jewish) believed in the "catholicism" of gold as the monetary base, whereas the Péreires (also Jewish) put their faith in paper. When the crash came, the paper proved worthless while gold never lost its luster, and indeed glittered more tantalizingly than ever.

The tension between paper credit and commodity moneys (such as gold) is omnipresent in these chapters. Marx treats of it most explicitly fairly late on, in the midst of an otherwise rambling chapter on precious metal and the rate of exchange:

> It is precisely the development of the credit and banking system which on the one hand seeks to press all money capital into the service of production, while on the other hand it reduces the metal reserve in a given phase of the cycle to a minimum, at which it can no longer perform the functions ascribed to it—it is this elaborate credit and banking system that makes the entire organism oversensitive.

The metal reserve functions "as the pivot of the entire credit system" by guaranteeing the convertibility of banknotes. The structure that emerges is that

> the central bank is the pivot of the credit system. And the metal reserve is in turn the pivot of the bank. It is inevitable that the credit system should collapse into the monetary system.... A certain quantity of

metal that is insignificant in comparison with production as a whole is the acknowledged pivot of the system. Hence, on top of the terrifying illustration of this pivotal character in crises, the beautiful theoretical dualism. (C3, 706)

Figure 4

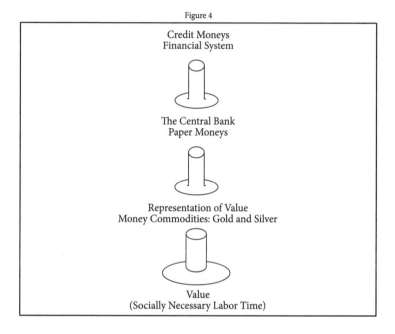

Credit Moneys
Financial System

The Central Bank
Paper Moneys

Representation of Value
Money Commodities: Gold and Silver

Value
(Socially Necessary Labor Time)

While even the pretense of a metallic or commodity base to the global credit and money system was abandoned in the early 1970s (though so-called "gold bugs" who advocate a return to a gold standard still abound), the idea of a hierarchical structure of pivots (with the US dollar central) to the global financial system still seems an appropriate conception. It is even more true now than when Marx was alive, that

credit, being . . . a social form of wealth, displaces money and usurps its position. It is the confidence in the social character of production that makes the money form of products appear as something merely evanescent and ideal, as a mere notion. But as soon as credit is shaken, and this is a regular and necessary phase in the cycle of modern industry, all real wealth is supposed to be actually and suddenly transformed into money, into gold and silver—a crazy demand, but one that necessarily grows out of the system itself. And the gold and silver that is supposed to satisfy these immense claims amounts in all to a few million in the vault of the bank. (C3, 708)

Earlier, Marx had provided an even richer account of these relations: "It is the foundation of capitalist production that money confronts commodities as an autonomous form of value, or that exchange-value must obtain an autonomous form in money." Commodity money as the universal equivalent is that autonomous form. What then happens when credit moneys and credit operations replace the money commodity? "In times of pressure, when credit contracts or dries up altogether, money suddenly confronts commodities absolutely as the only means of payment and the true existence of value. Hence the general devaluation of commodities and the difficulty or even impossibility of transforming them into money, i.e. into their own purely fantastic form." The allusion to the theory of fetishism is here unmistakable. Secondly, "credit money is itself only money in so far as it absolutely represents real money." When gold gets drained abroad, the convertibility of credit into gold

becomes problematic. Hence we get forcible measures, putting up the rate of interest, etc. in order to guarantee . . . convertibility. . . . A devaluation of credit money (not to speak of a complete loss of its monetary character, which is in any case purely imaginary) would destroy all the existing relationships. The value of commodities is thus sacrificed to ensure the fantastic and autonomous existence of this value in money. . . . This is why many millions' worth of commodities have to be sacrificed for a few millions in money. This is unavoidable in capitalist production, and forms one of its particular charms. . . . As long as the social character of labour appears as the monetary existence of the commodity and hence as a thing outside actual production, monetary crises, independent of real crises or as an intensification of them, are unavoidable. (C3, 648–9)

Is this what broadly happened in the 1930s depression? And is this the "unavoidability" that Keynesianism strove to correct?

While this tension between credit and "real" money had long been identifiable, it is only with this system that the most striking and grotesque form of this absurd contradiction and paradox arises, because (1) in the capitalist system production for direct use-value, for the producer's own use, is most completely abolished, so that wealth exists only as a social process expressed as the entwinement of production and circulation; and (2) because with the development of the credit system, capitalist production constantly strives to overcome this metallic barrier which is both a material and an imaginary barrier to wealth and its movement, while time and again breaking its head on it. (C3, 707–8)

So the form of commodity moneys is an obstacle to expansion that is overcome or circumvented by credit moneys, but at some point the quality and reliability of credit moneys can be validated only by their exchangeability against commodity moneys.

One of the things that is difficult for all analysts (including Marx) to grapple with is the difference between wealth circulating in the financial and credit system on the one hand and supposedly "real" wealth production on the other. The relation between Wall Street and Main Street (or, as the British refer to it, between the City and the High Street) puzzles everyone. The current arguments over what to do about the euro provide a wonderful demonstration of the confusions that reign. What Marx suggests is that a monetary system based purely on commodity moneys acts as a barrier to further capital accumulation because there is only so much gold to be had. There is a clear and constant danger of what is now called "financial repression," which occurs when there is not enough money (of any sort) to circulate the expanding volume of commodities being produced as capital accumulation proceeds. Credit moneys therefore become not only necessary but crucial to the continuous expansion of capitalism. There is prima facie evidence to suggest (though to my knowledge it has never been empirically studied) that the history of capital accumulation has been paralleled by an accumulation of credit moneys and their concomitant debts. Only in this way can capital be accumulated "without limit." But if capital accumulation depends upon a parallel accumulation of credit moneys and credit instruments, then it necessarily produces a fetish monster of its own design, based on faith, confidence and expectation, that periodically lurches out of control. Credit moneys do not simply replace metallic money: they shift the monetary system and the conception of money on to a wholly new plane that embraces rather than punctures the fetishisms implicit in the credit system. Credit "froth," asset bubbles, and speculative booms and busts are the price that capital has to pay for temporarily liberating itself from money-commodity restraints.

These restraints reappear, however, during phases of crisis. The volume of credit obligations periodically goes way beyond that of real value production (however that may be measured); then commodity moneys (the representatives of value) bring the craziness of credit moneys back to earth in the course of a financial crisis. It is the discipline of real hard money that connects Wall Street to Main Street. This is the "catholicism" of the monetary base in action. The religious reference, by the way, reflects the Catholic Church's long-standing proscription of interest (a stance which continues under contemporary Islamic law, and which the Catholic Church abandoned only late in the nineteenth century). Martin Luther's famous distinction between the evils of usury and the legitimacy of a "fair" rate of interest was critical to the protestant movement's break with Rome.

What is so crucial about the credit system is its ability to burst through any and all monetary barriers to accumulation into a world of unlimited growth. Limitless possibilities exist for the creation of paper money (IOUs). This is what happened with the housing bubble after 2001 in the United States. Prices were going up, and everyone was cashing in on rising housing asset values—and the more they cashed in, the more the prices went up. Houses seemed like ATMs, with no limit placed on withdrawals until people realized that housing prices had become far, far out of line with incomes. The crash then followed. The same thing happened with the Japanese land boom of the 1980s. When the crash comes, the liquidity of the owners (command of real hard cash) is all that then matters. To the degree that this is found wanting, the foreclosures, losses and asset devaluations pile up and up.

So what is the general contemporary significance of this? The metallic base to the world's money system was formally abandoned in the early 1970s. This would seem to render Marx's thinking irrelevant. Did he not say that "money in the form of precious metal remains the foundation from which the credit system can *never* break free?" Gold still plays an important residual role, of course. When faith in paper and credit moneys gets badly shaken, gold prices surge, as they have over the past few years. A minority still feels that gold is the safest way to store real money values. Advertisements to invest in the safety of gold now abound. Maybe there is some truth to this (and we will all kick ourselves for not investing if the gold price triples in the next five years!). But there is little likelihood of a contemporary return to the gold standard. Conventional wisdom has it that this would be an unmitigated disaster for the continuous expansion of world trade, and plunge the world into permanent depression. The world economy rests on the plane of the credit economy, and cannot get off.

But, if the metallic "pivot" to the whole monetary system disappears, then what replaces it? The answer is the world's central banks in combination with state regulatory authorities (a state-finance nexus, as I call it). Together, these now form the "pivot" of the global money and credit system. For Marx, this pivot was the Bank of England, and for us it is the Federal Reserve Bank of the United States (coupled with the US Treasury) and the world's other central banks and regulatory authorities, such as those of Britain, Japan and the European Union. The effect, however, is to replace a regulating mechanism that rests on real commodity production (of gold and silver) with a human institution. Human judgment is the only discipline exerted over credit creation. But will this human institution do the right thing? Critical focus must then shift to how central banks are structured and regulated, and how policies are formulated within the state apparatus to deal with the periodic excesses that occur within the credit system.

If the central bank and the regulatory authorities are badly structured, or if they operate on the basis of some erroneous economic theory (like monetarism), then policy can become deeply implicated in the processes of crisis formation and/or resolution. Central bank policy is believed by many to have played an important role in exacerbating the great depression of the 1930s (as did Winston Churchill's disastrous decision, when chancellor of the exchequer, to put Britain back on the gold standard in the 1920s). Some now claim that Bernanke's policies at the Federal Reserve are taking the US in entirely the wrong direction, and that Alan Greenspan's years at the helm of the Fed that looked so wonderful at the time played a role in the devastating crash of 2007–08. Certainly, the idea of regulatory failure is now widely canvassed as having affected recent events, and a better regulatory structure is touted by some as one important answer to the crisis in the United States, and even globally. But what are we to make of a European Central Bank that is mandated to keep inflation under control without any regard for unemployment, and that consequently appears paralyzed over the question of how to respond to the Greek debt crisis other than by promoting a debilitating and ever-deepening austerity? Human institutions are fallible, and subject to all manner of social forces and conflicting opinions. They create a very different regulatory mechanism to that which prevails when commodity moneys still operated as the pivot upon which central bank policy had to turn.

Even in Marx's time, the fallibility of the financial institutions and their policies played an important role. Marx cites the "mistaken" British Bank Act of 1844 as his prime example. That legislation divided the Bank of England into "an Issue Department and a Banking Department" (C3, 688). The former department held government securities and the metal reserve, and issued banknotes backed by these reserves. It exchanged its notes (which were far more convenient for trading purposes) for gold, and the notes promised in return "to pay the bearer" (on British banknotes that language of promising to pay the bearer can still be found) in gold if necessary. So, at any time, I could go to the bank with the notes and get the gold back. The notes were, in short, "convertible." (The suspension of convertibility was always then a political option, and had actually already occurred in Britain at one point during the Napoleonic Wars.) The other part of the bank discounted bills of exchange, passed checks, issued bonds and engaged in other conventional bank business. The legislation of 1844 created a firewall between the two parts of the bank. But in 1848 a crisis of confidence hit the latter banking part. There was a run on the bank as people lost trust in the discounted commercial paper and the bonds. The Banking Department ran out of gold while the Issue Department was flush with it:

> The separation of the Bank into two independent departments withdrew the directors' power of free disposal of their entire available means at decisive moments, so that situations could come about in which the Banking Department was faced with bankruptcy while the Issue Department still had several millions in gold. . . . The Bank Act of 1844 thus directly provokes the entire world of commerce into meeting the outbreak of crisis by putting aside a reserve stock of banknotes, thereby accelerating and intensifying the crisis. And by this artificial

intensification of the demand for monetary accommodation . . . it drives the interest rate in crisis times up to a previously unheard-of level.

The parallels with what happened to the interest rate on Greek bonds in the crisis of 2011 is striking:

Thus instead of abolishing crises, [the Bank of England] rather intensifies them to a point at which either the entire world of industry has to collapse, or else the Bank Act. On two occasions, 25 October 1847 and 12 November 1857, the crisis reached such a height; the government then freed the Bank from the restriction on its note issue, by suspending the Act of 1844, and this was sufficient on both occasions to curb the crisis. (C3, 689)

I do not read Marx as here saying that the Bank Act of 1844 was the cause of a crisis: but it did serve to intensify and accelerate a crisis that had arisen for other reasons (what they were, Marx does not say). But what kind of institutional arrangement is it that cannot respond adequately to the inevitability of periodic crises? This is, surely, the foundational question that was being asked of the European Central Bank during the debt crises that engulfed not only Greece, but also Ireland, Portugal, Spain and Italy during 2011. To depict the Bank Act of 1844 as "mistaken" is to infer that Marx believed a Bank Act possible that would not exacerbate crises. Human credit and banking institutions might be constituted that would be flexible enough to accommodate changing outputs and prices and, even more importantly, changing sentiments among investors. But were financial institutions possible that could contain the foundational contradictions that underpinned crisis formation? For Keynesians this was the holy grail of public policy. Marx did not think it was possible. "Ignorant and confused banking laws, such as those of 1844–5, may intensify the monetary crisis. But no bank legislation can abolish crises themselves" (C3, 621).

So what does it mean that the rootedness of credit in commodity moneys was entirely and formally abandoned from the early 1970s onwards (it had been informally bypassed by Keynesian policies after the 1930s)? Where Marx might stand on such contemporary shifts is hard to tell. He would certainly have lined up far more closely with the Keynesians than with the monetarists (he repeatedly criticizes the quantity theory of money as advanced by Ricardo). But he would never, I think, have believed that the crisis tendencies of capitalism could ever be contained, let alone overcome, by financial reforms. A careful reading of these chapters, I believe, supports that view. It is important to pose these questions here because, with the analysis of credit, Marx seems to take his concept of capital into a radically different dimension.

The evident, if periodic, craziness that arises within the financial system provokes the question: Why on earth does any society tolerate it? Marx's answer is very clear. Credit is absolutely essential if the expansionary thrust of perpetual capital accumulation is to be accommodated in monetary terms. The barrier constituted by the metallic base (and banknotes convertible into gold) has to be overcome, because the amount of gold and silver is both inadequate (because relatively inflexible in relation to fluctuations in commodity output) and in the end insufficient, because finite. Furthermore, the speculative character of all forms of capital investment (all of which presuppose that expansion in the form of more surplus-value will be produced at the end of the day) is ineluctably embedded in the circulation of interest-bearing money capital. And, as we have seen again and again throughout Volume II of *Capital*, the vagaries of different circulation times (of fixed capital in particular) can only be accommodated by way of an active credit system; the release of "dead capital" from the hoards that would otherwise be required plays a critical role in accelerating rather than retarding accumulation. The Péreire brothers represented all of this and more. They broke through the restrictions of the monetary base, to the horror of the conservative House of Rothschild, which controlled so much of the gold. But the crash of 1867 showed the weakness of the Péreires' position, and seemed therefore to prove Rothschild's (and Marx's?) belief in the ultimate power of gold. But the Péreires had helped successfully to absorb surpluses of capital and labor for fifteen years, and they had also left behind a radically transformed built environment that we can to this day still admire when we stroll along the Parisian boulevards, enjoy the parks, and still benefit from the water supply and sewage-disposal systems that serve the stately if standardized boulevard housing that still characterizes much of central Paris. The Péreires were the visionaries and the adventurers, the real entrepreneurial capitalists; they had faith and got things done, whereas the House of Rothschild dragged its feet.

This raises some interesting questions of faith, beliefs and psychology. Zola's novel *Money*, which centers on the rivalry between Saccard (the Péreires) and Gunderman (Rothschild) during the Second Empire, pivots on the clash of sentiments and the mentalities at work in financial speculation. Here is what Saccard says as he seeks to persuade his demure, respectable and thoughtful niece, Mme Caroline, of the justice of what she worries to be his shady speculative activities:

> "Look here," cried Saccard . . . "you will behold a complete resurrection over these depopulated plains, those deserted passes, which our railways will traverse—Yes! Fields will be cleared, roads and canals built, new cities will spring from the soil, life will return as it returns to a sick body, when we stimulate the system by injecting new blood into exhausted veins. Yes! Money will work the miracles . . .
>
> "You must understand that speculation, gambling, is the central mechanism, the heart itself, of a vast affair like ours. Yes, it attracts blood, takes it from every source in little streamlets, collects it, sends it back in rivers in all directions, and establishes an enormous circulation of money, which is the very life of great enterprises.
>
> "Speculation—why it is the one inducement that we have to live, it is the eternal desire that compels us to live and struggle. Without speculation, my dear friend, there would be no business of any kind. . . . It is the same as in love. In love as in speculation there is much filth; in love also, people think only of their own gratification; yet without love there would be no life and the world would come to an end."[1]

It is in the context of such sentiments that it becomes much easier to understand what Marx meant when he referred to Isaac Péreire as having "the charming character of swindler and prophet."

The credit system appears on the surface to be lawless, chaotic and seemingly unbridled in its capacity for incubating speculative fevers and periodic crashes. This might be expected because interest is, in the language of the *Grundrisse*, a particularity, and it is regulated (if at all) by other particularities—notably, as we have seen, the supply of and demand for money capital, along with competition between

---

1   Émile Zola, *Money* (Stroud, UK: Alan Sutton, translated by Ernest Vizetelly, 1991), 232.

different factions of capital. It is bound therefore to be accidental, lawless and conjunctural. It also depends upon faith. The psychology of it all, as Keynes later was at pains to emphasize (and which Zola so brilliantly depicts), becomes crucial. But for Marx, that question is posed in a rather different way. It boils down to asking how capitals and capitalists might function when they are locked into the inherent fetishisms of capital's surface forms. Once lost in the labyrinth of their own fetish constructs, how can capitalists possibly divine the root of their own dilemmas, let alone find a way out? This is, I suspect, the "confusion" that Marx wanted to expose. Its unraveling depends on a closer understanding of the category of fictitious capital, which I will take up shortly.

Marx also suggests that the tendency toward overproduction and the overaccumulation of capital—or what he later refers to as a "plethora" of capital—earlier identified as fundamental features of the general laws of motion of capital, act as triggers, or even as underlying causes, of the crises of confidence that periodically wrack the credit system. The "catholicism" of the monetary base, where real value is represented by the money commodities of gold and silver, is positioned by Marx as the ultimate reality check on speculative fevers. So, even when commodity moneys—the precious metals—are relieved from their mediating role as representations of value, it would surely be unlikely that Marx would agree to removing value itself from its central role as arbiter of the laws of motion of capital. The question of the relation between the immaterial but objective powers of value and the efflorescences of the credit system then moves into the foreground of theoretical concern.

While he does not come to definitive answers, Marx generates insights in these chapters upon which it might be possible to build. Chief among these is the role of fictitious and speculative forms of capital in shaping ("disrupting" might be a better word) the actual as opposed to general laws of motion of capital accumulation. But the relations between Wall Street and Main Street remain as opaque and controversial today as they were for Marx. Can Marx's intuitive ability to ask the right critical questions be helpful for further enquiry? This is the question it is useful to keep in mind as we delve a little more closely into the individual chapters. I will begin, however, with chapter 36, which takes up the prehistory of the credit system.

ON CHAPTER 36: THE PREHISTORY OF THE CREDIT SYSTEM

"Interest-bearing capital, or, to describe it in its archaic form, usurer's capital, belongs together with its twin brother, merchant's capital, to the antediluvian forms of capital which long precede the capitalist mode of production and are to be found in the most diverse socio-economic formations" (C3, 728). This formulation parallels that given elsewhere (for example, C1, 267). Notice that interest-bearing capital exists *before* the capitalist mode of production. This roundly contradicts the mistaken story that Marx occasionally repeats from Adam Smith, that there was a natural evolution from barter to a money economy, and finally to the credit economy (see C2, 195). Commodification, money and the buying and selling of labor-power all had to exist prior to the capitalist mode of production (as we saw in the first chapters of Volume II). But we now see that even money as interest-bearing capital had to preexist the rise of its own distinctive mode of production.

Surplus moneys (hoards) were always and necessarily to be found in precapitalist societies. But they only became capital when the hoarder "transform[ed] himself into a money lender." This requires that "money can be valorized as capital," that it can be lent out to appropriate the labor of others (C3, 729). "The development of usurer's capital is bound up with that of merchant's capital, and particularly with that of money-dealing capital." In ancient Rome these two forms of capital "were developed to their highest point." In the chapter on merchant's capital, Marx complained of "the confusion" of the economists who treated money and merchants' capital as branches of production (like agriculture, industry and other divisions of labor) rather than as categories embedded within circulation.

In precapitalist times, usurious lending took two forms—"firstly, usury by lending money to extravagant magnates, essentially to landed proprietors; secondly, usury by lending money to small producers who possess their own conditions of labour, including artisans, but particularly and especially peasants." Usury therefore "works on the one hand to undermine and destroy ancient and feudal wealth and ancient and feudal property." It also "undermines and ruins small peasant and petty-bourgeois production." In short, it completes the process of primitive accumulation described in Volume I (though Marx does not use that term here). In the process, "usurer's capital and mercantile wealth bring about the formation of a monetary wealth independent of landed property" (C3, 732–3). This echoes an argument in the *Communist Manifesto* where the superior mobility of money (the "butterfly" form of capital) and of commodities contributes to the domination of merchant capital over feudal land-based powers.

Whether, however, the resultant "concentration of large money capitals" leads to the establishment of "the capitalist mode of production in its place, depends entirely on the historical level of development and the conditions that this provides" (C3, 729). Usury may have helped undermine and destroy feudal and ancient modes of production, but it did not and could not in itself give rise to a capitalist mode of production. While usury concentrates money power, "usurer's capital impoverishes the mode of production, cripples the productive forces instead of developing them, and simultaneously perpetuates these lamentable conditions in which the social productivity of labour is not developed even at the cost of the worker himself, as it is in capitalist production" (C3, 731–2). It "does not change the mode of production, but clings on to it like a parasite and impoverishes it. It sucks it dry, emasculates it and forces reproduction to proceed under ever more pitiable conditions," even as "the mode of production remains unaltered" (C3, 731).

The destructive powers of usury provoked popular abhorrence and resistance on the part of many powerful institutions, such as the Catholic Church, which proscribed usury along with interest until the late nineteenth century. At the end of the chapter, Martin Luther's distinction is duly noted between usury and a "fair and just" rate of interest—one dimension of the break with Rome that constituted the Protestant Reformation.

Marx considers it

> quite absurd to compare the level of *this* interest [that of the usurer] in which *all* surplus-value save that which accrues to the state is appropriated, with the level of the modern interest rate, where interest, at least the normal interest, forms only one part of this surplus-value. This is to forget that the wage-labourer produces and yields to the capitalist who employs him profit, interest and ground-rent, in short the entire surplus-value.

Wage-laborers cannot therefore be debt-slaves in their role as producers under capitalism, though they can be so, Marx presciently notes, in their "capacity as consumer"(C3, 730). This is one of the rare occasions when Marx mentions the possibility of consumer debt on the part of the worker.

So "usury has a revolutionary effect on pre-capitalist modes of production only in so far as it destroys and dissolves the forms of ownership which provide a firm basis for the articulation of political life and whose constant reproduction in the same form is a necessity for that life," and "it is only where and when the other conditions for the capitalist mode of production are present that usury appears as one of the means of formation of this new mode of production, by ruining feudal lords and petty production on the one hand, and by centralizing the conditions of labour on the other" (C3, 732). Marx does not elaborate on what these "other conditions" might be, but his caginess in not designating any one condition (such as a revolution in productive forces or a radical transformation of mental conceptions of the world) suggests that he has in mind a variety of conditions rather than a "single-bullet" explanation of the transition from feudalism to capitalism, with usury playing a potentially important role.

"The credit system develops as a reaction against usury. But this should not be misconstrued, nor by any means taken in the sense of the ancient writers, the Fathers of the Church, Luther or the early socialists. It means neither more nor less than the subordination of interest-bearing capital to the conditions and requirements of the capitalist mode of production." What does this imply?

> Interest-bearing capital retains the form of usurer's capital vis-à-vis persons and classes, or in conditions where borrowing in the sense appropriate to the capitalist mode of production does not and cannot occur; where borrowing results from individual need, as at the pawnshop; where borrowing is for extravagant consumption; or where the producer is a non-capitalist producer, a small peasant, artisan, etc. . . . finally where the capitalist producer himself operates on so small a scale that his situation approaches that of those producers who work for themselves. (C3, 735)

We have to expect, in short, the continuation of usurious practices within capitalism, from the contemporary impoverished inner cities of the United States (where the pawnshop is a vital institution) to the ubiquitous moneylenders that live parasitically off Indian peasant populations.

What sets interest-bearing capital apart under capitalism are "the changed conditions under which it functions" and "the totally transformed figure of the borrower who confronts the money lender." That borrower is given credit "as a potential capitalist" even if the borrower is himself without means. "A man without wealth but with energy, determination, ability and business acumen can transform himself into a capitalist in this way." This is seen as something admirable by the economic apologists, when it "actually reinforces the rule of capital itself, widens its basis and enables it to recruit ever new forces from the lower strata of society. . . . The more a dominant class is able to absorb the best people from the dominated classes, the more solid and dangerous is its rule" (C3, 735–6). The "rags to riches" myth of capital thus serves as a powerful ideological justification for the perpetuation of this class relation at the same time as it serves to rejuvenate the capitalist class and preserve its energy and power. The lack of upward mobility (or its diminution, as in the United States in recent times) is therefore often viewed as dangerous to the perpetuation of the capitalist social order. To the degree that the modern credit system facilitates this mobility and flexibility, it was and is viewed in a positive light.

Marx then goes on to give a brief description of how usury was tamed, and how the circulation of interest-bearing capital was subordinated "to commercial and industrial capital, instead of vice versa" (C3, 738). He sees the pioneering role of the credit associations that formed in Venice and Genoa in the twelfth and fourteenth centuries as crucial, followed by the developments centered in Holland in the seventeenth century, where "commercial credit and dealing in money did develop along with trade and manufacture, and by the course of development itself, interest-bearing capital became subordinate to industrial and commercial capital."

This is fairly standard economic history by now, and those familiar with Giovanni Arrighi's account of the role of financialization in facilitating the shift in hegemony within global capitalism from the Italian city-states to Holland, Britain, and later the United States will notice the parallels. But there is one aspect of Marx's account that has particular significance. With respect to Venice and Genoa, he notes that the banks proper that were founded in these urban republics were at the same time institutions for public credit, from which the state received advances against taxes anticipated. It should not be forgotten that the merchants who formed these associations were themselves the most prominent people in those states and were equally interested in emancipating both their government and themselves from usury, while at the same time subordinating the state more securely to themselves.

This points to the crucial importance of what I call a "state-finance nexus" in the rise of capital as a distinctive mode of production. The underlying importance of this state-finance nexus in the history of capital has not been fully appreciated. There is now a substantial literature on the formation of what is called the "military-fiscal state" from the late medieval period onwards, which focuses on how state power merged with financialization in the perpetual wars of the late medieval period, and how this form of the state became an important agent in dictating those "conditions" to which Marx vaguely alludes as being necessary for the transition to a capitalist mode of production. To those who prefer a literary rendition of this process, I refer you to Hilary Mantel's historical novel, *Wolf Hall*, which is about the life of Thomas Cromwell, who became financial advisor to Henry VIII and played a crucial role in the merging of state and capital during that period. Of course, the novel is about all the court intrigues (everything from the marriage and execution of Anne Boleyn to the execution of Sir Thomas More); but, beneath the surface, we see the nature of the British state evolving in crucial ways. It is still the case that, at crucial moments, the pinnacle of the banking system (currently the Federal Reserve in the United States) must come together with that aspect of state power that deals in monetary questions (currently the US Treasury) to devise common policies to confront crisis conditions that threaten jointly both state and capital. Those common policies have to deal with both commercial and state debts, and the relations between them. It was no accident that, in the wake of the Lehman Brothers collapse, the two figures who dominated the media in the United States were Hank Paulson (secretary of the Treasury) and Ben Bernanke (chair of the Federal Reserve), while the President had little or nothing to say. This was the state-finance nexus in action, both exposed (it prefers to remain in the shadows) and personified. The crisis of the euro has been as deep as it has precisely because this state-finance nexus has yet to cohere and perform adequately within the European Union as a whole, even as the appointed "technocratic" governments that temporarily replaced the democratically elected governments of Italy and Greece actually signify the assertion of direct rule on the part of the state-finance nexus. The president of France and the German chancellor now seem to recognize the necessity (to a considerable degree in opposition to their own stated political beliefs) to modify or renegotiate the European charter (and revise the powers of the European Central Bank) to confront the same sorts of issues (perhaps even in the same way) that arose in Venice and Genoa so long ago.

Be that as it may,

> this violent struggle against usury, the demand for the subjection of interest-bearing capital to industrial capital, is simply the prelude to the organic creation that these conditions of capitalist production produce in the form of the modern banking system, which on the one hand robs usurer's capital of its monopoly, since it concentrates all dormant money reserves together and places them on the money market, while on the other hand restricting the monopoly of the precious metals themselves by creating credit money. (C3, 738)

In Britain, this transition was greeted by a "howl of rage" on the part of goldsmiths (who had a vested interest in preserving the monopoly power of the precious metals) and the pawnbrokers against the formation of the Bank of England, which was designed to consolidate the functioning of an open money market. The hegemonic demand at the time was for "the subjugation of interest-bearing capital and loanable means of production in general" as one of "the preconditions" for a fully functioning capitalist mode of production. Marx amusedly noted, "If we just look at the phrases used, the way they coincide with the banking and credit illusions of the Saint-Simonians is often astonishing, right down to the very words" (C3, 740). This leads him into some commentary on the "religion saint-simonienne" and the role of the Péreire brothers, which I have already elaborated upon.

> It must never be forgotten, however, firstly that money in the form of precious metal remains the foundation from which the credit system can *never* break free, by the very nature of the case. Secondly, that the

credit system presupposes the monopoly possession of the social means of production (in the form of capital and landed property) on the part of private individuals and that it is itself on the one hand an immanent form of the capitalist mode of production and on the other hand a driving force of this development into its highest and last possible form. (C3, 741)

Marx evidently forgot the golden rule that one should "never say never," because we now have a monetary system without a metallic base. We might also view with some skepticism the teleological idea, promoted by Lenin a century ago, that finance capital is the "highest and last possible form" that a capitalist mode of production can assume. While historical phases undoubtedly exist in which finance capital becomes more prominent, and even hegemonic, I do not believe that the balance of forces between factions of capital is destined to evolve in one direction only.

But we may now have arrived at the point where the "immanent relation" between money and the state has become so tightly bound that it is impossible to imagine a state power that can regulate and control financialization from the outside. Evidence for this can be seen in the recent Dodd-Frank financial regulatory reform act in the United States, which was basically written by bankers and, to the degree that its implementation was left vague, is being undermined clause by clause largely according to the desires of the banking lobby. But if I am right about the long-lasting role of the state-finance nexus in the history of capitalism, then this "immanence" goes back to the origins of capital itself. Does this mean that the state is simply a tool of capital, or has the long-standing fusion of state and finance (and note it is finance and not capital in general) morphed into something radically different in recent years? Certainly, the overt power of the bondholders over state policies now seems greater than before. But I can also remember Harold Wilson, British Labour prime minister back in the 1960s, complaining about the power of the "gnomes of Zurich" to dictate his economic policy, even as he conceded to the demands of the financiers of the City of London against the interests of productive capital in Britain. There is a parallel with Bill Clinton's famous frustrated exclamation as he sat down with his economic advisors before his first inauguration: "You mean to say my economic policy and my prospects for reelection depend on the views of a bunch of fucking bond traders?" To which the answer was a resounding "Yes!" We do not, I think, have a sufficiently sophisticated history of the intertwining powers of state and finance to tell whether we are now in a different situation or not, although we do know for sure that the problems of financial regulation and institutional reform are now international in scope, and beyond the power of any one state to dictate.

But Marx gives a peculiar twist to where this "immanent force" within the credit system might lead. The "social character of capital is mediated and completely realized only by the full development of the credit and banking system. . . . It thereby abolishes the private character of capital and thus inherently bears within it, though only inherently, the abolition of capital itself." This is a pretty astonishing statement, but it will be repeated elsewhere, as we shall see. Banking and credit "also become the most powerful means for driving capitalist production beyond its own barriers and one of the most effective vehicles for crises and swindling" (C3, 742). So which direction will capital go? This is, of course, the question that underpins the characterization of Isaac Péreire as both "swindler and prophet."

The prophetic aspect is important to Marx:

> There can be no doubt that the credit system will serve as a powerful lever in the course of transition from the capitalist mode of production to the mode of production of associated labour; however, only as one element in connection with other large-scale organic revolutions in the mode of production itself. On the other hand, illusions about the miraculous power of the credit and banking system, in the socialist sense, arise from complete ignorance about the capitalist mode of production and about the credit system as one of its forms. (C3, 743)

The ignoramus in this case, it soon becomes clear, is Proudhon, with his proposal for free credit as the socialist panacea.

What Marx seems to be proposing here is that, in the same way that usury played an important precursive if antediluvian role in the rise of capitalism, but had to be revolutionized into the sociality of the money market and the circulation of interest-bearing capital, so the latter is destined to play a precursive role in the transition to socialism. The "organic transition" to socialism will depend, however, upon many other conditions and factors. What this leaves us with is a tantalizing set of open questions about the role of money, banking and credit not only in the transition but within socialist/communist society itself.

One further point in this chapter is worthy of note:

> We have seen how merchant's capital and interest-bearing capital are the oldest forms of capital. But it lies in the very nature of the matter that interest-bearing capital should appear to the popular mind as the form of capital *par excellence*. . . . In interest-bearing capital . . . the self-reproducing character of capital, self-valorizing value, the production of surplus-value, appears as a purely occult quality. (C3, 744)

Everything therefore seems derivative of it. The result is that "the internal articulation of the capitalist mode of production is misconstrued." Interest-bearing capital can and does take paths other than those defined directly by the production of surplus-value. These other paths will later be examined under the heading of fictitious capital. But here, says Marx, it is

> irrelevant and senseless to drag in the renting of houses, etc., for individual consumption. It is plain enough that the working class is swindled in this form too, and to an enormous extent, but it is equally exploited by the petty trader who supplies the worker with means of subsistence. This is secondary exploitation, which proceeds alongside the original exploitation that takes place directly within the production process. (C3, 745)

Marx is not often very sensitive to these "secondary" forms of exploitation, no matter how vicious. This is one of the rare moments when they at least rate a mention. It implies the possibility of a serious gap between where surplus-value is produced and where and how it is recuperated and realized by the capitalist class as a whole.

CHAPTER SEVEN

The Role of Credit
and the Banking System
(Chapter 27 Onwards in Volume III)

So why, then, is credit necessary for the production and reproduction of capital? In what sense is it possible to view the activities of the financial sector as productive of value and/or of surplus-value? In chapter 27, Marx lists a number of crucial roles that it plays. Summarizing:

1. It facilitates the smooth flows of money capital between sectors and industries in such a way that the profit rate is everywhere equalized. This is, I think, what Marx primarily had in mind when he referred earlier to credit as functioning as "the common capital of the class." The "butterfly" form of capital moves to standardize the rate of return across different industries, activities and places.

2. It significantly reduces (a) the costs of circulation by dispensing with the use of commodity moneys, replacing gold with paper and reducing the necessity for a reserve fund (hoarding) to accommodate fluctuations in commodity exchange, while (b) reducing turnover times (or, what amounts to the same thing, "accelerating the velocity of the metamorphoses of commodities" and increasing "the velocity of monetary circulation"). This acceleration of circulation carries over to the reproduction process of capital in general. In short, it facilitates speed-up (which is clear from the analysis of turnover times).

3. It allows the formation of joint-stock companies, which dramatically expand the scale of possible production enterprises, permit the privatization of formerly government functions, and help centralize capitals (as mentioned in Volume I). This means that many capitalist enterprises now take on a social as opposed to a private and individual character. Marx somewhat surprisingly concludes that "this is the abolition of capital as private property within the confines of the capitalist mode of production itself." It consolidates the "transformation

of the actual functioning capitalist into a mere manager, in charge of other people's capital and of the capital owner into a mere owner, a mere money capitalist" (C3, 567).

A variety of consequences flow from this last transformation. If the manager does indeed merely earn wages of superintendence, then capital now appears as the property right inherent in the ownership of pure money capital seeking interest "vis-à-vis all individuals really active in production from the manager down to the lowest day-labourer" (C3, 568). The production of surplus-value appears as a mere means to satisfy that right. The capitalist as direct producer becomes a manager of other people's money capital:

> In joint-stock companies, [production] is separated from capital ownership, so labour is also completely separate from ownership of the means of production and of surplus labour. This result of capitalist production in its highest development is a necessary point of transition towards the transformation of capital back into the property of the producers, though no longer as the private property of individual producers but rather as their property as associated producers, as directly social property. It is furthermore a point of transition towards the transformation of all functions formerly bound up with capital ownership in the reproduction process into simple functions of the associated producers, into social functions. (C3,568)

Whenever the concept of the "associated producers" enters into Marx's argument, it usually holds out some progressive possibilities. The "socialization" of capital through the formation of joint-stock companies suggests a transitional state that has the potential to evolve in different directions. There are implications for how the laws of motion of capital operate:

> Since profit here simply assumes the form of interest, enterprises that merely yield an interest are possible, and this is one of the reasons that hold up the fall in the general rate of profit, since these enterprises, where the constant capital stands in such a tremendous ratio to the variable, do not necessarily go into the equalization of the general rate of profit. (C3, 568)

Paul Boccara, chief theorist of the French Communist Party in the late 1960s, argued this was a major force counteracting the tendency for the rate of profit to fall during those years. Capital invested in large-scale infrastructures (no matter whether financed by the state or by joint-stock companies) can indeed, and generally does, circulate in this way—commanding interest only—in effect subsidizing profits elsewhere. Individual capitalists may also choose to rent much of their constant capital (such as forklift trucks and other forms of machinery), and in so doing they reduce the cost (to them) of that constant capital considerably. They simply pay the equivalent of interest on the loan of that capital in commodity form, rather than paying the equivalent of the commodity's full value (interest plus profit).

The physical mass of the fixed capital now embedded in the built environment (a physical mass that gives credence to the idea of a massive rise in the ratio of constant to variable capital circulating in production) for the most part circulates as interest-bearing capital capturing rents, rather than through the direct buying and selling of the commodities involved. The relationship between the extraction of rents and the circulation of interest-bearing capital (as best exemplified in the existence of huge mortgage markets) would then become an important feature in capitalist dynamics. This is a topic that Marx barely touches upon (though mortgages, as we shall shortly see, are defined as a form of "fictitious capital").

But the deeper possibility is this. The transformation of the productive capitalist into a mere manager entails "the abolition of the capitalist mode of production within the capitalist mode of production itself, and hence a self-abolishing contradiction, which presents itself prima facie as a mere point of transition to a new form of production" (C3, 569). This is a fairly astonishing statement. What does it signify? This transformation does not necessarily point in a progressive direction:

It gives rise to monopoly in certain spheres and hence provokes state intervention. It reproduces a new financial aristocracy, a new kind of parasite in the guise of company promoters, speculators and merely nominal directors; an entire system of swindling and cheating with respect to the promotion of companies, issues of shares and share dealings. It is private production unchecked by private ownership. (C3, 569)

This is what happens when capital and business become, as witty commentators in Second Empire Paris liked to call it, "other people's money." This was the world that the Péreire brothers constructed: Saint-Simonian utopianism become dystopian. The "financial aristocracy" to which Marx points is even more prominent today.

"Credit offers the individual capitalist, or the person who can pass as a capitalist, an absolute command over the capital and property of others . . . and through this, command over other people's labour. It is disposal over social capital, rather than his own, that gives him command over social labour." Marx attaches great potential importance to the sociality that is involved here. "The actual capital that someone possesses, or is taken to possess by public opinion, now becomes simply the basis for a superstructure of credit." As a result, "all standards of measurement, all explanatory reasons that were still more or less justified within the capitalist mode of production, now vanish. What the speculating trader risks is social property, not his own. Equally absurd now is the saying that the origin of capital is saving since what this speculator demands is precisely that *others* should save for him" (C3, 570).

Goodbye to the Weberian myth of the abstemious Protestant ethic and the rise of capitalism—the "illusion" that "capital is the offspring of a person's own work and savings is thereby demolished" (C3, 640). It gives the lie to the theory of abstinence and undermines the moral case for profit as a reward for bourgeois virtue. The capitalist merely borrows and makes money using the savings of others.

> Conceptions that still had a certain meaning at a less developed state of capitalist production now become completely meaningless. Success and failure lead in both cases to the centralization of capitals and hence to expropriation on the most enormous scale. Expropriation now extends from the immediate producers to the small and medium capitalists themselves. Expropriation is the starting-point of the capitalist mode of production, whose goal is to carry it through to completion, and even in the last instance to expropriate all individuals from the means of production. . . . Within the capitalist system itself, this expropriation takes the antithetical form of the appropriation of social property by a few, and credit gives these few ever more the character of simple adventurers. Since ownership now exists in the form of shares, its movement and

transfer become simply the result of stock-exchange dealings, where little fishes are gobbled up by the sharks and sheep by the stock-exchange wolves. (C3, 570–1)

The credit system, in short, becomes the main vehicle for that contemporary form of primitive accumulation that I call "accumulation by dispossession." How much of the wealth of today's financial aristocracy has been accumulated through the expropriation of the wealth of others (including other capitalists) through the machinations of the financial system?

But there is something deeply discordant about all this that Marx does not explicitly address. The general theme he enunciates in the history of money-dealing capital is that usury and interest had to be disciplined and rendered subservient to the requirements of a capitalist mode of production in general, and to the circulation of industrial capital in particular. Yet these passages suggest that the capitalist credit system is totally out of control, that it now returns to threaten the world of capital and surplus-value production in pernicious and perverted ways. It centers an economy of accumulation through dispossession rather than an economy of labor exploitation in production. It reinscribes usurious practices in the economy, though in a very different way from the usury of yore. Can this threaten the sustainability of capital accumulation? Marx gives no clear answer, but the possibility is certainly implied.

This question seems to permeate the subsequent investigations. The result is an interesting analytic description that has some relevance to an understanding of the global state we are currently in, and its financial contradictions. "If the credit system appears as the principal lever of overproduction and excessive speculation in commerce, this is simply because the reproduction process, which is elastic by nature, is now forced to its most extreme limit; and this is because a great part of the social capital is applied by those who are not its owners" (C3, 572). This was, of course, the rationale that led Adam Smith to voice his disapproval of joint-stock companies, except to finance large-scale transport enterprises (such as canals) and public utilities that could not otherwise be constructed. The rise of the credit system clearly shows "how the valorization of capital founded on the antithetical character of capitalist production permits actual free development only up to a certain point, which is constantly broken through by the credit system." Credit is, in short, the primary means by which the accumulation of capital evades all limits, because credit moneys can be created without limit. "The credit system," Marx continues, "accelerates the material development of the productive forces and the creation of the world market, which it is the historical task of the capitalist mode of production to bring to a certain level of development, as material foundations for the new form of production." (Note the teleology here, but note also that there is no immediate hint as to what this new form of production might look like.) From this standpoint, the credit system contributes mightily to the production of value and surplus-value: "At the same time, credit accelerates the violent outbreaks of this contradiction, crises, and with these the elements of the dissolution of the old mode of production." The credit system "develops the motive of capitalist production, enrichment by the exploitation of others' labour, into the purest and most colossal system of gambling and swindling, and restricts ever more the already small number of the exploiters of social wealth; on the other hand it constitutes the form of transition to a new mode of production"(C3, 571).

So what is it that the "swindler" Isaac Péreire prophesized? Marx takes up some positive possibilities. Joint-stock companies emphasize the sociality of production, and thus an "opposition between the character of wealth as something social" and the way this wealth "remains trapped" within "capitalist barriers" of private ownership. Can this sociality be liberated? Can this contradiction be exploited? Marx seems to think so:

> The cooperative factories run by the workers themselves are, within the old form, the first examples of the emergence of a new form, even though they naturally reproduce in all cases, in their present organization, all the defects of the existing system, and must reproduce them. But the opposition between capital and labour is abolished here, even if at first only in the form that the workers in association become their own capitalist. . . . These factories show how, at a certain stage of development of the material forces of production, and of the social forms of production corresponding to them, a new mode of production develops and is formed naturally out of the old. (C3, 571)

This development could not occur had it not been for the rise of the factory system, with its emphasis upon cooperation and organized detailed divisions of labor, while the credit system presents the means for the gradual extension of cooperative enterprise on a more or less national scale. Capitalist joint-stock companies as much as cooperative factories should be viewed as transition forms from the capitalist mode of production to the associated one, simply that in the one case the opposition is abolished in a negative way, and in the other in a positive way. (C3, 571–2)

This positive potentiality is periodically revisited by socialist thinkers in, for example, Peter Drucker's commentary on "pension fund socialism," or the more active Rudolf Meidner plan for the gradual displacement of capitalism by worker's corporate ownership, by the payment of workers partly through stock acquisitions that would ultimately confer worker ownership of the corporations that now employ them.[2] While hopes of such transitions continue to spring eternal, there is unfortunately no doubt whatsoever that the dominant historical trend has been of an opposite, negative sort.

This brings us back to the idea, occasionally broached throughout all three volumes of *Capital*, that collective and associated labor constitutes the basis for the construction of an anticapitalist alternative. Since this is one of the few occasions where Marx actually describes a transitional mechanism from capitalism to socialism and communism, it cries out for some commentary. After Marx had drafted this chapter, Engels inserted a couple of pages describing the evolution of the power of corporate capital. The inference is that Engels thought that the moment at which anything progressive might be constructed out of all of this had long passed. Engels elsewhere notes Marx's profound respect for the ideas of Saint-Simon, which centered on the power of associated capitals to be mobilized for progressive purposes. Marx here embellishes on that idea, and takes up the prospects for associated capital to be managed through workers' cooperative control. While he concedes that such worker cooperatives are bound to reproduce many of the defects of the existing system, they at least provide a basis for the conquest of a national space through the spread of cooperative movements and practices. Marx seems to have thought this possibility to be very real back in

---

2   Peter Drucker, *The Unseen Revolution: How Pension Fund Socialism Came to America* (New York: Harpercollins, 1976); Robin Blackburn, "Rudolf Meidner: A Visionary Pragmatist," *Counterpunch*, December 22, 2005.

the 1850s and 1860s. Engels seems to think that this moment of possibility quickly passed. But was it real even then?

This question is important, since there are many movements in motion in our own times that believe that this moment has come again—that the democratization of production through factory takeovers, the development of alternative solidarity economies, bartering networks and other cooperative forms can in itself be a path towards a radical anticapitalist reconstruction of political and economic life. Even as many participants recognize the difficulty of self-exploitation and the inevitable reproduction within the cooperative forms of many of the defects of the capitalist system they seek to displace, this path is often depicted as the only one possible for a democratic anticapitalist movement. It seems as if the rise of the credit system and the socialization of capital provides a "natural" basis upon which cooperatives and worker control might flourish. There is no mention here, however, of the demand articulated in the *Communist Manifesto* for the centralization of all credit in the hands of a worker-controlled state.

We come back in our own time to the compelling example of Mondragon. It succeeds without state support. But it survives, as we have seen, partly because it builds relations across the circulations of production, money and commodity capital. It has its own credit and retail structures. Differentials in remuneration between the shareholders are much circumscribed, and decision-making is democratized. Ironically, the main left criticism of Mondragon is that it acts like a corporation and like a joint-stock company. There appears, therefore, to be something to Marx's intuitive sense of some underlying continuities between the association of capitals of which Saint-Simon made so much and the creation and survival of alternative cooperative worker structures within the framework of capitalism. If the earth were covered with Mondragons, if the recuperated worker-controlled enterprises in Argentina could survive and proliferate, even as they necessarily reproduced capitalist forms of competition and self-exploitation, then we would be living in a very different and potentially far more progressive world. Is this what Marx means when he refers to the abolition of the capitalist mode of production within the capitalist mode of production, and depicts it as a self-dissolving contradiction? These are interesting questions.

But there are also plenty of cautionary tales. Some years back, in an influential book by Piore and Sabel called *The Second Industrial Divide*, the argument was made that new labor practices of flexible specialization and small-batch production were opening a space (similar to that which existed in 1848) where small-scale cooperative production under the control of workers (as exhibited in places like the Third Italy of Emilia-Romagna) would drive out the corporate-dominated factory form and provide a transitional mechanism to a decentralized socialism.[3] Piore and Sabel waged a quite effective campaign (particularly in Europe) to persuade organized labor to drop opposition to these new technological and organizational forms and embrace flexible specialization as liberatory (they were very much enamored of Proudhon's ideas, which Marx, of course, could not abide). What Piore and Sabel did not recognize was that flexible specialization was to underpin the viciously exploitative practices of flexible accumulation so central to the neoliberal project. Flexible specialization became the primary means to discipline and repress the workforce everywhere it was deployed. Nobody now speaks favorably of its emancipatory possibilities. There is, sadly, a long history of seemingly liberatory possibilities being recuperated into the dominant practices of capitalist exploitation. So, be careful what you wish for.

ON CHAPTER 28 OF VOLUME III: MEANS OF CIRCULATION AND CAPITAL

Chapter 28 is largely taken up with disputing the views of Tooke and others who held there was a distinction between money as capital and money as currency in circulation. I will not examine Marx's critique (or Engels's additions) in any detail. From Marx's perspective, the more relevant distinction is between money used by capitalists to buy the commodities to be used in production and money borrowed to purchase the commodities produced. The distinction is "between *the money form of revenue* and *the money form of capital*" (C3, 575). Both uses of money are incorporated into the circulation of industrial capital. Marx sometimes refers to the flow of credit into production as "money capital," as opposed to the "money-dealing capital" that flows to consumers to support the realization of value and surplus-value in the marketplace.

---

3   Michael Piore and Charles Sabel, *The Second Industrial Divide: Possibilities for Prosperity* (New York: Basic Books, 1986).

Bankers can furnish loan capital for production and credit to consumers to buy the commodities produced. For example, the same bankers can lend both to developers to build tract housing and to consumers to buy them with a mortgage. The demand for means of payment (consumer credit) and for means of purchase (loan capital) are neither synchronized nor equal. But the lack of either can constitute a barrier within the circulation of industrial capital. While Marx does not make the point, we can also infer the possibility that, under conditions of easy credit and much surplus liquidity, both the supply of and demand for a crucial commodity (such as housing) can create an investment "bubble" precisely because the flows of interest-bearing capital can operate so freely to influence both supply and demand conditions: "The two spheres of circulation have an inner connection, since on the one hand the amount of revenue to be spent expresses the scale of consumption, while on the other the amount of capital circulating in production and trade expresses the scale and speed of the reproduction process" of capital (C3, 578).

A number of ancillary features here come into focus, such as the velocity of circulation of money and the role of the credit system in accommodating these demands. That movements in availability can produce cyclical fluctuations of seeming prosperity followed by actual droughts is obvious, and Marx gives brief indications as to how the monetary and credit aspects of such movements typically behave. What we saw in the housing markets of many countries, from the US to Ireland and Spain in 2005–12, was the production of an asset bubble followed by a savage collapse of financial flows, as housing prices got way out of line with incomes.

ON CHAPTER 29 OF VOLUME III: THE PROBLEM OF BANKING AND FICTITIOUS CAPITAL

What is bank capital really about, and how does it circulate? This is the question that animates chapter 29, and it leads into a discussion of a very important category that Marx dubs "fictitious capital."

Banking capital itself consists of "(1) cash in the form of gold or notes; (2) securities." The securities are of two sorts: "commercial paper, current bills of exchange that fall due on specified dates, their discounting being the specific business of the banker; and public securities, such as government bonds, treasury bills and stocks of all kinds," including mortgages (C3, 594). The capital held by the bank can be divided between that of the banker himself and other people's money—i.e. deposits and savings, along with any notes that the bank has the right to issue.

Marx examines what happens when this banking capital is lent out in return for interest. Interest, he points out, can be viewed as equivalent to any flow of revenue. If the rate of interest is 5 percent, any "annual income of £25 is seen as the interest on a capital of £500." But this is, Marx comments, a "purely illusory notion." There does not have to be any actual money capital behind the flow of revenues. Many US citizens receive monthly social security checks, for example, but it is illusory to believe that this flow of money is the interest on some mass of capital held by the state. But, by promising to turn over the $25,000 a year that the social security recipient receives to the bank, the former can acquire money capital of $500,000 to buy a house. The annual flow of $25,000 is capitalized into $500,000 even though there is no original amount of money capital behind the social security payments (just a promise of the state to furnish the monthly income that it funds by placing a tax on wages). This brings us to consider one of Marx's most important concepts, that of fictitious capital.

"The state has to pay its creditors a certain sum of interest each year for the capital it borrows. In this case the creditor cannot recall his capital from the debtor but can only sell the claim, his title of ownership. The capital itself has been consumed, spent by the state. It no longer exists." It has, for example, been spent on waging a war in Iraq and Afghanistan.

> What the state's creditor possesses is (1) the state's promissory note for, say, £100; while (2) this note gives him a claim on the state's annual revenue, i.e. the proceeds of the year's taxation, to a certain amount, say £5 or 5 per cent; (3) he is free to sell this promissory note to anyone he likes. If the rate of interest is 5 per cent, and assuming the state's security is good [which is not the case now with Greek state debt] owner A can generally sell the note for £100 to B: since it is the same thing for B whether he lends out £100 at 5 per cent per year or assures himself of an annual tribute of £5 from the state by paying out £100. *But in all these cases, the capital from which the state's payment is taken as deriving, as interest, is illusory and fictitious.* (C3, 595; emphasis added)

So this is Marx's initial definition of fictitious capital. "It is not only," Marx goes on to explain, "that the sum that was lent to the state no longer has any kind of existence" because it has been spent. "It was never designed to be spent as capital, to be invested, and yet only by being invested as capital could it have been made into a self-maintaining value." In other words, no surplus-value is being produced through the state's actions, yet it appears as if extra value is being produced since the state is paying out interest (supposedly a portion of a surplus-value being produced somewhere) on the money it borrows. Furthermore, the trade in the buying and selling of the state's promissory notes make it seem as if an original capital can be recovered (sometimes even at an extra profit, if the demand for promissory notes exceeds the supply). But "no matter how these transactions are multiplied, the capital of the national debt remains purely fictitious, and the moment these promissory notes become unsaleable, the illusion of this capital disappears. Yet this fictitious capital has its characteristic movement for all that, as we shall see soon" (C3, 596). The "characteristic movement" to which Marx refers is of the sort that we see in the daily and even hourly fluctuations in values on the stock and bond markets.

Interest-bearing capital thus appears as "the mother of every insane form" (C3, 595). This insanity is even more dramatically registered when bourgeois theorists take the flow of wages accruing to the laborer and create out of it the fiction of capital embodied in the worker. The value of the worker is then calculated as the capitalized value of the annual wages earned. Human capital value can then be enhanced, so this theory goes, by the worker investing in education and the acquisition of skills, all of which should then pay off in the form of higher wages. Workers are, according to human capital theory, capitalists! "Here the absurdity of the capitalist's way of conceiving things reaches its climax, in so far as instead of deriving the valorization of capital from the exploitation of labour-power, they explain the productivity of labour-power by declaring that labour-power itself is this mystical thing, interest-bearing capital."

This very convenient view of labor has become hegemonic in our perverted neoliberal times. If workers command low wages, then it is their own fault, it is said, for not taking the trouble to invest in their own human capital. If they all invested properly, then everyone would have much higher wages. Why, then, do we see taxi drivers these days with doctoral degrees? In any case, if workers truly were capitalists they would have the choice, as regular capitalists do, of actually working for a wage or lolling in a hammock and living off the interest on their capital.

Behind all of this lies a simple but crucial principle—that of capitalization: "The formation of fictitious capital is known as capitalization. Any regular periodic income can be capitalized by reckoning it up, on the basis of the average rate of interest, as the sum that a capital lent out at this interest rate would yield." The legal title to this flow of revenue can be traded at this capitalized price. "In this way, all connection with the actual process of capital's valorization is lost right down to the last trace, *confirming the notion that capital is automatically valorized by its own powers*" (C3, 597; emphasis added).

I cannot overemphasize the significance of this argument. In Volume I, Marx had commented on the conception of capital that made it seem as if it was "the goose that laid its own golden eggs," and here we see how the fetish appearance of self-valorization takes on a very specific form called fictitious capital, wrapping itself in mystery even as it becomes all too real in the bond, security and other markets in which property rights over different income and revenue streams become capitalized and sold as capital

> Even when the promissory note—the security—does not represent a purely illusory capital, as it does in the case of national debts, the capital value of this security is still pure illusion. We have already seen how the credit system produces joint-stock capital. Securities purport to be ownership titles representing this capital. The shares in railway, mining, shipping companies, etc. represent real capital, i.e. capital invested and functioning in these enterprises, or the sum of money that was advanced by the shareholders to be spent in these enterprises as capital. It is in no way ruled out here that these shares may be simply a fraud. But the capital does not exist twice over, once as the capital value of the ownership titles, the shares, and then again as the capital actually invested or to be invested in the enterprises in question. It exists only in the latter form, and the share is nothing but an ownership title, *pro rata*, to the surplus-value which this capital is to realize. (C3, 597)

It is, in effect, a claim on the future labor that will supposedly produce the surplus-value of which interest (a return to pure ownership) will be a part.

The markets for these bonds, stocks and shares are, of course, fluctuating: "The independent movement of these ownership titles' values . . . strengthens the illusion that they constitute real capital besides the capital or claim to which they may give title. . . . The market value of these securities is partly speculative, since it is determined not just by the actual revenue but rather by the anticipated revenue as reckoned in advance." Prices can move up or down, depending upon the prospects for future surplus-value production. Falling prices and crises bring devaluations of asset values, but "once the storm is over, these securities rise again to their former level" (assuming they were viable and not fraudulent). The loss of housing asset values in the United States after 2007 was huge, and there is little sign of recovery five years later. But, Marx presciently notes, the depreciation of these asset values in a crisis "is a powerful means of centralizing money wealth." Or, as the banker Andrew Mellon put it long ago, "in a crisis, assets return to their rightful owners" i.e. to him. Increasing centralization of wealth and power in the course of a crisis is an important historical fact (borne out in the financial crisis of 2007–12).

Speculative movements are not necessarily harmful. "As long as their depreciation was not the expression of any standstill in production and in railway and canal traffic, or an abandonment of undertakings already begun, or a squandering of capital in positively worthless enterprises, the nation was not a penny poorer by the bursting of these soap bubbles of nominal money capital" (C3, 599). This is so because

> all these securities actually represent nothing but accumulated claims, legal titles, to future production. . . . In all countries of capitalist production, there is a tremendous amount of so-called interest-bearing capital or "moneyed capital" in this form. And an accumulation of money capital means for the most part nothing more than an accumulation of these claims to production, and an accumulation of the market price of these claims, of their illusory capital value. (C3, 599)

If there was a "tremendous amount" of this kind of capital floating around in Marx's time, what kind of adjective would we need now to deploy?

"With the development of interest-bearing capital and the credit system, all capital seems to be duplicated, and at some points triplicated, by which the various ways in which the same capital, or even the same claim, appears in various hands in different guises. The greater part of this 'money capital' is purely fictitious" (C3, 601). This is nowhere more apparent than within the banking system itself:

> The greater part of banker's capital is therefore purely fictitious and consists of claims (bills of exchange) and shares (drafts on future revenues). It should not be forgotten here that this capital's money value, as represented by these papers in the banker's safe, is completely fictitious even in so far as they are drafts on certain assured revenues (as with government securities) or ownership titles to real capital (as with shares), their money value being determined differently from the value of the actual capital that they at least partially represent; or, where they represent only a claim to revenue and not capital at all, the claim to the same revenue is expressed in a constantly changing fictitious money capital. Added to this is the fact that this fictitious capital of the banker represents to a large extent not his own capital but rather that of the public who deposit with him, whether with interest or without. (C3, 600)

A Synthetic View of the Credit System According to Marx

Is there some way to synthesize Marx's general conception of the role of the credit system within the capitalist mode of production? Let us imagine a vast pot of money held by bankers, brokers, money dealers and so on, within some bounded entity called the credit system. At the base of the credit system lies the central bank, and beneath that lie commodity moneys, gold and silver in particular. These commodity moneys represent value, which is in turn based upon the sociality of human labor on the world market. Marx postulates a vertical hierarchical structure of this sort to the monetary system.

To what degree is each layer in the structure disciplined by the operations of the others? In a tightly coupled system, the behavior of the credit system would be very closely controlled by value requirements through the mediating layers of money commodities and the central bank. Clearly, Marx envisages a loosely coupled system. Credit operations are autonomous and independent from value production. Operations within the credit system likewise escape the controls of the central bank no matter how hard the latter struggles to discipline them. The design and actions of the central bank can be at odds (as Marx shows with respect to the 1844 Bank Act) with what would be required to preserve "real values" as represented by the money commodities.

But, in Volume I, Marx also identified several deep contradictions in the way money commodities represent value (for example, a particular concrete use-value like gold is used to measure abstract, universal, socially necessary labor time). To the degree that the sociality of labor is perpetually undergoing changes, so value relations are unstable. The disciplinary impulses imposed from one layer to another within this hierarchically organized monetary system are omnipresent but weakly articulated. By this, I mean that strong influences are perpetually percolating through the different layers, but that the signals they create are often confusing and contradictory.

This, I think, is the reason that Marx construed the credit system as "autonomous" and "independent" but still subsumed under the general laws of motion of capital. We have encountered this formulation of "autonomous and independent but subsumed under" before and plainly in the instance of the pivots structured into the money and credit system it requires some sort of interpretation. My favorite analogy is to say it is a bit like teenagers: on the one hand they are perpetually demanding and claiming their right to independence and autonomy, while on the other their financial and legal security is anchored in the household so that when things go wrong they come running home to mommy and daddy. In some ways this seems an apt analogy with the whole way in which the money and credit system works, with each layer within the pivots populated by ever more rambunctious teenagers with the most rambunctious operating at the very top as the so-called "masters of the universe." When the system crashes they all rush back to the parental state hoping they will get bailed out, which the state, being an indulgent and loving parent, invariably does.

The flow of disciplinary influences within this hierarchy of pivots is certainly not one-way. The deep base in the sociality of human labor does not exercise some determining if shadowy power over events within the "crazy" superstructures of credit. Commodity moneys (which Marx construed as being an ultimate and insuperable barrier that could "never" be transcended) have now been abolished in favor of an uninhibited credit system to accommodate endless compound growth. Periodically, events both within the credit system and in the dynamics of value production create pressures for a radical reform and repositioning of the central banks and other regulatory powers within the monetary system. (Is this what we are now experiencing?) While each layer "pivots" (to use Marx's term) on the conditions prevalent in the layer below it, there is no necessary presumption that these are mechanical pivots that have a permanent and unchanging form.

But, particularly in times of crisis, there seems to be some sort of disciplinary power, located in the world of value relations, that restores order to the system. Marx also concedes, however, that crises of confidence and of expectations within the credit system can wreak havoc on value and surplus-value production.

This is, roughly, the hierarchical structure of the money and credit system as Marx reconstructs it. Marx seems to be deeply ambivalent as to how best to understand its functioning. There is no clear theory to guide us here. The problem is to figure out, in a given conjuncture, what is actually happening where. Each layer seems to be constructed like a double-edged sword. On the one hand, commodity moneys constituted a restrictive barrier to endless accumulation. On the other hand, they exercised a strong disciplinary power over the craziness of speculation and fictitious capital flows. The abolition of commodity moneys (a move that would not, I think, have surprised Marx at all if he had held it to be technically possible) liberates endless capital accumulation from monetary chains, but it shifts the burden of credit discipline to fallible and sometimes whimsical human institutions such as the central banks. The problem for the central bank (and other facets of the state regulatory apparatus) is then to restore order within the credit system without destroying the conditions for surplus-value production, which is seemingly impossible to do (though Keynesians continue to fantasize its possibility). The hierarchical structure is by no means stable.

But we also need to look more closely at how interest-bearing capital circulates horizontally. The flows of interest-bearing capital come from somewhere and get dispersed down all manner of different channels, only some of which have to do with surplus-value production.

The money capitalists that populate the credit system operate to some minor degree with their own funds. But their main source of money power comes from assembling the money surpluses of others who use the services of the bank either as an intermediary to transfer funds to others or as a safe place to deposit their idle cash balances (which would otherwise be hoarded)—either temporarily or in the longer term—in return for a rate of interest. These money surpluses

Figure 5

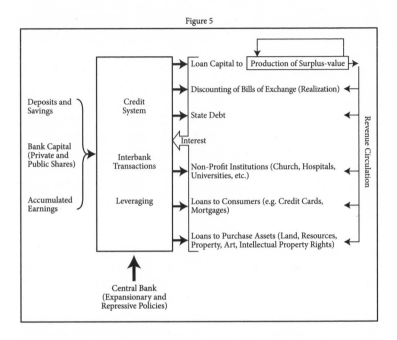

come from consumers of all sorts, as well as from capitalists who, as we saw in Volume II, need to hoard money to cover differential turnover times and fixed-capital investments and replacements. The banks make their money by offering, say, a 3 percent rate of interest on the money they borrow while lending out at, say, 5 percent. In this way, money is flowing into and constantly augmenting the pool of credit available. But where does the money so assembled flow to?

Lending out takes a variety of forms:

1)   *Loan capital*
Money is lent out to producers who use it to buy the constant and variable capital required to engage in surplus-value production. Suppose the production capitalist borrows money to buy machinery. The money is then repaid, along with interest, over the lifetime of the machine. The loan capital is thereby consumed, and returns to the original owner as it is consumed. This is money lent for real value and surplus-value production. There is nothing fictitious about it (although, of course, all investment of this sort is by definition speculative). Things

look different, however, when the money is procured by offering shares. The share is in fact a property right attached to pure money ownership. It is a legal claim to a share of future surplus-value production without any terminal date, even as the money is used up in productive consumption. The share can be bought and sold long after the machinery purchased with it has been amortized or become worn out (see C3, 608). The price of the share depends upon future expectations of surplus-value production. The movement of its value is open to all manner of speculative influences and is capable of all manner of manipulations, all the way to downright fraud. Stocks and shares are, therefore, a form of fictitious capital, but their fictitious character is mitigated by the fact that they retain a loose connection to value and surplus-value production (in money terms, the earnings of the company underpin the value of the shares). However, in the case of a company like Enron, it turned out that no surplus-value was actually being produced, even though the shares were trading high. The earnings posted were fraudulent.

2)   Loans for realization

Money can be lent to realize the value of commodities already produced (or even before, as with crops not yet harvested or houses yet to be built). The discount rate is equivalent to the rate of interest on bills of exchange which are due at some later date. The banker provides the money for realization of commodity values (at a discount), and takes over the bill of exchange in the hope of realizing its full value when it falls due. This operation is paralleled by the activities of merchants who also operate as money dealers. As Marx points out, however necessary this activity may be in smoothing out and shortening turnover times for the producer capitalists, there are all sorts of opportunities for chicanery and cheating. The piling up of bills of exchange drawn upon bills of exchange can in itself presage a collapse and a commercial crisis in its own right, which may or may not spill over to have profound effects on the conditions for the circulation and realization of capital. Loans for realization (means of purchase) can be integrated with loans to production (means of payment) such that the credit system can manage both the supply of and demand for a given commodity (such as housing), and it is easy to see how this can produce asset bubbles from time to time, such as that which arose in housing markets in the United States after 2000 or so.

3) Loans to the state and the national debt

The state can borrow capital sums against its power to raise revenues (through taxes and fees). It promises a share of anticipated future revenues in return for a capital sum. Titles to state debt can be traded long after the money borrowed has been used up. Much of what the state spends the money on has little or nothing to do directly with the production of surplus-value (although it often develops indirect relations by forming a viable market for, say, military hardware). This is fictitious capital par excellence. The state generally produces no value or surplus-value (it maintains a monarchy and fights wars, for example). Taxation of revenues is converted into a flow of interest payments that can be capitalized into a lump sum, and then traded as a claim on future revenues. Some categories of state expenditures do relate to surplus-value production. There are state-run enterprises (these were important in many parts of the world until the wave of neoliberal privatizations began after 1980 or so, and they continue to be important in China). While these enterprises do not necessarily have to earn a profit, they provide inputs to other firms at lower cost, which affects overall profit rates. The state also invests in physical infrastructures necessary for production (highways, public utilities, sewage and water provision, and the like). It can provide these constant capital inputs in return for interest only, and so help mitigate any tendency for the rate of profit to fall. The category of debt-financed "productive state expenditures" became very important early in the physical reconstruction of Second Empire Paris under Haussmann, for example. But most state debt is purely fictitious.

4) Loans to non-profit institutions

Here would be included private hospitals, universities, churches, museums and all manner of cultural institutions. Loans to them would also fall into the category of fictitious capital, since for the most part they produce no value or surplus-value (although some branches of universities and hospitals may be directly involved in surplus-value production through innovation and research). The revenues to pay the interest on loans can come from a variety of sources, but mainly depend in our times on user fees and donations.

5) Consumer loans

By far the most important form of consumer loan in the United States is the housing mortgage, which Marx explicitly lists as a form of fictitious capital. The mortgage market in the US at its peak, in 2007, amounted to $14 trillion (as compared to the total GDP for that year of around $15 trillion). In this case the revenue stream to pay the interest comes from wages, salaries and government redistributions. The house is not generally used for value or surplus-value production, hence the designation of mortgage finance as a form of fictitious capital. Of course, if I turned my house into a sweatshop it would then qualify as a form of fixed capital in production. And, while there is no direct value or surplus-value production taking place in the home, the role of household labor in fixing the value of labor-power clearly affects surplus-value production. Consumer debt is now huge business, and it plays a crucial role in the management of aggregate demand in an economy as well as providing abundant opportunities for the secondary forms of exploitation that Marx occasionally acknowledges but generally excludes as peripheral to his interests.

6)   Loans to acquire and purchase assets and other paper claims to revenues (such as royalties on natural resources, patents, and rents on land and property)

The proliferation of asset markets (everything from art investments to land and resource grabs) has been a marked feature of recent capitalist history, and a great deal of surplus money-dealing capital flows into these markets.

Bankers do not generally discriminate (though they may specialize) between these different loan options. Their capital can flow to wherever the demand, the rate of return and the security of the loan are strongest, and wherever future prospects look brightest. Expectations—faith in the future—play a prominent role in the movement of these markets. The possibility also exists for a "crowding out" of some investment possibilities by the high demand (and expectations) for others. (This is a frequent criticism of strong government borrowing or asset bubbles: that they crowd out investment in productive activities and raise interest costs for others.) The credit system does not typically discriminate between different forms of investment, and certainly not between those that are purely fictitious; those that are partially fictitious, because at least loosely connected to the production of surplus-value; and those directly engaged with the circuit of industrial capital as loan (money) capital. Imbalances in the flows of interest-bearing money capital will frequently occur. Precisely because these flows are independent and autonomous, they can affect the overall laws of motion of capitalist development while periodically precipitating a crisis on their own account. If, for example, a great deal of surplus money-dealing capital flows into the land and property markets (as happened in Japan in the late 1980s and in the United States, Spain, Ireland, and so on after 2000), then huge distortions in flows of credit and speculative booms in those asset values can result until the crash materializes to force a correction.

If we take a kaleidoscopic view of all these flows of credit, it becomes readily apparent that the banking and credit factions (or "classes" as Marx occasionally calls them) have a strong vested interest in sustaining, and if possible expanding, the different markets for the flows of fictitious capital, particularly if the channels are relatively easy to manipulate and exploit. For example, a vast amount of activity is taken up in the United States in extending credit to homeownership, even when bubble conditions are not in evidence. This is a primary way in which wealth can be recaptured by capital from consumers in general, and from labor in particular.

Extractive as opposed to productive activities have long predominated within these credit markets. There is no firewall within the banking system between the activities of lending to produce surplus-value, lending to realize surplus-value, and lending to fictitious capital markets. The money capitalists, working in their own interest in markets where signals are detached from the need to promote surplus-value production, make individual decisions that in aggregate may make absolutely no sense. Hence the instabilities and periodic crises emanating from within the credit system.

Money Capital, Real Capital and the Industrial Cycle

I shall not attempt any close reading or interpretation of the remaining chapters on money and credit. But there are some issues posed that command our attention, particularly in chapters 30 and 31.

Marx, while plainly perplexed by the volatility and speculative insecurity that characterized the world of money, banking and credit, sought to understand the logic (if any) behind the cyclical booms and crashes going on around him. These clearly posed a major threat to the reproduction of capital, and forced periodic devaluations of much of the capital in circulation. The continuity of the circulation process of capital emphasized in Volume II is plainly subject to disruption in ways that were posited as possible in that volume but not elaborated upon.

The question that hovers over these chapters in Volume III is: Why might this be inevitable and necessary, given the nature of the contradictions to which the circulation of industrial capital is prone? And what might be the overall impacts of the "crazy" and "insane" aspects of this financial system upon the laws of motion of capital? To what degree, for example, is the accumulation of money capital

> an index of genuine capital accumulation, i.e. of reproduction on an expanded scale? Is the phenomenon of a "plethora" of capital, an expression used only of interest-bearing capital, i.e. money capital, simply a particular expression of industrial overproduction, or does it form a separate phenomenon alongside this? Does such a plethora and oversupply of money capital, coincide with the presence of stagnant sums of money . . . so that this excess of actual money is an expression and form of appearance of this plethora of loan capital?

In contemporary parlance, when the world is "awash in surplus liquidity" (as the IMF regularly claimed before the collapse of 2008), does this signal an overaccumulation of real capital or simply an excess of money as potential loan capital? Conversely, "to what extent does monetary scarcity, i.e. a shortage of loan capital, express a lack of real capital (commodity capital and productive capital)"? Or does it simply indicate "a lack of means of circulation?" (C3, 607).

Again, in contemporary parlance, is the contraction of the money supply and the freezing of interbank credit flows a sign of financial repression imposed by central banks and state authorities, or does it signal a lack of profitable investment opportunities?

Underlying this is a more general question: To what degree is there an association between the accumulation of debts and the accumulation of wealth? This is the question that the proliferation of forms of fictitious capital poses. "Accumulation of capital in the form of the national debt," for example, "means nothing more than the growth of a class of state creditors with a preferential claim to certain sums from the overall proceeds of taxation." Hence, "even an accumulation of debts can appear as an accumulation of capital" (C3, 608). As always, however, the word "appears" signals that something else is probably going on behind the fetish mask. But what? The problem is that an accumulation of promissory notes (fictitious capital) can be transformed into actual money capital, thus making fictitious capital real. This presumes, however, that the promissory notes can be traded. This in turn implies that fictitious capital continues to circulate as before. The same is true of stocks and shares, which are "nominal representatives of non-existent capitals":

> In so far as the accumulation of these securities expresses an accumulation of railways, mines, steamships, etc., it expresses an expansion of the actual reproduction process, just as the expansion of a tax list on personal property, for example, indicates an expansion of this property itself. But as duplicates that can themselves be exchanged as commodities, and hence circulate as capital values, they are illusory, and their values can rise and fall quite independently of the movement in value of the actual capital to which they are titles. (C3, 608)

We have many examples of exactly this process in recent times: in order to get sufficient capital to start a business many individuals refinanced the mortgage on their homes during the housing boom, only to find after the crash that the fictitious capital they had extracted and turned into investment capital no longer existed, and that they now owed more on the house than its current market price. But if in the meantime their business had been successful, then they might have recouped enough to compensate for their earlier conversion of fictitious capital, now exposed as such, into real money capital. Many people who engaged in the fraudulent trading of fictitious capitals in housing mortgage markets became enormously rich, having transformed the fraudulent claims into real money power.

This highlights something about how Marx uses categories in a relational and fluid manner. In the same way that a particular use-value can shift from being fixed capital to being circulating capital or part of the consumption fund overnight, through a change of use, so what is fictitious capital at one moment can instantaneously be transformed into real money power (for capital or consumption) at another moment. When mortgages were packaged into collateralized debt obligations they existed, as it were, in a doubly fictitious state; but when a hedge fund manager traded them to unsuspecting and gullible investors and made a cool billion, he acquired real money power that was not, unfortunately, in any way fictitious.

Marx has some very acute and acerbic observations on the class consequences of such forms of wealth accumulation:

> Profits and losses that result from fluctuations in the price of these ownership titles, and also their centralization in the hands of railway magnates etc., are by the nature of the case more and more the result of gambling, which now appears in place of labour as the original source of capital ownership. . . . This kind of imaginary money wealth makes up a very considerable part not only of the money wealth of private individuals but also of banking capital.
>
> . . . The entire immense extension of the credit system, and credit as a whole, is exploited by the bankers as their private capital. These fellows have their capital and revenue permanently in the money form or in the form of direct claims to money. The accumulation of wealth by this class may proceed in a very different way from that of actual accumulation, but it proves in any case that they put away a good proportion of the latter. (C3, 609)

The behavior of this "class" of capitalists—the fraudulent and speculative swindling that goes on using "other people's money," and even the exploitation of the industrial capitalists—comes in for some severe pummeling in these chapters. But while the class consequences of this are plain enough to see, the question of what is happening to aggregate wealth creation and the laws of motion of capital through surplus-value production is much harder to elucidate.

In the passages that follow, Marx attempts to uncover the limits that might exist, both internal and external, to the functioning of the credit system, particularly with respect to commercial credits that capitalists extend to each other. The limits are set by "the wealth of the industrialists and merchants," and how quickly loans return to their point of origin. As "markets expand and become further removed from the point of production," so "credit must be prolonged," which in turn means that "the speculative element must come more and more to dominate transactions." "Large-scale production for distant markets" makes credit "indispensable." Indeed, credit "grows in volume with the growing value of production and grows in duration with the increasing distance of the markets" (C3, 612). Marx posits this as a reciprocal relation. The growth of credit facilitates the creation of the world market, while the expansion of the geographical range of commerce requires an expansion of the credit system. In this way, the production and revolutionizing of global spatial relations is intimately tied to the growth of the credit system. In the language of the *Grundrisse*, the credit system is the primary means producing capital's "annihilation of space through time."

But the central issue with which Marx attempts to come to grips in these chapters is the role of credit in fueling the booms and busts of industrial (or business) cycles. These were obvious features of capital's development in Marx's times, and were roughly ten years long (1836–37, 1847–48 and 1857 were all dramatic peak/crash years). Marx nowhere provides a coherent theory of these fluctuations from within his understanding of the general laws of motion of capital, though he does associate the periodic "plethora" of money capital with the theory of the overaccumulation of capital laid out in earlier chapters of Volume III. But he does provide a general description of the typical course of an industrial cycle, showing how the demand for and supply of money capital, and the distinctive activities and agendas of the moneyed capitalists (the bankers and other intermediaries), affect the course of that cycle. He also pays some attention to how the various "pivots" within the system of money and credit (the role of central bank policy and of commodity moneys) come into play. We end up with a somewhat different perspective on crisis theory, because the details he uncovers shed a brighter light on underlying contradictions.

Marx makes several attempts to describe the cycle. The best of them, in my view, occurs on pages 614–15, and I can do no better than replicate it here:

> As long as the reproduction process is fluid, so that returns remain assured . . . credit persists and extends, and its extension is based on the extension of the reproduction process itself. As soon as any stagnation occurs, as a result of delayed returns, overstocked markets or fallen prices, there is a surplus of industrial capital, but in a form in which it cannot accomplish its function. A great deal of commodity capital; but unsaleable. A great deal of fixed capital; but in large measure unemployed as a result of the stagnation in reproduction.

This faithfully replicates the points of potential disruption identified in the opening chapters of Volume II. The question is then posed of what happens within the money circuit. The general pattern goes something like this: "as the new crisis breaks out, credit suddenly dries up, payments congeal, the reproduction process is paralysed and . . . there is an almost absolute lack of loan capital alongside a surplus of unoccupied industrial capital." All of which is a pretty exact description of the conditions that pertained in the wake of the Lehman Brothers bankruptcy of September 2008.

An accumulation of loan capital can "precipitate out" of normal capital accumulation. "With genuine accumulation constantly expanding, this expanded accumulation of money capital can be in part its result, in part the result of elements that accompany it but are quite different from it"— for example, rising stock and share values in productive companies—"and in part also the result even of blockages in genuine accumulation"— commodity surpluses not sold but whose discounted value is realized through bills of exchange. But "this accumulation can also express elements that are very different from genuine accumulation"—for example, through rising asset values from capitalization, and fictitious capital formation of state or consumer debt. The aggregate result is "a plethora of money-capital at certain phases of the cycle" (C3, 639–40).

Credit then subsequently contracts, "(1) because this capital is unoccupied[;] (2) because confidence in the fluidity of the reproduction process is broken; (3) because the demand for this commercial credit declines." The lack of credit makes it

> more difficult to obtain goods on credit. . . . In the crisis itself, since everyone has goods to sell and cannot sell, even though they have to sell in order to pay, the quantity of capital blocked in its reproduction process, though not of unoccupied capital to be invested, is precisely at its greatest, even if the lack of credit is also most acute. . . . Capital already invested is in fact massively unemployed, since the reproduction process is stagnant. Factories stand idle, raw materials pile up, finished products flood the market as commodities. Nothing could be more wrong, therefore, than to ascribe such a situation to a lack of productive capital. It is precisely then that there is a surplus of productive capital, partly in relation to the normal though temporarily contracted scale of reproduction and partly in relation to crippled consumption. (C3, 614)

The role of the capital surplus, and the problems that attach to finding profitable means to absorb such capital surpluses, are here strongly posed. In raising the issue of "crippled consumption," Marx is echoing a theme that gradually emerges as critical in Volume II. Here he builds a very simple model of dynamic relations between classes across the cyclical movement.

"Let us conceive the whole society as composed simply of industrial capitalists and wage labourers"—let us ignore all other features such as price fluctuations and

> the fraudulent businesses and the speculative dealings that the credit system fosters. In this case a crisis would be explicable only in terms of a disproportion in production between different branches and a disproportion between the consumption of the capitalists themselves and their accumulation. But as things actually are, the replacement of the capitals invested in production depends to a large extent on the consumption capacity of the non-productive classes; while the consumption capacity of the workers is restricted partly by the laws governing wages and partly by the fact that they are employed only as long as they can be employed at a profit for the capitalist class. *The ultimate reason for all real crises always remains the poverty and restricted consumption of the masses*, in the face of the drive of capitalist production to develop the productive forces as if only the absolute consumption capacity of society set a limit to them. (C3, 615; emphasis added)

This is, of course, one of those famous declarations (see also Volume II, 391), on a par with his assertion that the falling rate of profit is "the most important law of modern political economy," which needs to be contextualized in order to be understood. What the study of the industrial cycle reveals is that there is no necessary opposition between these two statements. Profit rates may fall in the short run because of the restricted consumption of the masses. This is very different from the mechanism usually deployed in explaining falling profit rates earlier in Volume III. But laying workers off reduces market demand, which leaves commodities unsold and productive capacity idle, and so induces capital to reduce wages and lay even more workers off. Marx clearly sees the possibility of such a downward spiral during the industrial cycle. Whether this constitutes a long-run secular trend is another matter entirely. The credit system permits capital to exceed such direct consumption constraints, at least for a time. "The maximum of credit is the same thing here as the fullest employment of industrial capital . . . irrespective of the limits of consumption" (C3, 613). Personal consumption was largely sustained during the neoliberal years of wage repression after 1980 or so by extending consumer credit.

Marx also sees how the downward spiral might be reversed with the aid of credit. The massive pool of idle loan and money capital—along with low rates of interest—that forms in the wake of a crisis, becomes critical to the revival. "In the period when business revives after the crisis . . . loan capital is demanded in order to buy, and to transform the money capital into productive or commercial capital. And then it is demanded either by the industrial capitalist or by the merchant. The industrial capitalist invests it in means of production and labour-power" (C3, 645). The low rates of interest make long-term investments in fixed capital and entirely new undertakings more attractive than usual (C3, 619–20). Interest rates typically remain low in the initial phases of expansion, when easy credit plays its most constructive role—and this facilitates, as we have seen, the further extension and integration of the world market.

Marx then focuses upon what is, in many respects, the culminating form of his argument, which rests on a depiction of the cyclical, temporal form that inevitably arises out of the mediations of the credit system in relation to a permanent tendency towards overaccumulation and overextension. I can do no better here than quote him at length. In his first attempt to explain how the cyclical movement might unfold, he writes as follows:

If the reproduction process has reached the flourishing stage that precedes that of over-exertion, commercial credit undergoes a very great expansion, this in turn actually forming the "healthy" basis for a ready flow of returns and an expansion of production. In this situation, the rate of interest is still low. . . . The ease and regularity of returns, combined with an expanded commercial credit, ensures the supply of loan capital despite the increasing demand and prevents the interest level from rising. This is also the point when jobbers first enter the picture on a notable scale, operating without reserve capital or even without capital at all, i.e. completely on money credit. Added to this too is a great expansion of fixed capital in all forms and the opening of large numbers of new and far-reaching undertakings. Interest now rises to its average level. It reaches its maximum again as soon as the new crisis breaks out, credit suddenly dries up, payments congeal, the reproduction process is paralysed and . . . there is an almost absolute lack of loan capital alongside a surplus of unoccupied industrial capital. . . . This industrial cycle is such that the same circuit must periodically reproduce itself, once the first impulse has been given. (C3, 620)

Marx assumes here, of course, that there is no attempt to modify this sequence by state interventions in monetary and fiscal policies, though he does opine that "no bank legislation can abolish crises themselves." This whole process is then summarized in a passage that is of great importance because it acknowledges how the tension between credit and its monetary base is played out in relation to a tendency towards overaccumulation:

In a system of production where the entire interconnection of the reproduction process rests on credit, a crisis must evidently break out if credit is suddenly withdrawn and only cash payment is accepted, in the form of a violent scramble for means of payment. At first glance, therefore, the entire crisis presents itself as simply a credit and monetary crisis. And in fact all it does involve is simply the convertibility of bills of exchange into money. The majority of these bills represent actual purchases and sales, *the ultimate basis of the entire crisis being the expansion of these far beyond the social need.* On top of this, however, a tremendous number of these bills represent purely fraudulent deals, which now come to light and explode; as well as unsuccessful speculations conducted with borrowed capital, and finally commodity capitals that are either devalued or unsaleable, or returns that are never going to come in. It is clear that this entire artificial system of forced expansion of the reproduction process cannot be cured by now allowing one bank, e.g. the Bank of England, to give all the swindlers the capital they lack in paper money and to buy all the depreciated commodities at their old nominal values. Moreover, everything here appears upside down, since in this paper world the real price and its elements are nowhere to be seen, but simply bullion, metal coin, notes, bills and securities. This distortion is particularly evident in centres such as London, where the monetary business of an entire country is concentrated; here the whole process becomes incomprehensible. (C3, 621–2; emphasis added)

Marx finally turns to consider how these cyclical impulses take geographical form. As regards imports and exports, for example,

> all countries are successively caught up in the crisis, and . . . it is then apparent that they have all, with few exceptions, both exported and imported too much; i.e. the balance of payments is against them all, so that the root of the problem is actually not the balance of payments at all. England, for example, suffers from a drain of gold. It has imported too much. But at the same time every other country is overburdened with English goods. They too have imported too much.

Credit changes this picture, but not the underlying problem:

> The crisis may break out in England, the country that gives the most credit and takes the least because the balance of payments . . . is against it, even though the overall balance of trade is in its favour. . . . The crash in England, introduced and accompanied by a drain of gold, settles England's balance of payments, partly by bankrupting its importers . . . partly by driving part of its commodity capital abroad at low prices, and partly by the sale of foreign securities, the purchase of English ones, etc. The sequence now reaches another country. . . . In 1857 the crisis broke out in the United States. This led to a drain of gold from England to America. But as soon as the American bubble burst, the crisis reached England, with a drain of gold from America to England. Similarly between England and the Continent. In times of general crisis the balance of payments is against every country, at least against every commercially developed country, but always against each of these in succession—like volley firing—as soon as the sequence of payments reaches it. (C3, 623–4; cf. 650)

Geographical movements of this sort were all too clear in the wake of the crisis that broke out in the US in 2007–08, and which then spread to different parts of the world. This has indeed been "like volley firing"— though it is not always easy to predict where the crisis will next be registered. Capital, I have argued elsewhere, never solves its crisis tendencies: it merely moves them around, from one sector to another as well as from one part of the world to another.

In Marx's view, this all goes to show "by its very universality: (1) that the drain of gold is simply a phenomenon of the crisis and not its basis; (2) that the sequence in which this drain of gold affects the different countries simply indicates when the series reaches them, for a final settlement of accounts; when their own day of crisis comes . . ." (C3, 624). Despite Marx's claim to universality, this sequence with its focus on "drains of gold" is but one possible scenario by means of which the crisis these days takes geographical form. In our times, it was the burgeoning sovereign debt of, for example, Greece—produced partly by excessive Greek borrowing from German and French banks to pay for goods produced in Germany, in particular. All of this was facilitated through the creation of the euro, which benefited the more efficient producers (Germany) and undermined production in the less efficient economies of southern Europe. The result is that the value of the fictitious capital held by the German and French banks is threatened, which in turn may threaten the sovereign debt of France, and even ultimately Germany, unless there is concerted action across the whole eurozone. This turns out to be particularly difficult, given the "mistaken" constitution of the European Central Bank. Volley-firing, indeed.

The movement associated with credit markets in all this is palpable. But Marx does not believe that these movements lie at the root of the crisis. The root lies in a combination of a basic tendency towards overaccumulation of capital and the independent and autonomous production of a plethora of money capital that piles up on its own account. Recall that

> the very fact that the accumulation of loan capital is augmented by these elements that are independent of genuine accumulation, even if they accompany it, must lead to a regular plethora of money-capital at certain phases of the cycle, and this plethora develops as the credit system improves. At the same time as this, there develops the need to pursue the production process beyond its capitalist barriers: too much trade, too much production, too much credit. This must also happen always in forms that bring about a reaction. (C3, 640)

This combination is what I generally refer to as "the capital surplus disposal problem." The thesis that this tendency to produce surpluses of capital, and particularly surpluses in the money form, lies at the root of all crises is surely worthy of exploration. The fact that these surpluses are so easily sucked into channels of fictitious capital formation and circulation then becomes a central problem that can be neither evaded nor repressed given the positive role that capital in money form, backed by the sheer power of the moneyed capitalists, has to play in overcoming the necessity for hoarding.

From Volumes Two to Three and Back Again: A Concluding Comment

It would have been ridiculous for Marx to pursue the holy grail of a complete specification of the laws of motion of capital in its pure state without finding a way to use a knowledge of those laws to dissect the two major crises he experienced in his lifetime as an active scholar of and participant in events. The financial and commercial crises of 1847–48 and 1857 cried out for adequate interpretation (as did the crash of 1873, though by then much of Marx's theoretical production lay behind him). It is tempting, therefore, to interpret the materials in Volume III as following on sequentially from the Volume II analysis, since it is only in these chapters on finance that the crises of these years are actively addressed. This forced Marx to leave behind the rigorous (and to no small degree rigid) self-constraints so evident in Volume II in order to evoke the fetishisms and the fictions, the insanity and the craziness, that so evidently bedeviled the world of finance and commerce in those crisis years. The language of much of Volume III is, as a consequence, radically different from the restrained and technical language of Volume II. From the casual reader's perspective, it seems as if Marx has liberated himself from the boring scientist constraints that dominate Volume II. By reanimating the concept of fetishism, for example, he places himself far closer to the seething turbulence of capital's surface appearances and the multiple potentialities they hold for future transformations, both negative and positive.

The trouble with this interpretation is that it does not conform to the chronology of the writing. Most of Volume II was written after Volume III was drafted. So why was it that Marx went back to the dry and technocratic accounting style of argument in Volume II after writing the more dramatic and viscerally engaging (though frustratingly incomplete and occasionally incoherent) materials on merchants' capital and finance?

I have no definitive answer to that question, nor any special claim to privileged insights. But I do have a theory that I favor. Marx certainly knew that he needed to get to the bottom of what happened in 1847–48 and 1857 (in much the same way that we need to get to the bottom of 2007–12). Marx's studies of these crises showed how much the events themselves, as well as the interpretations of them by contemporary commentators, were riddled with fetishistic understandings. This poses the problem of understanding the obvious insanity of speculative dealings, particularly with fictitious capitals, against the background of Marx's emerging understandings of the laws of motion of capital. Marx was in no way deterred by his encounters with fetishisms of theory and practice. On the contrary, he relished the prospect of unmasking what they concealed. His typical response was to dig deeper to unearth the necessities and contradictions that underpinned them. He believed it would thus be possible to make more sense of all the surface turbulence and all the manifest contradictions that characterized the world of finance and credit, and the crises with which they were associated.

It is in this context that his return to the question of capital's inner nature in Volume II makes sense. What Marx is seeking is a kind of x-ray of that inner nature that will elucidate how and why the contradictory craziness of the credit system must necessarily come about. Why is it that the fundamental, underlying contradictions of capital always take the form of financial and commercial crises? To uncover all of this, he excludes the credit system and the circulation of interest-bearing capital from the study of capital accumulation and circulation in Volume II in order to understand what it is about the circulation and accumulation of capital that makes credit and the "autonomous and independent" functioning of money capital so necessary. From Volume II, in short, we get to understand why it is that capital cannot exist without a credit system, why it is that an accumulation of wealth is necessarily paralleled by an accumulation of debts, and why the central contradiction between value and its monetary representation internalizes the never-ending and necessary nonequivalence between supply and demand within a capitalist system of surplus-value production. This, it seems to me, is what the lengthy passage cited above from page 621 of Volume III fully acknowledges.

Adam Smith held that banking and finance were unproductive activities. From the Volume III account it is tempting to believe that Marx concurs in this judgment, that the parasitical excrescences of money capital, and the height of insanity exhibited within the financial system, stand self-condemned as a monumental distraction from (if not a pernicious tax upon) real wealth and value production. Popular opinion in our times is inclined towards such a view. This immediately poses the question: Why does capitalism tolerate this? What Volume II shows, however, is the crucial necessity of credit not only in facilitating value production, but also in expanding the capacity to create and capture surplus-value directly. The analogy with the role of machinery in Volume I is helpful here. Machinery is constant (usually fixed) capital, and hence unproductive of value. Marx then goes on to show how it can be a source of relative surplus-value both for the individual capitalist (my superior technology yields me excess profits) and for the whole capitalist class (rising productivity in the production of wage goods diminishes the value of labor-power and expands the surplus-value for the capitalist). Credit is likewise in itself unproductive of value; but it can facilitate a vast expansion in the production and realization of surplus-value by, for example, reducing the necessity of hoarding.

The hoarding question is, in fact, crucial. What becomes obvious from a study of Volume II is that, in the absence of a credit system, so much capital would need to be hoarded to cover everything from fixed-capital circulation to disparate circulation times, that capital accumulation would at best be tightly confined and at worst become so gummed up as to grind to a halt. Whether or not the money released from hoards can be converted into money capital to produce surplus-value depends, of course, on the availability of labor-power and means of production, as well as on the conditions prevailing within all the other circuits of capital (including the vitality of effective demand). But without the release of hoarded money there would be little potential money capital available. This is what Marx clearly shows us in Volume II.

Whether Marx successfully situated the role of credit and finance (as well as commercial capital) in relation to the laws of motion of capital is a matter of opinion, and can surely be debated (I feel he was only partially successful, and that he unnecessarily constrained himself out of some sort of vision of scientism to which he felt he had to conform in order to maintain credibility). But, if I am right that one of the key aims of Volume II is to get beneath the fetishisms so virulently on display in the finance chapters of Volume III, then this repositions Volume II in

Marx's oeuvre in a way that mandates far more careful study than it usually receives. Marx clearly understood that he needed to construct from the standpoint of circulation an equally powerful model of the laws of motion of capital to that which he constructs in Volume I from the standpoint of production. The tragedy is that he did not complete the work, and that he never lived to synthesize the two perspectives of production and circulation into a working whole.

CHAPTER EIGHT

The Time and Space of Capital (Chapters 12–14 of Volume II)

Chapters 12 through 14 of Volume II are, thankfully, fairly simple and lucidly written. They pose no particular difficulties, and in any case are somewhat repetitive of themes on turnover time presented in chapters 5 and 6. So this provides an easy point of reentry into the world of Volume II, after suffering the turmoil and confusions of financial speculation in Volume III.

Marx here takes up some obvious material facts of production and circulation that affect the overall turnover times of capital. The overall turnover time is made up of production time plus circulation time, but production time divides into a working period—when value-producing labor is actually applied to the production of commodities—and time needed for the production process to be completed without any labor input (as in much of agricultural production, for example). Chapter 12 is about "the working period," which is defined as "the succession of more or less numerous interrelated working days" required to congeal value and surplus-value into a given commodity, such as a locomotive or cotton. Chapter 13 is about "production time," which is defined as the working time plus whatever extra time is needed to finish the commodity without expending labor (for example, time for fermenting, ripening, maturing, and so on). Chapter 14 deals with "circulation time," which is the time taken to get the commodity to its final destination for consumption. This chapter is of particular interest to me, since circulation time is much affected by the time and cost of transportation (a topic we have also encountered before), and by location decisions (such as the tendency for suppliers of inputs to cluster around major production sites in order to minimize the time and cost of transportation). It opens up the question of the role of space relations, of agglomeration economies, and of the production of space in capital circulation and accumulation.

The heterogeneity of temporalities of working periods, production times and circulation times is, Marx notes, "infinite." This poses potential problems of coordination between different branches of production within the overall division of labor. While cotton spinning can take place continuously over the year, the cotton harvest occurs only once a year. This generates complex issues of how much capital comes to be tied up (hoarded as either commodities or money) to cover disjunctions between different turnover times. Hoarded capital is inactive, and therefore unproductive of surplus-value. Large stocks and inventories of raw cotton, for example, keep much of that commodity capital inactive. Such capital is, Marx points out, technically "devalued" or "fallow" capital. This, we have seen, is a critical problem that needs to be addressed either by the credit system or by other means.

A rising pressure therefore exists to find ways to reduce the amount of capital held in an idle state. This is where techniques such as accelerating turnover times and inventory management, and institutional arrangements such as the credit system, come into play. The competitive drive to shorten working periods and production times has had far-reaching effects. For example, technological and organizational innovations (such as the "just-in-time" system pioneered by the Japanese in the 1980s) have helped reduce inventories of commodity capital (and hence idle capital) to a minimum. While a cotton harvest occurs only once a year, different harvest times in different parts of the world help smooth out the availability of cotton throughout the year, and thus reduce the need for large inventories. There has also been a perpetual drive throughout the history of capitalism to economize on costs and times of movement.

ON CHAPTER 12 OF VOLUME II: THE WORKING PERIOD

Take two forms of production, cotton spinning and the manufacture of locomotives, each of which have the same ten-hour working day. In the first case, a certain quantity of finished product is "turned out every day and every week; in the other, the labour process must be repeated for perhaps three months in order to produce . . . one locomotive." There is therefore an initial contrast between continuous and discrete production processes. Significant differences also exist in the time taken for different discrete production processes to come to completion. "These differences in the duration of the act of production do not just occur between different branches of production, but also within the same branch." The examples Marx gives are instructive. "An ordinary dwelling-house is built in a shorter time than a large factory. . . . If the building of a locomotive takes three months, that of a battleship takes a year if not several. . . . A road can be built in a few months, while a railway requires years," and so on. "The differences in length of the act of production are thus of infinite variety," he concludes (306–7).

These differences affect turnover times. The longer the turnover time, the more circulating capital is required up front before the commodity is finished. The "speed of turnover" affects profitability (307).

Marx defines the "working period" as "the succession of more or less numerous interrelated working days" required to create a finished product (308). A hundred working days of ten hours each amounts to a working period of 1,000 hours. "Interruptions and disturbances of the social production process, as a result of crises," he points out "have a very different effect on those products of labour that are discrete in nature, and those whose production requires a longer connected period" (308). In the case of continuous production, the process shuts down, and not much circulating capital is lost; but in the case of a locomotive all the circulating capital already embodied in the product is either put on hold or lost, and this implies that a much greater risk attaches to undertaking such forms of production.

Of course, fixed capital is also involved in these different turnover processes, but the turnover of the fixed capital itself (for example, a steam engine) is unaffected by the differential turnover times of the products it helps to produce. But the expenditure on circulating capital is differentially affected. Wages have to be advanced on, say, a weekly basis, and means of production likewise purchased often on a continuing basis over the weeks or months that it might take to create a finished product. The longer the working period, the more circulating capital has to be advanced before the capital can be recuperated and the surplus-value realized through the sale of the final product. This can place a considerable burden on the individual capitalist. "At the less developed stages of capitalist production," Marx notes,

> enterprises that require a long working period, and thus a large capital outlay for a longer time, particularly if they can be conducted only on a large scale, are often not pursued capitalistically at all. Roads, canals, etc., for example, were built at the cost of the municipality or state (in earlier

periods mostly by forced labour . . .). Alternatively, products which require a long working period for their fabrication are manufactured only to a very minor extent with the financial means of the capitalist himself. (310–11)

In other words, they are built with the aid of credit. Marx goes on to cite the case of housing, in which

> the private individual for whom the house is being built pays advances to the builder in successive portions. He thus pays for the house bit by bit. . . . In the era of developed capitalism, however, where on the one hand massive capitals are concentrated in the hands of individuals, and on the other hand the associated capitalist (joint-stock companies) steps onto the scene alongside the individual capitalist—where credit, too, is developed—it is only in exceptional cases that a capitalist builder still builds houses to order for individual clients. He makes a business out of building rows of houses and whole districts of towns for the market, just as individual capitalists make a business out of building railways as contractors. (311)

Marx cites a Bank Act Committee Report of 1857 on the strategies of speculative house building, in which mortgage finance, land acquisition and leveraging of borrowed funds all feature: "It is impossible nowadays for any contractor to get along without speculative building and on a large scale at that. The profit on the actual construction is extremely slight; the main source of profit comes from raising the ground rent, and from the clever selection of exploitation of the building land" (and he cites the upscale neighborhood of Belgravia in London as an example). I think this process is far more important than is generally recognized, but since it involves the extraction and appropriation of rents Marx does not go into it further here, and I will also refrain from elaborating. But it is interesting to note how many of the examples Marx cites here involve investment in the built environment (a topic that comes up at odd moments like this, but which he does not isolate out for special consideration).

As we have seen so conspicuously in recent times, processes of this sort are ever crisis-prone:[1]

---

1   Property speculation appears to have played a role in the crisis of 1857,

Today the contractor no longer works directly for a client, but rather for the market. . . . Whereas previously a contractor might have built three or four houses at a time on speculation, he now has to buy an extensive piece of land . . . erect on it up to 100 or 200 houses, and thus involve himself in an undertaking that exceeds his own means some twenty to fifty times over. Funds are procured by taking out a mortgage, and this money is put at the contractor's disposal bit by bit as the building of the houses progresses. If a crisis breaks out, bringing the payment of these installments to a halt, then the whole undertaking generally collapses; in the best case, the houses remain uncompleted until better times, while in the worst they are auctioned off at half price. (311–12)

In much of the United States, Spain and Ireland, the worst-case scenario unfolded with a vengeance after 2008. Housing speculation in this last instance created an asset bubble that actually sparked the crisis when it burst, whereas Marx here sees the housing crash as resulting from a commercial and financial crisis that had its roots elsewhere.

"Large-scale jobs needing particularly long working periods are fully suitable for capitalist production only when the concentration of capital is already well advanced, and when the development of the credit system offers the capitalist the convenient expedient of advancing and thus risking other people's capital instead of his own" (312). The shift from individual entrepreneurial activity to one in which, as we saw in the chapters on finance and credit, business becomes "other people's money" has major consequences for how capital works, and I think it is no accident that Marx's prime example is of large-scale urban and infrastructural investments. While he does not say so here, it is plain also that the involvement of fictitious capital is not far away.

Marx's main concern, however, is with the "circumstances that increase the product of the individual working day," and "shorten the working period," such as "cooperation, division of labour, application of machinery" (312). "Thus machinery shortens the building time of houses, bridges, etc.," while "improved ship-building techniques, resulting in greater speed, shorten the turnover time of the capital invested" in ship construction. Many of these improvements depend, however, on the deployment of more fixed capital. This, in itself, generates a

which probably explains why it was the focus of a parliamentary enquiry.

significant tension (contradiction?), since the turnover of a portion of the capital has to be slowed down in order to facilitate the accelerated turnover of the rest. The latent tension between stasis and motion is omnipresent throughout much of Volume II.

Cooperation can be mobilized for the same purpose: "The completion of a railway is hastened by setting afoot great armies of workers and tackling the job from many different points in space" (312). Some of the most spectacular examples of the mobilization of both technologies and masses of labor for such purposes in recent years have come from China. In the lectures on which this book is based, I showed an astonishing video of the construction of a fifteen-story hotel in China in ninety hours to illustrate the point that Marx is making here. It can be seen on YouTube under "Build a Hotel 15 Floors in China in 90 Hours." There is now another video titled "China Puts Up a 30-Floor Building in 15 Days." In both instances, of course, the parts are prefabricated, but it is also interesting to watch and think about the nature of the labor process. The emphasis is not only upon cooperation, mechanization and coordination of divisions of labor, but also upon intensity, which in Volume I of *Capital* gradually emerges as a key contributor to surplus-value production. And, of course, labor has to be paid only for the 90 hours (of shift work).

The background to this is that capital has to be sufficiently concentrated and immediately available to set in motion such processes:

> It comes down to a question of the extent to which the means of production and subsistence . . . are fragmented, or united in the hands of individual capitalists, i.e. the extent reached by the concentration of capital. In so far as credit mediates, accelerates and intensifies the concentration of capital in a single hand, it contributes to shortening the working period, and with this also the turnover time. (313)

The association of accelerating turnover times with the centralization of capital, state activities, and the rise of the credit system is important to note. My casual observations on the topic through the study of the history of urbanization would suggest that Marx is quite correct to point to these tightening associations in pursuing ever-shorter turnover times.

The extent of this drive to shorten turnover times is illustrated most dramatically, in Marx's view, by the case of sheep breeding. "British sheep, just like French sheep as late as 1855, were not ready for slaughter before the fourth or fifth year." As a result most people ate mutton and not lamb (feasting on mutton chops is a recurrent habit in Dickens's novels). But along came Bakewell and his "New Leicester" breed of sheep, in which "one-year-old sheep can already be fattened, and in any case they are fully grown before the second year has elapsed," thereby cutting production time by more than half (315). So we now eat lamb, and not mutton chops. And spring lamb can be had in less than a year. Such interventions in so-called "natural" lifecycles are everywhere in evidence in agriculture. It has proved possible even to speed up the maturation of lobsters by judiciously moving lobster pots from one water temperature regime to another. "Natural" reproduction cycles are by no means sacrosanct in the world of capitalist production.

ON CHAPTER 13 OF VOLUME II: PRODUCTION TIME

Production processes often involve interruptions in production "independent of the length of the labour process." Marx provides a number of examples such as wine that has to go through a maturing process, pottery that has to dry, time-consuming chemical processes such as bleaching—and of course, in many arenas of agricultural production, there are long periods when no labor is applied at all (most conspicuously in forestry, where it may take a century for the tree to grow to maturity).

I spend some time each year on the land in Argentina, and on a given day in January a huge machine appears along with a truck and three operatives to harvest 20 hectares of wheat in one day. The next day another machine appears with three people to plant 20 hectares of soy beans in one day. Two months later, another machine arrives to spray the soy beans with horrible insecticide and, three months later, a machine appears to harvest all the soy beans; a couple of months later yet another machine comes to fertilize the land, and then another to plant the wheat. The fixed capital involved is considerable, but the labor input and the working periods very brief compared to the production time. "In all these cases, additional labour is added only occasionally for a large part of the production time" (317).

Plainly, there are strong incentives to reduce production times to the degree that this is physically possible. Marx thus cites the gains made in the history of iron production "from the invention of puddling in 1780 to the modern Bessemer process and the latest procedures introduced since then." While "the production time has been enormously curtailed . . . the application of fixed capital has also increased to the same extent," once again emphasizing a potential contradiction between slowing down and speeding up.

Agriculture is the sphere where, as might be expected, it is hardest of all to reduce production times, and this has implications for capital, and even more importantly for labor. Marx quotes extensively from the work of Kirchhof, who emphasizes the differential impacts of these distinctions upon capital and labor. For the latter, the seasonality of work possibilities in agriculture constitutes a major problem. In Russia, for example, agricultural labor is possible for only 130 to 150 days of the year, which would pose very serious problems were it not for village-organized production, as "weavers, tanners, shoemakers, locksmiths, cutlers, etc." The "unification of agriculture with rural subsidiary industries" was an effective way to deal with this naturally imposed seasonal structure of employment. "In so far as capitalist production later manages to complete the separation between manufacture and agriculture, the rural worker becomes ever more dependent on merely accidental subsidiary employments and his condition thereby worsens. As far as capital is concerned, as we shall see later on, all these differences in the turnover balance out. Not so for the worker" (319). The problem of seasonal labor in agriculture does not go away. In the United States migrant workers pass up both the East and West Coast agricultural regions harvesting seasonal crops such as fruits and vegetables in migrant gangs, living for the most part under appalling conditions and exposed to a wide range of toxic pesticides, before returning in the dead season to Mexico or the Caribbean.

While Marx acknowledges that there are many industries in which such seasonality problems or large gaps between working periods and production times do not occur (except under conditions of crisis), there are several forms of investment that are plagued with such problems. The result is "great unevenness in the outlay of circulating capital in the course of the different periods of the year" (319). The fixed capital deployed is not used for part of the year and so its circulation is also interrupted, and this gives rise to "a certain depreciation." The most interesting case is forestry, where the production time and the working time are so hugely different as to make "forest culture a line of business unsuited to private and hence to capitalist production. . . . The development of civilization and industry in general has always shown itself so active in the destruction of forests that everything that has been done for their conservation and production is completely insignificant in comparison" (322). If this was true for Marx's day, then it is an even more widespread problem today, as the depletion of the tropical rain forests throughout Latin America, Southeast Asia and Africa continues apace—but now with documented impacts upon global warming and loss of biodiversity, as well as the loss of the forests themselves.

In closing, Marx returns to the question broached in chapter 6 on the formation of stocks and inventories as a circulatory cost, but, in this instance, as a problem of temporality. For any production system "a quantity of means of production . . . has to be held in reserve . . . in order to go into the production process bit by bit." How large does this stock have to be? Its size, Marx argues, "depends on the greater or lesser difficulty of its replacement, its relative proximity to the supplying markets, the development of means of transport and communications, etc." (323). But it is also sensitive to changing conditions in "the circulation sphere." While Marx does not say what these might be, the most obvious recent example available to us would be the so-called "just-in-time" production systems and their variants, first introduced in Japanese industry in the late 1970s. Optimal scheduling of deliveries, facilitated by a networked information system (subsequently computerized) and a reliable transport system, reduced to a minimum the need to keep stocks of inputs on hand, thus releasing a vast wave of "dead" or "fallow" capital for active use. These systems quickly became widespread in all spheres of capitalist economic activity.

The "wide range of possibilities" that exist in the relation between working times and production times, Marx ends by observing, arise partly out of the nature of the production process itself and partly reflect the changing conditions within the circulation sphere (such as ease of access to supplies and markets). It is therefore to this latter part of the problem that we now turn.

ON CHAPTER 14: CIRCULATION TIME

This is the chapter where Marx is most explicit about the role that spatial structures and dynamics play in the laws of motion of capital. This topic often crops up in Marx's writings, but usually in a highly condensed and more often than not cryptic way. While its fundamental importance is never denied, and sometimes even stressed, there is little attempt, except here in this chapter and then in only a few pages, at a systematic presentation. We have to rely, then, on this chapter in *Capital*, where the commentary is mainly technical (and thereby consistent with the overall tenor of Volume II) and various other occasional commentaries if we wish to reconstruct Marx's views on the spatial and geographical dynamics of capital accumulation and their inner contradictions. This I sought to do in a paper published back in 1975 in *Antipode*, which was the leading radical geography journal of that time. Nobody took much notice, of course, even when I incorporated many of these findings into the last part of *The Limits to Capital* in order to emphasize how important the production of space and of spatial (and territorial) relations had been in the historical geography of capitalism.[2] Unfortunately, until recently, the question of the production of space, of spatial relations and of territorial forms ("places") has largely been ignored in expositions of Marx's thought. Either that or it is viewed as transparently obvious, and therefore not worth examining. Only recently has this aspect of capital accumulation and the changing dynamics of daily life come to be more accepted as fundamental, rather than peripheral. When Marx does mention it, he does so with remarkable vigor.

Consider, for example, the presentation in the *Communist Manifesto* which constitutes a neat description of what we now call globalization:

> The need for a constantly expanding market for its products chases the bourgeoisie over the entire surface of the globe. It must nestle everywhere, settle everywhere, establish connections everywhere. The bourgeoisie has through its exploitation of the world market given a cosmopolitan character to production and consumption in every country. To the great chagrin of the Reactionists, it has drawn from under the feet of industry the ground on which it stood. All old-established national industries have been destroyed or are daily being destroyed. They are dislodged by new industries, whose introduction becomes a life

---

2 David Harvey, "The Geography of Capitalist Accumulation: A Reconstruction of the Marxian Theory," *Antipode* 7: 2 (1975), 9–21; reprinted in *Spaces of Capital: Towards a Critical Geography* (Edinburgh: Edinburgh University Press, 2001).

and death question for all civilised nations, by industries that no longer work up indigenous raw material, but raw material drawn from the remotest zones; industries whose products are consumed not only at home, but in every quarter of the globe. In place of the old wants, satisfied by the productions of the country, we find new wants, requiring for their satisfaction the products of distant lands and climes. In place of the old local and national seclusion and self-sufficiency, we have intercourse in every direction, universal inter-dependence of nations. And as in material, so also in intellectual production. The intellectual creations of individual nations become common property. National one-sidedness and narrow-mindedness become more and more impossible, and from numerous national and local literatures, there arises a world literature.

The bourgeoisie, by the rapid improvement of all instruments of production, by the immensely facilitated means of communication, draws all, even the most barbarian, nations into civilisation. The cheap prices of its commodities are the heavy artillery with which it batters down all Chinese walls, with which it forces the barbarians' intensely obstinate hatred of foreigners to capitulate. It compels all nations, on pain of extinction, to adopt the bourgeois mode of production; it compels them to introduce what it calls civilisation into their midst, i.e., to become bourgeois themselves. In one word, it creates a world after its own image. (*The Communist Manifesto*, 38–9)

Small wonder, then, that the motto of CNN, the international news channel oriented to the business elite, is that it "goes beyond borders" (without, of course, ever mentioning class!). The "cosmopolitanism" that capitalism produces—that of the "frequent flyer," is abundantly on show.

Or consider this, just one of many similar passages from the *Grundrisse*:

Whether I extract metals from mines or take commodities to the site of their consumption, both movements are equally spatial. The improvement of the means of transport and communication likewise falls into the category of the development of the productive forces generally.

. . .

The more production comes to rest on exchange value, hence on exchange, the more important do the physical conditions of exchange— the means of communication and transport—become for the costs of circulation. Capital by its nature drives beyond every spatial barrier. Thus the creation of the physical conditions of exchange—of the means of communication and transport—the annihilation of space by time— becomes an extraordinary necessity for it. (*Grundrisse*, 523–4)

. . .

Circulation time therefore determines value only in so far as it appears as a natural barrier to the realization of labour time. It thus appears as a barrier to the productivity of labour. . . . Thus while capital must on one side strive to tear down every spatial barrier to intercourse, i.e. to exchange, and conquer the whole earth for its market, it strives on the other hand to annihilate this space with time, i.e. to reduce to a minimum the time spent in motion from one place to another. The more developed the capital, therefore, the more extensive the market over which it circulates, which forms the spatial orbit of its circulation, the more does it strive simultaneously for an even greater extension of the market and for greater annihilation of space by time. (*Grundrisse*, 539)

This is so because "the constant continuity of the process, the unobstructed and fluid transition of value from one form into the other, or from one phase of the process into the next, appears as a fundamental condition for production based on capital to a much greater degree than for all earlier forms of production" (*Grundrisse*, 535).

It is important to preface the discussion of chapter 14 on circulation time with these commentaries from elsewhere, partly to emphasize that the materials rather cursorily put together in this chapter are far from being a minor, one-off set of observations. They set out some principles for understanding the spatial dynamics of a capitalist mode of production, and thus call for study and, where necessary, elaboration. The principle that focuses Marx's attention is that "with the development of the means of transport, the speed of movement in space is accelerated and spatial distance is thus shortened in time" (327).

Marx begins chapter 14, however, with a simple statement: "A permanently effective cause of differentiation in the selling time, and hence in the turnover time in general, is the distance of the market where the commodities are sold from their place of production. For the whole period of its journey to the market, capital is confined to the state of commodity capital" (327). Capital cannot, therefore, make the transition into the money form, unless, as we have seen in the discussion of the credit system, a money capitalist is prepared to discount the bill of exchange attached to the movement of the commodity (hence the strong historical relation between long-distance trade and the credit system). What Marx calls the "selling time" is the most important component of circulation time. Clearly there is a strong competitive incentive to try to reduce this selling time to a minimum (as we saw in the analysis of commercial capital from Volume III, but which is here examined as if the producer acts as his own selling agent). "A permanently effective cause of differentiation in the selling time, and hence in the turnover time in general, is the distance of the market where the commodities are sold from their place of production" (327).

How long it takes to get to the market depends on the nature of the commodity (its weight and perishability, for example), and upon the means of transport and communications available. Differences in selling time occur not only between different commodities, but also between producers of similar commodities. However,

> improvement in the means of communication and transport shortens absolutely the period in which commodities migrate in this way, but it does not abolish the relative difference in the circulation time of different commodity capitals. . . . Improved sailing ships and steamships, for instance, which shorten the journey, shorten it just as much for nearby ports as for distant ones. [The relative differences, however, may] be displaced by the development of the means of communication and transport in a way that does not correspond to the natural distances. For instance, a railway leading from the place of production to a major inland centre of population may lengthen the distance to a nearer inland point which is not served by a railway, absolutely or relatively, in comparison to the one naturally more distant; similarly the relative distances of places of production from the major market outlets may be altered as a result of the same circumstances, which explains the demise of old centres of production and the emergence of new ones . . . (327)

On the following page Marx elaborates further:

> A place of production which possessed a particularly advantageous position through being situated on a main road or canal now finds itself on a single railway branch line that operates only at relatively long intervals,

while another point, which previously lay completely off the major traffic routes, now lies at the intersection of several lines. The second place rises, the first declines. (328)

The implications for capital (for example, the devaluation of capital locked into the first place) and for labor (for example, the shift in employment opportunities from the first to the second place) are wide-ranging. Local crises of devaluation of both capital and labor-power are omnipresent. The competitive churning within the geographical landscape of capitalism comes sharply into focus. But Marx attempts no deep analysis of the processes and consequences of such uneven geographical developments.

Innovations and investments in the means of communication and transportation are perpetually revolutionizing the geographical landscape that capital creates. The relative spaces of the space-economy are perpetually changing. Whole cities of capitalist activity are created only to decline as relative locational advantages change within the overall landscape of capitalist competition. Vast amounts of fixed capital are embedded in the land, the value of which is either enhanced or threatened with the building of new communication links and transport facilities that encourage activities elsewhere. Marx does not go into such matters in any detail, but the perpetual threat of revaluation and devaluation of these fixed capital asset values is a considerable source of instability within the history of capitalism: witness the incredibly difficult processes of deindustrialization in many of the core areas of capitalist development—the older manufacturing cities such as Detroit, Baltimore, Manchester, Sheffield, Essen, Lille, and many others—after 1980 or so, as the dynamics of a long-standing process of globalization underwent a radical change of direction, with production moving on a large scale, mainly but not exclusively to East Asia. Geographical shifts within countries—from the Midwest and Northeast to the South and Southwest of the United States—are just as important as international shifts in creating the unstable and uneven geographical developments of capitalism.

None of this is explicitly taken up in Marx's analysis here. What is presented, in a way that is consistent with the overall concerns of Volume II, is a simple theoretical and purely technical basis for developing such an analysis. This basis is constituted simply by the circulation time (and cost of movement) of commodity capitals, and the dependence of that circulation time and cost on the spatial conditions of production and realization of surplus-value.

The principles are simple. When the "time in which capital is confined to the form of commodity capital is prolonged, by the greater the distance to the market, this directly gives rise to a delayed reflux of money, and thus also delays the transformation of capital from money capital into productive capital" (331). "With the development of the means of transport, the speed of movement in space is accelerated, and spatial distance is thus shortened in time." The reference to the idea of the "annihilation of space through time," as set out in the *Grundrisse*, is clear. The scale and frequency of service reduces costs. "The relatively cheaper cost of transport for longer distances as compared to shorter" is important in stretching out the geographical space of commodity circulation. The main reason for this, which Marx fails to mention, is the high cost of loading and unloading cargo relative to the cost of movement. This high cost of transshipment was radically reduced after the 1960s by containerization. This was a key innovation that redirected the form and paths of globalization in commodity movements.

Frequency and reliability of service reduce the stocks of commodity capital that need to be kept on hand by producers (Marx spots here the tendency to create what later became known as the "just-in-time" systems of supply of inputs into production, which gave Japanese industry such a powerful competitive edge in the 1980s, until the rest of the world caught up). Marx also recognizes the importance of what are called agglomeration economies—the benefit to be had in the reduction of circulation times by gathering together many producers of the same goods along with all their suppliers in the same location.

At first the greater or lesser frequency with which the means of transport function, e.g. the number of trains on a railway, develops with the degree to which a place of production produces more, and becomes a major centre of production, and this is a development in the direction of the already existing market, i.e. towards the major centres of production and populations, towards export ports, etc. On the other hand, however, and conversely, this particular ease of commerce and the consequent acceleration in the turnover of capital (in as much as this is determined by the circulation time) gives rise to an accelerated concentration of both the centre of production and its market. With this accelerated concentration of people and capital at given points, the concentration of these masses of capital in a few hands makes rapid progress. (328)

What Marx is articulating here is a theory of what we geographers call relative space relations.[3] This space is fixed not by physical distance but by the friction of distances, which is measured by the changing costs and times of movement across physical space. Physical space in itself does not matter for capital. All that capital cares about is the cost and time of movement, and it will do everything in its power to seek to minimize these costs and times, and to reduce spatial barriers to movement. To do this, it must radically and continuously revolutionize space relations. This is what Marx means in the *Grundrisse* when he writes of the "annihilation of space through time." The history of innovations under capitalism that contribute to this goal of reducing spatial barriers and the friction of distance is simply stunning. But the barriers are not only physical: they are also social and political. The reduction of tariff barriers and other political obstacles to the movement of capital (not necessarily of people) has become part of the holy grail of the emergent international capitalist order (a process that is not without contradictions and which is frequently a focus of political conflict and social struggles). But it is hard to imagine how much capital accumulation would have been curbed had the gradual removal of barriers to trade across the European space after 1950 or so had not taken place. By the mid-1970s, the long lines of trucks stuck at border customs inspection points across Europe were becoming intolerable.

There is thus a distinction between absolute and relative space. The territorial units that emerge in the organization of capitalist space (everything from bounded individual and collective property rights on the land to the state itself) tend to fix things in space, which contrasts with the fluid movement across space of capital in all of its forms (as money, as commodities, and as production activity). These, at least, are my glosses on the arguments that Marx briefly advances.

Marx takes up this question a bit later in the chapter from the angle of productive consumption—the supply of inputs into production:

---

3   See David Harvey, "Space as a Key Word," in *Spaces of Global Capitalism: Towards a Theory of Uneven Geographical Development* (London: Verso, 2006).

The time of purchase, and the greater or lesser distance from the major sources of raw materials makes it necessary to buy raw materials for longer periods and keep them available in the form of productive stock, latent or potential productive capital . . . this increases the mass of capital that must be advanced at one stroke, and the time for which it must be advanced. (331)

Reduction in the necessity to hold stocks of raw materials and other inputs on hand reduces the amount of capital that has to be advanced relative to that employed.

Locational shifts of producers to take advantage of proximity to means of production, labor supplies, and final markets make only a brief appearance in this text, but they are nonetheless of considerable importance. Since Marx mentions breweries in large cities, let me elaborate on that. In the eighteenth century in Britain, beer was very much a local, often home-brewed drink, and it was only in big cities, as Marx notes, that large breweries could be found. There they tended to configure into local monopolies protected from competition by high transport costs. But the introduction of preservative ingredients, most notably hops, into brewing allowed beer to be transported over much longer distances.[4] The time beer as a commodity could spend on the market was increased by hop flavoring. One consequence was the rise in the nineteenth century of hop production as a distinctive form of agriculture, mainly located in my home county of Kent—and this, you should know, provided me with the subject of my doctoral dissertation. Most people I tell this to stare in astonishment: How could you spend all that time on such a trivial topic? Actually it turned out to be fascinating, as well as a great learning experience that I still draw upon. Hop cultivation was a capital-intensive form of agriculture, and was connected to London's financial and credit markets by way of merchant capital and the brewing companies. The hop-acreage fluctuated with credit availability and the business cycle. It needed lots of fertilizer, and London night-soil was shipped down into Kent along with rags and other wastes, giving

---

4   Though this required people to get used to the bitter taste—which is still with us as a cultural habit even though hops have since been replaced by chemical preservatives. The much sweeter malt beers sold earlier as home brews had the disadvantage that they quickly went sour.

employment to recyclers in London. At certain times of year massive amounts of labor were also required. The annual migrations of the impoverished working classes from London's East End at hop-picking time was an astonishing scene. I still remember it from my early days. Imagine my pleasure when I took a cab in London just last year and the elderly driver told me of his many happy memories of hop-picking in his youth (it is all done mechanically now).

By the mid-nineteenth century, certain heavily hopped beers were even being exported to British expatriates in India (the so-called "India pale ales" that are still produced by certain brewers, such as Bass, located along the River Trent in the English Midlands). But, in the 1950s, most beers still did not travel far. It was too expensive to transport, and monopolies still prevailed in local markets. So I drank local draft beer (I had to go to the next town to sample draft Guinness when I was a kid). My move from Kent to Cambridge, where I was a student, meant I had to change my beer from Courage to Flowers! The same was true in the United States in the 1960s. If you lived in Baltimore you drank National Bohemian, and if you lived in Pittsburgh it was Iron City. Falling transport costs from the mid-1960s then led to beer coming from all over, while the containerization of ocean transport along with the emergence of keg (rather than barreled) beers that began in the 1960s meant that imported beers could compete in national markets. Beer production consolidated through mergers into mega-companies—though an antidote later arrived in the form of local brews. But now you can drink beer from almost anywhere; there is a bar in New York where you can drink local brews from all over the world.

The introduction of refrigeration, as well as falling transport costs, made all sorts of new locational configurations of food supply possible. The implications of refrigeration for the supply of fresh vegetables from California and of frozen meat from the US Midwest to the East Coast cities of the US and well beyond is beautifully set out in William Cronon's book about nineteenth-century Chicago, *Nature's Metropolis*.[5] The telegraph also made it possible to communicate commodity prices worldwide, and so to coordinate global markets in increasingly efficient ways. The patterns of urbanization that arose after 1945 would not have been possible without assurance of a steady supply of perishable food

5   William Cronon, *Nature's Metropolis: Chicago and the Great West* (New York: Norton, 1992).

products, courtesy of both refrigeration and a transport delivery system that is efficient, fast and relatively cheap. None of this would have occurred had it not been for the colonization of space and the transformation of space relations under the influence of intercapitalist competition. Even when transport and communication innovations have had their origin in military imperatives (as has often been the case), their immediate adoption by capital has played a crucial role in the reconfiguration of urbanization, and the production of space and daily life. It has also been a mainstay of my own argument that the absorption of surplus-value and of surplus product through the production of space in general and urbanization in particular has been crucial to sustaining capital accumulation. These are, for me, some of the exciting projections that arise out Marx's brief notes on the development of transport and communications in Volume II.

But Marx does note some burgeoning potential contradictions in the drive to reduce circulation times:

> If the progress of capitalist production and the consequent development of the means of transport and communication shortens the circulation time for a given quantity of commodities, the same progress and the opportunity provided by the development of the means of transport and communications conversely introduces the necessity of working for ever more distant markets, in a word, for the world market. The mass of commodities in transit grows enormously, and hence so does the part of social capital that stays for long periods in the stage of commodity capital, in circulation time—both absolutely and relatively.

Traffic planners have long noticed a tendency for traffic to increase up to the capacity of the network, thus making attempts to relieve congestion in any traffic network self-defeating in the long run (some studies suggest that traffic moved at an average speed of 11 miles per hour in the London of the horse-and-buggy era, and that in the automobile era the average speed is not much different).

The second contradiction we have encountered before: "A simultaneous and associated growth occurs in the portion of social wealth that, instead of serving as direct means of production, is laid out on means of transport and communication, and on the fixed and circulating capital required to keep these in operation" (329).

Other complications arise out of the system of money flows that does not necessarily correspond with the commodity flows due to various mechanisms for discounting. Variations in turnover "form one of the material bases for differing periods of credit, just as overseas trade in general, in Venice and Genoa, for instance, formed one of the original sources of the credit system in its true sense" (329). In the chapters on the credit system in Volume III, Marx paid considerable attention to these phenomena but here he merely notes them without much additional commentary.

While much of this chapter is given over to looking at the circulation process from the standpoint of the transformation of the commodity into the money form, Marx closes with some brief remarks on the problems that arise in the transformation of money into commodities to be used in production. He had shown in chapter 6

> how the time of purchase, and the greater or lesser distance from the major sources of raw material, makes it necessary to buy raw materials for longer periods and keep them available in the form of productive stock, latent or potential productive capital; how this increases the mass of capital that must be advanced at one stroke, and the time for which it must be advanced, the scale of production being otherwise the same. (331–2)

This plunges Marx back into the seasonality of supply, and the particular times at which certain commodities are thrown upon the market.

Marx ends by reminding us that all of these considerations have to be inserted into a circulatory world in which capital in its money, commodity and productive forms continues to interpenetrate, and that capital cannot exist without taking on these specific forms in a continuity of movement that occurs in space and time. Plainly, these different forms of capital are spatially mobile in different ways, and the relations between these movements of money, productive activity and commodities are never entirely consistent with each other. Some of these inconsistencies are taken up in the next chapters of Volume II.

CHAPTER NINE

Circulation and Turnover Times (Chapters 15–17 of Volume II)

These three chapters are hard to understand and assess. I am still not sure how best to read them. The problem, as is too often the case with Marx, is to untangle the perpetual disputatious dialogue he is having with the political economists of the time from the advances he may be making in his own theoretical exposition. Marx also, as we know, often gets lost in numerical trivia—and here, as even Engels editorializes, Marx is at his very worst. To add to the confusion, Marx at certain points abandons the usual political reticence that characterizes Volume II and takes to speculating both on where capital in general is headed and what communism might entail (much as he does in Volume III). This either leaves us with quite a lot of work to do on our own account or invites us to skim over the trivia and the disputes and seek to identify and dwell upon the moments where he broaches more important business.

ON CHAPTER 15 OF VOLUME II: CIRCULATION TIME AND THE MAGNITUDE OF CAPITAL ADVANCED

This chapter may qualify as perhaps the most tedious of all in Volume II—though, as usual, there are some important problems posed and a key insight or two to be gained. Matters could, by Engels's account, have been much worse, because Marx left behind "a thick sheaf of notebooks in which he worked through all the various kinds of commercial calculation." Engels spared us from going over these, cryptically noting that Marx "was never at ease in reckoning with figures . . . and in his turnover calculations Marx became confused, with the result that, apart from being incomplete, they contain many errors and contradictions." The "uncertain results of this tiresome calculation business," Engels suggests, led Marx to attribute unwarranted significance to rather trivial matters.

So what is going on here? To begin with, Marx complains that "the economists, who have never produced a clear account of the turnover mechanism, constantly overlook this basic aspect, i.e. the fact that only a part of the industrial capital can be actually engaged in the production process, if production is to proceed *without interruption*" (emphasis added). Marx then adds, significantly, that "since this is overlooked, so also is the importance and role of money capital in general" (342). This is at least one of the key insights, which, as I have noted in the case of the circulation of interest-bearing capital, has vital implications for understanding the laws of motion of capital in general.

"Continuity," Marx reiterates, "is a productive force of labour" (356). It is crucial that it be maintained. Any interruption or delay in capital flow is costly and to be avoided like the plague. The difficulties of maintaining continuity as a productive force open up an important role for the money market and the credit system (as we saw in the study of finance capital and the credit system in Volume III). By the way, in the discussions on the nature of productive forces in the general Marxist literature, it is rather rare for "continuity" to be mentioned, and its extensive implications are usually ignored.

Smoothing out turnover processes reduces the capital that has to be advanced:

> This money capital that is set free by the mechanism of the turnover movement (together with the money capital set free by the successive reflux of the fixed capital and that needed for variable capital in every labour process) must play a significant role, as soon as the credit system has developed, *and must also form one of the foundations for this.* (357; emphasis added)

Note that Marx does not say that this turnover movement gives rise to the circulation of interest-bearing capital and the credit system. The implication (which is explicit in the historical chapter on credit in Volume III) is that credit that had long been in existence had to be disciplined, redesigned and redirected to meet this compelling need.

If this is a foundational statement (which I believe it is) and not merely a casual, offhand remark of the type that can sometimes be found in Marx's incomplete writings, then it is by far the most important observation to be taken from this chapter. It has huge significance for the whole architecture of Marx's project. His studies of the laws of motion of capital have in effect brought him (rather late in the day) to the point of concluding that these laws dictate (and I use that word advisedly) the existence of a money market and a credit system that functions in a particular way. If such a functioning money market and credit system did not already exist, it would have to be created. Furthermore, as we saw in Volume III, the money market and the credit system, far from being constituted as mere speculative froth (though there is plenty of that) on the top of basic surplus-value production, move center stage in explicating how the generality and continuity of sustained capital accumulation actually work. This forces Marx out of the strict framework defined in the *Grundrisse*: the particularities of distribution here have powerful internal effects within the laws of motion of capital.

Engels's objections that the numerical examples to which Marx appeals offer relatively insignificant support for this thesis do not constitute a denial of the thesis. The process of "freeing up" capital in money form is far more general and extensive (and we only have to go back over the chapter on fixed capital, as Marx himself notes, to recognize this). "The main thing in the text," says Engels, "is the proof that a considerable part of industrial capital is always present in the money form, while a still more considerable part must assume this form from time to time" (360).

So what is Marx's argument about the necessary "freeing up" of money capital within the logic of turnover time? In effect, it goes like this:

The capitalist produces a commodity in a working period of nine weeks and lays out £900 at the beginning, so she is spending £100 a week on labor and means of production (the problem of fixed capital is mentioned but mostly assumed away). We also assume the working period is the same as the production time. The circulation time when the commodity capital is on the market is three weeks, and for that period the capitalist has no money to continue production. The continuity of value production is broken. How can the three-week gap be filled? There are two solutions. The first is to cut back on weekly outlays and use the money saved to keep production going in the three-week circulation time (but this may be impossible if the capitalist has to operate at a certain scale in order to produce effectively). The second option is to find another £300 to cover the dead period when the commodity is on the market. I really cannot see why Marx makes such a fuss of the difference between these two strategies, since essentially they amount to the same thing, and he thereafter refers solely to the latter case. After the three weeks taken up by circulation time, the commodity will be converted into money and the capitalist will have the whole £900 in her pocket. But she only needs £600 to complete the next working period because she has already laid out the £300 to cover the dead circulation time. This frees up £300, which sits idle until the next circulation period occurs. The general point, as Engels points out, is that more money is always needed in a production process than is actually used up, and that the amount needed or available fluctuates depending on the phasing of production and circulation. So why not take the surplus money and put it on the money market until it is needed? Or why not borrow the £300 needed to cover the three weeks of circulation time and then pay it off when the whole £900 comes back to the capitalist after the circulation time is over? There is, of course, yet another option that Marx does not consider here (except incidentally): the capitalist sells immediately to a merchant at a discount (say, of less than £300), and so reduces her effective circulation time to zero.

Marx works through three different detailed examples in which the circulation time is shorter, equal to, and longer than the working period. He does so in excruciating detail and, of course, discovers some oddities (provided the credit system does not intervene). In particular, he shows that there are instances—as when the circulation time and working period are equal or when one is a simple multiple of the other—when no capital is freed up at all. But these are clearly special cases. In all other instances, the amount of capital freed up varies according to the turnover time and the ratio between working period and circulation time. The amount of free money capital created will also fluctuate according to the overlapping turnover processes that ensure the continuity of production.

But the main point is prefigured and somewhat obvious already (even though conventional economists had failed to spot it): "If we consider the total social capital, then a more or less significant part of this additional capital exists for a prolonged time in the state of money capital." For the individual capital, the

> intervention of the additional capital required for the conversion of . . . circulation time into production time thus not only increases the size of the capital advanced and the length of time for which the total

capital has to be advanced, but it also specifically increases that part of the capital advanced that exists as a money reserve, i.e. exists in the state of money capital and possesses the form of potential money capital. (341)

As usual, Marx uses this insight to go after the economists

who have never produced a clear account of the turnover mechanism, [and who] constantly overlook this basic aspect, i.e. the fact that only a part of the industrial capital can be actually engaged in the production process, if production is to proceed without interruption. In other words, one part can function as productive capital only on condition that another part is withdrawn from production proper in the form of commodity or money capital. Since this is overlooked, so also is the importance and role of money capital in general. (342)

By extension, this must surely apply also to money markets and credit, although this is an issue that is not directly taken up here.

Plainly, if there is some reduction in circulation time (due, for example, to improvements in transportation and marketing) in relation to production time, then this too will release excess money capital for use elsewhere. Under such conditions, some of the

value originally advanced is precipitated out in the form of money capital. As such it enters the money market and forms an additional part of the capital functioning there. We can see from this how a surfeit of money capital can arise—and not only in the sense that the supply of money capital is greater than the demand for it; the latter is never more than a relative surplus, which is found for instance in the depressed period that opens the new business cycle after the crisis is over. It is rather in the sense that a definite part of the capital advanced is superfluous for the overall process of social reproduction (which includes the circulation process) and is therefore precipitated out in the form of money capital; it is thus a surplus which has arisen . . . simply by a contraction in the turnover period. (358)

We can thus imagine a scenario in which the reductions in the time of transport outlined in the previous chapter may dramatically reduce circulation times, and so release a flood of surplus money capital onto the money markets, which will bring interest rates down. Conversely, if the circulation time is for some reason extended (for example, the Suez Canal gets blocked), then "additional capital will have to be obtained . . . from the money market"; and if this is widespread then it may "exert pressure on the money market," by which Marx presumably means that the extra demand for money capital will, other things being equal, drive up interest rates (358–9). This will have a definite impact upon the supply and demand for money capital which, as we saw earlier, is the key determinant of interest rates.

I think this is about all there is to say on the constructive aspects of this chapter. I really think the details do not matter too much. But the inner connectivity that here begins to emerge, on the one hand, between turnover time and its components of working period, production time and circulation time, and, on the other, the functioning of money capital both internal to production and externally through a viable money market and credit system, is of great significance in how we understand the unfolding of Marx's project. And that project is, of course, to uncover the general laws of motion of capital.

ON CHAPTER 16 OF VOLUME II: THE TURNOVER OF VARIABLE CAPITAL

This is likewise a frustrating chapter. But it also has some substantial insights. "The variable circulating capital expended in the course of production can serve again in the circulation process only to the extent that the product in which its value is reproduced is sold, transformed from commodity capital into money capital, so that it can be laid out anew in payment for labour-power." The same is also true for constant circulating capital. So, in order to take up the question of how variable capital circulates and how it produces surplus-value, Marx separates it off from constant capital and treats "the variable part of the circulating capital as if it alone formed the circulating capital" (370). This is a pretty dramatic abstraction: variable capital is the only form of capital there is.

Marx then defines the annual rate of surplus-value. Suppose £500 of variable capital is advanced on a turnover time of every five weeks, producing £100 surplus-value per week; then, by the end of the year (which is by assumption only fifty weeks long) the repeated advance of £500 every five weeks produces an annual surplus-value of £5,000, or 1,000 percent. This is case A. The result looks completely different when the whole £5,000 has to be advanced for the whole year, rather than in ten £500 installments. Presuming the same weekly rate of exploitation, the annual rate of surplus-value is only 100 percent. This is case B. The annual rate of surplus-value (and hence the profit rate) is dramatically influenced by turnover time. The significance of this finding cannot be overestimated. The advantages that accrue to capital from shorter turnover times are manifold. The sooner the variable capital advanced is turned into a commodity and then back into the money form, the shorter the "time for which the capitalist has to advance money from his own funds." From this, it also follows that "the smaller the total capital he needs to work at a given scale of production" and "the relatively greater . . . is the mass of surplus-value that the capitalist extracts in the course of the year" (389).

So why is this significant? We have first to refer to Marx's ongoing critique of classical political economy. Such differences in the annual rate of surplus-value make it seem as if the rate of surplus-value (and hence, profitability) depends on "influences deriving from the circulation process" rather than from the exploitation of living labor in production. "Since the beginning of the 1820s, this phenomenon" (which might best be described as a fetishistic attribution of surplus-value to circulatory conditions rather than to production) "has led to the complete destruction of the Ricardian school" (373).

Surplus-value, in Marx's view, cannot arise from circulation, and any theory that makes it seems so, such as that propounded by the Ricardians, is profoundly in error. But the "strangeness" of Marx's finding does pose a problem. To defend against the Ricardian position, Marx has somehow to reconcile his own theory of surplus-value production with the fact that the annual rates of exploitation plainly differ as a result of different turnover times, and that shortening turnover time does indeed increase the annual rate of surplus-value. Marx's answer is to draw a distinction between capital advanced and capital applied. Both capitals, A and B, apply variable capital at the same weekly rate, and produce the same surplus-value per week. The difference lies in the capital that has to be advanced. Capital A can get back the £500 capital advanced in five weeks and apply the capital again, while capital B has gradually to draw down the £5,000 initially advanced over the whole year. At the end of the first five weeks, capital B still has £4,500 in reserve, hoarded in effect, to pay laborers over the rest of the year. The point made much of in the previous chapter is again apparent—a good deal of surplus money has to exist within production to accommodate differences in turnover time.

The difference between cases A and B is not that faster turnover times generate higher rates of surplus-value, but that faster turnover times tie up less hoarded and inactive money capital over the course of a turnover period. If labor is paid £100 on a weekly basis, then capital A needs to advance five times that, while capital B needs to advance fifty times the weekly wage. This creates yet another reason to bring credit to the rescue, although Marx for some reason does not mention that here. Plainly, the idle money capital in case B could be sitting on the money market up until the point when it is actively needed. But

> the variable capital advanced functions as variable capital only to the extent that it is actually applied, and during the time for which it is applied; not during the time in which it remains advanced in reserve without being applied. But all circumstances that differentiate the ratio between advanced and applied variable capital can be summed up in the difference in turnover periods. . . . The law of surplus-value production is that, with the same rate of surplus-value, equal amounts of functioning variable capital create equal masses of surplus-value.

The equal amounts of variable capital applied by A and B produce equal amounts of surplus-value no matter what the differences are in the ratios of capital advanced and capital applied. The variation in "the ratio between the mass of the surplus-value produced and the total variable capital advanced, rather than actually applied," is simply "an inescapable consequence" of the "laws put forward for the production of surplus-value" (375). Everything boils down to the difference between capital advanced and capital applied.

After excavation of some tedious arithmetic examples, Marx produces a formula for the annual rate of surplus-value as "s'n, i.e. the real rate of surplus-value produced in a turnover period by the variable capital consumed during this period, multiplied by the number of turnovers." Marx's overall point is not that the differences in the annual rates of surplus-value are illusory or "merely subjective," but that they are "produced by the actual movement of capital itself" (381). Marx does not, therefore, dismiss the annual rate of surplus-value as illusory or insignificant, but he does show how it can be reconciled with the underlying laws of surplus-value production. Once we understand how the different annual rates are produced, then we can clearly see that the differences have nothing to do with purely circulatory phenomena but rest, as always, on the conditions of production and realization of surplus-value.

The significance of the annual rate of turnover remains to be emphasized, since it clearly has an impact on profit rates, and therefore must be taken into account in any discussion of the tendency for the rate of profit to fall. Marx intended a chapter on this in Volume III but did not write it. So Engels felt compelled to insert his own interpretation (based on the Volume II materials) in a separate chapter. He there clearly states that "the profit rates of two [similar] capitals vary inversely as their turnover times," and that the "direct effect of the abbreviated turnover time"—most spectacularly associated in his time with a revolution in transport and communications—"on the production of surplus-value, and therefore also on profit, consists in the increased effectiveness which this gives to the variable portion of capital," as articulated in the chapter we are here considering (C3, 165).

The implications for Marx's own arguments are potentially far-reaching. As is well known, Marx is often identified with a theory of a tendency for the rate of profit to fall. But we here see two direct and one indirect forces that may lead the profit rate to rise. The issue here is whether the profit rate is calculated on the basis of the capital applied or the capital advanced. For the capitalist, it is plainly the latter that matters. From the arguments set out in this and the preceding chapter, we can see that any reductions in circulation times relative to the working period will reduce the excess money capital needed to support the continuous production of surplus-value. Less money will need to be advanced, and profit rates (assuming a constant rate of exploitation in production) will rise. The same result will occur with any reduction in turnover times due to either shorter working periods and/or shorter circulation times. Engels plainly states in his Volume III chapter that shorter turnovers (other things held constant) mean higher profits. He also notes the astonishing reductions in turnover times then occurring through revolutions in transport and communications, which, by radically cutting back on the capital advanced, would surely be having a major impact on increasing the profit rate. We forget how dramatic some of these innovations were. The telegraph, for example, reduced the transmission time of information flow by a factor of 2,500 relative to sending letters in the mail (the internet decreased transmission times by a factor of only five relative to the fax). The coming of the railroads and of steamships had a far greater relative impact in the nineteenth century than did jet air transport in the twentieth.

We see here an added incentive, of which individual capitalists are all too aware, to find ways to further annihilate space with time, and to engage in the active pursuit of time-space compression in their business strategies. Capitalists who find ways to shorten working periods and/or circulation times (by finding quicker ways to get their commodities to market, for example) gain a higher profit on the capital they advance (even though the profit on capital applied is identical), provided that the costs associated with new production and circulation strategies do not offset their higher profits.

But the indirect way of dealing with these problems of circulation and turnover times, which hovers in the background of this chapter, is located in the development of the money market and the credit system. The industrial capitalist can cut down on the capital advanced to cover disparate circulation times by resort either to the services of the merchant capitalist and the banker, who will discount bills of exchange, or, more directly, by entering and exiting the money market with short-term borrowings and deposits of surplus capital. The former has the effect of reducing circulation time to zero, while the latter obviates the problem of advancing capital to cover the whole turnover time. What Marx clearly establishes here in Volume II is that a lot of surplus money capital has to be freely available to support the continuity of production activities. And he suggests, more or less in passing, that it is this that makes a money market and a credit system so necessary for the proper functioning of capitalism. In Volume III, as we saw earlier, he takes the argument further. The industrial circulation system is disaggregated into a duality of money and interest-bearing capital, on the one hand, and the extraction of surplus-value from production, on the other. How all of this impacts profit rates is unclear. Much depends on the relationship between the rate of interest and the rate of profit—and that, as is argued in Volume III, depends on the particularities of supply and demand conditions and competition. It is in this direction that these chapters help to advance Marx's own theoretical understandings, but unfortunately he fails to take up the full implications. This leaves a lot of unresolved problems for the general theory.

Towards the end of chapter 16, however, Marx does take up some of the more general social and political implications by looking at the market impacts of the circulation of variable capital. The £500 initially laid out as variable capital in his example ceases to be capital once workers receive it as wages. The workers "pay it out again in purchasing their means of subsistence . . . to the value of £500. A mass of commodities amounting altogether to this value is thereby annihilated. . . . It is consumed unproductively, as far as the worker is concerned, except in as much as he thereby maintains his labour-power, which is an indispensable instrument for the capitalist, in working condition" (384). Once again we encounter a concept of "unproductive" activity that seems strange, given that the reproduction of workers is fundamental for the sustenance of capital. But the logic is impeccable when we go back to Marx's stipulation that, for capital, the only form of production that matters is that of surplus-value, and that is not happening when the worker spends money on commodities and eats and sleeps at home. When the worker returns to the workplace, production of surplus-value is renewed. The £500 the capitalist gets back at the end of the first turnover period has been produced by the worker. So the £500 advanced by the capitalist as variable capital for the second period is in fact the equivalent of the worker's own product. Marx is here reiterating a claim made in Volume I, that in truth that product should belong to the direct producer (the laborer), and that it is only according to bourgeois right that it can be said to belong to the capitalist. The aim here, as in Volume I, is to delegitimize the general theory of bourgeois property rights and point up the contradiction within the Lockean view maintaining that rights to private property accrue to those who fruitfully mix their labor with the land while also asserting the right to exploit labor-power under the rule of capital.

The broader effects within the market also need to be considered. The capitalist A, who turns over the variable capital in five weeks, puts a weekly demand of £100 for wage goods into the market, and supplies an equivalent product of £500 value after five weeks. Capitalist B places the same weekly demand for wage goods, but does not supply the equivalent commodity value for £5,000 until the end of the year. The monetary imbalances in supply and demand conditions can become problematic, and we will take up the full consequences of this shortly.

Marx does offer a somewhat unusual commentary on this situation that warrants some consideration:

> If we were to consider a communist society in place of a capitalist one, then money capital would immediately be done away with, and so too the disguises that transactions acquire through it. The matter would simply be reduced to the fact that the society must reckon in advance how much labour, means of production and means of subsistence it can spend, without dislocation, on branches of industry which, like the building of railways, for instance, supply neither means of production nor means of subsistence, nor any kind of useful effect, for a long period, a year or more, though they certainly do withdraw labour, means of production and means of subsistence from the total annual product. (390)

Up until this point, the idea of communism has been largely confined to that of associated laborers freely managing and organizing their own labor for a social purpose. But here there looms a larger problem of coordination in the production of long-term improvements and infrastructures that will absorb large amounts of labor and means of production for a considerable period of time without providing immediate benefits. Notice that Marx appeals not to the state, but to some unspecified way in which "society must reckon" and presumably decide on the prosecution of such large-scale infrastructural projects. Notice, also, that he also asserts that, under communism, "money capital will immediately be done away with," which presumes the existence of some other form of value determination (such as social use-values), which remains unspecified. This commentary also suggests (and there are other passages that support this view) that a central problem within a capitalist mode of production lies in the monetization of circulation and the profit-oriented circulation of money capital.

While Engels may have been correct to complain of Volume II that "it does not contain much material for agitation," this passage signals a significant development in Marx's political vision of communism. It will become even more compelling (though largely unstated) in Part 3 of Volume II. It raises questions of how "society" might rationally coordinate and "reckon" aggregate divisions of labor and manage long-term developmental projects in the absence of market signals in a way that enhances rather than hinders the freedom of associated laborers to pursue their collective interests. What the analysis here shows, for the first but not the last time in *Capital*, is the existence of a central contradiction at the heart of the communist project. For in the same way that individual bourgeois liberty and freedom only became possible in the context of the draconian private-property-based disciplinary apparatus that underpins a capitalist mode of production, so communism has to find a way to redefine and protect the liberty and freedom of associated labor within an overall framework of calculation, coordination and reckoning that circumscribes and disciplines the production of necessary social and physical infrastructures even as it enhances prospects for human emancipation.

> In capitalist society, on the other hand, where any kind of social rationality asserts itself only *post festum*, major disturbances can and must occur constantly. On the one hand there is pressure on the money market, while conversely the absence of this pressure itself calls into being a mass of such undertakings, and therefore the precise circumstances that later provoke a pressure on the money market. The money market is under pressure because large-scale advances of money capital for long periods of time are always needed here. This is quite apart from the fact that industrialists and merchants throw the money capital they need for the carrying on of their business into railway speculations, etc. and replace it with loans from the money market. (390)

This process provides a technical basis for all of the "insane forms" and "crazy" behaviors identified in the Volume III investigations of finance capital and the credit system:

> Since elements of productive capital are constantly being withdrawn from the market and all that is put into the market is an equivalent in money, the effective demand rises, without this in itself providing any element of supply. Hence prices rise, both for the means of subsistence and for the material elements of production, during this time, too, there are regular business swindles, and great transfers of capital. A band of speculators, contractors, engineers, lawyers, etc. enrich themselves. These exert a strong consumer demand on the market, and wages rise as well. As far as foodstuffs are concerned, agriculture is given a boost by

this process. But since these foodstuffs cannot be suddenly increased within the year, imports grow, as well as the import of exotic foods (coffee sugar, wine, etc.) and objects of luxury. Hence over-supply and speculation in this part of the import trade. On the other hand, in those branches of industry in which production can be increased more quickly (manufacture proper, mining, etc.) the price rise leads to sudden expansion, soon followed by collapse. (390–1)

This is a radical departure from the usual language of Volume II and links up directly, and rather marvelously, with the chapters on finance and credit in Volume III, confirming the underlying unity between the two volumes. But Marx goes even further when he examines the effect on labor:

> The same effect occurs on the labour market, drawing great numbers of the latent relative surplus population, and even workers already employed, into the new lines of business. Undertakings of this kind, such as railways, generally withdraw from the labour market on a large scale a certain quantity of force, which can derive only from branches such as agriculture, etc. where only strong lads are needed. This still occurs even after the new undertakings have already become an established branch of industry and the migrant working class needed for them has already been formed e.g. when railway construction is temporarily pursued on a scale greater than the average. A part of the reserve army of workers whose pressure keeps wages down is absorbed. Wages generally rise, even in the formerly well-employed sections of the labour market. This lasts until, with the inevitable crash, the reserve army of workers is again released and wages are pressed down once more to their minimum and below it. (391)

The unity expressed with the theses of chapter 25 of Volume I is clear. But to this Marx adds an even more pertinent and potentially explosive theoretical observation in a footnote:

> Contradiction in the capitalist mode of production. The workers are important for the market as buyers of commodities. But as sellers of their commodity—labour-power—capitalist society has the tendency to restrict them to their minimum price. Further contradiction: the periods in which capitalist production exerts all its forces regularly show

themselves to be periods of over-production; because the limit to the application of the productive powers is not simply the production of value, but also its realization. However, the sale of commodities, the realization of commodity capital, and thus of surplus-value as well, is restricted not by the consumer needs of society in general, but by the consumer needs of a society in which the great majority are always poor and must always remain poor. (391)

That wage repression in the interest of surplus-value extraction for capital poses such a difficulty of sustained effective demand has long been one of the central contradictions within the laws of motion of capital. It is here explicitly recognized as such. The significance of workers as consumers, and hence as agents for the realization of the value of commodity capital in the market, is in fact an important emergent theme throughout the whole of Volume II. In Volume I, this issue was ignored simply by assuming that all commodities trade at their value. This is one of those moments in *Capital* where wages—an aspect of distribution largely ruled out as a particularity—are reintroduced into the heart of the circulation process of industrial capital in general, with major impacts upon the contradictions within the laws of motion of capital.

In bringing this chapter to a close, Marx extends his thinking beyond his normal assumption of a closed system of trade. The distance of the market has to be considered "as a specific material basis" for longer circulation, and hence turnover times. The example is that of cotton cloth and yarn sold to India. The producer sells to the merchant, who resorts to the money market for means of payment. The exporter later sells on the Indian market. Only then can the equivalent value flow back to Britain (either in money or commodity form) to provide means of payment equivalent to that required for new production (the money, of course, flows back into the money market). The gaps between supply and effective demand are similar to those already outlined in the case of the annual turnover of capital B. The gap between supply and demand has to be covered by resort to the money market or credit. But there is much that can go wrong here:

> It is also possible that the yarn is sold on credit in India itself. With this credit, products are bought in India and sent as a return shipment to England, or else drafts are remitted to this amount. If this process is

delayed, the pressure builds up on the Indian money market, which may react on England to produce a crisis here. This crisis, in its turn, even if it is combined with the export of precious metals to India, provokes a new crisis in that country, on account of the bankruptcy of English firms and their Indian branches, who were given credit by Indian banks. Thus a simultaneous crisis arises both on the market for which the trade balance is unfavourable, and on that for which it is favourable. The phenomenon can be still more complicated. England may have sent silver bullion to India, but India's creditors now press their demands here, and in a short while India will have to send its silver back to England.

The point, of course, is that "what appears as a crisis on the money market in actual fact expresses anomalies in the production and repro-duction process itself" (393). This is the true insight that comes from the study of differential turnover times, particularly those involved in the long-distance trade.

I cite this instance to show two things. Firstly, that there is nothing new about monetary crises rumbling around contagiously from one place and one moment in the circulatory process to another. It is, so to speak, very much in capital's nature to perform in such a way. But, secondly, and internally to Marx's own theorizing, there are plainly strong underlying connectivities between all three often seemingly disparate volumes of capital. There are innumerable threads through which "the whole is joined together" into that "organic totality" envis-aged in the introduction to the *Grundrisse*. These relations are only tentatively, and in this chapter rather tenuously, established. But that Marx perpetually managed to keep them constantly in mind over more than a quarter-century of relentless study, I find simply amazing.

ON CHAPTER 17 OF VOLUME II: THE CIRCULATION OF SURPLUS-VALUE

In this chapter Marx isolates the circulation of surplus-value for close inspection. The chapter generates high expectations but does not really deliver, leaving a critical aspect of theory in a somewhat ambiguous but tantalizing state. The central question it poses, articulated well into the chapter, "is not: where does surplus-value come from? But rather: where does the money come from which it is turned into?" (404). Does the production of gold as the preeminent money commodity provide the extra money needed to realize the surplus-value? If not (and it is fairly clear that Marx rejects this possibility, though without denying the peculiar role of the gold producers), then this leaves us with the awkward question: Where does the effective demand come from to realize the surplus-value that is perpetually being thrown upon the market?

Marx begins the chapter by going back to the case of the two capitalists, A and B, the second of whom does not realize the total value of £5,000 until the end of the year. In this latter case, "the surplus-value is not realized and can therefore be consumed neither individually nor productively. So far as individual consumption is concerned surplus-value is anticipated. Funds for this must be advanced" (394). The funds advanced have to cover not only the capitalist's consumption but also all the repairs and maintenance of fixed capital. For the capitalist operating on a very short turnover time, these funds come out of already realized surplus-value, and do not have to be advanced. When the surplus-value is realized as capital—"capitalized," as Marx puts it—is therefore a crucial question. The longer the capitalist has to wait before putting the commodity on the market, the more that capitalist has to have money in reserve to cover his consumption and incidental expenses (such as repairs and maintenance).

The "relation between the capital originally advanced and the capitalized surplus-value becomes still more intricate" when the credit system intervenes, but Marx, as usual in Volume II, does not explore that question in any great detail here. The main issue is what happens to the surplus-value when it is capitalized. Marx refers back to chapter 24 of Volume I to remind us of the necessity for capital to be reproduced on an expanding scale (the rule of "accumulation for accumulation's sake," as he put it there). So part of the surplus-value must be put to expansion either "extensively in the form of the addition of new factories to old ones, or intensively in the enlargement of the former scale of operations" (395).

Marx describes the various forms this expansion can take. But, in each case, the relation between the amount of surplus-value capitalized and the amount required to expand production places limits on the capacity to expand immediately. Hoarding capitalized surplus-value over several turnover periods may be required, until sufficient funds are built up to invest in expansion at a given scale of operations (building an additional new factory and equipping it with machinery, for example). During this period "the money capital that the capitalist cannot yet apply in his own business is employed by others from whom he receives interest. It functions for him as money capital," but "in someone else's hands . . . it actually operates as capital." Over time, the amount of money available on the money market tends to increase, so that a large part of the surplus-value produced "is absorbed again from the money market for the expansion of production." While Marx does not mention it, the increasing supply of money into the money market increases the supply of loanable capital, and therefore presumably leads to lower rates of interest.

After a brief return to what happens under conditions of hoarding, Marx offers us two pages of long quotations from the political philosopher William Thompson, who published his *An Inquiry into the Principles of the Distribution of Wealth* in 1824. I will not go over these, but I think it is very useful to read what Thompson has to say, because it is clear that there were bourgeois analysts who held very perceptive and deeply critical views of the capitalist development going on around them. It is significant that Marx does not offer any critical commentary on Thompson's account here (nor does he elsewhere, to my knowledge, when he cites Thompson's work).

Throughout *Capital*, Marx typically adopts the tactic of examining the reproduction of capital first as if it is engaged in simple reproduction, and secondly under the far more realistic conditions of continuous expanded reproduction. He did so in Volume I and will do so again in Part 3 of Volume II, which I will shortly consider. The reason for this separation is that it is far easier to determine basic relations in the case of simple reproduction.

So the circulation of surplus-value is first looked at through the lens of simple reproduction. The surplus-value produced and realized over several turnovers "is consumed individually, i.e. unproductively, by its owners, the capitalists" (399). Some of the surplus-value has to take on money form, otherwise there would not be the money to buy the commodities needed for workers and capitalists to consume. When we look back at the chapter on money in Volume I, we see that the "mass of metallic money existing in a country cannot just be enough to circulate commodities" because it has "to cope with fluctuations in the circulation of money" which arise for a number of different reasons (fluctuations in commodity outputs and prices, and so on). Growth in the economy in general calls for growth in the annual production of gold and silver, unless the growth can be accommodated by increasing the velocity of circulation or using money more and more as a means of payment. Hence, "a part of the social labour-power and a part of the social means of production must therefore be spent each year in the production of gold and silver." This leads Marx to a detailed analysis of what happens in the case of the production of gold. I will not consider the details of this case here, because I think it is irrelevant to the general conditions of money creation and use in contemporary capitalism and, in any case, does not help answer the real question that is then posed: Where does the money come from into which surplus-value is turned?

The problem is "that the capitalist . . . casts into circulation an excess over and above his capital and withdraws this excess from it again. The commodity capital that the capitalist casts into circulation is of greater value . . . than the productive capital he has withdrawn in labour-power and means of production from the circulation sphere" (404). "But before the commodity capital is transformed back into productive capital and the surplus-value contained in it is spent, it must be turned into money. Where does the money for this come from?" This was, Marx claimed, a problem for which no one in classical political economy had an adequate answer.

Let me give a simple explanation of the structure of this problem. Throughout *Capital*, Marx assumes (at least up until the chapters on money capital and finance) that demand and supply are in equilibrium. But we here encounter a situation not only where that is not the case, but where the capitalist strives mightily to widen the gap between supply and demand as far as possible. Put simply, the capitalist's demand is for means of production (c) and for labor-power (v), but he supplies to the market commodity values that are equivalent to $c + v + s$, so that the supply of commodity values systematically exceeds the demand. Furthermore, the desire to maximize surplus-value pushes this discrepancy to a maximum. Where does the extra effective demand equivalent to the surplus-value come from? If it does not materialize, then capital circulation ceases to be.

The extra surplus-value "is cast into circulation in the commodity form. . . . But the extra money needed for the circulation of this additional commodity value is not provided by the same operation." This difficulty, Marx warns, "should not be circumvented by plausible subterfuges."

Marx then goes through some of these "plausible subterfuges." Most of these rest on the timing through which different capitals enter the market at different moments, on the flows of constant and fixed capitals in relation to each other, or upon the time-structure of how the revenues of workers and of capitalists are expended. But "the general answer has already been given." Now this is one of those moments where we have to be sure whether this is Marx's general answer or the general answer of the political economists which merely constitutes a "plausible subterfuge": "if a mass of commodities of x times £1000 is to circulate, it in no way affects the quantity of money needed for this circulation whether the value of this commodity mass contains surplus-value or not, or whether the mass of commodities is produced under capitalist conditions or not. *Thus the problem itself does not exist*" (407). The problem is then reduced to that of regulating the supply of money in a country sufficient to lubricate all commodity exchanges. This, I think Marx is saying, is the greatest and most plausible subterfuge of all: it is equivalent to the "childish babble" of Say's law criticized so savagely in Volume I.

But it does leave behind "the *semblance* of a special problem. For here it is the capitalist, the man who casts the money into circulation, who appears as the point of departure." The capitalist lays out variable capital (v) and money for constant fixed and fluid capital (c):

> Beyond this, however, the capitalist no longer appears as the point of departure for the quantity of money that exists in circulation. All that exist now are two starting points, the capitalist and the worker. All third parties either must receive money from these two classes for the performance of services, or, in so far as they receive money without providing services in return, they are co-proprietors of surplus-value in the forms of rent, interest, etc. (408)

What Marx is boldly doing here, is proposing a simple two-class model—constituted by workers and capitalists—of a capitalist mode of production, and then posing the question of who furnishes the extra demand to realize the surplus-value in such a world. "As far as the workers are concerned, it has already been said that they are only a secondary point of departure, whereas the capitalist is the primary point of departure for the money cast into circulation by the workers." So the solution to the problem must lie with the capitalists: "How can the capitalist class continue to extract £600 from circulation if it only ever puts £500 in? Out of nothing, nothing comes. The entire class cannot extract anything from the circulation sphere that was not put into it already" (408). The answer is simply stunning:

> In point of fact, paradoxical as it may seem at the first glance, the capitalist class itself casts into circulation the money that serves towards the realization of the surplus-value contained in its commodities. But note well: it does not cast this in as money advanced, and therefore not as capital. It spends it as a means of purchase for its individual consumption. Thus the money is not advanced by the capitalist class, even though this class is the starting point of its circulation. (409)

Marx illustrates this with the case of a capitalist who advances money capital of £5,000 with £1,000 for variable capital, producing £1,000 surplus-value over the course of a whole year. The capitalist "has to cover his individual consumption for the first year out of his own pocket, instead of using the product produced for nothing by his workers. He does not advance this money as capital. He spends it" on commodities whose value he consumes away until he gets his surplus-value at the end of the year (409). Marx assumes here

> that the sum of money that the capitalist casts into circulation to cover his individual consumption until the first reflux of his capital is exactly equal to the surplus-value that he produces and hence has to convert into money. This is obviously an arbitrary assumption in relation to the individual capitalist. But it must be correct for the capitalist class as a whole, on the assumption of simple reproduction. (410)

This is a beautiful example of Marx using drastic powers of simplification and abstraction to identify a vitally important feature of a capitalist mode of production. He invokes this result elsewhere—as we have seen, for example, in Volume III, though there he concedes the importance of an autonomous class of nonproductive consumers. But the implications are far-reaching. For one thing, this result punches a hole in the theory of the rise of capitalism as a result of the abstinence of a capitalist class who virtuously scraped and saved to get capital to invest. Historically, if this happened (as may have been the case with the early Quaker capitalists in Britain), then it would indeed require a parallel class of non-virtuous consumers whose only role was to consume to the hilt without producing anything. The existence of such a class in Britain in the eighteenth century was not only patently obvious (read a Jane Austen novel), but was justified by Malthus in his own efforts to answer the question of where the aggregate demand might come from to absorb the ever-expanding surplus product (the other solution was expanding foreign trade, which Rosa Luxemburg, in *The Accumulation of Capital*, converted into imperial and colonial domination of foreign markets). The result also has implications for how we might interpret the reproduction schemas of Part 3 of Volume II, which we will shortly be considering—though, in the extensive and controversial Marxist literature that has accumulated around the interpretation of these, I rarely if ever see this very important result mentioned.

After the first turnover period, during which the capitalist pays for his own consumption, the capitalist can then utilize the surplus-value produced by the workers and realized through his own expenditures on consumption to circulate as revenues over all successive turnover periods (assuming simple reproduction). This corresponds to Marx's argument that the capitalist may indeed advance his own money capital for production and use his own money reserves for consumption. But, over time, those money reserves increasingly represent products of the laborer, who has produced not only the variable capital needed to reproduce himself but also the surplus-value that the capitalist appropriates as revenues for purposes of consumption. How this all works under conditions of expanded reproduction has yet to be determined.

Instead of developing these insights, however, Marx returns to the question of the gold producers and the complicating fact that the surplus-value produced in gold production is itself already in money commodity form, so the question of how it is to be turned into money cannot arise. In fact "the gold-producing group constantly pump more money in than they withdraw from it in means of production" (411). This has implications for trade relations between countries, some of which produce gold while others do not. But, even though they inject more money value into circulation than they withdraw from it for purposes of production, that excess cannot possibly match the vast amount of surplus-value needing to be realized in the market.

Marx then considers the more interesting question of how the circulation of variable capital intersects, as it must, with the circulation of surplus-value. Plainly, a significant part of aggregate effective demand in a capitalist mode of production is constituted by workers' consumption, and this depends on wage rates and employment: "A greater outlay of variable money capital means a correspondingly greater quantity of monetary means in the hands of the workers. . . . This gives rise to a greater demand on the part of the workers. A further consequence is a rise in the price of commodities" (414). There has been a long-standing tendency on the part of bourgeois analysts to attribute inflation to wage pressures and relatively full employment, but Marx appears here to be somewhat critical of this line of reasoning. It is certainly the case that, "as a result of rising wages the demand of the workers for necessary means of subsistence will grow. Their demand for luxury articles will increase to a smaller degree, or else a demand will arise for articles that previously did not enter the area of their consumption" (414). There will undoubtedly be "temporary oscillations" in prices and outputs, along with adaptations in the market to these new conditions, but Marx is very skeptical of any long-term trend toward inflation: "If it were within the capacity of the capitalist producers to increase the prices of their commodities at will, then they could and would do so even without any rise in wages. Nor would wages rise with a fall in commodity prices." Deflation is, in short, just as likely as inflation: "The capitalist class would never oppose trade unions, since they would always and in all circumstances be able to do what they now do exceptionally under certain particular and so to speak, local conditions—i.e. use any increase in wages to raise commodity prices to a far higher degree, and thus tuck away a greater profit" (414). These were, of course, precisely the "exceptional conditions" that prevailed in the post-1945 period in the US and much of Europe, when capital was forced by political circumstances to accept some greater degree of trade-union and working-class power, and responded with inflationary tactics that allowed corporations to "tuck away" immense profits in spite of rising wages and relatively full employment.

When it comes to expanded reproduction, Marx fails to pursue an obvious line of enquiry that derives from the simple fact that part of the surplus-value now has to be invested in productive consumption (new means of production and augmentation of labor-power) that diminishes the capacity for bourgeois consumption. If the capitalist has to abstain on personal consumption in order to launch capital into further productive consumption, then he cannot possibly mop up the extra surplus-value then produced without again delving even deeper into his own monetary reserves. The idea that those reserves are bottomless is patently absurd. The problem of where the expanded aggregate demand can come from needs to be addressed, but Marx fails to do so adequately.

The clearest answer I can find is that capitalists solve the difficulty by the simple and long-standing practice of buying now (thus realizing the surplus-value) and paying later (after the surplus-value has been monetized). In other words, they deficit-finance the expansion. This involves the money market and the credit system with which, as we have seen, Marx is reluctant to engage (even as he concedes its absolute necessity) throughout Volume II. Hints that this might be the solution can be found, as we have seen, in the Volume III exploration of the role of the money markets, finance capital and the credit system. Pursued to its ultimate point, this line of argument would suggest that that accumulation of capital through the production of surplus-value would have to be paralleled by an accumulation of debt in the realization of that surplus-value in the market.

Marx comes close to tentatively admitting as much. A part of the surplus-value is invested in expansion, which diminishes the amount available to circulate as revenue for realization. Extra surplus-value is produced. "The same question comes up again as before. Where does the extra money come from to realize the extra surplus-value that now exists in the commodity form?" (419). Marx, as before, goes through a variety of solutions proposed in classical political economy that attempt to solve the problem through an examination of monetary circulation, and ultimately through the activities of the gold producers. He seems skeptical of all such solutions apart from the resort to credit, which has at least some technical possibilities: "in as much as the auxiliary means that develop with credit have this effect [i.e. solve the problem of where the extra money might come from] they directly increase capitalist wealth. . . . This also disposes of the pointless question of whether capitalist production on its present scale would be possible without credit . . . i.e. with a merely metallic circulation. It would clearly not be possible. It would come up against the limited scale of precious-metal production. On the other hand, we should not get any mystical ideas about the productive power of the credit system, just because this makes money capital available or fluid." Unfortunately, and frustratingly, he then adds: "but the further development of this point does not belong here" (420–1).

I think we can infer from this that the accumulation of wealth is accompanied by an accumulation of debts within the credit system. But this does not mean that the accumulation of such debts leads to the accumulation of wealth. The latter always depends upon the productive powers of labor.

The final section of the chapter considers how money for new investments is first built up into a hoard of latent capital, until there is enough to build a new factory or whatever, assuming the credit system "is non-existent" (421). Under these circumstances, the capitalist who "stores money up" must have first "sold without buying." Among many individual capitalists this poses no particular problem. "But difficulties start to arise" in the case of "general accumulation within the capitalist class. Outside this class, on our assumption—that of universal and exclusive domination of capitalist production—there is no other class except the working class. The total purchases of the working class are equal to the sum of their wages, i.e. the sum of the variable capital advanced by the entire capitalist class as a whole. This money flows back to the latter through the sale of their product to the working class." But the working class can never "buy the part of the product which contains the constant capital let alone the surplus-value which belongs to the capitalists." There has to be, as already argued, "a monetary fund" that functions as a "circulation fund," as distinct from the "latent money capital" required for expanded reproduction (422–3). When Marx considers where the latent money capital might be found, he identifies bank deposits, government paper and shares. But where is the circulation fund to be used to realize the surplus-value? And what happens when money has to be used and even hoarded for this purpose? Marx unfortunately gives no answer.

CHAPTER TEN

The Reproduction of Capital (Chapters 18–20 of Volume II)

In Part 3 of Volume II, Marx imagines an economy divided into two grand departments. Department 1 produces means of production for other capitalists (everything from raw materials and partially finished products to machinery and other fixed-capital items including the built environment for production). Department 2 produces goods to be consumed individually by workers and capitalists (also including the built environment for consumption). The department producing consumer goods has to buy its means of production from department 1. The workers and capitalists operating in department 1 have to purchase their consumer goods from department 2. If such an economy is to work smoothly, then the exchanges between the two departments have to balance each other. Under conditions of simple reproduction (no expansion), the value of the means of production that flow to department 2 has to be equivalent to the value of the consumer goods that flow to workers and capitalists in department 1.

This is the basic model of the economy that is examined in these chapters. It is useful to describe the general character of the model at the outset. Once we have firmly grasped the general form of it, then it is much easier to deal with the detailed enquiry with which Marx surrounds it.

The so-called "reproduction schemas" are described on pages 471–4. While Marx uses an arithmetic example, it is easy to give it algebraic form. The total output of each department in a given year can be represented in value terms as constant capital (c) + variable capital (v) + surplus-value (s). Marx sets aside the question of fixed capital and different turnover times, and assumes that everything is produced and consumed on an annual basis. He then sets up a simple arithmetic example, calculated in units of value, in which the rate of surplus-value (s/v) and the value composition (the ratio of c/v) are equal in the two departments. So, on an annual basis, he postulates:

Department I 4,000c + 1,000v + 1,000s = 6,000 means of production
Department II 2,000c + 500v + 500s = 3,000 consumption goods

Algebraically, this can be represented as:

Department I $c_1 + v_1 + s_1 = w_1$ (the total value output of means of production)
Department II $c_2 + v_2 + s_2 = w_2$ (the total value output of consumption goods)

The total demand for means of production is $c_1 + c_2$. The total demand for consumption goods is $v_1 + v_2 + s_1 + s_2$. If we assume that demand and supply are in equilibrium (474), then:

$$w_2 = c_2 + v_2 + s_2 = v_1 + v_2 + s_1 + s_2$$

which, after eliminating similar terms on both sides, reduces to

$$c_2 = v_1 + s_1$$

The demand for means of production in department 2 must equal the demand for consumer goods emanating from department 1 if the necessary value proportionalities to assure continuous and balanced reproduction are to be achieved. In the arithmetic example, the 2,000c needed to produce consumer goods in department 2 is equivalent to the 1,000v + 1,000s personal consumption of the workers and capitalists operating in department 1. "The result of all this," as Marx puts it, "is that, in the case of simple reproduction, the value component v + s of the commodity capital in department 1 (and therefore a corresponding proportionate part of department 1's total commodity product) must be equal to the constant capital . . . precipitated out by department II as a proportionate part of its total commodity product" (478).

Plainly, there are all sorts of questions that then follow: How, for example, can the processes of capitalist production and realization be so arranged that the correct proportionalities are (at least roughly) achieved? What happens when fixed capital is unevenly deployed between departments and when a variety of turnover times are encountered? And, above all, in chapter 21 the all-important question is posed of how accumulation can proceed on an ever-expanding scale while keeping the proportionalities in line?

The schemas as Marx devised them incorporate all manner of assumptions—there are only two classes of workers and capitalists (as briefly laid out in chapter 17); only two sectors, producing means of production and means of consumption (though at one point he does divide means of consumption into necessities and luxuries); demand and supply are in equilibrium; everything turns over in one year; there is no technological change; and everything exchanges at its value—just to mention the main ones. While Marx initially recognizes that he ought to examine the processes of reproduction "both in value and in material" (use-value) terms (469), in practice he works out the proportionate relations between the two departments solely in values, thus assuming that the physical quantitative requirements for reproduction are automatically met. There are plenty of problems that derive from these assumptions. The complexities that arise from their relaxation are mind-boggling.

Part 3 of Volume II presents a working model of how a capitalist mode of production as a whole gets reproduced through the continuous circulation of capital. It is clearly meant as the culmination of the argument in Volume II. It therefore parallels how Part 7 of Volume I brings together the many insights earlier generated in that volume. Both volumes contain preparatory chapters on simple and then expanded reproduction. But there are some significant differences. In Volume I, the "General Law" synthesizes many of the findings earlier established, to produce a working model that explains the production of an expanding industrial reserve army of workers that is subject to unemployment and increasing impoverishment. While Volume II uses the distinctions between the different circuits of capital set out in the first four chapters to good effect, it abstracts from many of the other key findings—particularly regarding fixed-capital circulation and differential turnover times—to construct a tentative schema of the expanding reproduction of capital.

In these schemas, it should be noted, the consumption of workers takes a "relatively decisive share" (490). If the schemas point to anything in the way of a politics, therefore, it is to the necessity to stabilize worker incomes in order to harmonize the relationship between the total output of means of production and the total demand for consumer goods. This contradicts the findings of Volume I, where Marx envisages the increasing impoverishment of the working class as an inevitable outcome of free-market capitalism. Marx only hints at this contradiction, however, because the equivalent chapter to the "General Law" chapter is missing from Volume II. It is interesting to surmise how we might have read Volume I if the "General Law" chapter had not been written—and we therefore had only the chapters on simple and expanded reproduction.

Conversely, we need to imagine what the equivalent chapter in Volume II to the "General Law" chapter might have looked like. Would it, for example, have imagined a significant number of workers in a significant number of places being increasingly drawn into endless and increasingly mindless consumerism in order to stabilize the conditions for realization of values in the market? Would it have shown, furthermore, how uninterested such workers might become in socialist revolution given how wrapped up they were in seductive capitalist consumerism? What role would anti-consumerism (of the sort that indeed flourished in the 1960s in some parts of the world, and which is now central to much environmental politics) play in revolutionary movements? It is hard to imagine, of course, that Marx would ever have written such a chapter, and to most dedicated Marxists the very idea would almost certainly be denounced as scandalous.

But what is so interesting about Marx's reproduction schemas is that they in no way deny such possibilities (which is almost certainly why Rosa Luxemburg, for one, was so upset at their contents). And, to the degree that 70 percent of economic activity in the United States and other advanced capitalist countries is now driven by consumerism (as opposed to half that in contemporary China, which is probably closer to the conditions that prevailed in Marx's own time), and that many so-called "affluent" workers are indeed deeply enamored of the consumerism of the capitalist world they inhabit (with all its evident faults), so we have here at hand some tools to analyze a political-economic situation of this kind. Clearly, the contradiction with the thesis of increasing impoverishment of chapter 25 in Volume I poses serious problems. But good Marxists should surely never flee from the site of such a contradiction merely because it is serious as well as awkward.

But there are ways to finesse this central contradiction. Marx on a couple of occasions notes the existence of what we now refer to as a "middle class" (407). The primary role of that class under contemporary conditions is to provide the backbone of consumption, as well as general political support for a functioning capitalist democracy. This layer in the population was even invoked in Volume I, when Marx noted how the regulation of the working day came to fruition as "capital's power of resistance gradually weakened, while at the same time the working class's power of attack grew with the number of its allies in those social layers not directly interested in the question" (C1, 408–9). Something similar is also suggested in one of the several study plans that Marx devised in the *Grundrisse* (264), where he promises studies on "Taxes or the existence of the unproductive classes." And in his seminal account of the political forces that produced the Paris Commune of 1871, Marx gives considerable prominence to the role of the debt-encumbered "nascent middle classes" (the "petite bourgeoisie" described also in *The Eighteenth Brumaire of Louis Bonaparte*, which analyzed the counterrevolutionary movement after 1848) in the political struggles of these times.[6]

The importance of such social layers in supplying the necessary effective demand was first set out by Malthus (though the class of consumers he had in mind were more purely aristocratic and parasitic than would now be politically feasible—except in, say, the Gulf states). Since it has long been accepted that the growth of a middle class, employed largely in managerial, administrative and service roles on steady and adequate salaries, has been critical to the economic, social and political stabilization of capitalism, it could then be argued that the contradiction we are here encountering derives more from Marx's assumption of a two-class model than from any real situation. The contradiction in a three-class situation could then play out as wage repression of the sort envisaged in Volume I for the lower working classes (for example, in China), and a flow of revenues to a middle class (incorporating a layer of affluent workers as well as unproductive classes) of consumers (for example, in the US, where some workers have achieved home ownership and a suburban lifestyle) adequate to supply the necessary effective demand as envisaged in Volume II. Middle-class revenues, in Marx's scheme of things,

---

6   Karl Marx, *The Civil War in France* (New York: International Publishers, 1989).

would ultimately have to derive, of course, from value and surplus-value production, though under contemporary conditions this would undoubtedly be supplemented by debt-fueled state expenditures on the consumption fund and expanding credit availability to boost middle-class consumerism (particularly with respect to housing demand). Interestingly, it is now generally acknowledged that the standard of living of this middle class is seriously under threat in North America and much of Europe—partly because of excessive indebtedness—and this is directly associated with the loud laments of deficiencies in aggregate effective demand to sustain the economy. The potential growth of internal consumer demand through the formation of a middle class in China and other developing countries is then hopefully postulated as a compensating movement. The current pressure, both internal and external, for the Chinese policy-makers to take active steps to stimulate the internal market is very strong. Demands are also heard from influential policymakers that those countries with trade surpluses, such as Germany, relax their penchant for wage repression (Volume I) and boost their consumer-ism (Volume II) to aid overall economic growth (so far Germany has refused). Thinking about contemporary situations within the general framework of the reproduction schemas in mind is, I find, very help-ful, provided we deploy them flexibly and expansively.

But the other way to finesse the problem flows directly from the fact that productive consumption derives from reinvestment in expansion. There is no golden rule to fix the relation between capital-ist-class personal consumption and its incentives or needs to reinvest in expansion. In Volume I, this decision was depicted as a Faustian conflict in the breast of every capitalist between the desire for enjoy-ment and the need or urge to reinvest. But reinvestment depends not only on the power and intensity of the coercive laws of competition, but also on the expectations and prospects for high profits—which in turn depend on the capitalists' approach to future risk and uncer-tainty. Whatever the case, the expansion of aggregate demand is as sensitive to waves of expansion and reinvestment as it is to expan-sions in personal consumption of workers, capitalists, or some other layer of the population.

There are other significant differences to Volume I. Marx in Volume I seems much less interested in the technical details than in the reproduction of the class relation between capital and labor, and in "the historical mission" of a bourgeoisie that finds itself committed to endless accumulation ("accumulation for accumulation's sake"). He is more interested in the *why* than in the *how*. In Volume II, concern for the why largely disappears. Instead, he builds a technical model of *how* capital might accumulate in perpetuity. In reading these chapters, it is important to remember that the reproduction of the class relation, though rarely invoked, is still central.

Given the mathematical form of the reproduction schemas, it is not surprising to find that they have occasionally been elaborated upon using the high-powered mathematical tools available to contemporary economics. While, therefore, much of Volume II remains in the shadows of Marxist thinking and theorizing, the reproduction schemas are better known, and have been scrutinized and further developed by economists of both Marxist and non-Marxist persuasions. For this same reason, the schemas also seem to have played a subterranean role in the development of mainstream modern economic growth theory. So, while literary theorists, historians, theologians, philosophers and others of their ilk interested in Marx's writings rarely discuss the schemas and their interpretation, the economists have reveled in them. Some economists have even concluded that Marx was finally coming to his senses and abandoning his foolish dialectical and relational mode of enquiry in favor of embracing the methods of conventional economic science.

I disagree with this view. Certainly, the overt dialectical/relational content of Part 3 is muted, if not absent (the ghost of Hegel disappears). But we have seen all along that Marx is more than a little prepared to accept general (and non-dialectical) frameworks proposed in bourgeois political economy. He frequently embeds technical "modeling" exercises of a sort acceptable to conventional economics (such as that of the General Law of Capitalist Accumulation in Volume I) in a broader dialectical/relational and historical critique. That this broader critique is overtly lacking throughout much of Volume II proves nothing about any shift in method. As became clear when we connected the far more relational and historical analysis of merchants' and interest-bearing capital from Volume III with the technical expositions of Volume II, the overall nature of Marx's project in *Capital* entails a powerful dialectical, social and relational critique that emerges from the contradictions of bourgeois political-economic science. It is, I would argue, up to us either to uncover that critique or to inject it into the incomplete Part 3 of Volume II.

The obvious way to do this is to ask: Where are the hidden contradictions and antinomies in schemas that seem to describe the smooth and continuous expansion of capital accumulation? One obvious contradiction is the clash already identified between the tendency toward wage repression and increasing impoverishment laid out in Volume I and the "decisive" role of working-class consumption for the realization of values in Volume II. Another arises out of Marx's analysis of the impossibility of reconciling fixed-capital replacement, repair and maintenance with the equilibrium conditions described in the schemas except by way of crises. There are, as we shall see, other possibilities.

It is useful to insert here one example of the later development within mainstream economics of the basic ideas incorporated in Marx's schemas. I do so not only to indicate their subsequent importance, but also to give a clearer idea of what the schemas might be about, and to show their potentiality for practical application. Toward the end of the 1930s, Wassily Leontief, an economist of Russian origin who came first to Germany and then to the United States in the 1930s, elaborated on Marx's models to create what became known as "input-output analysis." Figure 6 illustrates a typical Leontief matrix, with data on inputs to different industries (the industries the inputs come to) inserted down the vertical columns and the data on outputs of those industries (where they go to) arranged horizontally. With such an input-output matrix, it is possible to estimate how much in the way of extra inputs (say of coal, energy and iron ore) will be required to raise the level of output in a given industry (such as steel), and to trace back iteratively the inputs into increasing the coal production (for example, the extra machinery and extra steel in that machinery) necessary to increase the steel production. Input-output analysis, for which Leontief received the Nobel Prize in economics in 1974, was widely deployed as a planning tool during the halcyon years of postwar boom conditions in the advanced capitalist economies, and to this day plays a crucial role in national accounting. This technique was also incorporated into the five- and ten-year plans typically devised by communist regimes, and was also used by many democratic and quasi-capitalist countries, such as India after independence. It became, in short, a key tool in centralized planning.

Figure 6

Output → Input ↓	Agriculture	Mining	Energy	Manufacturing	Construction	Services	Government	Total Output
Agriculture	300	10	100	20	40	10	200	680
Mining	30							
Energy	50							
Manufacturing	150							
Construction	40							
Services	70							
Government	40							
Total Input	680							

A Leontief Style Matrix of Inputs and Outputs

Reading down the columns records where all the inputs of each sector are coming from (n.b. Agricultural supplies things to agriculture such as seed or fodder for animals). Reading across tells us where all the outputs from each sector, e.g. agriculture, are going to. In this table inputs are set equal to outputs, so the economy is in a state of simple reproduction.

Leontief mainly constructed models of material (use-value) flows (Marx for the most part used value flows). Armed with adequate data on inputs and outputs in different industries, it is possible to allocate investment and labor to different aspects of the social division of labor, so as to ensure balanced growth. Otherwise there is always a danger that bottlenecks in, for example, steel or energy production could block growth everywhere else. The rational social allocation of investments and of labor became a vital aspect of public policy in many parts of the world, and under very diverse political circumstances. While centralized planning using such techniques has acquired a bad name, more sophisticated versions are now used within corporations to define optimal efficiency in complex production systems.

The main problem here, however, is to interpret what Marx himself intended the schemas to mean. He assumes the outputs and inputs of the two sectors producing consumption goods and means of production respectively are in equilibrium in value flows (he does not actually use the word "equilibrium," but refers to "necessary proportionalities"). Does this presume that harmonious and never-ending capital accumulation is actually possible within a capitalist mode of production? Engels, in his preface, worried that the materials provided no support for political agitation, while Rosa Luxemburg thought that accepting the validity of these schemas made political struggles pointless. Or does Marx mean to show that harmonious accumulation is impossible under capitalism because market allocations could not possibly converge on the correct proportionalities? Would it then follow that a rational proportionate allocation of labor to different aspects of the division of labor would be possible only under communism? "Later," Marx writes hopefully, "we shall go on to investigate how different things would look if it were assumed that production was collective and did not have the form of commodity production" (527). Unfortunately, he never made good on the promise.

Even if, as Marx certainly does argue, individual capitalists working in their own self-interest in response to market signals were unlikely to hit the right proportionalities "except by accident," it could be that mini-crises of "disproportionality" might work to keep the system as a whole oscillating around a sustainable equilibrium growth path. After all, he had already argued in Volume I that the "constant tendency on the part of the various spheres of production towards equilibrium comes into play only as a reaction against the constant upsetting of this equilibrium" (C1, 478). The ultimate breakdown of the Volume I model of accumulation was not attributable to any technical unsustainability. It resulted from the increasing impoverishment of the growing masses, who would rise up and expropriate the ever-diminishing group of increasingly wealthy expropriators. Marx does not assert any parallel revolutionary imperative at the end of Volume II. To the degree that Volume II shows how the working class actively contribute to realization through their consumption, the Volume I politics is, as we have already seen, attenuated if not contradicted.

The ideas presented in Part 3 of Volume II were first conceived of in the early 1860s but only elaborated in the 1870s, culminating in 1878 when Marx devoted his very last theoretical work to elaborating on them further. These chapters were therefore written after most of Volume III had been drafted, and after Volume I had been published. They were also written at a time when wages in Britain had been steadily rising for nearly a quarter of a century, as workers shared some of the benefits to be had from rising productivity (a shift, as it were, from absolute to relative surplus-value production). The ideas are explored in a technical and largely non-dialectical way. They leave broader historical and social questions, as well as issues of crisis formation, largely unaddressed (even as many possibilities for crises are revealed). Subsequent studies have elaborated upon the technical qualities of the schemas in many different directions, and improved enormously upon the mathematical sophistication of the presentation. These elaborations have not resolved but, if anything, have instead deepened the mystery that Marx left behind. It has been said in a recent study by Andrew Trigg, for example, that, "in the absence of any clear statement of the purpose of the reproduction tables, there is no agreement as to what they are for, how they relate to the rest of *Capital Volume II*, and how they relate to *Capital* as a whole."[7] Interpreting Marx in Marx's own terms is, in short, close to impossible in this case.

Presenting these chapters to an audience largely unfamiliar with both Marxist and contemporary economic theory poses all manner of difficulties, far beyond the usual textual problems of incomplete and digressive argument and complex languages of critique and counter-critique, to say nothing of Marx's penchant for dabbling endlessly in accounting trivia and using tortuous arithmetic examples. The subsequent mathematical explorations of the schemas take us onto grounds upon which ordinary mortals rarely tread, while Marx's exposition is almost as rarefied. This problem is serious because the way in which we interpret these schemas affects the interpretation of foundational concepts like value and price, while, when treated on a par with Volume I, it creates an entirely different picture of the dynamics of capital's reproduction. The best I can do under these circumstances is to keep fairly close to the text and to the subject matter, while skimming over that which appears most redundant or trivial. I attach a short reading list for those who wish to go into matters further.[8] But, at some point, I

---

7 Andrew Trigg, *Marxian Reproduction Schema: Money and Aggregate Demand in a Capitalist Economy* (New York: Routledge, 2006), 2.

8 There is an extensive literature on the reproduction schemas. Some of it requires higher-order mathematics, and the overall emphasis is upon exploring the technical aspects of the reproduction process while relaxing some of Marx's more restrictive assumptions. The classic texts include Henryk Grossmann, *The Law of Accumulation and the Breakdown of the Capitalist System: Being Also a Theory of Crises* (London: Pluto, 1992); and Paul M. Sweezy, *The Theory of Capitalist Development: Principles of Marxian Political Economy* (New York: Monthly Review Press, 1942). For Luxemburg's objections, see Rosa Luxemburg, *The Accumulation of Capital* (London: Routledge, 1951). Survey works include Meghnad Desai,

and you, the reader, have to take a crack at the thorny problem of what the schemas might be about.

ON CHAPTER 18 OF VOLUME II: INTRODUCTION

Marx's main stated purpose in this introductory chapter (from which he very quickly deviates) is to consider how the economy as a social totality is constituted out of myriad individual activities, and how that totality is structured. He opens by reminding us of the importance of continuity in the flow of capital—of how the money circuit appears to mediate the productive circuit of capital (and vice versa) in a process of "constant repetition." The result is the "perpetual re-emergence" of the capital "as productive capital" conditioned by "its transformations in the circulation process." It is very important to keep in mind the idea of the constant metamorphoses in form (from money into production into a commodity back to money). This conception of capital as process and as flow is, after all, what makes Marx's concept of the economy and of capital so very special.

"But each individual capital," says Marx, "forms only a fraction of the total social capital, a fraction that has acquired independence and been endowed with individual life, so to speak, just as each individual capitalist is not more than an element of the capitalist class. The movement of the social capital is made up of the totality of movement of these autonomous fractions" (427).

The independence and autonomy of individual capital is vital to keep in mind as a foundational feature of a capitalist mode of production. Individuality and autonomy do not derive, we perpetually have to remind ourselves, from rights given by nature, but are a historical product of the rise of a market society, of bourgeois law, of monetization and commodification, all of which were necessary preconditions for the emergence of a capitalist mode of production. I find it odd that Marx is

---

Marxian Economics (Oxford: Blackwell, 1979); Michael C. Howard and John E. King, *The Political Economy of Marx* (London: Longman, 1975); and Shinzaburō Koshimura, *Theory of Capital Reproduction and Accumulation* (Kitchener, Ontario: DPG Publishers, 1975). For those interested in a mathematically rigorous development of the argument from a Keynesian perspective, see Trigg, *Marxian Reproduction Schema*, cited earlier. For a sophisticated neoclassical exploration of the schemas, see Michio Morishima, *Marx's Economics: A Dual Theory of Value and Growth* (London: Cambridge University Press, 1973).

so often depicted as denying individuality and the possibility of autonomy when he is in fact perpetually citing its importance, while giving an account of how it came to be.

Productive consumption, furthermore, entails the "conversion of variable capital into labour-power." The worker enters the scene as bearer of the commodity labor-power (yet another precondition for the emergence of a capitalist mode of production). But the workers also purchase commodities for their individual consumption. "Here the working class appears as a buyer of commodities, and the capitalists as sellers of commodities to the workers" (428). The individuals within the two great classes relate to each other as buyers and sellers, which is a very different relation to that of producers and expropriators of surplus-value. The consumption of the working class (its consumerism) becomes an important moment in the realization of values in the market. And the worker, like everyone else, has autonomy and choice as a buyer.

> The circuits of the individual capitals, therefore, when considered as combined into the social capital, i.e. considered in their totality, do not encompass just the circulation of capital, but also commodity circulations in general. In its fundamentals, the latter can consist of only two components: (1) the specific circuit of capital, and (2) the circuit of those commodities that go into individual consumption, i.e. the commodities on which the workers spend their wages and the capitalists their surplus-value (or part of it). (428)

Marx then explicitly reviews the relation between the presentation given here and that laid out in Volume I. The assumption that everything was exchanged at its value permitted him in Volume I to abstract from questions of circulation apart from the buying and selling of labor-power. Parts 1 and 2 of Volume II, however, focus on circulation rather than production processes, and introduce us to the complexities of circulation time. But the analysis mainly stayed at the level of "an individual capital, the movement of an autonomous part of the social capital" (429). "What we now have to consider, is the circulation process of the individual capitals as components of the total social capital, i.e. the circulation process of this total social capital. *Taken in its entirety, this circulation process is a form of the reproduction process*" (430; emphasis added). It should always be recalled that this is about the reproduction of class relations as well as the reproduction of commodities and capital through circulation.

So we now have arrived at the point of considering how the total social capital reproduces. But what immediately follows is a diversion (or perhaps we should better call it an "insertion") on the role of money capital in all of this. While Marx says he believes this should come later in the analysis, he decides to consider it here. The shift has some significance. With commodity flows, the question of the uses of the commodities is in the forefront. With money flows, it is possible to abstract from uses and concentrate on quantities and quantitative relations. I will come back to this difference later. If there is a serious problem with expanded reproduction, it seems it is somehow connected with the interventions of money capital. He certainly argues on more than one occasion that the social and rational use of the schemas to plan production would first require the abolition of the powers of money capital.

From the standpoint of the individual capital, money capital "appears as prime mover, giving the first impulse to the whole process." Note, once more, the significance of the word "appears." Capitalist commodity production, "whether we consider it socially or individually," presupposes money capital "both as the prime mover for each business when it first begins, and as a permanent driving force. Circulating capital, especially, presupposes the constantly repeated appearance, at short intervals, of the motor of money capital" (431). This is, on the surface, a rather different conception of money to that laid out at the beginning of Volume II, where money was not defined as capital because money can only perform the money functions of buying and selling. That it here appears as capital presumably rests on its fetish character (which is central to the analysis of money capital in Volume III). Furthermore, as was shown in Volume I, the amount of this money capital has no absolute or inherent limits.

The implications are legion. Money is a form of social power appropriable by private persons. From the standpoint of the individual there is no limit to the amount of that money power that a capitalist can accumulate. But there does seem to be a limit in society as a whole, particularly if we live in a world where gold is the "pivot" of the whole monetary system. There are various ways we can get around the limit posed by gold—increasing velocity, issuing paper moneys, using money as a means of payment, and creating a credit system. You should never approach an aggregate economy with the idea that there is some limit to the amount of money available. Since money has now lost its metallic base, it can be created without limit by the central banks. It is remarkable that the Federal Reserve can announce that it will inject another trillion dollars into the economy whenever it fancies. While there may in practice be political constraints (leading to financial repression), these can always be circumvented.

But Marx again switches tracks: "The elements of production that are incorporated into capital are independent in extent, within certain limits, of the magnitude of the money capital advanced." Marx is here referring back to that section of chapter 24 in Volume I entitled "The circumstances which independently of the division of surplus-value into capital and revenue, determine the extent of accumulation . . ." These means include working laborers harder; increasing the efficiency of production by all manner of ways, including through the application of scientific advances "which cost capital nothing"; extracting "free gifts" from nature as well as from past investments in the built environment which have long ago been amortized ("landed property has long since been redeemed by society, and redeemed time and again at that"); science and technology; the reorganization of cooperation; the reduction of turnover times (C1, 747–57).

All of these are in effect free goods out of which the capitalist can extract extra value without paying anything or advancing any extra money capital. "All this clearly has nothing to do with the specific question of money capital as such. It simply indicates that the capital advanced . . . contains, once it has been transformed into productive capital, productive powers whose limits are not given by the bounds of its own value, but, within a given field of action, can operate differently, both in extent and intensity" (433). Why Marx felt compelled to remind us of all this here is not at all clear. While money capital appears as the prime mover and as the self-sustaining motor of value and surplus-value production (and hence for the reproduction of capital), it is obviously not the only thing that matters. So on the one hand he seems to want to diminish its significance, but on the other, he also has to recognize that "extended operations of long duration require greater advances of money capital for a longer time. Production in these branches is therefore dependent on the extent of the money capital which the individual capitalist has at his disposal. This limit"—surprise, surprise!—"is overcome by the credit system and the forms of association related to it, e.g. joint stock companies. Disturbances in the money market therefore bring such businesses to a halt, while those same businesses, for their part, induce disturbances in the money market" (433–4).

This issue of long-term investments comes back again and again in Volume II as a serious question. If a case is being made here for a total breakdown in the dynamics of capital accumulation, then the main focus would be the problem of fixed capital investments of long duration. The trouble is that such investments are largely assumed away in the reproduction schemas, though not without our first being reminded of their potential disruptive effects for both capital and any alternative. "On the basis of social production"—I assume he means socialist or communist production, though he could also be referring to associated capitals—

> it would be necessary to determine to what extent it was possible to pursue these operations, which withdraw labour-power and means of production for a relatively long period without providing any product or useful effect during this time, without damaging those branches of production that not only withdraw labour-power and means of production continuously or several times in the course of a year, but also supply means of subsistence and means of production. With social production just as with capitalist production, workers in branches of industry with short working periods will withdraw products only for a short time without giving other products back in return, while branches of industry with long working periods will continue to withdraw products for a long time before they give anything back. This circumstance arises from the material conditions of the labour process in question, and not from its social form. With collective production, money capital is completely dispensed with. The society distributes labour-power and means of production between the various branches of industry. There is no reason why the producers should not receive paper tokens permitting them to withdraw an amount corresponding to their labour time from the social consumption stocks, but these tokens are not money; they do not circulate. (434)

Passages of this sort introduce us to an idea that recurs throughout these chapters: the potential role of these schemas in the construction of an alternative socialist or communist economy. I will not comment further on this point here except to say that this issue of how to deal with large-scale long-term projects is as foundational for the construction of any substantive anti-capitalist alternative mode of production as it is problematic within the laws of motion of capital. There is also an important hint of a potential contradiction between the material form balances and the flows of value balances—a topic to which I will also return. And how the power of money capital will be dispensed with is an open question. But, throughout these chapters, Marx frequently suggests that commodity circulation "can proceed quite well on the basis of non-capitalist production" (430). It did so before the rise of a capitalist mode of production, and presumably can continue to do so after its demise.

ON CHAPTER 19 OF VOLUME II: FORMER PRESENTATIONS ON THE SUBJECT

It is generally acknowledged that Marx based his schemas upon the *tableau économique* devised by the French surgeon and economist François Quesnay (first published in 1757–59). So who was Quesnay, and why was his formulation so special and so important? Quesnay (1694–1774) was a surgeon at the court of Louis XV. As a privileged medical practitioner and confidante of the king, Quesnay not only followed advances in medical knowledge but also thought a lot about the nature of the body politic. He was much impressed with William Harvey's discovery of the circulation of the blood that revolutionized medical knowledge, and saw parallels with the circulation of capital in the body politic.

I have always liked the parallel between the circulation of capital and the circulation of blood (perhaps because I happened to be born some forty miles away from William Harvey's birthplace!). I invoked the idea as foundational in the introduction to *The Enigma of Capital*, but I had forgotten, until rudely reminded when rereading Volume II for this book, that the parallel was first invoked by Quesnay.

William Harvey's theory of circulation of the blood displaced that of Galen, which had dominated for several centuries. In Galen's theory, the heart was the center for the production of blood, which flowed out to the various organs where it was consumed away. This is a one-way-street model of production flowing to consumption. William Harvey, by contrast, saw the heart as a pump that kept the blood in continuous circulation throughout the body while being replenished and cleansed by a metabolic transformation of matter from outside sources. Quesnay applied Harvey's conception to the field of political economy, and Marx, with his intense concern for fluidity, continuity and flows of value, was obviously drawn to Quesnay's way of thinking. The problem was that Quesnay insisted that value was produced in agriculture alone, and that industrial production was parasitic on agriculture. Quesnay dared not criticize the conspicuous consumption at Versailles or the consumerism of the aristocracy, so he pretended that both the peasantry and the landed aristocracy were engaging in value production, thus masking the extraction of surpluses from the peasantry. This "physiocratic" (predominantly French) vision contrasted with a "mercantilism" (predominantly British at that time) that saw the amassing of gold reserves through trade as the holy grail of economic policy.

Marx was antagonistic to both schools of thought. But, given the industrial structures that then prevailed in France, Quesnay's physiocratic notions had some plausibility, since it was the surplus extracted from agriculture that supported an artisanal industrial structure (very different from the factories that Marx saw) largely given over to producing luxury items (jewelry, fine raiments, pottery, carpets, and so on) for aristocratic consumption (take a visit to Versailles, where Quesnay lived, to see what was typically produced by the so-called industry of the times).

While Marx obviously rejected Quesnay's physiocratic theories, the flow model of the economy was of interest. It seemed to offer a scientific way to break out of the "weak syllogistic" model of classical political economy in which, Galen-like, the centrality of production dominated over the particularities of distribution, until being totally consumed through the singular activities of consumption. As Piero Sraffa, a close colleague of Keynes and editor of all of Ricardo's work, put it in a text of great significance to the argument being developed here: "It is of course in Quesnay's Tableau Économique that is found the original picture of the system of production and consumption as a circular process, and it stands in striking contrast to the view presented by modern theory, of a one-way avenue that leads from 'Factors of Production' to 'Consumption Goods.'"[9] The latter, I think it

---

9 Piero Sraffa, *The Production of Commodities by Means of Commodities* (Cambridge: Cambridge University Press, 1960). What Sraffa showed was that the whole of the neoclassical framework of economics was founded on a tautology. But his techniques were actually put to use by some Marxist economists—most notably

is important to note, is pure Galen, and still dominates conventional economic thinking.

I know I am departing from Marx's text at this point. But I do so because I think the argument here is of vital import. If it is still the case, as Sraffa suggests, that contemporary economic theory is stuck in the Galen-model mode, and if Marx moved to embrace the Quesnay/ William Harvey model, then there is still a radical disjunction in the field of political economy between bourgeois economic theory and Marx. I used this radical disjunction in *The Enigma of Capital* to explain not only why bourgeois political economy failed to notice the threat of systemic risk and possible failure, but how Marx's theory of disruptions in the continuity of capital flow and the potential emergence of serious blockages (everything from labor supplies to natural resources or the absence of effective demand) revealed whence crises might come. Failure to circumvent or transcend the barriers, or to relieve the blockages, would lead to the collapse of capital movement and the death of the capitalist body politic as surely as arterial blockages end the lives of persons. While the metaphor is undoubtedly over-dramatized, it has some interesting corollaries. Under the Galen theory, remedies were typically of the bloodletting sort (read: austerity), or later accompanied by transfusions (read: quantitative easing and release of liquidity by the world's central banks), neither of which make any sense from the standpoint of Marx's theory. The policies of stabilization in the face of crises that emerge from Marx's theory would require an analysis of the main barriers and blockage points to the continuity of capital flow; and a simultaneous attack upon all of them to try to bring the system back closer to that equilibrium which the reproduction schemas do show might be possible—and I emphasize "might," since it is by no means a certainty.

But Marx's basic proposition remains: interrupt the flow of capital for very long, and capital dies. We need a flow model to understand these dynamics, and it was Marx, building on Quesnay, who first showed

---

in Ian Steedman, *Marx After Sraffa* (London: Verso, 1977)—to destroy the prevailing (non-dialectical) notion of value theory in Marx, while the neoclassical theorists just decided, after some controversy, to ignore his mathematical proofs and findings entirely! The only way the neoclassicals could get out of the tautology would be to reformulate their arguments dialectically, but they would not have the foggiest idea how to do this.

how this might be constructed. So it is hardly surprising that those bourgeois thinkers who have moved in this direction (for example, some of the macroeconomic theorists) would to some degree take inspiration, if they dared to confess it, from Marx's key innovations, even as they in turn pose difficult questions regarding the status of these reproduction schemas in Marx's general theory of the laws of motion of capital.

There is one other important point about Quesnay's formulation. Precisely because he was interested in the continuity of flow, Quesnay became a strong advocate for freedom of circulation and movement. This was much hindered in France at that time, not only by physical barriers to transportation, but also because of the innumerable tolls and tariffs on the roads and bridges imposed by local powers. Quesnay advocated for the reduction and abolition of all such social and political barriers to movement. He was the first to use the term "laisser-faire"—a term rendered all too familiar by Adam Smith and subsequently the whole Ricardian school of free traders.

Marx actually pays scant attention to Quesnay in chapter 19. The chapter is dominated by a critique of what Marx elsewhere calls Adam Smith's "incredible blunder" in interpreting Quesnay. Smith rightly corrected Quesnay's erroneous view that value could only be created in agricultural production. But, in so doing, he erroneously proposed a theory of value that amounted to adding up the revenues attached to each of the so-called basic factors of production—land, labor and capital—that Quesnay had identified. This is, of course, a radically different theory of value than that given in both traditional and Marxist versions of the labor theory of value. This was, says Marx, an "absurd idea" that dominated political economy right down to Ricardo (461–7). Smith's additive theory of value was later modified by the neoclassical move to establish prices by combining the marginal costs (rather than the absolute values) of these basic factors of production, land, labor and capital (this is the Galen model in action). The relative scarcities of the different factors of production moved into the center of bourgeois economic thinking. Smith's "absurd formula" is thus perpetuated until this day.

Marx will have none of this. He was obsessed throughout his works with countering Adam Smith's "incredible blunder," and one of his aims in developing the reproduction schemas certainly was to discredit

Smith's interpretation and its subsequent influences.[10] If value was equated with revenues on land, labor and capital, there was no place in the theory for the replacement of the constant capital used up. Under those conditions, the reproduction of capital would be impossible:

> The narrowness of this conception lies in Smith's failure to see what Quesnay had already seen namely the reappearance of the value of constant capital in a renewed form. Instead, he saw here only a further illustration, and moreover a false one, of his distinction between fixed and circulating capital; hence he missed an important aspect of the reproduction process. (438)

There is a connection here, therefore, with Marx's critique of Smith's categories of fixed and circulating capital, outlined above (in chapter 4 of this book). Marx concludes that "Smith's confusion persists to this day, and his dogma forms an article of orthodox belief in political economy" (467).

ON CHAPTER 20 OF VOLUME II: SIMPLE REPRODUCTION

Chapter 20 parallels chapter 23 of Volume I, which has the same title. Recall that, in Volume I, Marx subordinated the technical issues of how capital gets reproduced to the reproduction of the class relation between capital and labor. While the Volume II analysis foregrounds the technical aspects to the problem of how capital gets reproduced, it is helpful to read these materials against the background of the need to reproduce the capital-labor relation as emphasized in Volume I.

Marx's aim is to look at the circulation of the total social capital. He wants to know "what characteristics distinguish the reproduction process" of the total social capital "from the reproduction process of an individual capital and what characteristics are common to both." He starts from the Volume I position:

> The annual product includes both the parts of the social product that replace capital, social reproduction, and the parts that accrue to the

---

10   This is the main argument in Fred Moseley, "Marx's Reproduction Schemes and Smith's Dogma," in Christopher John Arthur and Geert A. Reuten, eds., *The Circulation of Capital: Essays on Volume Two of Marx's* Capital (New York: Routledge, 1998).

consumption fund and are consumed by workers and capitalists: i.e. both productive and unproductive consumption. This consumption thus includes the reproduction (i.e. maintenance) of the capitalist class and the working class, and hence too the reproduction of the capitalist character of the entire production process. (468)

The focus, as noted earlier, is on capital in its commodity form: "the process of reproduction has to be considered from the standpoint of the replacement of the individual component of C' both in value and in material" (469). This is so because we need to focus on what commodities are used for what purpose (individual consumption of workers and capitalists versus productive consumption), and because we can no longer assume, as happens in the case of the circulation of individual capitals, that there is an untroubled passage from the conversion of C' into money form and then back into the purchase of means of production and labor-power. We need to know how it is that both the means of production and the labor-power are going to be available on the market in the right quantities and at the right times. Furthermore,

> the movement of the part of the social commodity product that is consumed by the worker in spending his wage, and by the capitalist in spending surplus-value, not only forms an integral link in the movement of the total product, but is also interwoven with the movements of the individual capitals, so that its course too, cannot be explained by being simply presupposed. (469)

The general assumptions that prevailed in the Volume I analysis can no longer hold. In particular, working-class and capitalist consumption, as pure consumption, here enter into the picture in ways that were excluded from the purview of Volume I, but have been articulated as important at various points earlier in Volume II: "The immediate form in which the problem presents itself is this. How is the *capital* consumed in production replaced in its value out of the annual product, and how is the movement of this replacement intertwined with the consumption of surplus-value by the capitalists and of wages by the workers?" (469).

But, in order to probe this question, some assumptions are required. We begin with the general presumptions of much of the Volume II analysis: "we assume not only that products are exchanged at their values, but also that no revolution in values takes place in the components of productive capital" (i.e. there is no technological change). The fact that prices may diverge systematically from values (a proposition that derives from the Volume III analysis) and that there are continuous value revolutions because of technological and organizational changes (a Volume I argument) "in no way affects" (470), he boldly claims, the general outlines of his argument. There are also some tacit assumptions that run throughout most of Volume II which have a prominent role to play in the reproduction schemas. We deal exclusively, for example, with a two-class model of capitalism in which capitalists and workers provide all of the aggregate demand and supply within a closed system (only occasionally are other classes or global trade with noncapitalist formations mentioned). In what follows, we will also specifically assume that both capitalists and workers spend all of their available revenues on consumption, that everything turns over on an annual basis (the fixed capital problem is briefly taken up but does not really enter into the argument), and that there are no unproductive activities (such as those that Marx calls the *faux frais* of capitalist circulation). Marx plainly hoped to use this "stripped down" model of capitalist production and circulation to explore theoretically the conditions that might make for balanced growth.

> The transformation of one portion of the product's value back into capital, the entry of another part into the individual consumption of the capitalist and working classes, forms a movement within the value of the product in which the total capital has resulted; and this movement is not only a replacement of values, but a replacement of materials, and is therefore conditioned not just by the mutual relations of the value components of the social product but equally by their use-value, their material shape. (470)

But there is a difficulty here. What have to be replaced in this process of reproduction are not only values, but use-values. For example, the specific use-values that enter into the value of labor-power have to be produced in the right quantities if the working class is to be reproduced. The specific use-values needed for productive consumption also need to be reproduced. It has to be assumed that these physical requirements match the necessary reproduction of value relations. But this is not automatically the case. In a typical Leontief model of an input-output system, the amounts of iron ore and coal needed to produce the steel that is used to make the engines that go into cars can all be modeled as a physical process within a matrix of inputs and outputs. The modeling is materially and use-value based. The financial flows that accompany these use-value relations are an entirely different matter. While one may work smoothly, the other may not. Which basis do we choose? Marx seems to want it both ways. In what follows, however, use-values and the material modeling of the process of social reproduction either gradually drop out of the picture or are presumed to so shape the prices and the money and the value flows as to be unproblematic. What we get, after an initial broad distinction between departments of production defined in use-value terms, is a pure value/monetary analysis of the movement of the total social capital reflective of use-value distinctions and requirements. Potential contradictions between the value and monetary analysis and the material use-value flows are not examined.

Given Marx's habit, from the very outset of *Capital*, of emphasizing the contradictions between use- and exchange-values, the burying of this tension would suggest that here is one point from whence crises will arise, and that this is where we should look for breakdowns within the reproduction schemas. This disjunction has in fact given rise to a conflict between those who interpret the schemas in material, use-value terms (generally referred to as neo-Ricardians, including Piero Sraffa) and those who view them in monetary terms (closer to Keynesians). The fact that Marx thought the rational use of the schemas for social coordination would require the prior abolition of the role of money capital suggests that this is where the primary contradiction within the schemas might lie—while the fact that the material requirements of fixed capital formation also throw a monkey wrench into the smoothness and continuity of things from the standpoint of monetary flows also suggests a form of contradiction arising from the material side in relation to monetary movements. In a certain sense, I suspect that Marx might have seen the subsequent schism between the neo-Ricardian and the Keynesian reading of the schemas as a classic case of the internal contradictions of capital becoming externalized in the realms of thought. None of this is, of course, even hinted at in the text.

This would, however, be my bet for the site of fundamental contradiction within the schemas. But given that much of the work of exploring these schemas has been done by those trained in mathematical economics, and that such experts exhibit at best a weak appreciation of, if not downright aversion to, dialectics and contradiction, it is hardly surprising that this potential point for crisis formation has remained largely unexplored. The rest of us, partly intimidated by the mathematical prowess of our economist colleagues, have largely failed to press the issue. But back to the text . . .

Sections 2 and 3: Exchanges Within and Between Departments

In the following pages Marx works out the necessary proportionalities in the production of means of production and of means of consumption, as outlined above. But there are some wrinkles that need to be ironed out:

> This mutual exchange [between the departments] is brought about by a money circulation, which both mediates it and makes it harder to comprehend, even though it is of decisive importance, since the component of variable capital must always reappear in the money form, as money capital which is converted from the money form into labour-power. Variable capital must be advanced in the money form in all the branches of production simultaneously pursued alongside one another across the entire surface of the society, irrespective of whether these belong to departments I or II. (474)

Thus, the workers in department 1 use their wages to purchase means of consumption from department 2, and in so doing transform half of department 2's constant capital into a money form that can flow back to department 1, where it can again function as money capital to purchase labor-power. If the capitalists delay payment to their laborers, then they delay the monetary flow that will convert into money the constant capital they have already produced and marketed to department 2. For this reason, "certain reserves of money—whether for capital advance or for expenditure of revenue—must always be taken as present in the hands of the capitalists alongside their productive capital" (476). As in the case of differential turnover times and circulation times, more money has to be in circulation than the amount that matches actual production. Capital has to be advanced by some capitalists and anticipated by others in the exchanges between the two departments. So, while "ultimately, the two departments pay one another fully by the exchange of their respective commodity equivalents," and while "the money that they cast into circulation over and above the total value of their commodities, as a means for exchanging these commodities, returns to each of them from the circulation sphere to the exact amount that each of the two cast into it.... neither has become a farthing richer from all this." Furthermore, embedded in "all this" is the necessity that workers do their part in consuming their wages in ways that match production in department 2, while the bourgeoisie must likewise do its duty by capital and completely consume the equivalent of its revenues in appropriate ways.

Section 4: Necessities and Luxuries

This last point leads Marx to open up the question of a distinction between the consumption of necessary means of subsistence, on the one hand, and of luxury goods on the other. The workers in department 2 in effect buy back part of the value of the goods they produce, and thereby furnish the capitalists with some of the money they need to continue production. The "company store" relation between capital and labor in the realm of consumption has been a frequent motif in *Capital* (including in Volume I, where Marx depicts the laborers as an "appendage" of capital not only in production, but also with respect to consumption). But there is an important shift, because the working class here "appears as buyer and the capitalist class as seller" (479).

Department 2 in effect divides into two. One part produces "those means of consumption that enter the consumption of the working class, and, in so far as they are necessary means of subsistence, also form part of the consumption of the capitalist class." Marx notes, however—almost certainly with his own consumption habits in mind—that it is "quite immaterial whether a product such as tobacco, for example, is from the physiological point of view a necessary means of consumption or not; it suffices that it is such a means of consumption by custom" (479). Luxury means of consumption, however, "enter into the consumption of the capitalist class only." Though produced by workers, these items are unavailable for workers to consume.

The luxury goods industries have some special characteristics. In Volume I, for example, Marx pointed out that revolutions in productivity in such industries have no role in changing the value of labor-power, and therefore are not a source of permanent relative surplus-value. Here, however, Marx enjoys himself going over—in the usual intricate detail, and with the familiar abundant arithmetic examples—the forms of circulation that link workers and capitalists operating in the luxury goods industries vis-à-vis those engaged in the production of necessities, given that the capitalists themselves split their allocation of revenues in some proportion between necessities and luxuries. Intricate circulation processes are set up in which capitalists pay for luxuries, and in so doing realize the value of luxury goods such that the capitalists producing them take part of their surplus-value to purchase more luxury goods, along with whatever necessities they need. Meanwhile, the workers in the luxury goods industries in department 2b spend their freshly monetized variable capital on the necessities produced in department 2a. Much depends, of course, on how the capitalist class splits its revenues between demand for necessities and luxuries.

Clearly, the "quota of labour-power . . . absorbed in luxury production . . . is conditioned by the prodigality of the capitalist class, the conversion of a significant part of their surplus-value into luxury items." But this is sensitive to economic conditions. Crises temporarily decrease luxury consumption, which then diminishes outlays on variable capital—and this in turn diminishes the general demand for non-luxury wage goods. "The reverse is the case in periods of prosperity, and particularly during the phase of hyper-activity" when a fully employed working class with higher wages may in fact purchase some marginal luxury goods.

This leads Marx to make the following very important general observation (which I cited earlier):

> It is a pure tautology to say that crises are provoked by a lack of effective demand or effective consumption. The capitalist system does not recognize any forms of consumer other than those who can pay, if we exclude the consumption of paupers and swindlers. The fact that commodities are unsaleable means no more than that no effective buyers have been found for them, i.e. no consumers (no matter whether the commodities are ultimately sold to meet the needs of productive or individual consumption). If the attempt is made to give this tautology the semblance of greater profundity, by the statement that the working class receives

too small a portion of its own product, and that the evil would be remedied if it received a bigger share, i.e. if its wages rose, we need only note
that crises are always prepared by a period in which wages generally rise,
and the working class actually does receive a great share of the annual
product destined for consumption. From the standpoint of these advocates of sound and "simple"(!) common sense, such periods should
rather avert the crisis. It thus appears that capitalist production involves
certain conditions independent of people's good or bad intentions,
which permit the relative prosperity of the working class only temporarily, and moreover always as a harbinger of crisis. (486–7)

At first blush, it seems difficult to reconcile this statement with the footnote on page 391, where the "realization of commodity capital and thus
of surplus-value as well, is restricted not by the consumer needs of society in general, but by the consumer needs of a society in which the great
majority are always poor and must always remain poor." In fact, the
"tautology" of which Marx speaks does not deny the importance of
effective demand, but merely insists that the only demand that counts is
that which is backed by ability to pay. This once more directs our attention to how money (exchange-values) circulates without regard for the
real need for use-values.

It is clear, from the context, that the purchasing power of the working
classes is dependent on such factors as the prodigality of the capitalist class
and the rise and fall of employment over the course of business cycles
whose movement is dictated by, among other things, waves of fixed capital
investment. System-wide changes in the productivity of labor will likewise
reduce the number of laborers engaged in value and surplus-value production. The "underconsumption" that appears as an immediate barrier to the
realization of surplus-value cannot therefore be construed as the unique
cause of crises. This is why lack of effective demand appears in this chapter
as a tautology. It is for this reason that I prefer to move away from the idea
of any one unique source of crises to that of multiple potential blockage
points, all of which can appear as the proximate cause of crises at any
historical moment. Capital does not resolve its crisis tendencies but, as I
argue in *The Enigma of Capital*, moves them around. The effective demand
problem, which I think Marx correctly depicts as one possible barrier to
further accumulation, can be removed, but that cannot stabilize capital
accumulation. It merely moves the contradictions elsewhere.

I do not think Marx is empirically correct, however, to argue that rising working-class incomes precede the onset of crises. While this was the case in, say, the crises of the 1970s, it would be hard to make that argument for the crisis that broke out in 2007–08. So I would propose to modify Marx's general statement that effective demand has nothing to do with the real inner contradictions of capital, and argue that the lack of effective demand can be a form of appearance of those inner contradictions under certain circumstances. But this is my own personal opinion, with which many will surely disagree.

Section 5: Monetary Circulation and the Schemas

In the section on "the mediation of the exchanges by monetary circulation," Marx explains why more money has to be advanced within the system than would strictly be necessary for the volume of value exchanges, because of the differences in timing of purchases throughout the year. An immediate problem arises, however, when capital is organized through the financial system into the "common capital of the class," as described in Volume III:

> Wherever there is a money capitalist behind the commodity producers, and it is he who first advances the money capital to the industrial capitalist . . . the actual point of return of this money is the pocket of the money capitalist. In this way, even if the money circulates through the hands of more or less all concerned, the mass of the circulating money belongs to the department of money capital organized and concentrated in the form of banks, etc. (488–9)

The main problem lies, however, with the way money circulates "through the hands of more or less all concerned." The sequences and the timing problems involved are intricately described, as wages paid in the sector producing means of production flow first to the sector producing means of consumption, only to flow back to the sector producing means of production as the capitalists producing consumption goods spend their money on procuring the means of production they need. As usual, Marx goes to considerable length to document the various sequences that are possible in order to indicate complicated timing issues in the flows. But the upshot is that the money capital transformed into variable capital, i.e. the money advanced as wages, plays a major role in actual monetary circulation. Since the working class has to live from hand to mouth, i.e. since it cannot give the industrial capitalists any long-term credit, variable capital has to be advanced at the same time in money at countless different points in society, and at definite and short intervals, such as a week, etc.

—no matter what the turnover time of the capitals involved. "In every country of capitalist production, the money capital advanced in this way *forms a relatively decisive share* in the total circulation" (490; emphasis added). But the timing problems (for example, the frequency with which wages are paid) are of consequence because enough spare money has to be in the system to deal with the gaps that arise. "On the other hand, the natural form into which the variable capital existing in the money form has to be converted—i.e. labour-power—has to be maintained, reproduced by consumption, and be present once again as the only article of trade of its proprietors, who have to sell this if they want to live. *In this way the relationship between wage labourers and capitalists is also reproduced*" (492; emphasis added). I emphasize this passage because it is one of the few points where the reproduction of the class relation, so vital in the Volume I presentation, is brought back into the argument. Marx may have viewed it as so obvious as to require no further elaboration or emphasis.

Marx then turns his attention to the role of capitalist personal consumption. "Once a capitalist spends his money on means of consumption, he is then done with it, it has gone the way of all flesh." If the money returns to him it is because the commodity capital he produces is thrown into circulation for realization in money form. "It is therefore literally correct, in the present case, that the capitalist himself cast into circulation the money into which he converts his surplus-value . . . by spending this on means of consumption. . . . In practice this occurs in two ways. If the business was started only within the current year, then it takes a good while, at best a few months, before the capitalist can spend money for his personal consumption out of his income from this actual business. He does not on this account suspend his consumption for a moment. He advances himself money against the surplus-value that he still has to hunt out." If, on the other hand, the business is long-established, then the capitalist merely anticipates receipts from sales yet to be made, though "if our capitalist goes bankrupt, then his creditors and the courts" may question his consumption habits (496–7). Notice, however, the role of anticipations and monetary advances relative to real production in all of this.

> In relation to the capitalist class as a whole, however, the proposition that it must itself cast into circulation the money needed to realize its surplus-value (and also to circulate its capital, constant and variable) is not only far from paradoxical, it is in fact a necessary condition of the overall mechanism. For here there are just two classes: the working class, which only disposes of its labour-power, and the capitalist class, which has the monopoly of the means of social production, and of money.

The individual capitalist does so, however, "by acting as buyer, *spending* money on the purchase of means of consumption or *advancing* money on the purchase of elements of his productive capital. . . . He advances money to circulation only in the same way that he advances commodities to it. In both cases, he acts as the starting point of their circulation" (497). We encountered much of this argument before, in chapter 17.

But this "real course of events" is obscured by the interventions of "a special kind of capitalist" (commercial and money capital) and the claims of government, of merchant capital, and of landlords extracting taxes, profits and rents, respectively. All of them advance money, but "what is always forgotten" are "the sources from which they originally obtained this money, and continue to obtain it" (497). The value this money represents must ultimately originate in production. But whether it originated in the past or is anticipated to originate in the future (for example, through debt creation) seems to me to be a very important distinction that is not fully articulated here.

Sections 6 and 7: The Circulation of Constant and Variable Capital and Surplus-Value Within Their Respective Departments

Marx first looks at the circulation of constant capital in department 1. Part of the output goes directly back into production in that same department, because corn is needed to produce corn, "coal into coal production, iron in the form of machines into iron production etc." And of course coal goes into steel production that goes into the production of the machinery needed to mine the coal. So the exchange of means of production for means of production is vigorous, and the question is posed as to how effectively these exchanges are coordinated through the market. To this, Marx adds a comment that gives fuel to those who look to the schemas to provide a means of social planning:

> If production were social instead of capitalist, it is evident that these products of department 1 would be no less constantly redistributed among the branches of production in this department as means of production according to the needs of reproduction; one part directly remaining in the sphere of production from which it emerged as a product, another part being shifted to other points of production, and so there would be a constant to and fro between the various points of production in this department. (501)

These are, of course, the input-output relations that Leontief later modeled in his matrices.

In section 7, the movement of variable capital and surplus-value within and between the departments is put under the microscope. We start with the obvious identity under conditions of simple reproduction that the total value of the means of consumption is equivalent to the total variable capital plus surplus-value. But, as the formulae outlined above show, the equivalence arises because the value of the new constant capital output from department 1 that flows to department 2 is realized through the application of labor in department 2. This poses the question, which will be looked at more concretely later, as to which department is in the driving seat of these exchanges. It also poses other problems. Constant capital cannot produce value in itself, and its value is simply passed on into the value of the product by the laborer engaging in productive consumption. But the production of fresh constant capital in department 1 produces both value and surplus-value. Adam Smith was therefore wrong to conclude that the total social product was equivalent to $v + s$ (though it was understandable that he might be misled to think so). The total social product is $c + v + s$, as Marx has maintained all along.

Section 8: *The Flows of Constant Capital Through Both Departments*

Marx applies the usual accounting method to look at the flows of constant capital through the two departments. He here encounters an interesting difficulty that is germane to my argument that there is a contradiction between use-value and value relations within the schemas. "The difficulty does not lie," says Marx, "in analyzing the value of the social product itself. It arises when the *value* components of the social product are compared with its *material* components" (506). From the standpoint of individual capital, this comparison is irrelevant—all that is required is that the product be a use-value, and that is that. But

> it is different with the product of the total social capital. All material elements of the reproduction must be parts of this product in their natural form. The portion of constant capital consumed can be replaced by the overall production only if the entire reappearing constant portion of the capital reappears in the product in the natural form of new means of production that actually can function as constant capital. On the assumption of simple reproduction, therefore, the value of the portion of the product that consists of means of production must be equal to the (consumed) constant portion of the value of the social capital. (508)

All of which is a rather tortuous way of saying that, if something is produced as constant capital but proves to be useless as a material product, it would have no value. It is very important to ensure that department 1 only produces products "in their natural form" (by which Marx means a physical, material use-value) that can serve to "realize the value of the variable capital and the surplus-value" in both departments (509).

Section 10: Capital and Revenues: Variable Capital and Wages

I leave section 9—a look back to Smith, Storch and Ramsey—to one side, before moving on to section 10. The first issue taken up here is the distinction between the value produced and the value transferred. From the standpoint of the individual capitalist, constant capital produces no value. Its value is simply transferred to the final product through the act of laboring. From the social standpoint, we see department 1 producing constant capital for department 2 "both in its entire value and in its natural form." Please note that, when Marx refers, as he frequently does in this text, to "natural form," he means material use-value form. In fact, "the greater part of the annual social labour is . . . spent on the production of new constant capital . . . to replace the constant capital value spent on the production of means of consumption" (514). The active production of means of production produces both value and surplus-value. This was what the economists in general, and Adam Smith in particular, could not understand. They took what is true for the individual capitalist—that constant capital produces no value—and wrongly projected it upon society as a whole, to infer that the production of means of production was not productive of value and surplus-value (that the total social product was v + s). A number of other confusions arise that are a bit difficult to follow.

First, it is important to understand that "the variable capital functions as capital in the hands of the capitalist and as revenue in the hands of the wage-worker." In other words, variable capital does not circulate through the body of the laborer (as I have sometimes been prone to think). The money capital is simply turned into money that circulates as revenue as the workers use their wages to buy commodities. The same money here appears as capital in the hands of the capitalist and there takes on the form of revenue in the hands of the worker.

Under this conception, Marx can resist the idea that the worker ever possesses capital. "In point of fact, labour-power is his capacity (ever renewing and reproducing itself), not his capital. It is the only commodity that he can constantly sell, and he has to sell it in order to live, but it operates as capital (variable capital) only in the hands of the buyer, the capitalist." Marx will have nothing to do with the economist's view of what we now call human capital theory. "If a man is perpetually forced to sell his labour-power over and over again, i.e. to sell himself, to someone else, this proves according to these economists, that he is a capitalist, because he always has a 'commodity' (himself) for sale" (516). By the same logic, Marx ironically notes, "even a slave would be a capitalist." We have encountered this rejection of human capital theory before. Capitalists always have a choice whether to engage in production or simply put their capital on the money market and live off the interest. Workers never have that choice. If they did they could loll in a hammock and live off the interest on their human capital! The worker is in the C-M-C circuit, only able to circulate wages as revenues. "His wage is realized in means of consumption, it is spent as revenue, and taking the working class as a whole, it goes on being spent as revenue continuously" (517).

In order for the flows between the departments to reach the equilibrium point of demand and supply, the market must operate with all agents, both capitalists and workers, taking on the active role of buyers and sellers: "All agents in this exchange simply appear as buyers or sellers, or both; the workers appear in it simply as commodity buyers; the capitalists alternatively as buyers and sellers; and, within certain limits simply as unilateral buyers and sellers" (518). Only in this way can it be ensured that "department 1 once more possesses the variable portion of capital, the only form from which it is directly convertible back into labour-power. . . . On the other hand, in order to reappear as a buyer of commodities, the worker must firstly reappear as the seller of a commodity, as the seller of his own labour-power" (518-19). It is important to remember, Marx is reminding us, that the exchange between the two departments is mediated through the operation of freely functioning labor markets.

Within this labor market there are, however, some asymmetries: "Since the working class lives from hand to mouth, it buys as long as it is able to. It is different with the capitalists. . . . The capitalist does not live from hand to mouth. His driving motive is the greatest possible valorization of his capital." It is sometimes advantageous or necessary for the capitalist to save (hoard) and not to spend. Indeed, "reserve capital in money is generally necessary in order to be able to continue operations without interruption, regardless of whether the reflux of the variable capital value in money is quicker or slower" (521).

The main point here is that, when the annual product as a whole is under consideration, many of the important distinctions and interrelations remain invisible. Only when the economy is disaggregated and broken down into departments is it possible to see clearly what the "real" relations are. What the interchanges between departments show, for example, is that laborers live permanently in a world in which money capital becomes money that they spend as revenue in order to live and return to work (they are permanently denied access to capital). The capitalist, on the other hand, continuously circulates variable capital through the moments of money capital used to purchase labor-power, to put that labor-power to work, and to convert the labor value congealed in the commodities produced back into the money capital form. In this case "*it can in no way be said [that variable capital is] converted into revenue for anyone*" (522-3).

This way of looking at things is helpful. What looks odd at the level of the total circulation process, when it is said, for example, that the capitalist must furnish the effective demand equivalent to the surplus-value produced, no longer looks so when we think of the flows of capital and the interchanges occurring between the different departments. Marx does not make this point, but he well could have. In laying out their capital to produce consumer goods, for example, the capitalists in department 2 provide an important part of the effective demand for the capitalists producing means of production in department 1, thereby realizing the surplus-value already congealed in the commodities they have produced. The productive consumption organized in both departments is far more important than personal consumption in furnishing the effective demand for means of production. The idea that the capitalists have to furnish the demand for realizing the surpluses produced no longer looks as ridiculous as it did when the economy was not disaggregated.

Section 12: *The Supply of the Money Commodity*

I leave aside until later consideration the problem of fixed capital, and take up Marx's brief consideration of the role of gold producers in section 12. "It is self-evident," he says, "that the greater the maturity of capitalist production, the greater is the quantity of money accumulated on all sides, and the smaller therefore the proportion that the new gold production of each year adds to this quantity [of money], even though this addition may be quite significant in absolute terms" (549). If this was so in Marx's day, then it would surely be even more so now. So while the gold and silver producers have a special role, it is not a determinant of the reproduction of capital accumulation.

This still leaves unresolved, however, the question: "How is it possible for each capitalist to withdraw a surplus-value from the annual product in money, i.e. to withdraw more money from the circulation sphere than he cast into it, since in the final analysis the capitalist class itself must be seen as the origin of all money in circulation?"

Marx considers the question ill-posed: "The only assumption required here is that there should always be sufficient money to convert the various elements of the commodity mass annually reproduced." This is the key question, and not "Where does the money come from to realize the surplus-value?" To be sure, there is a difference between the money circulating as capital and the money that circulates as revenue: "The mass of money . . . exists in the hands of the capitalist class, which is by and large the total quantity of money that exists in the society, one part [of which] circulates the capitalists' revenue" (549–50). To illustrate, he resurrects the case of a capitalist setting up a new business who lives off his own revenues for the purposes of consumption, and "fishes back" the money equivalent later.

Part of the problem derives from the way we typically personify the capitalist as a producer and not a consumer. In the latter role, "the capitalist class casts a certain sum of money into circulation in the shape of revenue." It then "appears as if it paid an equivalent for this part of the total annual product, and that this has thereby ceased to represent surplus-value. But the surplus-product in which the surplus-value is represented costs the capitalist class nothing. As a class, it possesses it and enjoys it free of charge, and the monetary circulation cannot alter this in any way." Each capitalist "withdraws commodities of all kinds from the total stock to the amount of the surplus-value that he appropriated, and appropriates these." The circulation mechanism shows that the capitalist class "casts money into circulation to be spent as revenue" and then "withdraws the same money from circulation." Thus "the same process can always begin anew; considered as a capitalist class, therefore, it remains now as before in possession of this sum of money needed for the realization of its surplus-value."

The logic here is a little hard to follow. But, in essence, Marx is saying that, in withdrawing commodities (which congeal surplus-value) for purposes of consumption, and in selling produced commodities (which congeal surplus-value) at the same time, the capitalist gets a free good. "If I buy commodities for £1 sterling, and the seller of these commodities gives me back my £1 in exchange for a surplus product that cost me nothing, then I have obviously received the commodities for nothing."

Marx is here assuming that the exchanges are simultaneous and that there are no problems of turnover time. But "in all branches of industry whose production periods (as distinct from their working periods) extend over a relatively long time, money is constantly cast into circulation" to realize values and surplus-values without placing any equivalent commodity value on the market. "This factor becomes very important in developed capitalist production, in connection with long drawn-out enterprises undertaken by joint-stock companies, etc. such as the building of railways, canals, docks, large municipal buildings, the construction of iron ships, the draining of land on a large scale, etc." One of the attractions of these forms of investment, I note in passing, is that they can absorb vast amounts of surplus money capital without producing much in the way of commodity capital until much later. It is also the case "that all kinds of things circulate as commodities that were not produced within the year: plots of land, houses, etc., as well as products whose production period extends over longer than a year, such as cattle, wood, wine, etc." In these cases, "it is important to establish . . . that besides the sum of money required for direct circulation, there is always a certain quantity in a latent and non functioning state, which can come out and function on a given impulse. The value of these products also often circulates bit by bit and gradually: for example the value of houses circulates in rent over a series of years" (553).

This then leads, finally, into the almost ritual, Volume II-style invocation of how "a system of credit and certain aspects of the credit mechanism have developed on this basis." All of the complications of circulation he then cites "had only to be noted and brought to light by experience, in order to give rise both to a methodical use of the mechanical aids of the credit system and to the actual fishing out of available loan capital" (555–6). The reproduction schemas as here studied do not include any attempt to examine what happens when the circulation of interest-bearing capital becomes a central means by which the collective capitalist may regulate affairs or, as in this instance, may attempt to coordinate the flows between the two departments. What the examination of the credit system shows, as we saw, is that the positive virtues and necessity of credit are inevitably and unfortunately accompanied by the permanent threat of disruptive speculative fevers.

Chapter 20 ends with a consideration of the views of Destutt de Tracy. Marx offers these as a prime example of "bourgeois cretinism in its ultimate state of bliss!" (564). I refrain from any comment.

CHAPTER ELEVEN

The Problem of Fixed Capital and Expanded Reproduction (Chapters 20 and 21 of Volume II)

THE CASE OF FIXED CAPITAL

In section 11 of chapter 20, Marx takes up the problem of how the reproduction schemas might be affected by fixed capital formation and circulation. I have delayed consideration of this topic until now because here, at least, Marx's intent and interest are relatively clear. "This example of fixed capital—in the context of reproduction on a constant scale—is a striking one," he writes.

> A disproportionate production of fixed and circulating capital is a factor much favoured by the economists in their explanation of crises. It is something new to them that a disproportion of this kind can and must arise from the mere maintenance of the fixed capital; that it can and must arise on the assumption of an ideal normal production, with simple reproduction of the social capital already functioning. (545)

Crises of disproportionality are, in short, inevitable. How deep and widespread they might be is hard to determine. But Marx clearly concludes that crises arise even when the exchanges between the departments are occurring normally.

There are two ways to interpret this. First, there is the view that the disruptions imparted by fixed capital circulation confirm that there is absolutely no way that the smooth reproduction process can actually be realized, and that crises of disproportionality are therefore both endemic and inevitable throughout. The second is that such crises specifically arise out of fixed capital circulation. In this case crises might be averted through the socialization of fixed capital circulation. This could take a variety of forms, varying from state provision or intervention to more radical forms of social planning, including the decommodification of fixed capital investment under communism. But Marx does not rule out, as we earlier saw, that capitalists themselves may overcome the difficulties with the aid of the credit system and joint-stock company formation. The problem with the latter solution (as we saw in Volume III) is that it opens the Pandora's box of speculative booms and crashes centered on the monetary movements associated with fixed capital circulation. While one problem, that of fixed capital, is solved, another far more serious problem, that of autonomous financial crises, takes its place. Let us examine the case more closely.

Marx opens his commentary in section 11 by reminding us of the complexities that arise when not all of the capital is used up in a given turnover time (in this case, the yearly turnover time that is assumed throughout). Different fixed capitals turn over at different rates, many fixed capitals are renewed piecemeal and in parts, and there is therefore a murky distinction between maintenance, repairs and replacements. But he reintroduces these fine points only to suggest they do not really affect the essential nature of the problem. He then launches into tedious arithmetic calculations on how the exchanges between departments work when some of the means or production in both departments take a fixed capital form. I will not attempt to replicate these.

Problems arise, he shows, from the monetary aspects of the circulation. Marx more than once claims that the problems would disappear if the monetary aspects were excluded. The essence of the problem is that the part of money "which is equal to the wear and tear of the fixed capital is not transformed back again into the component of productive capital whose loss of value it replaces. It settles down alongside the productive capital and persists in its money form." It continues in this money form all the while the fixed capital functions, and does so until the time comes to replace it. "Once the fixed element—buildings, machinery, etc.—has expired . . . its value exists alongside it completely converted into money." It is then and only then expended on the replacement (Marx does not go into the problems of different replacement costs and moral depreciation that we considered in chapter 4).

"The hoard formation"—as we have encountered several times in Volume II—"is therefore itself an element of the capitalist reproduction process," and hoarded money comes to play a very special role. It is here that Marx proposes that he will later "go on to investigate how different things would look if it were assumed that production was collective and *did not have the form of commodity production*" (526-7; emphasis added). He did not do so, but this is the kind of remark, as I argued earlier, that has led to speculation as to the potential role of the schemas under conditions of social(ist) production. It also reinforces the view that the problems that arise within the schemas are attributable to the distinctive role of money capital, the abolition of which is a necessary condition for more "rational" coordination of inputs and outputs. But the whole framework would also look very different when the credit system, operating as "the common capital of the class," enters the picture.

Unfortunately, Marx proceeds as if there is no credit system, and focuses on the imbalances that arise through hoarding. The sort of example he has in mind is this: department 2 would have a money fund against the wear and tear of its fixed capital; "on the other side, however, that of department I, there would be an overproduction of means of production . . . and in this way the whole basis of the schema would be destroyed, i.e. reproduction on the same scale, which presupposes complete proportionality between the various systems of production. One difficulty would have only been displaced by another much more inconvenient one." Then, rather ominously, he goes on to say that since political economists have ignored this problem, he intends to investigate "all possible (at least seemingly possible) solutions of the problem, or rather formulations of it" (530). I say "ominously" since this usually signals that we are in for some more endless and tedious calculations.

This seems to me, however, to be an important passage for those looking for clues as to the nature of Marx's intent in constructing the schemas. He seems bent on determining the proportionalities that must hold, and then investigating in what ways such proportionalities might or might not be achieved given the monetary coordinating mechanisms available. His scientific reticence precludes saying at the very outset how impossible this monetary coordination might be, but I somehow doubt that, by the end of his investigations, we would be persuaded that untroubled reproduction would be remotely possible.

He then elaborates on all sorts of possibilities. In his summary of the results, he makes a couple of interesting observations. Consider the case I have already described in which department 2 creates a hoard to cover the wear and tear of its fixed capital. Obviously, there is "some monetary dislocation." Department 1 "has either to contract its production, which means a crisis for their workers and capitalists engaged in it, or to supply a surplus, which again leads to crisis." This is what proves that crises are immanent within this system. But Marx then suggests that, "of themselves, these surpluses are no evil, rather an advantage; in capitalist production, however they are an evil." The reason is that "once we dispense with the capitalist form of reproduction, then the whole problem boils down to the fact that the magnitude of the part of fixed capital that becomes defunct and has therefore to be replaced in kind varies in successive years." A lot is needed in one year, and much less in others. This problem can "only be remedied by perpetual relative over-production; on the one hand a greater quantity of fixed capital is produced than is directly needed; on the other hand . . . a stock of raw materials, etc. is produced that surpasses the immediate annual need (this is particularly true of means of subsistence). *Over-production of this kind is equivalent to control by the society over the objective means of its own reproduction.* Within capitalist society, however, it is an anarchic element" (544–50; emphasis added).

Overproduction of use-values is socially a good thing, since it opens up new potentialities for human reproduction. But, under capitalism, the overproduction of surpluses becomes a bad thing, because it results in lower profits and even traumatic devaluations of capital. It is therefore the anarchy of market determinations and money considerations that lies at the root of the problem, and not the production of material surpluses per se. But reproduction does not have to be so anarchic, even under capitalism. Many long-term fixed capital investments are undertaken by the state, and are therefore open to rational social engineering and planning. The formation of associated capitals (joint-stock companies) and the "abolition of the capitalist mode of production within the capitalist mode of production" opens up new modes of coordination that may or may not be more or less anarchic (the speculative booms around built-environment investment being the downside, while the upside is collective production of the collective means of production and consumption).

One aside in this section is, I think, also illuminating. For the most part, throughout *Capital* Marx assumes he is dealing with a closed system—either capitalism in one country or a global capitalist economy. Only occasionally does he depart from this to comment on the role and significance of foreign trade. Plainly, under conditions of imbalances between the departments because of hoarding for fixed capital, foreign trade could help bring back the necessary proportionalities. "But foreign trade, in so far as it does not just replace elements (and their value), only shifts the contradictions to a broader sphere, and gives them a wider orbit" (544). This is a very neat formulation of how to understand capital's struggle to overcome its internal contradictions by resort to external "spatial fixes" (as I call them) through geographical expansion, colonialism and imperialism, and the globalization of the world market. While "capitalist production never exists without foreign trade," he later comments, "bringing foreign trade into an analysis of the value of the product annually reproduced can therefore only confuse things, without supplying any new factor either to the problem or to its solution" (546). Whether or not Marx was right to assume so may be debated. But that this is what he does throughout is clear. Expanding foreign trade and forming the world market may be temporary palliatives to crises, but at the end of the day they merely shift the contradictions of capital onto a broader geographical scale.

ON CHAPTER 21 OF VOLUME II: EXPANDED REPRODUCTION

In the relatively short chapter 21, Marx takes up the case of expanded reproduction. I propose to follow the text fairly closely, before commenting more generally on its meaning and significance. Marx begins by referring us back to the parallel chapter 24 of Volume I. There he describes how the individual capitalist, having realized the surplus-value embedded in the commodity in money form, is forced by the coercive laws of competition continuously to expand accumulation by using some of that extra money to purchase more means of production (constant capital) and more labor-power (variable capital) to produce even more surplus-value. If this is true for individual capitalists, it must also be true, says Marx, for the total social capital. The expansion may not be smooth and continuous, since it may take several years to hoard enough money capital to open up a new factory or build a railroad. But saving up the money is not the only issue. More constant and variable capital must be readily available for purchase in the market to build the new factory or railroad. "Reproduction on an expanded scale" must therefore already have occurred in commodity form. Hence "money in itself is not an element of real reproduction" (566), because, if there are no surplus commodities available, then the saved money is useless.

There is, obviously, a chicken-and-egg problem here that can only be circumvented by emphasizing the continuity and interconnectedness of the different moments within the overall circulation of capital.

Hoarding (saving) money may not constitute new wealth in itself, but it does create "*potential* new money capital." But, if everyone hoards in anticipation of future expansion, then no one is buying commodities in the here and now, and the circulation process stops. Unsold commodities clog the system. The only form of money creation that does add to real wealth directly is gold production, since gold is a commodity which contains surplus-value (567). In the event of everyone saving and not buying, the only fund available to realize everyone's surplus-value would be the surplus-value of the gold producers. This, says Marx, is of course an "absurd" idea. We need to get to the bottom of the difficulty that saving reduces spending, and therefore diminishes the prospects for realization. To do this we have to look at how the accumulation process works in and between the two departments.

ACCUMULATION IN DEPARTMENT 1

Within department 1 there are two kinds of capitalists—those who are hoarding (designated as A, A', and A" . . .) and those who are in the process of spending their hoard on buying new constant and variable capital (designated as B, B', B" . . .). These two categories "relate to each other as buyers and sellers respectively." The activities of these two categories partially compensate each other. As one capitalist withdraws money from circulation to hoard, the other pours extra purchasing power back into the market. With a bit of luck the activities of the hoarders and the spenders will balance each other. Even if they do, "these several points at which money is withdrawn from circulation and accumulated in individual hoards or potential money capitals appear as an equal number of obstacles to circulation, because they immobilize the money and deprive it of its capacity for circulation" (568). And there is always the danger of an imbalance—too much hoarding and not enough buying.

The credit system offers a solution: "It is easy to understand the satisfaction evinced when the credit system concentrates all these potential capitals in the hands of banks, etc. makes them into disposable capital—'loanable capital' i.e. money capital, no longer passive, as it were, a castle in the air, but active, usurious, proliferating capital" (569). It is interesting that he here calls this money capital "usurious." As is his wont throughout Volume II, however, the potential "satisfaction" to be gained from this credit-based solution is laid aside. A solution has to be found without it. Only then will we be able to understand the nature of the problem that the credit system resolves.

A "real balance" in the production and realization of values (including surplus-values) would require that "equal values of commodities are reciprocally exchanged"(570). This "balance exists only on the assumption that the values of the one-sided purchases and one-sided sales cover each other. The fact that the production of commodities is the general form of capitalist production already implies that money plays a role, not just as means of circulation, but also as money capital within the circulation sphere." This

> gives rise to certain conditions for normal exchange that are peculiar to this mode of production, i.e. conditions for the normal course of reproduction, whether simple or on an expanded scale, which turn into an equal number of conditions for an abnormal course, possibilities of crisis, since, on the basis of the spontaneous pattern of this production, this balance is itself an accident. (570–1)

This implies that the interventions of money capital, while necessary, are potentially destabilizing. Again, it is money capital that seems to be at the root of the problem.

Are the proper balances restored through crises? Marx does not say. This is left as an open and important question. In the subsequent development of the schemas, he lays out exactly what the balances would have to be for equilibrium growth to be achieved (under certain assumptions, of course). I interpret Marx as saying (though I may be wrong) that such balances would at best be achieved by accident and at worst through the violent shakeouts occurring through crises.

Similar considerations affect the expansion of the variable capital employed. Expanding outlays on variable capital in department 1 creates further demand for the wage goods produced in department 2. The working class in department 1 "one-sidedly faces the capitalists in class II as buyer of commodities . . . and it faces the capitalists in department I one-sidedly as a seller . . . of its labour-power." So it buys from one department (2) and sells in the other (1). The "necessary preconditions" are that "all mutually require one another, but they are mediated by a very complicated process which involves three processes of circulation that proceed independently, even if they are intertwined with one another. The very complexity of the process provides many occasions for it to take an abnormal course" (571). Once again, the hint is that crises of some sort are highly likely.

To form their hoard, capitalists must first sell the commodity that contains the surplus-value produced by the worker. It is, in effect, the worker who produces the hoard, the potential money capital. Within department 1, we encounter the production of "the means of production of means of production" (572). An expansion of the production of means of production for means of production implies, however, a diminution in the production of means of production for the department producing consumer goods.

> Thus in order to make the transition from simple reproduction to expanded reproduction, production in department I must be in a position to produce fewer elements of constant capital for department II, but all the more for department I. This transition, which can never be achieved without difficulty, is made easier by the fact that a number of products of department I can serve as means of production in both departments. (572)

It is indeed important to note that many products—energy being the most obvious example—can serve equally well as means of production in either department. But the main thrust of this argument has had, I believe, enormous consequences. It underpins the view that has long dominated socialist development strategy, that priority must be given to expanding the output of department 1, if necessary at the expense of the production of consumer goods. The starting point is: develop heavy industry, invest in the fixed capital of production and of infrastructures, and restrict personal consumption. Eventually, when the capacity to produce means of production by means of production has reached a certain point, attention may be paid to the consumption needs of the masses. This was the path typically taken in the communist countries (the Soviet Union and China).

What Marx says here is consistent with that view. The actual example Marx constructs of an expanded reproduction schema is exactly of this sort, and confirms this bias. I say "bias" because Marx does not prove the necessity of this priority as a universal truth; and, given some of the historical results of the applications of this kind of development theory in socialist countries and beyond (it has often been built into the five-year plans adopted by democratic countries such as India), it may be wise to go back and take another look at what Marx here presumes to be the case and what he actually means.

Later in the text, however, Marx rejects "the idea that accumulation is achieved at the expense of consumption" as an "illusion that contradicts the essence of capitalist production, in as much as it assumes that the purpose and driving motive of this is consumption, and not the grabbing of surplus-value and its capitalization, i.e. accumulation" (579). In a purely capitalist mode of production, where the aim and objective is solely the further creation and consolidation of ever greater surplus-value, of ever-increasing capitalist class wealth, privilege and power, the strategy of concentrating investment on the production of means of production for the production of the means of production and ignoring consumption makes perfect sense. The conditions of consumption of the masses are of no direct interest. It is, therefore, the carrying over of that class-mandated priority to invest in department 1 into the practices of socialist planning that has to be questioned.

Marx goes on to argue that

> the greater the productive capital already functioning in a country (including the labour-power incorporated into it, the creator of the surplus product), and the more developed the productive power of labour and so also the technical means of rapid expansion of the production of means of production—the greater, accordingly, the mass of surplus product, both in value terms and in the quantity of use-value in which it is represented. (573–4)

But the question of who benefits from all of this expansion is left in the shadows. The unstated implication should surely be that it is the capitalist class that benefits.

Marx examines at length the relations between the A's and the B's in department 1. The A's repeatedly realize their surplus-value through a sale, but are now hoarding much of the money they are acquiring. The B's are buying (partly from the A's) in order to expand, but upon further expansion there is still the problem of who they can sell to if the A's are not buying. Where, in short, does the money come from to realize the value of their product?

The problem is that money is "absolutely unproductive . . . as a hoard and as virtual money capital that is formed bit by bit. In this form it runs parallel with the production process but lies outside of it. It is a 'dead weight' on capitalist production." It may be useful to note the importance of this category of "virtual money capital" here (is this the same as "potential capital" mentioned earlier? And in what relation does it stand to the "fictitious capital" of Volume III?). But, Marx continues, "the attempt to make use of this surplus-value that is being hoarded up as virtual money capital, either for profit or for revenue, culminates in the credit system and 'papers'. In this way money capital maintains an enormous influence in another form on the course of the capitalist system of production and its prodigious development" (574).

Here is yet another point in Volume II where Marx points to processes that either necessitate or culminate in the creation of the capitalist credit system. He also acknowledges its "enormous influence" over the course of capitalist development and therefore, presumably, over the laws of motion of capital. This further supports the view that one of Marx's purposes in Volume II is to show the absolute necessity of credit formation and the development of the credit system.

The advantage of making more and more of the virtual capital available to use via the credit system is that these moneys "can be invested more quickly in a particular business, whether in the hands of the same capitalist, or in others." The virtual capital can even be "completely separated from its parent capital, in order to be invested as new money capital in an independent business" (574). "Virtual money capital accumulated as a hoard, is supposed to function effectively as additional money capital," which means that it is released into circulation to buy new means of production and new variable capital. But this still does not answer the question of where the extra money comes from. Marx's answer is this:

> We already know, however, from considering simple reproduction, that a certain quantity of money must exist in the hands of the capitalists in departments I and II so that they may exchange their surplus product.

There the money whose only uses was to be spent as revenue on means of consumption returns to the capitalists to the extent that they advanced it for the exchange of their respective commodities; here the same money similarly reappears, but with its function changed. The A's and B's (department I) supply one another with the money for transforming their surplus products into additional virtual money capital, and alternately cast the newly formed money capital into the circulation sphere as a means of purchase. (575)

With expansion it has to be assumed, in short, that sufficient money (credit?) exists to accommodate both circulation and hoarding, so that the expansion of accumulation has to be accompanied by an expansion in the money supply or, what amounts to the same thing, an expansion of the facility to use money as a means of payment:

If this is true absolutely for the early phase of capitalist production, where the credit system is accompanied by a predominantly metallic circulation, it is just as true, too, for the most developed phase of the credit system, which still has metallic circulation as its basis. On the one hand, the extra production of precious metals, according to whether this makes them abundant or scarce, can now exert a disturbing influence on the price of commodities, not only in the long term, but also within very short periods; on the other hand, the whole credit mechanism must constantly be engaged in restricting the actual circulation of metal by all kinds of operations, methods, technical devices, to what is relatively an ever decreasing minimum—though this also increases in the same proportion the artificial character of the entire machinery and the chances of its normal course being disturbed. (576)

In other words, we have to contemplate the very real prospect of commercial and financial crises of the sort dealt with in Volume III. The ongoing battle between the credit system and its monetary base made so much of in that volume reappears here.[1] "It is important above all," says Marx here,

---

1 Recall from Volume III how "capitalist production constantly strives to overcome this metallic barrier, which is both a material and an imaginary barrier to wealth and its movement, while time and again breaking its head on it" (C3, 708).

to start by assuming metal circulation in its most simple original form, since in this way the flux or reflux, settlement of balances, in short all those aspects that appear in the credit system as consciously regulated processes present themselves as existing independently of the credit system, and the thing appears in its spontaneous form, instead of the form of subsequent reflection. (577)

It is not hard to see, given what we know about the role of credit systems operating as "the common capital of the class," that the credit system, far from being the source of crises, can be a primary mechanism not only for removing obstacles to monetary circulation but for crisis avoidance and crisis resolution more generally, even as "the artificial character of the entire machinery" increases "the chances of its normal course being disturbed." It is not surprising, therefore, that Marx makes frequent reference to the credit and banking system in these passages. But its contradictory character (as we have seen) presumably led Marx to reject any systematic attempt to incorporate its effects here. Having already considered Marx's analysis of the credit system as the "mother of all insane forms" allows us a clearer perspective on how credit gets us out of the frying pan of crises of disproportionality only at the expense of plunging us into the wild fires of financial and commercial crises.

The problem of hoarding, you will doubtless have noticed, is frequently invoked throughout Volume II. It is important because imbalances between supply and demand arise within departments, particularly in the department producing means of production. For example, sufficient money must first be acquired to buy the machinery required to mine coal or produce steel. Money must subsequently be set aside for replacement of these means of production even as they are being used up. During all these years the coal and steel producers may be producing and selling their commodity but not buying back the full value equivalent of what they are producing. This problem is exacerbated by the fact that much of the constant capital is fixed capital. This then raises all of the complications of the costs of maintenance, repairs and replacement of fixed capital examined in chapter 4. The upshot is that it is highly unlikely that trading even within department 1 will be harmonious and not subject to imbalances and disruptions. There will be swings, fluctuations, and waves of investment followed by phases when saving and hoard formation predominate.

While problems of this sort can be identified in the department producing consumer goods (it, too, requires fixed capital), the internal dynamic within the department is nowhere near as potentially disruptive. The reason is that wages, which constitute much of the demand for means of consumption, tend to be paid on a regular (usually weekly) basis, and workers, living as they usually do hand-to-mouth, tend to spend immediately that which they receive. They do not hoard (or at least Marx presumes so). Wage workers producing corn and paid the value of their labor-power have enough money to buy the milk they need on a regular basis. Since capitalists only pay for the labor they hire after the work is done, they do not have first to hoard money in preparation for hiring more workers in the same way they have to save to buy a new machine. Matters may be somewhat different when it comes to the consumption of the capitalist class. The demand for luxury goods may fluctuate more violently, depending upon economic conditions, expectations and the general level of confidence that prevails. This problem was mentioned in the previous chapter.

In advanced capitalist economies, such as that of the contemporary US, expectations and the state of consumer confidence among the mass of the working class have now also become critical in ways that Marx did not consider (though he does drop a hint of it, as we shall see). And workers save both voluntarily and involuntarily (through mandated pension schemes).

Not only must we presume that the money and the extra means of production are available for expansion to proceed. There must also be extra labor-power already in existence at the disposal of the capitalist. This elementary requirement leads into an examination of circulation within department 2. The demand for consumer goods emanating from department 1 will depend on the degree of hoarding. This entails the "formation of virtual extra money capital in department I (hence under-consumption from department II's standpoint); piling up of commodity stocks in department II which cannot be transformed back into productive capital (i.e. relative overproduction in department II; surplus money capital in department l and a shortfall in reproduction in department II" (578–9). Note that the contentious terms "under-consumption" and "overproduction" are here used relative to the standpoint of the particular department. Assuming that "there are neither merchants nor money dealers involved, nor classes that merely consume and are not directly involved in commodity production, it follows that the constant formation of commodity stocks is indispensable, in the hands of their respective producers themselves, in order to keep the machinery of reproduction going" (580). While Marx does not say so, commodity stocks are dead capital, and therefore a drag upon accumulation (in effect, hoarding takes commodity form). If department 1 is absorbing more means of production then, other things remaining equal, less will be available for the expansion of production in department 2.

But, as Marx points out in the following section, the capitalists in department 2 have an advantage because "the workers it employs have to buy back again from it the commodities they have themselves produced. . . . It not only buys labour-power but resells its commodities to its own workers." Capitalists in department 2 can benefit directly by repressing real wages below their value. But they have other means to claw back part of the variable capital they outlay:

> Even if the normal wage is nominally paid, a part of it can in actual fact be grabbed back without a corresponding equivalent, in other words stolen; this is achieved partly by way of the truck system, and partly by falsification of the circulating medium (even if possibly in a way that circumvents the law). This is what happens in England and the USA, for example.

Marx promises to expand on this theme later with "some nice examples."

Since this is one of the few places where this issue crops up in *Capital*, it is worth marking it. The recent fraudulent dispossession of millions of people's housing in the United States, by means of foreclosures, is an obvious contemporary case in point, as has been the whole politics of what I call accumulation by dispossession over the last forty years or so.

As usual, however, Marx rules out deep consideration of such matters, because "blemishes" of this sort "cannot be used as subterfuges for getting round theoretical difficulties" (585). In the purely capitalist mode of production that is the object of his "essentialist" enquiry, such blemishes have no place. In particular, they cannot help resolve the difficulty of lopsided demand and supply relations between the two departments.

The main problem in department 2 arises out of its relations with department 1. This contrasts with the more serious problems of circulation that arise within department 1. So how is this main problem resolved?

The Schemas for Expanded Reproduction

Marx's central aim is to model the trade relations between the departments. He does so assuming the conditions of "accumulation for accumulation's sake" set out in the parallel chapter 24 in Volume I. After a few pages of probing, he arrives at what he considers his most revealing model of dynamic relations between the departments in Section 3, on "Schematic Presentation of Accumulation." I will not go through all the preliminary arguments, but simply outline the solution he arrives at. His starting point is the schema he used for simple reproduction that we have already seen:

I 4,000c + 1,000v + 1,000s = 6,000
II 2,000 c + 500v + 500s = 3,000

The proper proportionality in exchange between the departments under conditions of simple reproduction required department 2 to purchase 2000c from department 1 against the purchase by workers and capitalists engaged in production of means of production of 1000v + 1000s from department 2 (or, algebraically, $c_2 = v_1 + s_1$). Notice that both the rate of surplus-value (s/v) and the value compositions of capital (c/v) are identical in the two departments.

To analyze the case of expanded reproduction, he chooses a different set of baseline figures to facilitate his calculations:

I 4,000c + 1,000v + 1,000s = 6,000
II 1,500c + 750v + 750s = 3,000

While the rate of surplus-value remains identical, the value composition has been changed such that productivity (the ratio c/v, otherwise known as the value composition of capital) in department 1 is double that in department 2. Marx evidently did this for ease of computation, but it is a change that has some significance. The equilibrium exchange required for simple reproduction—$c_2 = v_1 + s_1$—no longer holds. There is, in effect, overproduction of means of production and underproduction of means of consumption.

But this is the position at the beginning of the year. At the end of the year (assuming, as Marx does throughout, that everything turns over on an annual basis) the figures change if some of the surplus-value is reinvested in expansion at the expense of capitalists' personal consumption. Let us suppose that half of the surplus-value in department 1 (1,000s) is reinvested in expansion. Assuming the value composition of capital remains the same, the 500s that is reinvested will be used to purchase an extra 400c and 100v (giving totals of 4,400c + 1,100v) in department 1. Assuming the rate of surplus-value remains constant, then the surplus-value generated is now 1,100s and the total output in this department has increased from 6,000 to 6,600. This then forms the basis for accumulation in the following year. And so it goes from year to year in department 1.

For department 2, Marx presumes a different reinvestment rate, in which only 150s of the 750s available is reinvested. Given the value composition prevailing, this means purchasing 100c and 50v over and above the original 1,500c and the 750c. So the total purchases are now 1,600c and 800v, which produces a surplus-value of 800s for a total output of 3,200 as opposed to the 3,000 at the beginning of the year. This forms the basis for accumulation in the following year. And so it goes from year to year in department 2.

The total output of the two departments at the end of the first year is 9,800 compared to the 9,000 at the beginning of the year. But notice that 1,600c purchased in department 2 from department 1 is now equivalent to the 1,100v + 500s of demand for consumer goods emanating from department 1. A miraculous harmony is produced through the growth process: indeed, growth and fresh capital accumulation have produced a harmony where before there was imbalance! Of course, Marx has chosen his numbers and his conditions carefully to fit the result. But he thereby proves the possibility (but not in any way the probability) of harmonious capital accumulation. He makes it seem as if that process can go on forever. Table 1 shows the year-to-year movement over four years. It can go on indefinitely (everything else remaining equal).

Table 1

Year	Period	Equations
First Year	Beginning	I. 4000c + 1000v + 1000m = 6000 II. 1500c + 750v + 750m = 3000
	End	I. 4000c + 400Δc + 1000v + 100Δv + 500u II. 1500c + 100Δc + 750v + 50Δv + 600u
Second Year	Beginning	I. 4400c + 1100v + 1100m = 6600 II. 1600c + 800v + 800m = 3200
	End	I. 4400c + 440Δc + 1100v + 110Δv + 550u II. 1600c + 160Δc + 800v + 80Δv + 560u
Third Year	Beginning	I. 4840c + 1210v + 1210m = 7260 II. 1760c + 880v + 880m = 3520
	End	I. 4840c + 4840Δc + 1210v + 121Δv + 605u II. 1500c + 100Δc + 750v + 50Δv + 600u
Fourth Year	Beginning	I. 5324c + 1331v + 1331m = 7986 II. 1936c + 968v + 968m = 3872
	End	I. 5324c + 532Δc + 1331v + 133Δv + 666u II. 1936c + 194Δc + 968v + 97Δv + 677u

In algebraic terms, the reinvestment in department 1 is $c_1 + \Delta c_1 + v_1 + \Delta v_1 + s_{01}$ (where the last term stands for residual capitalist class consumption after reinvestment in expansion), and for department 2 it is $c_2 + \Delta c_2 + v_2 + \Delta v_2 + s_{02}$. The equilibrium exchange that keeps the dynamism going smoothly is $c_2 + \Delta c_2 = v_1 + \Delta v_1 + s_{01}$. Hit that proportionality and we could have harmonious capital accumulation for ever!

But this provides an answer to the question that has dogged Volume II from the end of chapter 4 onwards. Where does the extra demand come from to bridge the gap between the demand generated by launching c + v into circulation at the beginning of the day, when the supply at then end of the day is c +v + s? When viewed from the standpoint of the individual capitalist, it seems silly to say that the capitalist has to supply the extra demand to mop up the surplus-value. But, when disaggregated individually (the relationship between the A's and the B's in department 1) and across departments, we see that some capitalists are buying more than they are producing while others are producing more than they are buying, and that some combination of productive and personal consumption can be arrived at to establish a dynamic equilibrium between aggregate supply and demand.

The big question is what would be required to arrive at this equilibrium position. So what would it take for trading between the two departments to keep the proportionalities and ratios right, so that there is no overproduction in one department relative to the other that might otherwise experience underconsumption? Obviously, the schemas are totally unrealistic, and Marx has cooked the figures to fit his case. But are the schemas so unrealistic as to reveal nothing about the nature of the stresses, strains and contradictions, as well as the dynamic capacities, of a capitalist mode of production? If not, what are the schemas intended for?

These crucial questions require general evaluation. But before dealing with them, there is one other issue raised in this chapter that deserves some comment.

The Problem (Again) of Working-Class Consumption

Throughout Volume II of *Capital*, the issue of working-class consumption has frequently been raised in ways that were totally ignored in Volume I. First, working-class consumption constitutes a "*a relatively decisive share* in the total circulation" (490; emphasis added). One of the fundamental contradictions of capitalism resides in the inability to realize values because of lack of consumer power in "a society in which the great majority are always poor and must always remain poor" (391). Marx has even gone so far as to suggest that "the ultimate reason for all real crises always remains the poverty and restricted consumption of the masses, in the face of the drive of capitalist production to develop the productive forces as if only the absolute consumption capacity of society set a limit to them" (C3, 615).

It is in this context that we have to accord some significance (although exactly how much is open to debate) to his "incidental" insertion of the following observations in this chapter. This concerns how "Mr Capitalist, as well as his press, is frequently discontent with the way in which labour-power spends its money, and with the commodities II in which it realizes this. On this occasion he philosophizes, waxes cultural and philanthropizes." He then cites an article in the *Nation* from 1879 (published after the last theoretical work had been done), which complained that "the working people have not kept up in culture with the growth of invention, and they have had things showered on them which they do not know how to use, and thus make no market for." The problem is "how to raise him as a consumer by rational and healthful processes," and this is not easy to do, because "his ambition does not go beyond a diminution of his hours of labour, the demagogues rather inciting him to this than to raising his condition by the improvement of his mental and moral powers." While Marx is scathing in his criticism of this sort of thing, he also accepts the idea that making the worker into a "rational consumer" is a necessary condition for workers' consumption to function as a "relatively decisive" part of capital circulation. What is meant by "rational consumption is shown when [the capitalist] is condescending enough to take a direct interest in the consumer behavior of his workers—i.e. in the truck system." He also uses the example of the model cotton factories of Lowell in Massachusetts, where the policing of the lodging and living conditions of the girls employed provides a beautiful example of "the rational consumer in all his or her glory." But Marx began his studies when wages in Britain (his prime example) were being held down while, after 1860 or so, the evidence suggests that wages were rising. Much later, when the $5, eight-hour day was introduced in the automobile industry in 1914, Henry Ford sent in an army of social workers to teach the workers how to consume soberly and rationally. The rationality is, of course, defined by the need for workers to "make a market" for whatever consumer goods the capitalists can produce. How the singularities of consumption might be rationalized through organized consumerism is a challenge that Marx does not take up. But this "insertion" opens the door for such considerations, even though Marx himself rejects them.

The Assumptions

In evaluating what is going on in these schemas, it is useful first to point out the assumptions built into the account. To begin with, Marx assumes there is no problem assigning activities to one or other of the departments. Ambiguities in definition (Is flour a means of production when it is used to make bread, which is in turn a means of production to make sandwiches, before finally being consumed?) and of dual uses and joint products (sheep produce meat to eat, as well as wool and hides for industrial manufacturers) are pushed to one side. There are only two classes—capitalists and laborers (so there are no bankers or merchants even, and certainly no middle class, however defined). The productivity of labor (the value composition, c/v), which in practice is constantly evolving (through the technological and organizational changes produced through the search for relative surplus-value, as described in Volume I) is held constant, except for a rather opportunistic differential in value composition between the two departments introduced into the expanded schemas in order to get the figures to balance. (Does this imply that there is a unique path of technological change required that can facilitate equilibrium in the schemas, as some commentators have suggested might be the case?) The value of labor-power is fixed, and the reinvestment rates are considered (with one exception) constant. Reinvestments are confined within departments so that capital cannot flow from one department to another (and there is an odd blip in the reinvestment/savings rate in the second year of the arithmetic example, designed to keep everything in balance).

The fact that investment funds cannot flow between the departments implies that there is no mechanism for the equalization of the profit rate across the departments. Since this is a vital aspect of Marx's theory in relation to the falling profit rates examined in Volume III, there is an obvious theoretical problem here that needs attention. The exchanges are established in value terms on the assumption that everything exchanges at its value (and not according to the prices of production, as laid out in the early chapters of Volume III). Though the interventions of money capital frequently appear to disrupt matters, the monetary aspects of circulation are not fully integrated into the analysis. Everything turns over in one year, and the serious problem of fixed capital formation and circulation is for the most part assumed away. Other forms of appropriation and exploitation through rent, interest, profit on merchants' capital, and taxes are sidelined.

It is, I think, obvious from this that the schemas as stated form a completely unrealistic model of how a capitalist economy might work. But the purpose of modeling in this way is not necessarily to arrive at a realistic representation (though successful modeling of this sort may lay a basis for ultimately doing so). It is to highlight, as Marx would put it, key relations—the essence—in the inner structure of a capitalist mode of production and, in this case, reproduction. So what is it that the schemas reveal? Quite simply, it is that the reproduction of accumulation of capital through the continuous flow of capital by way of the three circuits of money, commodity and production capital is bound to be a tricky business and therefore crisis-prone, and that crises of one sort (of fixed capital flows, and of disproportionalities more generally) may be resolved only at the expense of generating even more problematic crises elsewhere (most notably in the financial system). I am fond of suggesting that, in Marx's analyses, crisis tendencies do not get resolved but are merely moved around, and I may be guilty of superimposing that idea on what is happening here. But I think a close reading of the text, particularly taken in conjunction with a close reading of the Volume III materials on credit and finance, is far more supportive of this reading than not.

The Schemas Under Capitalism: The Role of Money and Credit

What happens when the credit system operating as a common capital of the class is brought to bear upon these problems of macro-coordination of capital flows in a capitalist society? Why can't we imagine that the credit system can somehow exercise a controlling power over all of this, and even rationalize capital flows rather than leave them in the anarchic state that Marx depicts as the case under raw market determinations? The credit system, after all, plays a crucial role in rationalizing turnover times, and solves many of the problems of differential turnover times. It also finesses the circulation of fixed capital by reducing the associated monthly hoarding to the simple monthly payment. We encounter a similar problem of coordination between different sectors—and maybe the signals transmitted and worked out via the credit system as a system of periodic payments at a stated rate of interest could be used in macro-planning, by a state apparatus or some equivalent. Is this not in effect what central bank policies, being the pivot of the credit system and backed by the state, are largely mandated to do?

What this signals, once more, is the ambivalent role of the credit system. A realistic model of how this all works cannot be arrived at, I believe, without integrating the credit system into the framework. This is something that subsequent work should have done, but which still remains for the most part an uncultivated field of endeavor.

The Meaning of the Schemas and their Subsequent Development

Subsequent discussion and debate over the status and meaning of Marx's reproduction schemas has revealed some major disagreements on how best to interpret them. While I argue that Marx's purpose in setting up a harmonious equilibrium version of the relations was to show what an impossible condition this was, there are others who argue that he was in fact demonstrating the possibility of such a harmonious developmental path, and that diversions from this harmonious condition, when corrected by minor crises here and there, can in principle be controlled.

Rosa Luxemburg, in *The Accumulation of Capital*, thought that the schemas showed that "accumulation, production, realization and exchange run smoothly with clockwork precision, and no doubt this particular kind of 'accumulation' can continue ad infinitum." Fiercely resisting what she saw as the political passivity that was implied by the schemas, she charged that they were fatally flawed. Marx had totally failed to answer his own question: "Where does the effective demand come from to pay for the surplus product?" This is, of course, a question that Marx confronts in chapter 17, and attempts to resolve in chapters 20 and 21. This is also a question that is central to Keynesian economic theory. Marx's reproduction schemas seem to have had a hidden role in animating certain strains of Keynesian thought, as well as the macroeconomic models of economic growth that evolved from the 1930s onwards. There has consequently arisen a substantial literature on the relations between Marx and Keynes, in which the questions of aggregate effective demand and of rates of reinvestment, along with paths of technological change, loom large. For Keynes, the argument leads to the necessity for adequate fiscal and monetary policies on the part of the state (or states and international financial institutions such as the IMF) if anything like harmonious growth is to be achieved. Other economists of a Keynesian persuasion have shown that correct proportionalities could be sustained only by a unique path of technological and organizational change (the evolution of the productivity ratio of c/v). It would be unlikely, however, that the actual path of technological change would correspond to that required to achieve balanced growth. The more technological change deviated from that which would secure balanced growth, the more severe the crises of disproportionality would become.

As we earlier saw in the case of money and financial capital and credit, Marx does not appear to believe it possible to evade serious crises (as opposed to regulatory crises to correct disproportionalities) in this way. Almost certainly, this is how Marx would have differentiated himself from Keynes, who believed the crises and hence the contradictions were broadly manageable by state interventions. Before Marx, there had been little attempt—other than that of Quesnay, mentioned above—to build a macroeconomic model of the flows whereby capital is reproduced. Quesnay believed that the basis of all capital and wealth lay in production on the land, but Marx's version focuses on industrial production, and seeks to define the necessary flows and balances between the two departments he identifies. The "spontaneous pattern" of capitalist production (by which he means individual capitalists operating in their own self-interest) would mean, he said, that "balance is itself an accident," and that "conditions for the normal course of reproduction, whether simple or on an expanded scale," could all too easily "turn into an equal number of conditions for an abnormal course, possibilities of crisis." The "necessary preconditions" for balanced growth "all mutually require one another, but they are mediated by a very complicated process which involves three processes of circulation that proceed independently, even if they are intertwined with one another. The very complexity of the process provides many occasions for it to take an abnormal course" (571).

These kinds of crises are generally referred to in the Marxist literature as "crises of disproportionality." How deep and broad they may become is unclear, but a contemporary version of this sort of argument can be found in the frequent references in IMF reports and other documents to "global imbalances." To be sure, this usually refers under contemporary conditions to trade imbalances between national economies (such as those of the United States and China), but in a way this can be understood as a version of the uneven development and imbalances that can and do arise between sectors. This overlap and the extensive subsequent work to which it has given rise pose problems for a geographical version of the potential identified here of imbalances in the dynamic interactions between production and consumption.

The schemas show what capital would need to do to achieve harmonious and balanced growth at the same time as they set the stage for understanding the sheer impossibility of doing so. There are also some potential contradictions that remain unexplored. The technical analysis, as is the case throughout Volume II, points to possibilities of disruptions and dislocations. In the grander scheme of things, such as that portrayed in Volume III, we see how these possibilities are more fully realized in practice.

The schemas were first applied in the early years of the Soviet Union, when a Polish economist called Feldman began to explore their utility for building five-year economic development plans. Marx's schemas were then picked up by economists such as Michał Kalecki (also Polish) and others of a more straightforwardly Keynesian persuasion to formulate macroeconomic growth models and theories of economic development in bourgeois economics. Evsey Domar, jointly credited in the creation of what became known as Harrod–Domar macroeconomic growth models in the 1940s, was emphatic in acknowledging his debt to Marx's schemas. The whole field of macroeconomic growth modeling in bourgeois economics owes something to this heritage. Conventional economists would have saved themselves a lot of trouble, and actually moved ahead towards macroeconomic modeling and public policy planning seventy or so years before, had they taken Marx's schemas more seriously.

These ideas were also taken up theoretically, and with devastating effects, in Piero Sraffa's *Production of Commodities by Means of Commodities*, whose title says it all. There is, therefore, an overlap between Marx's achievements in creating the reproduction schemas and the development of bourgeois economics, normative economic and socialist planning.

The structure of relations Marx uncovers appears in fact to have a universal significance, beyond the specific historical relations of a capitalist mode of production. Its special capitalistic qualities seem to rest on the distinctive role of money capital flows as a grand coordinator of the relations between sectors and departments of production and consumption. But what if the schemas were set up in terms of physical use-value (rather than value or exchange-value)? Could they be used for planning of physical relations between different sectors of the economy without reference to capital accumulation? Marx clearly states that the circulatory process "can proceed quite well on the basis of non-capitalist production" (430).

The highly sophisticated explorations of the mathematics of Marx's "model" by mathematical economists—both Marxist and non-Marxist—have certainly developed Marx's insights, though in a non-dialectical way. But, given the way Marx presents the materials, it is very hard to see any other way forward. And if this is the dominant way forward, then how far should one go in presenting these materials for the first time to a relatively new audience, and in following up developments that require a familiarity with some pretty high-powered mathematical economics? The best I have been able to do under these circumstances (particularly since my own command of the mathematics required is minimal) is to indicate some references with which those inclined to push further down the mathematical road might begin to do so.

There are broadly two schools of development of the schemas that depend on the framework of economic thinking that is brought to bear on what Marx appears to have been doing. For example, Michio Morishima converts the schemas into that of neoclassical equilibrium theory, and deploys highly sophisticated mathematical techniques to show what the schemas actually imply about economic growth trajectories. The results are interesting. When the assumption that accumulation occurs separately in each department is dropped, Marx's numerical examples depict "explosive oscillations . . . around the balanced growth path, if department II, producing wage and luxury goods, is higher in the value composition of capital (or more capital-intensive) than department I." When "the value composition of capital is higher in department I than in department II, the result would be a monotonic divergence from a balanced growth path." Exercises of this sort are fascinating, since they illustrate how difficult it is to calculate even with fairly simple models what a balanced growth path would look like.

The other school of thought, broadly Keynesian, has also gone over the numbers in order to show that everything depends on the creation of a viable technology that can equilibrate the physical and value exchanges between departments simultaneously, and that rates of re-investment and employment must all move in tandem within a very strictly defined band. Again, the implication is that balanced growth is extremely unlikely, and that Marx's intuition that it could only be achieved "by accident" is right on the mark.

The conclusion that Marx arrives at elsewhere—that crises are violent restorations of equilibrium conditions for a balanced growth that can at best be momentary, and never permanent—then stands as entirely plausible, if not thoroughly justifiable. The intensely discomfiting corollary is the difficult question of how these dynamic relations can be articulated through conscious social planning and design to accommodate the needs of a noncapitalist mode of production.

The Possibility of Rational Socialist Planning

Several times throughout these chapters (as well as elsewhere) Marx refers to the problem of rationally allocating labor across different facets of the division of labor within society as a whole. He suggests that social means have to be devised to do this. This contrasts with the anarchy of allocations arrived at through money flows and market processes, and the irrationality of the crises that result. Some substance is given to the view that balanced growth might in principle be possible by applying the reproduction schemas. They have therefore been invoked as useful tools for the rational planning of production and consumption under socialism and communism. In a "communist society," says Marx,

> society *must reckon in advance* how much labour, means of production and means of subsistence it can spend, without dislocation, on branches of industry which, like the building of railways, for instance supply neither means of production nor means of subsistence nor any kind of useful effect, for a long period . . . though they certainly do withdraw labour, means of production and means of subsistence from the total annual product. (390)

He also stated, in chapter 49 of Volume III (written before the major theoretical studies of the 1870s, but where the reproduction schemas put in a cameo appearance), that "even after the capitalist mode of production is abolished, though social production remains, the determination of value still prevails in the sense that the regulation of labour time and the distribution of social labour among the various production groups becomes more essential than ever, as well as the keeping of accounts on this" (C3, 991). The implication is that Marx thought the schemas had some sort of role to play in the development of rational socialist planning. As they are, the reproduction schemas go nowhere near solving such problems. But they do show in principle how much new means of production might be needed to expand the production of both means of production and wage goods in order to establish balanced growth in a rationally ordered society. In any alternative society, coordinations of this sort would have to be socially organized, given Marx's repeated insistence that the role of money capital in such coordinations is too problematic and would have to be abolished. In other words, the schemas would have to be rewritten in purely use-value and physical terms (of the sort that Leontief later devised), rather than being guided by monetary flow and profitability considerations.

Throughout *Capital*, Marx also frequently invoked the exploitative capital-labor class relation in production as the fundamental problem that needed to be addressed and displaced by "associated laborers" freely organizing their production on a collective basis. This is the conception of "the alternative" at the level of individual enterprise. But this alternative is, as he recognizes in Volume III, limited in that it would in the end merely replicate the problems of capitalist enterprises (and even lead to chronic self-exploitation) unless steps were taken to gain control of all three circuits of capital simultaneously and subject them to social control.

Marx seems to be implying here that the anticapitalist alternative of control by the associated workers of production has to be supplemented, if not superseded, by social means to coordinate the allocation of labor across the various interrelated divisions of labor in society as a whole. The distinction here examined between the production of means of production and of means of consumption is but one variant of this. But it would surely continue to be as important under communism as under capitalism. This part of the anticapitalist project is far more difficult to conceptualize and to organize, even as it is absolutely critical in defining what an anticapitalist alternative might look like. Marx shies away from any further or deep consideration of it here.

It is fair to say that, in the present conjuncture, far more weight is given to the "associated laborer" aspects of the anticapitalist project than to the problem of the rational allocation of labor in society as a whole. This is partly because the latter is associated with the past dominations and repressions of the communist and even social-democratic state—institutions which no one is now prone (in my view rightly) to trust—and partly because the experience of communist and social-democratic planning has been in aggregate far from benign (though it would be wrong to dismiss it as totally unsuccessful). But, as Marx puts it in another context, we can ill afford to use such blemishes "as a subterfuge to avoid theoretical difficulties."

Unfortunately, it is generally the case that the contemporary left is all too prone to avoid such theoretical difficulties. In a complex socialist society, there are coordinations that need to be established to avoid overproduction, lack of supply, and bottlenecks in the physical flows required to reproduce daily life at an acceptable level of material well-being, and with an acceptable if not far more benign relation to ecological conditions. How to do this in the absence of the coordinations of money flows and profit-seeking in uncontrolled markets is the big question that cannot be evaded. And how to do it without developing something like a state apparatus is a huge challenge.

The sorts of things that can go wrong are illustrated by just one facet of Marx's schemas that, unthinkingly and without any justification, became a standard practice. In Marx's arithmetic example, the whole expansion is driven by changes in department 1. From this derived the view, already mentioned, that economic and developmental planning should concentrate investment in the production of capital goods and means of production, and then let the production of consumption goods follow on later. The socialist development model adopted this convention to the letter. Postcolonial governments, such as that of Ghana, also fell victim to this style of thinking in the 1960s, and have still not fully recovered from its effects.

There is absolutely no reason why department 2 should depend on department 1. This all arose because of an arbitrary choice by Marx and because of the lopsided character of relations between the two departments that arose from the differential impact of a greater level of hoarding in department 1 relative to department 2. The point of a socialist transition would, of course, be to eradicate that differential. This would make it entirely possible to reverse the relation and put department 1 at the service of department 2. Under capitalist social relations that would be impossible, as Marx has pointed out, because the objective of capital is to accumulate capital, not to satisfy the bodily and consumer needs of the mass of the people. But, surely, the aim in a socialist/communist world would be exactly the converse.

CHAPTER TWELVE

Reflections

So what can we conclude about the "contradictory unity between production and realization" that frames the relationship between volumes I and II of *Capital*?

What Volume II shows is that the continuity of the circulation of capital is again and again threatened by the limits and barriers that arise within the realization process. These barriers are different from those with which most Marxists are all too familiar in the labor market and within the realm of production. But, as Marx insists in the *Grundrisse* (404–10), the various limits and barriers to realization constitute a permanent threat to the dynamics of continuous accumulation, and frequently spawn major crises. He even goes so far as to suggest that "the universality towards which [capital] irresistibly strives encounters barriers in its own nature, which will, at a certain stage of its development, allow it to be recognized as being itself the greatest barrier to this tendency, and hence will drive towards its own suspension."

These barriers can be viewed collectively as barriers of consumption and of coordination in a context dictated by "accumulation for accumulation's sake." But consumption is far too crude a category by itself to capture all of the issues involved. To begin with, it is vital to distinguish between productive consumption (the consumption by capital of raw materials, energy, partially finished products and fixed capital items) and final consumption (the purchase and consumption of wage goods and luxuries by wage laborers, capitalists and the "unproductive classes"). Reinvestment of surplus-value to create more surplus-value continuously expands productive consumption. But, as Volume II shows, productive consumption generates a demand for the specific use-values required to produce each particular commodity. The nature and quantities of these specific use-values is perpetually changing according to technological requirements. These are in constant flux, as the coercive laws of competition drive dramatic shifts in the search for increasing labor productivity (the relative surplus-value so thoroughly examined in Volume I). At the same time, the creation of new wants and needs (for example, cell phones in recent times) calls for an ever wider range of commodity inputs, which have to be at the ready whenever capital requires them. While it is not impossible, as Marx demonstrates in his investigation of the reproduction schemas, for capital to achieve a rational coordination of all of these demands with supplies through market mechanisms, the likelihood of achieving balanced growth without many a mismatch is surely very low, thus presaging periodic crises of disproportionality (too many or too few use-values available to satisfy the needs of a given mix of production processes). Oscillating departures from equilibria are one thing, whereas monotonic divergence for one reason or another is quite a different proposition.

But it is not only the flows of physical use-values that require coordination. The money (and value) flows also have to match the purposive pursuit of balanced growth. While money, as the material representation of the sociality of labor, is entirely indifferent to the specificity of use-values, its quantitative flows have to be kept in balance in a situation where there are abundant opportunities for the monetary coordinations within the divisions of labor to go radically wrong. The problem is not that the total quantity of money may be insufficient to the task, for, as Marx convincingly argues, there are many monetary mechanisms to accommodate increases in commodity exchanges (for example, resorting to money of account). The problem is the mobilization of effective demand (demand backed by ability to pay) in a way that does not frustrate the possibility of realizing profit at every exchange point within the intricate pattern of exchanges.

When any of this goes wrong, as it surely will, we will likely witness crises of overproduction, which may be registered (as Marx shows in the first four chapters of Volume II) as idle money capital, idle productive capacity, and surpluses of commodities that cannot be sold at a remunerative (i.e. profitable) price. The consequence is a crisis of *devaluation* of capital. How long that crisis lasts and how deep it goes depends on the circumstances in each case.

The intricate trading that arises between capitalists with respect to commodities that form the means of production is ultimately conditional, however, upon the realization of commodities in the sphere of final consumption.

In this sphere, we immediately encounter a potential contradiction between the fact that the expansion of value and its monetary representation is potentially limitless, while the demand for specific use-values is not. Products that are not useful (in the sense that no one wants, needs or desires them) are valueless, and by extension all the commodities required to produce such products are likewise devalued. While there is a long history within capitalism of the creation of new wants and needs, along with the mobilization of all manner of desires (however stupid or meaningless we might judge them), the human capacity to consume is never infinite (even though Imelda Marcos, the wife of the disgraced Filipino dictator, had 6,000 or so pairs of shoes in her closets). The perpetual thrust to expand value thus runs up against what Marx in the *Grundrisse* (407) calls "alien consumption" as a universal potential barrier that cannot easily be surpassed.

There is, however, a distinction between necessities and luxuries with respect to final consumption. The limits and barriers in the sphere of necessities look different from those related to luxuries, because in the former case the wants, needs and desires are limited not by the human incapacity to absorb ever more use-values, but by the lack of effective demand (wants and needs backed by ability to pay) consequent upon the imposition of a wage contract upon labor that is more concerned to maximize immediate profitability rather than to expand the market. So, for the workers, the possibility of acquiring adequate consumer goods for a reasonable standard of living is strictly limited. As Marx points out at several points, this creates a major contradiction that has no easy resolution, and consequently is a frequent harbinger of crises in aggregate demand.

The situation is quite different with respect to the consumption of the bourgeoisie, as constituted by the capitalist classes themselves along with what Marx calls the "unproductive classes" that consume without producing anything. Marx generally excludes these unproductive classes from his analysis, but he clearly acknowledges their importance in the various outlines he devised for *Capital*. But, even if we insert these unproductive classes into the mix, at some point it becomes clear that their revenues depend ultimately upon extractions from value and surplus-value production by some means or other (for example, the taxation that funds the military). This leaves the question of how to overcome what Marx identifies in Volume II as a deeply problematic structural imbalance between supply of value ($c + v + s$) against the demand ($c + v$) that the capitalist class launches into circulation. While, ultimately, it can be argued that the appropriation of the surplus-value by the capitalists and the unproductive classes ultimately furnishes the demand, the time-structure of this entails buying now and paying later or—more emphatically, resort to credit (on which more anon).

In none of what we have so far outlined do we consider the impacts of differential turnover times (working periods, production times, circulation times). In particular, we have paid absolutely no mind to the thorny question of the circulation of fixed capital (and its parallel of fixed items of long life, such as housing, within the consumption fund). Volume II painstakingly reconstructs how all of these circulation processes work to shape the time-space of capital accumulation without—and this is a key point—any resort to the credit system. As noted in the first lecture, what results is the hoarding of ever greater quantities of money capital in a dead and unproductive state. Money needs to be held in reserve to deal with disparate turnover times and to renew fixed capital on a periodic basis. The more complex and intricate the capitalist production system becomes, the more money has to be hoarded. This hoarding constitutes an increasing barrier to the expansion of accumulation. This makes it more and more imperative to create an adequate money market and a sophisticated credit system. The result is that capital itself radically changes its spots, such that "in a general crisis of overproduction the contradiction is not between the different kinds of productive capital, but between industrial and loanable capital—between capital as directly involved in the production process and capital as money existing (relatively) outside of it" (*Grundrisse*, 413).

It is for this reason that integrating into the analysis the readings on merchants' and money capital from Volume III becomes so crucial, because it then becomes possible to understand why the liberation of the credit system as an independent and autonomous force within capitalism is so necessary. Marx began his studies with the idea that rent, interest and the profit on merchants' capital would end up being disciplined to the rules of circulation of industrial capital. While he considered that he had showed how such a disciplined posture was achievable with respect to merchants', capital and went to enormous lengths to try and show (unsuccessfully in my view) how land rent might end up in the same position, he clearly saw that this could never be the case with interest-bearing and money capital. Its autonomy and independence, and its consequent power as an external force in relation to if not over the circulation of industrial capital, was necessary to facilitate and lubricate the path towards continuous and perpetual capital accumulation. This was what money capital, organized as "the common capital of the class," had to do. And it is not hard to see, as in the case of mortgage finance, that rental appropriations were far more likely to be thrown together with the circuit of interest-bearing money capital rather than disciplined strictly to the requirements of the circulation of industrial capital. Recall that "all rent is now the payment of interest on capital previously invested in the land" (C3, 521). But, while the rise of the modern credit system liberated vast amounts of hoarded money and turned it into money capital, active and fructiferous in the production of surplus-value, it let loose the rogue force of fictitious capital circulation upon the land, converting the primary agents of capital accumulation (capital and labor) into a clash of industrial and loanable capital (about which workers had very little direct say). Hence the transformation of the crisis tendencies of capital into the financial and commercial crises with which we are now all too familiar.

I may, in all of this, be reasonably accused of stretching Marx's argument on to a terrain of my own rather than Marx's making. In defense, I would say that there are many signs in the chapters on money and finance of a radical reconstruction of Marx's thought—though, when set against the background of the whole corpus of his writing this can be taken more as a deepening of than a radical departure from his initial stance. This is why, for example, I put such emphasis upon his resurrection of the concept of fetishism and its translation into the concept of fictitious capital. Marx's penetrating revelations concerning the illusions and fictions of money capital, that fantasy of capitalization of any stream of revenues, and the consequent creation of a plethora of money capital (what the IMF routinely refers to as surpluses of liquidity) that can pile up without limit, led him to insist: "If we were to consider a communist society in place of a capitalist one, then money capital would immediately be done away with, and so too the disguises that transactions acquire through it" (390). This requirement for the immediate abolition of money capital only makes sense in relation to the primary role it was then beginning to assume in Marx's time in fostering perpetual accumulation through the increasing repression of the aspirations of wage labor. If this was becoming true in Marx's time, then surely money capital has now reached its pinnacle of influence and power.

While a careful and critical reading of Volume II and the chapters on distribution from Volume III can inspire and inform across an enormously wide range of topics—varying from disparate turnover times to the volatility of credit provision—it is still hard to draw any definitive conclusions as to how the laws of motion of capital actually work under today's conditions. Plainly, much work needs to be done to complete and straighten out what Marx had accomplished by 1878, and to understand where he might have been headed in the enormous enterprise he had set for himself around the time that the *Grundrisse* was written, in 1856–57. It is useful here firstly to recall the astonishing breadth and depth of Marx's original conception. In one of the several outlines he creates in the *Grundrisse*, he writes:

> I. (1) General concept of capital.—(2) Particularity of capital: circulating capital, fixed capital. (Capital as necessaries of life, as raw material, as instrument of labour.) (3) Capital as money. II (1) *Quantity of capital. Accumulation.* (2) *Capital measured by itself. Profit. Interest. Value of capital:* i.e. capital as distinct from itself as interest and profit. (3) *The circulation of capitals.* (α) Exchange of capital and capital. Exchange of capital with revenue. Capital and *prices.* (β) *Competitions of capitals.* (γ) *Concentration of capitals.* III Capital as credit. IV Capital as share capital. V. *Capital as money market.* VI Capital as source of wealth. The capitalist. After capital, landed property would be dealt with. After that, wage labour. All three presupposed, the *movement of prices*, as circulation now defined in its inner totality. On the other side, the three classes, as production posited in its three basic forms and presuppositions of circulation. Then the *state*. (State and bourgeois society.—Taxes, or the existence of the unproductive classes.—The state debt.—Population.— The state externally: colonies. External trade. Rate of Exchange. Money as international coin.—Finally the world market. Encroachment of bourgeois society over the state. Crises. Dissolution of the mode of production and form of society based on exchange value. Real positing of individual labour as social and vice versa). (*Grundrisse*, 264)

Marx would have had to become Methuselah to have completed this gargantuan project. And there is no doubt from this and his subsequent language in the *Grundrisse* that his grand ambition was to depict the becoming of bourgeois society as an organic totality.

It is against this background that we can lay down some general markers that help us understand critically and in more detail what he was doing and why in Volume II. To begin with, I think it is undeniable that, in this volume, he is working within the framework of the "shallow syllogism" constructed in classical political economy. The clarity of his argument depends on a strict adherence to reconstructing the dynamics of accumulation and realization at the level of generality without appeal to universalities, particularities and singularities. Volume II is by far the most spectacular example of Marx's adoption of the shallow syllogistic framework he attributed to classical political economy in order to pursue his enquiries. From this, he seeks to build a theoretical understanding of a capitalist mode of production "in its pure state." Once this work was done, he could slot his finding into the more organic modes of thinking as broadly articulated in the *Grundrisse*.

While Marx sticks fairly rigidly to this framework, he always acknowledges that there are occasions when the universalities, the particularities and even the singularities may directly affect the laws of motion of capital. While he excludes supply and demand from Volume I, for example, the gap between aggregate supply and demand and how to fill it become critical questions in Volume II. While consumption (and the relation between productive and personal consumption) is mentioned but not analyzed in Volume I, it emerges as a more and more critical topic for analysis in Volume II. And while Marx seems to have believed he had disciplined the return on merchant capital and the role of rent to the requirements of productive capital in Volume III, the third main pillar of distribution, interest and finance necessarily escaped that disciplinary power such that the contingencies of competition and of supply and demand for money capital determined all, while the rise of associated forms of capital created a different situation, out of which socialism might or would have to arise.

The result is an incomplete edifice of theory that is robust across all the historical and geographical configurations that capitalism might assume, but not so helpful in explicating actual situations where divergences, imperfections and political contaminations of a pure capitalist mode of production brook large, and where the particularities of finance, for example, or the odd singularities of consumerism, dominate. Above all, the relation that might pertain between commercial and financial crises on the one hand and the already established contradictory laws of motion of capital on the other still remains undeveloped.

The question, therefore, of what Marx's theorizations can do for us, and what we have to do for ourselves to analyze present predicaments, must always feature prominently in any attempt to shape a Marxist-style understanding of capitalism's fraught history. We cannot, for example, take current events and plug them into some version of Marx's theory and expect ready-made answers to pop out. But what Marx does provide is a mode of thinking that gets behind the fetish world of appearances to identify the emancipatory possibilities immanent within our present condition.

In Volume I, of course, there is a dialogue of sorts between essence and form of historical appearance that helps overcome the theory-history divide. Having derived the theory of absolute surplus-value, we plunge into the details of the historical struggle over the length of the working day, against a background of an even longer precapitalist history in which the appropriation of the time and labor of others had formed the basis for the formation of some form of class society. Having derived the theory of relative surplus-value, we plunge into the whole history of changing organizational forms (cooperation, divisions of labor, and the factory system) and new technologies (the rise of a machine-tool industry—the production of machines by way of machines—automation and the application of science) that are expressive of this theoretical movement. Having theoretically established a general law of capitalist accumulation that entails the production of unemployment and of an industrial reserve army of labor, Marx looks concretely at the historical forms taken by this industrial reserve army and its conditions of life as rural, immigrant and ultimately urbanized workers.

There is no attempt whatsoever in Volume II to put such historical flesh on the bare bones of the theoretical argument. It could be said that there are certain inherent difficulties in so doing that derive from the focus on circulation as opposed to production. I do not believe that to be the case. Even the first three chapters—which disaggregate the unity of the circulation of industrial capital laid out in chapter 4 into the different circulations of money, productive and commodity capital—could have been presented in a way that was more grounded in history. This is in fact what we find when we read the historical chapters from

Volume III, on merchants' capital and the history of credit relations. In a way, these chapters perform the same function as the chapter on struggles over the length of the working day, which refers back to serfdom and other modes of mobilizing and appropriating the surplus labor of others. Marx had already written the historical chapters on merchants' capital and credit when he wrote much of Volume II, but he rarely refers us to the Volume III materials for historical enlightenment.

It is not only the history that is missing in Volume II. When we plunge into the materials on finance and credit in Volume III, we find ourselves embroiled for the first and only time in *Capital* in a concrete analysis of the actual crises of 1848 and 1857. Although these are depicted as commercial and financial crises, in some way "independent and autonomous" of the deeper laws of motion with which Marx is elsewhere concerned, it is not hard to see how the many possibilities for disruption and blockages, as outlined in the first chapters of Volume II, are here converted into historical events and realities.

There are, however, some major absences in Marx's theorizations that are of particular importance. In the conclusion to *The Limits to Capital*, I noted two general topics that required immediate attention: the nature of the capitalist state and questions of social reproduction. Interestingly, in the discussion that took place in the very last session of the lectures on Volume II, the participants converged almost exclusively, without any prompting from me, on these two topics. To these questions, I would now add the issue of the dynamics of the relation to nature, which Marx fully recognizes as being of universal significance but fails to investigate in sufficient detail within the generality of a capitalist mode of production. There are now, of course, substantial literatures dealing with all of these topics, but the exhaustion that resulted from the intense debate over the Marxist theory of the capitalist state in the 1970s, the pulling away of issues to do with social reproduction and political subjectivity from the field of political economy, and the antagonism of much of the environmental movement toward Marxist thinking, have in some regards exacerbated rather than assuaged the difficulties.

For example, the metabolic relation to nature that is occasionally invoked in Volume I rates no mention in Volume II, except when it enters into the material conditions that determine perishability, rates of "natural" decay, production as opposed to working times, the lifetime of fixed capitals, the cost and time of overcoming physical distances, and the capacity to annihilate space through time. We are thus alerted to the changing space and time of capital, but almost no attention is paid to the consequences (or the contradictions) that might flow therefrom, and in what relation this exists to the construction of the world market and structures of geopolitical domination. And while Marx sticks by his utter contempt for Malthus's "natural" explanation for the poverty and distress of the mass of the population, he does not deny that natural scarcities (particularly when exacerbated by rental extractions and speculation) and the dynamics of population growth materially affect the ability to procure both means of production and adequate labor supplies.

There are also some themes gently inserted into the analysis that have consequences for understanding Marx's so-called "deterministic" and "teleological" bent. For example, the phrase "autonomous and independent" crops up at various key points in the text and warrants some commentary, since much of the hostile and ill-informed criticism of Marx dwells on how he supposedly gives no credit to the importance and power of individual initiative, and depicts everyone as automata blindly obeying abstract forces over which they have no control. This criticism is very strange, given that it was the much-admired and frequently cited Adam Smith who came up with the idea that it was the power of the hidden hand of the market over which no one individual had control, and that determined aggregate outcomes. Marx merely adopts Smith's position in chapter 2 of Volume I, sticking with its utopian pretensions pretty much throughout. That the libertarian right continues to embrace Smith's utopian pretensions while excoriating Marx seems mighty odd—except of course when it is realized that Marx's purpose in embracing the Smithian model is to show how it cannot possibly work for the benefit of all. It exacerbates and deepens class inequalities, which is precisely why, one suspects, the bourgeoisie so happily embraces the Smithian but not the Marxist version of the same theory.

The point here, of course, is not to deny individual independence and autonomy, but to recognize (a) the particular socioeconomic conditions under which such individual initiative might flourish, and (b) how the aggregate consequences might be very different from individual intentions when mediated through the coercive laws of competition and market exchange, where the law of value ultimately holds sway.

But Marx extends this theme of "independent and autonomous" in considering the circulations of merchants', interest-bearing and money (finance) capitals. I take this to mean that, being particularities, these forms of circulation need not, and most of the time do not, conform directly and mechanically to the general laws of motion of capital. Yet, as the structure of "pivots" upon which the credit system turns indicates, and as the unfolding of commercial and financial crises illustrates, some sort of power disciplines the independent and autonomous movements in the worlds of commerce and finance to the necessity of surplus-value production and realization.

It is not clear to me exactly how this disciplinary apparatus works. I believe that Marx was only at the beginning of his studies of it. I suspect this is why Engels considered the chapters on finance as perhaps the most important chapters in Volume III. There are, of course, certain minimal principles that Marx cites (for example, that if all capitalists abandoned production to live on interest, then capital accumulation would quickly grind to a halt). And there is a presumption that crises somehow do bring a measure of concordance in the relation between surplus-value production and the proliferation of, for example, credit arrangements.

In the introduction to this *Companion*, I identified what might be termed a "theory of determination" in Marx. I suggested that a wide range of particular distributive and institutional (political) arrangements and of consumption regimes might be possible throughout the world at any one historical moment, "*provided that they do not unduly restrict or destroy the capacity to produce surplus-value on an ever-expanding scale*." To the degree that some arrangements and regimes are more successful than others, so competitive pressures would likely force adaptations over time toward the more successful model of accumulation. We have seen this sort of thing going on historically. In the 1980s, it was West Germany and Japan that were leading the way. Then it was the so-called Washington Consensus; and now it is the East Asian model. But, as the history of shifts in global hegemony illustrates, the independent and autonomous elements never go away. Uneven geographical development keeps the question of what is the most successful model of accumulation for different times and places very much on the boil. It is, in my view, a crucial means of capital's successful reproduction. The same is also true for the independent and autonomous forms of circulation, and the crises they regularly foment. Without such independence and autonomy, capital could not adapt, reproduce and grow.

This illustrates how robust and flexible capital can be in relation, for example, to the singularities of consumption. Since this is perhaps one of the more problematic aspects of Marx's theorizing—his failure to discuss, let alone theorize, consumerism—let me give a strange, personal and definitively singular example. I had until recently a passionate attachment to British bitter marmalade. It seems a peculiar taste for which we Brits either have a genetic predisposition or a perverted cultural sense, but many of us can only face the day by consuming something bitter for breakfast. I got used, when back in Britain in the early 1990s, to making my own marmalade (like my mother and grandmother before me). I was incidentally surprised to find that so many of my academic colleagues did the same. So, every January and February, kitchens all over Britain are activated to make marmalade. I could not get the bitter oranges when I got back to the US. I would therefore always find an excuse to be in Europe in January and February, to get the bitter oranges and make the pulp, from which I would then make the marmalade when I returned to the US. I even engineered a January invitation to Córdoba, where the bitter oranges lie all around on the ground in the beautiful Islamic garden next to the spectacular mosque. I gathered up the oranges (much to the surprise of the locals, who kept telling me that these oranges were inedible) and made the pulp in my hotel room—causing an uproar with the room staff, who couldn't stand the pungent smell. They plainly thought I was mad. Could anything be more singular than this?

But there is, in fact, a fascinating Marxist-style story to be told that puts my strange consumer behavior very much in context. I had discovered, when researching my doctoral dissertation on hop and fruit cultivation in Kent during the nineteenth century, that there had emerged a strange and unlikely alliance in the 1840s between the mid-Kent yeoman farmers and the West Indian sugar-plantation owners. Both groups were agitating for the reduction of the sugar duties. For the fruit growers, this meant cheaper sugar and more demand for fruit to go into jams and conserves. This was the period when free-trade agitation in Britain was at its height, led by the Manchester manufacturers who wanted cheap foodstuffs to lower the value of labor-power and thereby increase the surplus-value they could appropriate. While this agitation mainly focused on the price of bread, the workers needed something to put on the bread. Sugar-laden conserves (along with sweetened tea) provided an instant source of energy for factory workers with long working hours. So, as Sidney Mintz points out in his brilliant book on *Sweetness and Power*, the industrial interest promoted the consumption of such instant energy for their workers (hence the long-lasting significance of the tea break in British working-class life). The analysis in Volume I of *Capital* of trade policy in relation to the value and intensity of labor-power (in the chapter on "The Working Day") sets the context for the promotion of these forms of working-class consumption.

But it does not explain why bitter marmalade. For this we have to go to Volume II of *Capital*. The conserve and jam manufacturers typically ran out of fresh fruit and fruit pulp by around December. Somebody saw all these inedible oranges dropping off the trees in Spain in January and February (where they liked the orange blossoms but did not want the trees being raided for edible fruit). Using the bitter oranges from Spain provided a marvelous way to keep fixed capital fully employed (a Volume II problem) all around the year. So problems in the turnover time of fixed capital played a critical role in promoting bitter marmalade for breakfast. Heavy on sugar and Vitamin C, this cultural habit of eating bitter marmalade became deeply engrained, and has lasted in Britain to this day.

There is nothing here that determines my peculiar and singular cultural habit. I can drop it if I like (and recently have). But capital creates certain "conditions of possibility" for the formation and perpetuation of seemingly singular cultural habits. Homeownership and the "American Dream" are other obvious examples. I take great pleasure in uncovering what these conditions of possibility might look like, and find it fascinating that a spot of Marxist-style theorizing helps me understand where some of my own peculiar habits and tastes might come from.

I cite this seemingly trivial personal anecdote because I believe deeply that Marx makes more and more sense as his abstract analysis is brought to earth, and that if the theory is incapable of illuminating not only the abstract processes through which capital moves but also daily life as it is lived by all (including why so many Brits love bitter marmalade), then the theory is wanting as an emancipatory tool in the search to construct an alternative, more egalitarian and less violence-prone mode of production.

Interestingly, the concepts of socialism and communism do come up in Volume II more explicitly than elsewhere in *Capital*. It seems Marx had in mind some mix of associated workers controlling their own production processes and levels of reward, and embedded in a broader-based form of social organization capable of displacing the disruptive powers of money capital circulation with a rationally specified and coordinated pattern of flows of non-commodified goods (use-values) within an international division of labor. The abolition of a society based on exchange-value is central in all of Marx's anticapitalist formulations. The corollary is that a society based on equality and justice and dedicated to human emancipation can never be constructed in a world where money is a form of social power appropriable by private persons, and where the monetary coordination of exchange in commodity markets is the primary social relation through which daily life is reproduced. Plainly, Marx's minimum specifications constitute a wholly inadequate and utopian program. But they do highlight the problem of international coordination within a deepening division of labor that the anticapitalist left is notoriously reluctant to confront, partly because of an understandable distrust of anything that looks like reliance upon state power in the transition to an anticapitalist alternative. What Volume II also illuminates are the complex processes of intertwining circuits of capital that have been built so as to sustain the production and realization of surplus-value seemingly ad infinitum—and that these are designed to perpetuate a singularly capitalist class power. What Marx convincingly shows is that no one aspect of circulation (such as money capital) can be radically changed without equally radical transformations occurring in the sequential circuits of production and of commodities.

What a noncapitalist alternative might look like will have to be determined by future generations of activists and scholars in the light of contemporary possibilities (including electronic modes of social coordination undreamt of by Marx). But the basis that Marx laid so long ago furnishes a stunning picture of the systemic if contradictory character of capital flow that has to be transformed into flows of use-values that can feed, house, clothe, nurture and sustain more than eight billion people on planet Earth. For someone who so famously said that our task is to change the world rather than to understand it, Marx spends an inordinate amount of time and energy dissecting, understanding and illuminating that which has to be changed. There is still a great deal of work to be done in this vein. But it is, as always, equally imperative that we begin upon the task of changing it—particularly since there are abundant signs that capitalism as a social system has outlived its shelf-life and cannot endlessly and mindlessly grow at a compounding rate through "alien consumerism," no matter what the social, political and environmental consequences. Only capital, says Marx, "has subjugated historical progress to the service of wealth." The

> growing incompatibility between the productive development of society and its hitherto existing relations of production expresses itself in bitter contradictions, crises, spasms. The violent destruction of capital not by relations external to it, but rather as a condition of its self-preservation is the most striking form in which advice is given it to be gone and give room to a higher state of social production. (*Grundrisse*, 590, 749–50)

It is surely time we all listened to that advice.

Index